PATRIOTIC TOIL

PATRIOTIC TOIL

NORTHERN WOMEN
AND THE
AMERICAN CIVIL WAR

JEANIE ATTIE

CORNELL UNIVERSITY PRESS

ITHACA AND LONDON

First published 1998 by Cornell University Press

Printed in the United States of America

Library of Congress Cataloging-in-Publication Data
Attie, Jeanie.
    Patriotic toil : Northern women and the American Civil War /
Jeanie Attie.
        p.   cm.
    Includes bibliographical references (p.   ) and index.
    ISBN 0-8014-2224-8 (cloth : alk. paper)
    1. United States—History—Civil War, 1861–1865—Women.   2. United
States—History—Civil War, 1861–1865—Health aspects.   3. United
States Sanitary Commission. 4. Women—United States—History—19th
century.   5. United States. Army—Sanitary affairs.
    E628.A87   1998
    973.7'082—dc21   98-25717

Cornell University Press strives to use environmentally responsible suppliers and materials to the fullest extent possible in the publishing of its books. Such materials include vegetable-based, low-VOC inks and acid-free papers that are recycled, totally chlorine-free, or partly composed of nonwood fibers.

Cloth printing   10   9   8   7   6   5   4   3   2   1

For my mother and in memory of my father

CONTENTS

ILLUSTRATIONS

ACKNOWLEDGMENTS

I have lived with this book for more years than I care to record. Thankfully, I did not live with it alone. Just as many Union soldiers would not have survived the Civil War without the "relief" provided by thousands of home-front women, so I have been fortunate throughout my struggles with this study to have had the support of numerous gifted historians and good friends, often one and the same.

I owe a long-standing intellectual debt to Jim Shenton, my friend and graduate adviser at Columbia University, whose teaching shaped my development as a historian and whose passion for the Civil War is reflected in my choice of subject. I extend a warm thanks to Eric Foner, who offered important insights and has been a steadfast mentor and friend.

I cannot overstate my gratitude to Betsy Blackmar. As a teacher and a friend, she engaged my every idea for revisions and in countless discussions challenged me to clarify my thinking about nineteenth-century gender and class relations. I thank her for imparting her wealth of historical and theoretical knowledge and for her abiding enthusiasm for this project.

Josh Brown has been the most supportive and generous friend, reading every draft of every chapter. Beyond his scholarly expertise, meticulous editing skills, and unique knowledge of nineteenth-century illustrations,

Josh was always willing to drop work on his own projects to read something of mine.

For years Peter Buckley shared his profound understanding of mid-nineteenth-century New York liberals and more than anyone else helped me to make sense of Unitarianism. I thank him too for reading portions of the manuscript and providing me with important primary materials.

Iver Bernstein was one of the original anonymous readers of this manuscript. As chance would have it, we became friends and colleagues at Washington University in St. Louis, where he read chapter drafts and patiently listened to me explain each shift in my thinking, all the while imparting his scholarship about Civil War America.

Even before we met, Jeanne Boydston had a profound impact on my ideas about the nineteenth-century gender system, and in particular, the value of women's unpaid household labor. This book owes a great intellectual debt to her work. As the reader of the revised manuscript, she increased my awareness of the larger significance of this study, and offered warm words of encouragement.

As a fellow student of the United States Sanitary Commission, Kristie Ross shared her expertise of the complex workings of the organization; as a friend, she provided me with even more. Ann Fabian read the final version of this manuscript with a sharp eye and nuanced mind. I am deeply grateful to her for engaging this work as she did and offering help when I needed it. I also thank Ellen Dubois, Nancy Hewitt, Jan Lewis, Ann Firor Scott, and Robert Zussman for their critical readings and suggestions.

A number of historians neither read chapters nor engaged me in conversations about my work but provided me with a valued intellectual community in New York City. I thank Jean-Christophe Agnew, Peter Dimock, David Jaffee, Michael Lapp, David Rosner, and Herb Sloan.

Peter Agree has been a dependable editor and friend, always enthusiastic about the manuscript and ever patient with my delays. I was fortunate to have a skilled historian, Grey Osterud, copyedit the manuscript, which she did with great precision. Carol Betsch guided the book and me through the production process with care and good humor.

In the final stages of preparation, two young women gave me invaluable assistance. I am very grateful to Jessica Attie for the intelligence with which she edited the final manuscript. Marisol Martínez lent her artistic eye to the choice of graphics and skillfully negotiated with historical institutions.

During the years that this book was a part of my existence, I incurred debts of a more personal nature. I thank Alice Attie, Ilana Attie, Kenny Attie, Nancy Berg, Mary Ann Dzuback, Judith Evans, Claudio Gatti, Gail

Hammer, Mark Kornbluh, Angela Miller, Helen Power, Marci Reaven, Dorothea Von Moltke, and Cliff Simms for sticking by me. A special thanks to Justine and Gideon Kahn, who may not have always understood why their aunt was so busy but provided her with joyous hours away from the computer.

I dedicate this book to my mother, Muriel Attie, and to the memory of my father, Joseph Attie. I am deeply saddened that my father did not live to see it published. Through the many years of research and writing, my parents never lost faith in me or my project. Their love and support sustained me far beyond the life of this book, and for that I will always be grateful.

JEANIE ATTIE

New York City

PATRIOTIC TOIL

PROLOGUE

"The story of the war will never be fully or fairly written if the achievements of women in it are untold."

Frank Moore, 1867

Throughout the American Civil War, as federal forces fought to preserve the Union, and political and social leaders endeavored to generate a consistent patriotism to support them, northern women were important subjects of patriotic discourse. The goal of fostering public unity at the northern homefront went beyond gaining emotional support for the cause; defending the midcentury American state required that women and men voluntarily offer themselves and their resources to the fight. But whereas men's participation was defined by their identification as citizens endangered by southern secession, women's assistance was premised on their positions as the apolitical and altruistic members of society. In public ceremonies, political speeches, church pulpits, and, shortly after the war, commemorative volumes, Union women were heralded for energies that never flagged and patriotic spirits that stayed buoyed for the duration of the conflict. Sometimes the accolades were about the northern "woman," the ideal embodiment of self-sacrifice, virtue, and disinterested benevolence that symbolized the values threatened by the Confederacy.

Most often northern women were described in the aggregate, with an emphasis on the enormous efforts of the hundreds of thousands who helped to preserve the Union. "We may safely say," the writer Frank Moore declared in his postwar tribute, "that there is scarcely a loyal woman in the

North who did not do something in aid of the cause."[1] As most accounts went, brave women, having sent their husbands and sons to the war, scraped lint in church basements and scrimped on household necessities to produce socks, shirts, bedding, jams, and jellies for local soldiers' aid societies. Society members carefully packed their gifts and forwarded them to the United States Sanitary Commission, the largest and best-known national war relief organization, which distributed them with utmost efficiency to grateful soldiers languishing in military hospitals.

In their commemorative tribute to loyal women, Dr. Linus Brockett, the author of patriotic histories, and Mary Vaughan, an advocate of temperance and woman's rights, offered what they considered an example, "with but slight variation," of the history of "perhaps thousands of articles sent to soldiers' aid societies."[2] After the death of her only son in battle, an anonymous mother, "though her heart is wrapped in the darkness of sorrow," denies herself mourning clothes. "The little earnings," of the mother and her daughter, "are carefully hoarded, the pretty chintz curtains which had made their humble room cheerful are replaced by paper, and by dint of constant saving, enough money is raised to purchase the other materials for a hospital quilt, a pair of socks, and a shirt, to be sent to the Relief Association, to give comfort to some poor wounded soldier, tossing in agony in some distant hospital."[3] Other women left their cherished homes, venturing forth to nurse wounded soldiers in army hospitals or on hospital transports. (Invariably excluded from such praise were the hundreds of women who donned military attire and in cross-dressed disguise fought along Union lines.) The Reverend Henry Whitney Bellows, New York City's preeminent Unitarian minister and president of the Sanitary Commission, exulted that women were "not only softening the fibres of war, but . . . were actually

[1] Frank Moore, *Women of the War: Their Heroism and Self-Sacrifice* (Hartford, Conn., 1867), p. iv. Moore, who became a member of the New-York Historical Society in 1856, edited collections of American historical documents, speeches, ballads, and poetry, and was best known as the author of books with patriotic and historical themes. See *Dictionary of American Biography* (hereafter *DAB*), vol. 7 (New York, 1934), p. 122.
[2] Linus Pierpont Brockett was trained as a physician but left clinical practice to become a writer, contributing to domestic and foreign encyclopedias, a state government report on idiocy in the 1850s, and histories of education. Following the Civil War, he authored celebratory accounts of Abraham Lincoln and military leaders, in addition to his chronicle on women. See *DAB*, vol. 2 (New York, 1930), p. 60. Mary Vaughan was a temperance activist and supporter of woman's rights. See Nancy F. Cott, Jeanne Boydston, Ann Braude, Lori Ginzberg, and Molly Ladd-Taylor, eds., *Root of Bitterness: Documents of the Social History of American Women* (Boston, 1996), p. 208.
[3] L. P. Brockett and Mary C. Vaughan, *Woman's Work in the Civil War: A Record of Heroism, Patriotism, and Patience* (Philadelphia, 1867), p. 82.

strengthening its sinews by keeping up their own courage and that of their households."[4] The unsung heroines of the war did more than maintain the bodies of damaged soldiers; they kept the body politic together for four long years.

Though clearly fictions that employed antebellum conventions of sentiment to flatter female sacrifice, such narratives nonetheless attempted to render visible the prodigious toil of hundreds of thousands of northern women during the Civil War. Female participation in defense of the Union covered a wide range of labor, including assisting troops departing for battle, working as nurses in military hospitals, aiding released prisoners of war, and teaching the children of freedpeople in southern locales. The work that occupied the vast majority of women, however, was the household manufacture of army supplies for military hospitals. In thousands of soldiers' aid societies, which served as the community-based sites for assisting the war effort, women employed their household skills to produce uniforms, hospital garments, bedding, and foodstuffs. The Sanitary Commission claimed that between ten and twelve thousand such societies formed part of its network of northern relief, and produced goods worth over $15 million. Brockett and Vaughan judged that, including donations sent by women to local and state government agencies as well as other private organizations, the monetary value of women's gifts to the army totaled $50 million.[5]

But romanticized narratives about mythical women and female sacrifice obscured the ways countless women—white and black, elite, middle-class, and poor—undertook war relief. The stirring tales were silent about women's motivations for entering such work, the content of their labors, and the ways they negotiated their support for the army with private relief organizations and government agencies. Representations of selfless and tireless women, energized by war and compelled by nature to minister to those in need, served obvious military ends. For a state that depended so extensively on the voluntary support of its citizens to prosecute the war, invoking commonly held assumptions about inexhaustible female charity was an expedient way to secure aid needed for the Union army.

Beyond stimulating material contributions, such characterizations of fe-

---

[4] Henry Whitney Bellows, introduction to ibid., p. 63.

[5] The number of soldiers' aid societies fluctuated over the course of the war years, and historical accounts differ on the total. The official history of the Sanitary Commission stated that "more than seven thousand" were associated with the organization, and that the value of donated supplies shipped to Commission branches was "about fifteen millions." See Charles J. Stillé, *History of the United States Sanitary Commission: Being the General Report of Its Work during the War of the Rebellion* (Philadelphia, 1866), pp. 172, 488. Bellows put the number of aid societies at 10,000; see his introduction to Brockett and Vaughan, *Woman's Work*, pp. 59, 78–79.

male behavior formed part of a broader construction of northern nationalism that served distinctly political goals. Women who redirected their household labors to advance nationalist purposes conveyed a perfect symbiosis between public and private arenas of production. The support that emanated from supposedly "private" homes, provided by women who purportedly had no relation to partisan politics or to the labor and commodities markets, served a dominant discourse about the universality of northern patriotism. The participation of women, whose compassion inspired their patriotism, engendered a vision of northern nationalism that was inclusive and ecumenical.[6] Thus, by relating the voluntarily donated products of the sentimentalized "home" to the restoration of men injured defending the state, nationalist leaders claimed a unique legitimacy for the war. The Civil War was not merely a political struggle between northern and southern elites, nor was it aggression mandated by a distant state. Rather, the integrity of the Union was self-evident because it was embraced by the least partisan and most virtuous members of the community. The wartime construct of the generous, patriotic "woman" contributed to a northern national identity that claimed moral supremacy over southern malfeasance by asserting a social order rooted in what appeared to be harmonious gender relations.[7]

Invented descriptions of female wartime labors had direct consequences for women's abilities to enact their patriotism and their political will. Popular wartime culture deemed loyalty to the Union a gendered phenomenon that dictated the manner in which a woman was to act on her political be-

[6] Benedict Anderson's idea of the nation as an "imagined community" is especially useful not only in understanding the abstract character of any nation—the fact that people know their fellow citizens only through acts of imagination and creation—but also for its emphasis on civil society; as he writes, "regardless of the actual inequality and exploitation that may prevail in each, the nation is always conceived as a deep, horizontal comradeship." See *Imagined Communities: Reflections on the Origin and Spread of Nationalism* (1983; rpt., London, 1991), pp. 6–7.

[7] Confederate nationalists articulated similar paeans to female sacrifice and benevolence. As the war intensified, southern women, amid increasing deprivation, became engaged in widely publicized acts of defiance, such as the verbal assaults by New Orleans women on Union soldiers and the food riots staged by women in Richmond. Northern writers exploited such incidents as evidence of the unfeminine and unseemly character of southern women, a consequence of distorted social relations in a slave society. See Drew Gilpin Faust, *Mothers of Invention: Women of the Slaveholding South in the Civil War* (Chapel Hill, N.C., 1996), pp. 208–14, and George C. Rable, *Civil Wars: Women and the Crisis of Southern Nationalism* (Urbana, Ill., 1989), pp. 108–11. One document issued by the New York–based Loyal Publication Society in the middle of the war made direct comparisons between the "quiet and constant" sense of duty of the northern woman and the "violent" and "impetuous impulse" that characterized her southern counterpart. See Gail Hamilton [Mary A. Dodge], "A Few Words in Behalf of the Loyal Women of the United States by One of Themselves," *Loyal Publication Society*, no. 10 (New York, 1863), pp. 1–17.

liefs and how those acts would be interpreted. In war, northern women had to confront—many for the first time—assumptions that their citizenship, while pivotal to the maintenance of the republic, was evident not through direct participation in the political arena but as a consequence of their benevolent deeds and their status as housewives. In the context of dominant beliefs about women's dependent status, female political obligations were viewed as flowing from familial obligations that were, in turn, ensconced in a system of social and labor relations that gave women few ways to determine the purpose of their contributions. Women may have responded to the war as citizens, but they were constrained to perform as "women."

This book is a study of the economic, political, and ideological conflicts that surrounded northern women's unpaid labors in support of the Union army. More specifically, it explores the relationship between the female homefront and the United States Sanitary Commission (USSC), a privately run organization ostensibly founded to "inform" and "advise" the government on hospital procedure, medical personnel, training of recruits, and to maximize homefront charity by coordinating female war relief through one centralized agency. From its inception, however, the Sanitary Commission embodied larger political and personal goals of its founders. The spontaneous and generous voluntarism offered by northern women to war mobilization presented Sanitary leaders with an opportunity to experiment with a social welfare scheme that would mimic the functions of a strong federal government. At stake was the creation of a new consciousness, a new national culture. The elite, urban men who founded the commission glimpsed in female domesticity and benevolence a means through which they could achieve a national platform for their class and nationalist interests.

The Civil War erupted after decades of debate about women's place in the democratic polity and their status as citizens. In their attempts to manipulate women's charity in service to a masculinized vision of nationhood, the men who led the Sanitary Commission found themselves engaged in a contest for women's labor and trust. Throughout the war years, northern women struggled to make evident the value of their household products and the content of their political loyalties. In the course of "warwork"—the voluntary contribution of homemade goods to the Union Army—thousands resisted the claims made upon their patriotism and the assumptions made about their labors.

By calling on unpaid housework to serve nationalist purposes, the Sanitary Commission scheme reignited debates about the relationship between women's domestic economies and the nation's larger political economy. Moreover, it brought into sharp relief the subordinate, and increasingly anomalous, status of women as citizens. For three-quarters of a century, the issue of women's relationship to men in the American republic hovered over a nation premised on ideas of free political will, fair representation, and equality.

Female Labor and Citizenship

The Civil War was not the first time that women's household production and benevolent deeds were tied to the fortunes of the American state, nor would it be the last. During the American Revolution, women were heralded as essential contributors to the colonists' struggle for independence, their manufacture of homemade goods widely deemed a means for undermining the mercantile domination of imperial Britain. Recognition of the political as well as economic value of colonial wives' household labors was brief, however, and soon disappeared into a paradigm of political rights that narrowed the definition of the republican citizen as a male property owner and, significantly, head of a household.[8] Men in the early republic claimed political rights by means of their domination of the labor of household dependents. Moreover, as Jeanne Boydston has written, the construction of citizenship in the new republic was rooted not only on the ownership of property but on the "presence of economic *dependents*."[9]

While men asserted their political will as masters over property and individuals, they simultaneously dispossessed themselves from ownership of public virtue, the attribute upon which republics depended that made one put aside private interests in order to act in concert for a larger public good. As the early American republic took shape, the idea that public virtue was a prerequisite for participation in the political realm disappeared; in fact, with the emergence of political factions, public life was itself shedding the cloak of disinterestedness. Under an earlier confluence of classical republicanism and Protestant thought, public virtue had been deemed a masculine at-

[8] In the decades after the Revolutionary War, wives gained some "legal separateness" in statutes passed by state governments that gave widows and abandoned wives greater access to remarry or earn a living; see Norma Basch, *In the Eyes of the Law: Women, Marriage, and Property in Nineteenth Century New York* (Ithaca, N.Y., 1982), p. 25. Although unmarried women who owned property were permitted to vote for a brief period in the state of New Jersey, evidence suggests that this anomaly may have had more to do with partisan bids for power than with acknowledgments of women's political capacities, despite occasional specific appeals to female voters. See Judith Apter Klinghoffer and Lois Elkis, " 'The Petticoat Electors': Women's Suffrage in New Jersey, 1776–1807," *Journal of the Early Republic* 12 (Summer 1992): 159–93.
[9] Jeanne Boydston, *Home and Work: Housework, Wages, and the Ideology of Labor in the Early Republic* (New York, 1990), pp. 30–55.

tribute; indeed, the term *virtú* derived from the Latin term for manliness. In a subtle intellectual shift that crystallized after the revolutionary crisis, propertied men were uncoupled from their previous identification with political virtue. Ruth Bloch points to a confluence of religious, psychological, and literary forces that, by the late eighteenth century, transformed the meanings of public virtue in such a way that women were positioned as its custodians. In this new formulation, the association of public virtue with women hinged on their exclusion from formal political institutions.[10]

Though civic republicanism placed the household at the center of political morality, it also strengthened the identification of the political with men and the domestic with women. This gendering of citizenship had long roots in European liberal philosophy, and was reestablished in the early republic by a formulation of male citizenship that was predicated on female dependency.[11] In the years following the American Revolution, women's political status—now embodying public virtue—was characterized as one of "maternal influence." "Republican mothers," so the logic went, would elevate the level of public discourse through their love and nurturance of moral men.[12]

Female subordination and dependency relied on more than ideological constructions, of course, and were based on a system of property rights that was codified by law and enforced through adjudication. Throughout the nineteenth century, the dominant paradigm for female political rights was coverture, the common-law doctrine that asserted that a husband and wife were a single person and that wives had no rights in property or earnings of

---

[10] Ruth H. Bloch, "The Gendered Meanings of Virtue in Revolutionary America," *Signs* 13 (Autumn 1987):37–58; see also Linda K. Kerber, *Women of the Republic: Intellect and Ideology in Revolutionary America* (Chapel Hill, N.C., 1980), pp. 35–36, 73–113, on distrust of female patriotism during the Revolution; Mary Beth Norton, *Liberty's Daughters: The Revolutionary Experience of American Women, 1750–1800* (Boston, 1980), pp. 242–50.

[11] Although nineteenth-century female political subjecthood derived from transatlantic political and intellectual developments that themselves expressed profound changes in property and social relations, it had long roots in European ideas about civil society and rights. The philosopher Carole Pateman argues that the sources of modern political patriarchy can be found within the contract theory developed by eighteenth-century Enlightenment philosophers. These thinkers justified women's exclusion from the social contract (which created civil society) by subsuming women in an unspoken "sexual contract." The legacy of the sexual contract was the belief that the political individual was male. See *The Sexual Contract* (Stanford, Calif., 1988); see also Denise Riley, *"Am I That Name?": Feminism and the Category of "Women" in History* (Minneapolis, Minn., 1988), p. 41.

[12] Jan Lewis, "The Republican Wife: Virtue and Seduction in the Early Republic," *William and Mary Quarterly*, 3d ser., 44 (October 1987): 689–721. See Jean Bethke Elshtain, *Meditations on Modern Political Thought: Masculine/Feminine Themes from Luther to Arendt* (University Park, Pa., 1986, 1992), pp. 48–52, on Rousseau's thoughts about women as mothers of citizens rather than active political participants.

their own. Women's legal status was subsumed under that of their husbands or husbands in general.[13]

As capitalist production expanded in the early decades of the nineteenth century and independent proprietorship declined, more and more men stood to lose their republican status as property holders. To the degree that men's claims to citizenship were still based on property ownership, a husband's control of his household's property as the source of his political independence grew in importance. The spread of market relations was accompanied by the emergence of a cultural system of gender relations that identified separate spheres of social power and authority for men and women. Alternately termed by historians "the ideology of separate spheres," "the cult of true womanhood," or "the ideology of domesticity," the antebellum gender system signaled an important development in the way women's household labors were valued and not valued in a capitalist economy.[14] It also suggested a relationship between female household duties and the maintenance of a liberal democracy. If the virtuous republican marriage was the metaphor for the maintenance of the early republic, the antebellum ideology of gender separation positioned bourgeois women during the era of early industrial capitalism as the repositories of a morality that was fast disappearing from the world of the market.[15]

A system of ideas about gender that asserted that the sexes inhabited separate realms of work and influence grew directly out of the reorganization of labor, the spatial rearrangement of housing, and the reapportionment of political rights that all accompanied the spread of industrial capitalism.[16]

[13] Basch, *In the Eyes of the Law*, p. 17.

[14] Nearly all historians of nineteenth-century women have grappled with the problem of the ideology of separate spheres and the disjunction between the ideological construction of gender and the lives and practices of women. Among the earlier explications of the ideology, see Nancy Cott, *The Bonds of Womanhood: "Woman's Sphere" in New England, 1780–1835* (New Haven, 1977). Jeanne Boydston, Lori Ginzberg, and Nancy Grey Osterud have refined our understanding of the origins of the ideology and the ways in which women employed it to their own uses, as well as social settings in which men and women inhabited worlds more shared than separate. See Boydston, *Home and Work;* Lori D. Ginzberg, *Women and the Work of Benevolence: Morality, Politics, and Class in the Nineteenth-Century United States* (New Haven, 1990); Nancy Grey Osterud, *Bonds of Community: The Lives of Farm Women in Nineteenth-Century New York* (Ithaca, 1991). For a useful overview of the historiography of separate spheres ideology, see Linda K. Kerber, "Separate Spheres, Female Worlds, Woman's Place: The Rhetoric of Women's History," *Journal of American History* 75 (June 1988): 9–39.

[15] Boydston, *Home and Work*, pp. 43–45; Jan Lewis, "Motherhood and the Construction of the Male Citizen in the United States, 1750–1850," in *Construction of the Self*, ed. George Levine (New Brunswick, N.J., 1992), pp. 143–63.

[16] The rhetorical separation of home from work never corresponded to people's actual lives or dwellings, but its salience as a metaphor depended on the physical separation of industrial production from private residences. Elizabeth Blackmar demonstrates that in industrializing New

But such ideological formulations did not so much reflect the realities of women's lives as distort them. They hid the degree to which women of all classes engaged in market relations, whether in the marriage market or the wage-based labor market, and the extent to which, even in the early decades of the nineteenth century, middle-class white women had staked out claims to social authority in benevolence and reform work. These cultural myths about the domestic realm also bolstered the critiques of feminists who challenged the economic devaluation of women's unpaid labors and women's legal and political subordination.

Catharine Beecher's Political Compromise

There was one antebellum American who made explicit connections between women's unpaid household labors and the maintenance of American political liberties. With the publication in 1841 of *A Treatise on Domestic Economy*, Catharine Beecher, oldest daughter of Lyman Beecher, achieved not only financial independence but a preeminent voice in the debates over women's place in the new democracy. Beecher wrote her *Treatise* as a rejoinder to Alexis de Tocqueville's observation that American wives, relative to European wives of wealth, were decidedly disadvantaged in the respect accorded them and consigned to lives of comparative subordination.[17] (Single American daughters, on the other hand, exhibited more freedom than their European counterparts). While arguing that Tocqueville misread America's gender system, Beecher also employed his observation to demonstrate that American women carried out important political responsibilities unique to a democracy. Precisely because they inhabited a domain protected from partisan conflicts, American housewives were empowered to act as a moralizing force for society at large. Assuming that her American female audience needed greater specificity to understand her argument, Beecher devoted the rest of her book to explaining the political significance of household duties, which required that the homes women managed become well-ordered sites

---

York City, bourgeois houses acquired "new economic and cultural meanings" that "stood at the heart of new property and labor relations." Long after industrial processes removed some economic activities from the home and moved individual workers to sites of employment outside the household, housework remained a vital economic activity "immersed in economic relations" that extended far beyond consumerism and the employment of domestic servants. See *Manhattan for Rent: 1785–1850* (Ithaca, 1989), pp. 110–12, 127–38.

[17] See Kathryn Kish Sklar, *Catharine Beecher: A Study in American Domesticity* (New York, 1976), pp. 151–67. Sklar notes that the *Treatise* was "reprinted nearly every year from 1841 to 1856" (p. 151).

for labor, education, and benevolence. By rationalizing domestic labors, Beecher believed women would make visible their household labors while they themselves became cognizant of the national importance inherent in their ordinary tasks and seemingly inferior positions.

Beecher structured the bulk of her text as a manual for housekeepers, with detailed information on topics including human anatomy, nutrition, clothing, cleanliness, manners, gardening, charitable work, and familial relations. But her response to Tocqueville's criticisms of American women's position in a democracy formed the context for appreciating this advice. For Beecher, the rudiments of proper housekeeping were critical to the maintenance of a political democracy in an era of social mobility. As her biographer Kathryn Kish Sklar notes, Beecher proposed a view of domesticity that served the chaotic environment of the market and national unity by demonstrating the political value of positions of subservience.[18] "Everything is moving and changing," Beecher observed. "Persons in poverty, are rising to opulence, and persons of wealth, are sinking to poverty." Not only was class fluidity unsettling, but the "mingling of all grades of wealth, intellect, and education" created a milieu in which social distinctions and relationships needed to be elaborated to insure social order. With a "dearth of distinct classes" as well as of domestic servants, it behooved bourgeois homemakers to understand that the efficient maintenance of their homes was a responsibility of national importance. "A woman, who has charge of a large household, should regard her duties as dignified, important, and difficult," Beecher implored, for one "who feels that she is a cipher, and that it makes little difference how she performs her duties, has far less to sustain and invigorate her, than one, who truly estimates the importance of her station."[19]

Beecher was also concerned that propertied women were physically and spiritually ill equipped for their tasks, a fact that in her framework had large social implications. In a country "under the influence of high commercial, political, and religious stimulus, altogether greater than was ever known by any other nation," it was hardly surprising that so many women suffered poor health. "The anxieties, vexations, perplexities, and even hard labor, which come upon American women, from this state of domestic service, are endless," Beecher conceded, "and many a woman has, in consequence, been disheartened, discouraged, and ruined in health." Women's bodies reverberated with the tensions generated by the expansion of the market, as if

[18] Sklar, *Catharine Beecher,* pp. 155–62.
[19] Catharine Beecher, *A Treatise on Domestic Economy for the Use of Young Ladies at Home and at School,* rev. ed. (New York, 1854), pp. 39–41, 150–51.

one could read the extent of social upheaval by a calculation of female infirmities. The solution for Beecher was to systematize the "hard labor" of housework and educate women about the fortitude they needed to confront their work.[20]

What made the *Treatise* stand apart from the plethora of antebellum advice books was the way Beecher linked domestic economy to political economy. That she titled her text a treatise proclaimed her political intent. She expanded on the idea of female virtue to claim that if women relinquished their privileged positions as the guardians of society's righteousness, they lost whatever special powers they might possess. Equality endangered women by removing their claim to disinterestedness and plunging them into the self-serving arenas of politics and the market. Arguing for women's superior aptitude for housework, benevolence, and teaching, Beecher offered a political bargain to men in Jacksonian America: women would relinquish claims to political equality if in return they acquired recognition for their separate but equally important sphere of influence. "In civil and political affairs, American women take no interest or concern except so far as they sympathize with their family and personal friends," she asserted; but, as if to warn men of the consequences of not accepting her settlement, she noted that "in all cases, in which they do feel a concern, their opinions and feelings have a consideration, equal, or even superior, to that of the other sex." Women, Beecher declared, "are made subordinate in station, only where a regard to their best interests demands it, while *as if in compensation for this*, by custom and courtesy, they are always treated as superiors." Indeed, she reminded her readers that far more radical solutions than hers were available. "If those who are bewailing themselves over the fancied wrongs and injuries of women in the Nation," she wrote of feminists, "could only see things as they are, they would know, that, whatever remnants of a barbarous or aristocratic age may remain in our civil institutions, in reference to the interests of women, it is only because they are ignorant of them, or do not use their influence to have them rectified." Treat women fairly and they will refrain from extreme demands: "it is very certain that there is nothing reasonable, which American women would unite in asking, that would not readily be bestowed."[21]

Though many historians have ascribed to Beecher the essentialist thinking that permeated most of the popularized versions of the ideology of sep-

---

[20] Ibid., p. 41.
[21] Jeanne Boydston, Mary Kelley, and Anne Margolis, eds., *The Limits of Sisterhood: The Beecher Sisters on Women's Rights and Woman's Sphere* (Chapel Hill, N.C., 1988), pp. 114–22; Beecher, *A Treatise on Domestic Economy*, p. 33.

arate spheres, Beecher herself never asserted a distinct female nature dictated by biology and unshaped by environment or spiritual transformation. What gave her tract its political punch as a negotiated bargain between the sexes was the implied possibility of female equality with men; women were empowered by their expressed willingness to relinquish political rights in exchange for other forms of status and authority. "The discussion of the question of the equality of the sexes, in intellectual capacity, seems frivolous and useless," Beecher professed, "both because it can never be decided, and because there would be no possible advantage in the decision." Much more important, in Beecher's mind, was the "relative importance and difficulty of the duties a woman is called to perform."[22]

Beecher's explication of the political leverage offered by female submission offers us a means of understanding the ideology of separate spheres in a way that is often too little appreciated. This gender ideology was not a doctrine put forth to oppress women, nor was it a farsighted, though conservative, route to equality. Rather, it was a political compromise, a tenuous compact between men and women that, if broken, would lead to conflict that threatened the safety of the democratic experiment. Just as the American republic was maintained, from the Constitution to the Civil War, by a series of political compromises on slavery, so the polity was established by a bargain between the sexes, negotiated not in Congress but in print. Though not forged in as explicit a forum, the compromise on gender recognized women as political actors, but subordinate, distinct citizens with unique functions. During the Jacksonian era, when America was moving from a republic to a democracy and extending political rights to new groups of men, women's exclusion stood out in greater relief. It was in this context that the ideology of separate spheres offered a way out of the seemingly inherent contradictions of democratic rhetoric. If language about rights, freedom, and individual responsibility were not to appear hollow or fragile, the question of female political subjectivity had to be confronted.

Though the compromise on gender hinted at the idea that women had different political identities because they had different natures, it rested on the opposite premise: that women were inherently equal to men in ability, and it was only through a negotiated compact that they had acquiesced in a division of social power. The implication was that if the compromise broke down, if the female sphere of influence were not inviolate, women would be entitled to abandon their end of the bargain and demand the rights accorded to men. Yet the ideology of domesticity, as it was popularized in pe-

---

[22] Beecher, *Treatise on Domestic Economy*, p. 155.

riodicals such as *Godey's Lady's Book*, lost this contractual dimension and was reduced to an essentialist defense of the sexual division of labor and social responsibilities.

Beecher's explanation of the political purposes of housework had specific importance for the era when universal white manhood suffrage emerged. The "era of the common *man*" had far-reaching implications for the political standing of women. With the enfranchisement of all white men and their elevation by their status as men—and potential property holders—to the level of full citizens, women lost relative power.[23] Increased male access to political decision making denied such access to women. Indeed, just as free black men lost their political rights in concert with the gains made by white men, so women too surrendered, if only on a theoretical level, their claims to citizenship in order to insure the privileges of white men. Further, the identification of men with political rights reinforced assertions of women's moral superintendency and their immersion within a sentimentalized, disinterested world of domesticity.[24]

The Bonds of Compromise

This compromise, like most compromises, was effective for a time. Northern women gained much: dominion over their households, access to fields of employment, preeminence in social welfare, and an influential voice in reform movements. Middle-class white women who entered charity work in the early decades of the nineteenth century staked out claims for social power and influence that, though contested, nonetheless facilitated their entry into reform movements. But whether in moral reform, temperance, or abolitionist societies, the women's chief weapon was moral suasion, the application of religious and ethical argument to effect social change. As long as they refrained from challenging the basic structures of power, they were free to operate in the public arena.

But the compromise on gender, like all compromises, was highly unstable. As women organized to promote charity, temperance, and the abolition of slavery, they increasingly found the tools of female influence and religious temperament inadequate for their tasks. By the 1850s many looked to

[23] Joan B. Landes finds a similar effect in revolutionary France with the abolition of political distinctions among men based on status. She argues that the resulting intensification of "women's sense of sex identification" helped to shape a feminist consciousness. See *Women and the Public Sphere in the Age of the French Revolution* (Ithaca, 1988), p. 170.
[24] Klinghoffer and Elkis, "Petticoat Electors." See Harry L. Watson, *Liberty and Power: The Politics of Jacksonian America* (New York, 1990), on black men's loss of voting rights.

legislative solutions for causes they once deemed soluble by moral suasion. Some came to recognize that, without political equality, their domains of authority mattered less and less.[25] The limitations of moral influence led many reformers to appreciate the radical demands of the woman's rights movement.

By the time she coauthored a postwar tribute to northern women, Mary Vaughan had undergone one of the more dramatic transformations from moral reformer to feminist. Like other women who entered reform believing that their sex empowered them to transform the social behavior of others, Vaughan soon felt the constraints imposed by the antebellum gender system. A temperance activist and, as she put it, an "unflinching advocate for 'Women's Rights,' " she nevertheless saw those rights situated firmly in "property, educational privileges, and in the acknowledgment of her intellectual equality"—in other words, in the same terms outlined by Catharine Beecher. In late 1850, Vaughan categorically rejected the demand for female suffrage, arguing that it would "denude" women of the protection "which covers the female character as a garment."[26]

Vaughan's arguments on behalf of women's exclusion from politics belied increasing personal frustrations with established reform methods. By September 1851, she wrote Amelia Bloomer, the feminist editor of the *Lily*, that she had become "convinced that [woman] . . . can do little except through the medium of the ballot box." Increasingly skeptical about the capacity of female "influence" and concerned that the "effect of moral suasion upon men's habits and prejudices is daily lessening," Vaughan concluded that only legislative reform would effect change. Moreover, to enact legal remedies women needed access to the vote. "Less than a year since, as yourself and readers well know, the idea that women should go to the polls, was utterly repugnant to me," she admitted to Bloomer. But she was not "ashamed to change opinions when convinced that those heretofore held are erroneous."[27]

Becoming more agitated as her views changed, Vaughan wrote Bloomer again, this time to rehearse the significant but ultimately inadequate gains women had made under the umbrella of the gender compromise: "Women acquire a little of the self-reliance they so much need, in those associations; they learn to transact business; and they gain the power of arranging their

[25] Ginzberg, *Women and the Work of Benevolence*, chaps. 3, 4, 5.
[26] Letters to the editor, *Lily*, November 18, 1850, quoted in Cott et al., *Root of Bitterness*, pp. 208–9.
[27] Letters to the editor, *Lily*, September 16, 1851, quoted in ibid., p. 211.

ideas, and putting them into words and of talking on subjects of importance and interest." But experience convinced her "more and more of woman's right to the elective franchise," not solely to advance the cause of temperance, but "for every thing in which, as citizens, we can have an interest." By the end of the 1850s, Vaughan and other women reformers had come up against the limits of power accorded by the gender compromise. Having acquired organizational and political skills as well as increased confidence, they comprehended that distinct citizenship was not equal citizenship.[28]

The compromise never settled the ambiguities contained within universal white manhood suffrage, liberalism, or the gendering of market relations. In the decades before the war, feminists struggled from many vantage points to uncover its discriminatory tenets. Perhaps their most radical assault was against coverture, the legal basis for female dependency and political subordination. Coverture had already become vulnerable to the imperatives of an economic system that demanded that capital be free and mobile. It also became politically problematic with the advent of democracy and the removal of property qualifications for citizenship. The passage of married women's property acts in the antebellum decades signaled the freeing of capital from common-law constraints and a coming to terms with American women's increasingly anomalous status.[29]

For some feminists, the challenge to coverture extended beyond these demands for legal equality and required a formal appreciation of the economic value of housework. Reva Siegal has uncovered in debates over married women's property acts the demand by some feminists for a "joint property claim"—a call for economic rights in household labor—that constituted a direct challenge to the notion of marital unity. The joint property claim can only be understood in the historical moment at which it emerged. The redistribution of political rights under universal white manhood suffrage laws had diminished the relative position of wives in the early democracy, all the while providing a language of rights and equality that feminists employed to new purposes. Had feminists succeeded in gaining women joint rights in marital property by virtue of the unpaid labor wives con-

[28] Letters to the editor, *Lily*, October 20, 1851, quoted in ibid., p. 212. In the abolitionist movement, women who used their voices to challenge slavery—an enormous institution of political power and economic profit—were attacked as unwomanly. See Jean Fagan Yellin, *Women and Sisters: The Antislavery Feminists in American Culture* (New Haven, 1989).

[29] Basch, *Eyes of the Law*, pp. 137, 144. The first married women's property act was passed in 1839 in Mississippi, a result not of feminist pressures, but of the drive to protect family property from creditors' claims by placing them in wives' names.

tributed to the household, it would have constituted, according to Siegel, nothing less than "a redistribution of property in marriage."[30] Feminists' failure to achieve legal recognition for women's economic contributions had long-range ramifications. Even after married women's property acts began to chip away at wives' legal disadvantages, husbands' participation in political domains continued to be premised on their status as heads of households which persisted as the rationale for female political subjugation.[31] Without a social appreciation of the economic value of wives' household labors, the rationale for a gender division of labor remained intact. So did the belief that female housework was a complementary or compensatory activity, available to fill political and social vacuums.

Warwork—The Compromise Resurrected and Challenged

Although the compromise on gender was somewhat battered by the end of the 1850s, it gained a new lease on life when the Civil War erupted. War rhetoric and patriotic passions seized women as they did men. The occasion of participating in a nonpartisan, collective political experience presented many northern women with unique opportunities to express their political loyalties and demonstrate their benevolent skills. But when women across the homefront were called upon by nationalist leaders to support the war effort through warwork, the relationship between women's unpaid household labors and the maintenance of the political system was once again brought into relief.

In ways only barely recognized at the outset of the conflict, the Civil War became a testing ground for the gendering of political rights and the ideological separation of men's and women's domains of work and influence. Though assumptions about women's domestic labors and their relationship to the political order had come under attack in the decade before the war, the identification of property and citizenship with men remained strong and, arguably, was even strengthened by the political rhetoric that gave rise to the Republican wartime state. A political party that came into existence with the slogan, "free soil, free labor, free men," expressed a conspicuous set

[30] Reva B. Siegel, "Home as Work: The First Woman's Rights Claims Concerning Wives' Household Labor, 1850–1880," *Yale Law Journal* 103 (March 1994): 1073–217.
[31] Basch, *In the Eyes of the Law*; Norma Basch, "Equity vs. Equality: Emerging Concepts of Women's Political Status in the Age of Jackson," *Journal of the Early Republic* 3 (Fall 1983): 297–318. The devaluation of women's household labors also demonstrated a tenacious hold in transatlantic economic thought; see Nancy Folbre, "The Unproductive Housewife: Her Evolution in Nineteenth-Century Economic Thought," *Signs* 16 (Spring 1991): 463–84.

of assumptions about the relation of property, political power, and gender that were shared by the vast majority of northern men, regardless of previous party affiliation. Legal and social constraints on female economic autonomy all but guaranteed that free soil was meant for free men. For only if men were free to appropriate the labor of family members in support of the household economy or, given industrialization, in support of the chief wage laborer, could they stand ready to take advantage of the opportunities that free soil might offer.[32]

Debates about the value of women's household and benevolent labors appeared to vanish amidst the exigencies of war. Regardless of the disadvantages that might attend the expansion of a society based on free labor, thousands of northern women embraced the defense of the Union as their own struggle. Women's labors in support of the war did not go unnoticed, nor did questions of how such activities should be interpreted. Precisely because the war occurred after a decade of challenges to the gender compromise, female warwork became a critical site of patriotic discourse and controversy.

This book explores the wartime controversies that ensued over female household labors and political obligations. In their communications with the prominent men who led the Sanitary Commission and the propertied women who directed the organization's regional branches, women across the North left a unique record of their political concerns, the complexity of their household duties, and the difficulties they encountered in applying their benevolence to the Union army. While employing sources from across the North, the book pays special attention to the Woman's Central Relief Association (WCRA), the New York–based, female-led branch of the Sanitary Commission that had authority over aid societies in most of New York State, portions of New Jersey, as well as areas of Connecticut, and Massachusetts. The WCRA held a special position in the organization. Organized prior to the creation of the Sanitary Commission, it suggested the possibilities inherent in organizing northern women's charitable activities, which the commission's founders shaped to their own ends. But the women who ran the WCRA occupied contradictory positions. Closely tied to Sanitary Commission men by class, religious, and institutional affiliations, they also shared the gender and volunteer status of homefront women. At many mo-

[32] See Eric Foner, *Free Soil, Free Labor, Free Men: The Ideology of the Republican Party before the Civil War* (1970; rpt. New York, 1984), on the meanings of "free labor" rhetoric; see Nina Silber, *The Romance of Reunion: Northerners and the South, 1865–1900* (Chapel Hill, N.C., 1993), for analysis of how metaphors and rhetoric of gender conveyed and legitimized other relationships of power.

ments, the WCRA women embodied the complicated gender and class dynamics that beset the management of northern homefront war relief.

The ceaseless production of sentimental narratives about female sacrifice attested to the felt need by some northerners to make visible the dimensions of women's contributions to the Union cause. Such stories also suggested, however, an effort to dictate the political meanings attached to women's household labors. If nothing else, the stream of romanticized stories about magnanimous women who acted out of instinct and moral temperament to support the state hinted at the war's potential to upset customary assessments of women's unpaid labors. Any reconsideration of the relationship of women's domesticity and the political system would constitute a reevaluation of the American gender structure. Because the American Civil War, which depended so heavily on popular voluntarism, expanded the space for female economic and political participation, the disjuncture between the realities of women's lives and the myths embedded in the antebellum compromise threatened to become visible.

1

"WE ALL HAVE VIEWS NOW": TAPPING FEMALE PATRIOTISM

On April 12, 1861, as southern troops shelled the federal base at Fort Sumter, igniting the American Civil War, Mary Livermore, an abolitionist and temperance lecturer, became swept up by the war fervor that suddenly engrossed Boston. For Livermore, those "never-to-be-forgotten days of Sumter's bombardment" were days of deep ambivalence, marked by apprehension about the possibility of a long and calamitous war but, at the same time, by elation about the prospect of slavery's demise. More than anything else, she remembered the exhilarating outbursts of patriotism and civic unity. On the following Sunday, pulpits in Boston "thundered with denunciations of the rebellion," recalled Livermore, who was surprised by the radical sermons offered by antislavery clergy. Amid this "blaze of belligerent excitement" came Lincoln's call for 75,000 troops to protect Washington and federal property; in what seemed like no time, recruiting offices opened in "every city, town, and village." In her memoir, Livermore wrote admiringly about military volunteers who were escorted through Boston by throngs of supporters. "Merchants and clerks rushed out from stores, bareheaded, saluting them as they passed. Windows were flung up; and women leaned out into the rain waving flags and handkerchiefs." By the time she returned to Chicago a few days later, Livermore was deeply impressed by the popular demonstrations that she had witnessed across the northern landscape; the "war spirit was rampant," she wrote, and "engrossed everybody."[1]

Livermore's account echoed those of other northerners, who were astonished by the precipitous shift in public sentiment and the spirit of cohesiveness that characterized the first days and weeks of the war. In what became a familiar refrain among contemporaries, the North suddenly coalesced into a patriotic whole. Even in a society with a strong voluntarist tradition, and despite frequent evocations of comparable behavior during the Revolutionary War, the scope of civilian initiative during the Civil War seemed unprecedented. Given the contentious partisanship that had characterized the antebellum decades and the divisiveness generated by the secession of the southern states, the sudden disappearance of political differences elicited frequent comment. Ulysses Grant recalled that business activities in Galena, Illinois, ceased as townspeople turned their attention to the war effort: "all was excitement; for a time there were no party distinctions." Maria Lydig Daly, an upper-class New Yorker and the wife of a Democrat, observed that the firing on Fort Sumter "united all the North. . . . All feel that our very nationality is at stake." As recruitment drives commenced, the omnipresent expressions of political harmony made any public criticism unseemly. Remarking on the Seventh Regiment's grand march through New York City (fig. 1), Jane Stuart Woolsey concluded that "New York. . . is all on one side now—all ready to forget lesser differences." From the moment the war began, northerners boasted about the prodigious efforts with which they mobilized themselves into a loyal homefront.[2]

Not all were persuaded by the consensus that seemed to seize northern public opinion. Admittedly surprised by the apparent "unity of all parties," the radical abolitionist and writer Lydia Maria Child nonetheless suspected that economic self-interest and fear of social chaos lay at the heart of much of the fervor. "I do not think there is much of either right principle, or good feeling, at the foundation of this unanimous Union sentiment," she wrote to her friend Lucy Osgood. Observing that "our merchants are alarmed

[1] Mary A. Livermore, *My Story of the War: A Woman's Narrative of Four Years Personal Experience* . . . (Hartford, Conn., 1889), pp. 85–104.

[2] Ulysses Grant, *Memoirs*, quoted in *Life in the North during the Civil War: A Source History*, ed. George Winston Smith and Charles Judah (Albuquerque, N.M., 1966), pp. 42–49; Maria Lydig Daly, *Diary of a Union Lady, 1861–1865*, ed. Harold E. Hammond (New York, 1962), p. 12 January 31, 1861; J. S. W. to Margaret Hodge, April 1861, in *Letters of a Family during the War for the Union, 1861–1865*, ed. G. W. Bacon and E. W. Howland, 2 vols. (New York, 1899), 1:45. See also Ethel Alice Hurn, *Wisconsin Women in the War between the States* (Madison, Wis., 1911), pp. 1–11, for descriptions of Wisconsin flag raisings, war meetings, and "the soul-stirring and ear-splitting music of the fife and drum."

In his oil painting *Seventh Regiment Marching Down Broadway, April 16, 1861*, Thomas Nast depicted, somewhat romantically, the patriotic displays and popular support that characterized the early days of war mobilization. The Seventh Regiment Fund, Inc.

about dangers to commerce" and others had become suddenly defensive about "insults to the U.S. flag," Child judged that "great numbers of people think there is an imperious necessity of defending the government *now* lest there should soon be no government to protect us from utter anarchy." For the majority, Child concluded, patriotism represented the readiness of people "to rush into whatever is the fashion."[3]

Women and the Politics of War

"It is easy to understand how men catch the contagion of war," Livermore conjectured; what required explanation was why women, "who send forth their husbands, sons, brothers and lovers to the fearful chances of the battle-field," were willing to endure such "exquisite suffering." The answer, she believed, lay in "another kind of patriotism," a love for their men and their country that diverged from male loyalties and masculine combativeness and provided women with a special strength to maintain "their own courage and that of their households."[4]

Implicit in Livermore's commentary on female loyalty was not only the idea that men's patriotism was something ingrained but also the idea that women's support of the war represented a conscious decision to make unique sacrifices in defense of the nation. Many women took on soldier aid work out of concern for husbands, sons, and neighbors leaving for war. Others were propelled by the excitement and urgency that marked mobilization drives. Yet the war's appeal to northern women went deeper than personal attachments or susceptibility to popular passions. Although the ferment surrounding the outbreak of military conflict seemed to cut across all social categories, troop mobilization presented dist███████portunities for many northern women. In a nation with a weak cen███ ▓ernment and a long tradition of political obligations performed at t██ ▓ocal level, the urgent need for civilian support furnished women, especially white women of the middle class, with an occasion for presenting themselves as skilled members of the polity whose contributions were essential to the government's defense, a chance to enact their political beliefs on terms that both they and men appreciated and held to be legitimate.[5] In the emergency

[3] Lydia Maria Child to Lucy Osgood, Wayland, April 26, 1861, in *Lydia Maria Child: Selected Letters, 1817–1880*, ed. Milton Meltzer and Patricia Holland (Amherst, Mass., 1982), p. 380.
[4] Livermore, *My Story of the War*, pp. 110, 120.
[5] Dorothy Sterling notes that because, in the early years of the war, black men were not permitted to enlist in the Union army, black women "remained on the sidelines" of mobilization. Many black women did become active aiding contraband slaves arriving in Washington. See

conditions generated by war, women welcomed the sudden expansion of the emotional and physical spaces in which they could perform their citizenship. Although the antebellum gender divisions of labor and power meant that women would not be able to dictate either the extent of their political contributions or the measure of their sacrifices, many women nonetheless perceived that the military crisis might erase some of the boundaries that separated them from male preserves of power.

In their wartime letters and memoirs, women frequently discussed the meaning of the war in terms of their own inclusion and sense of belonging. Emotion was suddenly the measure of political commitment, and women could feel as deeply as any. Harriet Judd of New York reminisced that the "the whole country was aroused" by the sudden entry into military conflict, and the "feeling was intense."[6] The prospect of armed combat moved some to comment on the way national events focused their attentions on politics. "I enjoy public affairs now," wrote Elizabeth Neall Gay in January of 1861, acknowledging that she hoped the war would turn into a "splendid Revolution." In a May 1861, letter to her cousin Sarah Watson, Mary Marsh of Brooklyn, New York, observed that "it takes most all my time to read the newspapers." "The northern enthusiasm gives me a new idea of the love of country as an idea realized," Sarah Alden Ripley of Massachusetts confessed to her daughter. "Who could have dreamed a year ago of political cabals, private interests 'hunkerdom'. . . merged in one grand stream of men and money uniting to preserve the Union," she mused, adding, "I know, nor care for politics in any form, and yet I am drawn into the vortex." A few months into the war, Helen Grinnell, the wife of a New York banker and a mother of five children, recorded her prayers that "the 'Constitution,' and the Federal Government may be sustained, and that the Union may be preserved."[7]

Dorothy Sterling, ed., *We Are Your Sisters: Black Women in the Nineteenth Century* (New York, 1984), pp. 245–54.

[6] Harriet Steward Judd, Autobiography 1903–5, Harriet Steward Judd Papers; Helen Grinnell, Diary, July 11, 1861, Helen Grinnell, Papers. Civil War memoirs, like all narratives, were constructions, aided and impeded by the passage of time and written within specific historical contexts. The war generated scores of memoirs by soldiers, politicians, government workers, and homefront participants that served both personal and political needs. Authors staked their claims for authority on their personal experiences; in the case of women, memoirs were usually written by nurses or members of Sanitary Commission branches. Anne C. Rose argues that the Civil War memoir must be read in the context of the "fascination with the self and human experience" characteristic of Victorians, who "wrote not as rationalists but as romantics." See *Victorian America and the Civil War* (New York, 1992), p. 254.

[7] Elizabeth Neall Gay to Sarah Pugh, January 19, 186[1], Sidney Howard Gay Papers; Mary B. Marsh to Sarah Watson, May 27, 1861, Mary B. Marsh Papers; Sarah A. Ripley to Sophia

In the eyes of many, the specter of military conflict removed political questions from the grubby world of partisan squabbling, elevating them to a higher plane and imbuing them with a purer nationalist content. For Rachel Cormany, even her prior involvement in abolitionist activities could not rival the war as a vehicle for political expression. While a student at Oberlin College, she had been attracted to the antislavery movement and, in her husband's words, "had caught the 'underground R.R.' idea." Yet, when the sectional conflict broke, Samuel Cormany recognized that the war gave his young wife "a good position to make sacrifices—if needs be—in a different form to carry out her patriotic ideas."[8] The feminist newspaper *The Mayflower* summarized the correspondence from its readership by noting that "nearly every letter we receive breathes a spirit of deep feeling upon the war question. Mothers, wives and daughters are no less interested than their sons, fathers and husbands. There seems to be little disposition to think, speak, read or write of anything else."[9] When Jane Woolsey tried to explain to a friend the mood in New York City in May 1861, she declined to offer her own political opinions, but added: "Not, in passing, that I haven't any! We all have views now, men, women and little boys."[10]

Mary Livermore was struck by the ways in which the war created arenas for men and women to join together as a newly constituted public, which was sanctioned to support the military on the battlefield whatever the cost. When, at Boston's Faneuil Hall, men filed in military-like columns to answer Lincoln's first call for volunteers, Livermore observed that "men, women, and children seethed in a fervid excitement."[11] Amid the seemingly universal approbation for combat, women felt free to vent a belligerency toward the Confederacy and a fondness for military regalia that contravened the bourgeois socialization of women. Maria Lydig Daly was surprised to hear upper-class New York City women "admiring swords, pistols, etc., and seeming to wish to hear of the death of Southerners." Many women coveted masculine emblems of militarism. In Skowhegan, Maine, one group of women appropriated local artillery to stage "a salute of thirty-four guns." And then there were the famous cases—estimated at a minimum of four

Thayer, 1861, Sarah Alden Ripley Papers; Helen Grinnell, Diary, July 11, 1861, Grinnell Papers.
[8] Rachel Cormany and Samuel Cormany, *The Cormany Diaries: A Northern Family in the Civil War*, ed. James C. Mohr (Pittsburgh, Pa., 1982), p. 207.
[9] *Mayflower*, May 15, 1861. This semi-monthly paper was edited by Miss Lizzie Bunnell and Mary F. Thomas, M.D., and published in Peru, Ind.
[10] Jane Stuart Woolsey to "a friend," May 10, 1861, in Bacon and Howland, *Letters*, 1:66.
[11] Livermore, *My Story of the War*, p. 91.

hundred—of women who disguised themselves as men and joined the Union army.[12]

But the historic identification of militarism with masculinity also pointed to the disadvantages women faced in enacting their politics. When the ultimate gesture of political obligation was military service, offering one's life for the preservation of the state, more than a few women chafed at the legal constraints imposed on their sex. As soon as the war began, Louisa May Alcott confided in her diary: "I long to be a man; but as I can't fight, I will content myself with working for those who can."[13] Another woman who devoted herself to war relief work reasoned, "for. . . what else can we women do, at such a time as this? We cannot fight ourselves, but we can help those who can."[14]

Although legal and social codes prevented women from performing their loyalties in the same manner as men, war mobilization nonetheless presented women with ways of exploiting the very structures of gender inequality to demonstrate their politics and loyalties. In acts of production and self-denial, many women discovered distinctly feminine methods for increasing their visibility as members of the polity. "They lopped off superfluities, retrenched in expenditures, became deaf to the calls of pleasure, and heeded not the mandates of fashion," Livermore wrote of her middle-class peers.[15] In the production of uniforms and supplies for departing soldiers, women applied their mastery of domestic arts to political uses. Through military rallies, village parades, charity bazaars, and the household production of patriotic artifacts, they devised creative means to express their inclusion in the national crisis, while simultaneously underscoring their identities as women.

---

[12] Daly, November 7, 1861, in *Diary of a Union Lady*, p. 73; Agatha Young, *The Women and the Crisis: Women of the North in the Civil War* (New York, 1959), pp. 96–98; Bell Irvin Wiley, *The Life of Billy Yank: The Common Soldier of the Union* (Baton Rouge, La., 1952), p. 18. Jane Ellen Schultz notes that the figure of four hundred female soldiers which is repeated in numerous sources was based on the number of women who sought war pensions; her research revealed many more who went incognito to the front. See Schultz, "Women at the Front: Gender and Genre in Literature of the American Civil War" (Ph.D. diss., University of Michigan, 1988), pp. 272–73.

[13] Louisa May Alcott, *The Journals of Louisa May Alcott*, ed. Joel Myerson and Daniel Shealy (Boston, 1989), p. 105.

[14] *Six Hundred Dollars a Year, A Wife's Effort at Low Living, under High Prices* (Boston, 1867), p. 45. Southern women expressed similar frustrations at being unable to serve as men did to defend their society. See Drew Gilpin Faust, "Altars of Sacrifice: Confederate Women and the Narratives of War," in *Divided Houses: Gender and the Civil War*, ed. Catherine Clinton and Nina Silber (New York, 1992), pp. 177–99; George C. Rable, *Civil Wars: Women and the Crisis of Southern Nationalism* (Urbana, Ill., 1989), p. 151.

[15] Livermore, *My Story of the War*, p. 110.

The symbol women chose most often to signify their patriotism was the United States flag. This choice of symbol was not surprising; northerners everywhere embraced the flag as an expression of their loyalty to the Union. When Caroline Dunstan attended a mass Union meeting in New York in April 1861, she saw "every house dressed with Flags, and every one with flags or Union badges."[16] But in an economy still dominated by household manufacturing, nearly every woman possessed the ability to produce her own patriotic emblem; handcrafting a national flag allowed a woman to identify herself as a citizen of a larger public while at the same time expressing the distinctiveness of her domestic skills. Sarah Chauncey Woolsey and her neighbors expressed their dual and overlapping loyalties to their nation and their state by making a Union flag as well as a special flag for Connecticut's Second Regiment. "The regimental banner is worked with the arms of the state. . . with a heavy wreath of palm worked in gold-colored silk around the shield and mounted on a staff headed with a battle-axe and spear plated in gold. Won't it be beautiful?" she asked rhetorically.[17] While creating regimental banners may have permitted more individual creativity in design, replicating the national flag provided a concrete means of imagining the connections that flowed from one's home to the national community. After Mary Chapman of Malone, New York, donated the flag she made to the local recruiting station, she confided to her daughter a desire for one of her own: "I am childish enough to want a flag to adorn my place of retreat; think [I] shall have one of merino or silk; nice but small, shall worship it as long as I live."[18]

"Love for the old flag became a passion," Livermore recalled, as women "crocheted it prettily in silk, and wore it as a decoration on their bonnets and in their bosoms."[19] Household reproductions of the flag motif proliferated as women incorporated its design and colors in a variety of crafted items. Caroline Cowles Richards, a young New York girl, boasted in her diary of the myriad ways she and her peers employed the nationalist symbol. "We have flags on our paper and envelopes, and have all our stationery bordered with red, white and blue. We wear little flag pins for badges and tie our hair with red, white and blue ribbon and have pins and earrings made of the buttons the soldiers gave us. We are going to sew for them in our society," she recorded. "We are going to write notes and enclose them

[16] Caroline A. Dunstan, Diary, April 20, 1861, Caroline Dunstan Papers.
[17] Sarah Chauncy Woolsey to Georgeanna M. Woolsey, 1861, in Bacon and Howland, *Letters*, 1:52.
[18] Mary Chapman to Mary Adelaide Chapman, February 14, 1864, Mary S. Chapman Papers.
[19] Mary A. Livermore, *The Story of My Life* (Hartford, Conn., 1897), p. 465.

in the garments to cheer up the soldier boys."[20] Though gratified by the patriotic displays made by members of her sex, Jane Woolsey remained somewhat embarrassed by the sudden cachet attached to wearing the "Union bonnet," a headpiece she described as "composed of alternate layers of red, white and blue, with streaming ribbons 'of the first.' "[21]

Along with declaring one's nationalism, the flag could also embody more particular political content. For Livermore, the flag came to represent her antislavery sentiments. Prior to the war, the national flag had never "signified anything" in particular, but after seeing the men, women, and children of Boston fired up with enthusiasm during the first recruitment drive, her feelings changed. "As I saw it now, kissing the skies," she recorded, "all that it symbolized as representative of government and emblematic of national majesty became clear to my mental vision." The flag now symbolized a specific moral meaning: "It signified an advance in human government."[22]

While many women used symbolic means to identify with the Union cause, others displayed their political consciousness through patriotic demeanor and rhetoric. Young women and adolescent girls found both gendered and age-specific ways to exhibit their support for the cause. At Union meetings in Wisconsin, one observer noted that "young ladies were generally more enthusiastic than the boys."[23] Not yet saddled with the responsibilities of adult womanhood and belonging to the same age group as most male volunteers, some girls were especially anxious to experience a taste of army life. Mary Jackson parodied military phraseology to describe to her soldier brother the frustration felt by the young women in her household: "Well now for one glimpse at home: 'disposition of forces.' Mary P. and Helen up in the study. . . . The girls. . . in the parlor. . . . The girls making some noise, talking much of the rebels and what they would do if men. I wish some of us women about here could be soldiers in place of the laggards that stay at home."[24]

[20] Caroline Cowles Richards, *Village Life in America, 1852–1872, Including the Period of the American Civil War as Told in the Diary of a School-Girl* (New York, 1913), p. 131.
[21] Jane Stuart Woolsey to "a Friend in Paris," May 10, 1861, in Bacon and Howland, *Letters*, 1:67; the bonnet may have consisted of the red, white, and blue wreaths of tissue paper that young boys sold on the streets of New York. The *Evening Post* reported seeing "young ladies who grace the shady 'stoops' in the cool evening sporting them upon their heads," July 24, 1861.
[22] Livermore, *My Story of the War,* pp. 91–92.
[23] *Company E and the Twelfth Wisconsin in the War for the Union,* quoted in Hurn, *Wisconsin Women,* p. 3.
[24] Alice E. Jackson to William Sharpless Jackson, June 26, 1863, Alger Family Papers.

"Design for a New Fancy Ball Character, Suggested by the War Wagons in the Park," a September 1861 cartoon from the satirical weekly *Vanity Fair,* caricatured northern women's creative inventions with flag motifs and their support for military medical relief. Prints and Photographs Division, Library of Congress.

To influence potential Union recruits, young women exploited one of their obvious appeals by linking patriotism to romance. Some imitated their southern counterparts who, they heard, refused to be courted by men who did not volunteer for the army. Septima Collis remembered that "young girls were declaring they would never engage themselves to a man who refused to fight for his country." The inducements women devised to encourage men to enlist and resist temptations to desert were pivotal in generating a new definition of masculinity, shaped by war and infused with heroic courage. One soldier confirmed the new development in his diary: "If a fellow wants to go with a girl now he had better enlist. The girls sing 'I am Bound to be a Soldier's Wife or Die an Old Maid'."[25]

Amid the commotion of mobilization, women's ardor for war was kept in check by the realization that some sacrifices might be more than they could bear. The prospect of losing loved ones left many women ambivalent about armed combat. Even in the first month of the war, Jane Woolsey observed that "there is the most extraordinary mixture of feeling with everyone—so much resistless enthusiasm and yet so much sadness." "What sad work this war is making," fifteen-year-old Helen Hart wrote in her diary when her father left to join an Ohio regiment as a surgeon. Wives and mothers of enlisted men faced dilemmas, balancing their commitment to the war's goals with their personal anxieties. Mary Logan, the wife of General John A. Logan, confided to him the limits of her patriotism: "I wish I could lay my hands on my heart and say truthfully I felt patriotic enough to give you up freely to do what you could in this war. . . but I can't." Upon first witnessing a soldier's burial, Rachel Cormany feared for her husband. "I could not help shedding a tear for the brave soldier, perhaps thinking that such may be the fate of my poor Samuel makes me so sad." Thinking of her enlisted son, Cory, Mary Chapman wrote in her diary, "I hope he will survive this war for I think he will be capable of appreciating peace, home, liberty." Yet Livermore may have assumed too much about the "exquisite suffering" women were willing to endure. In 1864 Mary Hawley, who was overwhelmed by reports of both Union and Confederate losses, wrote in her diary: "I wept I could not control my feelings, they are all my Countrymen led on blindly to their ruin."[26]

---

[25] Though many southern women resented the Confederacy's demand for their husbands and sons, a popular trend emerged that encouraged women to bestow romantic favors only on those who enlisted. See Drew Gilpin Faust, *Mothers of Invention: Women of the Slaveholding South in the Civil War* (Chapel Hill, N.C., 1996), pp. 12–18; Septima M. Collis, *A Woman's War Record, 1861–1865* (New York, 1889), p. 12. For other instances of young women coaxing boyfriends to enlist, see Ethel Alice Hurn, *Wisconsin Women in the War Between the States* (Wisconsin History Commission, 1911), pp. 3–4; Gerald F. Linderman, *Embattled Courage: The Experience of Combat in the American Civil War* (New York, 1987), pp. 87–94; *With Sherman to the Sea: The Journal of Theodore F. Upson*, quoted in Wiley, *Billy Yank*, p. 21. See also Mary Elizabeth Massey, *Bonnet Brigades* (New York, 1966), p. 30.

[26] Jane S. Woolsey to Margaret Hodge, April 1861, in Bacon and Howland, *Letters*, 1:51; Helen Marcia Hart, Diary, September 7, 1861, Helen Marcia Hart Papers; Mary Logan to John A. Logan, February 12, 1862, John A. Logan Family Papers; Cormany and Cormany, *Cormany Diaries*, p. 256; Mary S. Chapman, July 31, 1863, Chapman Papers; Mary Hawley, Diary, May 13, 1864, Mary Hawley Papers.

Female Patriotism

In spite of the poignant emotions they voiced about the purposes of the war and the passion they displayed for political affairs, most northern women were depicted by the popular culture of the war years as personifying a special "female" patriotism. Though women believed they had responded to the war emergency as members of communities and citizens of a nation alongside men, their support of the military was frequently characterized as gender-specific behavior, the manifestation of an apolitical and charitable nature. Whether women expressed their patriotism through their domesticity or as a result of the gendered modes of thought that permeated midcentury American culture, wartime invocations of political cohesion went hand in hand with an intensely gendered nationalist rhetoric. Throughout the war, northern women worked in a context that cast their patriotism as reflecting "feminine" rather than universal political concerns.

The Civil War notion of female patriotism stressed the naturalness of female loyalty, implying that women engaged in mobilization drives and soldier relief out of moral instincts, not political reason. When northern women threw themselves into the war effort, male contemporaries had a readymade intellectual framework through which to comprehend such activities, and few were surprised or unduly impressed. In his account of northern war charity, the Sanitary Commission's chronicler noted that the "earliest movement that was made for army relief [was] begun, as it is hardly necessary to say, by the women of the country."[27] What appeared, rhetorically, to be a single patriotism was, in fact, a dichotomous concept, calling men to patriotic obligation as citizens who offered services to the state through their own free will and summoning women as citizens who were guided by apolitical and irrepressible propensities.

Wartime references to women's distinct political nature were plentiful. In 1863, the conservative *Godey's Lady's Book and Magazine* intoned that, although women could not "grasp all the subjects relating to the world," it was unimportant, for "moral sense is superior to mental power."[28] An 1862 article in *Arthur's Home Magazine* declared that while men dominated as statesmen, patriots, and conquerors, women were invisible but all-important heroines at home. Extolling the female heroism of "self-sacrifice [and] self-denial," the article explained that the "heroisms of the home"

---

[27] Charles J. Stillé, *History of the United States Sanitary Commission* (Philadelphia, 1866), p. 39.
[28] *Godey's Lady's Book and Magazine*, April 1863, p. 396.

were in fact undertaken unconsciously. "They are *only natural*. They are nothing more than the spontaneous impulses and instincts of the heart. Those who perform them could do no less."[29]

The idea of female patriotism repackaged domestic ideology for the war emergency, placing voluntarism and moral purity at the heart of women's political obligations to the state. Just as the antebellum ideology of separate spheres mystified the economic contributions of housework during the expansion of waged labor, so female patriotism veiled women's domestic labor in service to the Union with an aura of sentiment. Because the rhetoric of female patriotism was about love and not work, about sacrifices driven by nature rather than by calculation, women's wartime benevolence was assumed to be limitless. This dichotomous reading of patriotic loyalty elevated men's capacity to control women's unpaid domestic labor, moving from appropriating ownership of such labor in individual households to claiming authority over it for the nation. While men were never asked to perform labor for free, whether as soldiers or agents of benevolent organizations, women were expected to demonstrate their loyalty through donating labor.

One measure of the dominance of this gendered construction of northern patriotism was the effort many women made to distance themselves from it. As if to deflect the repercussions of their unequal access to military service and to question the double standard applied to their patriotic activities, women who wrote about the war frequently stressed the inherent parity of their political passions with those of men. In her autobiography, the feminist Elizabeth Cady Stanton made a point of noting that the "patriotism of woman shone forth as fervently and spontaneously as did that of man."[30] Other memoir writers recounted with pride the solidarity that the war evoked across the gender divide. Sarah Henshaw remembered that with the onset of war, "the habits of ordinary life were suspended," and as men from the Northwest went to the front, the women were "filled with a like patriotism." Explaining her decision to volunteer as a nurse in military hospitals, Sophronia Bucklin drew a pointed comparison between male and female behavior: "The same patriotism which took the young and brave from workshop and plow, from counting-rooms, and college halls... lent also to our hearts its thrilling measure."[31]

The sense of possibility that attended women's voluntary support of the

[29] "Heroism of Home," *Arthur's Home Magazine*, June 1862, p. 357.
[30] Elizabeth Cady Stanton, *Eighty Years and More: Reminiscences, 1815–1897* (1898; rpt. New York, 1971), pp. 233–37.
[31] Sarah Edwards Henshaw, *Our Branch and Its Tributaries: Being a History of the Work of the Northwestern Sanitary Commission and its Auxiliaries . . .* (Chicago, 1868), pp. 19, 21; Sophronia

Union grew out of the particular conditions of northern mobilization, predicated on the voluntary enlistment of soldiers and the freely offered support of their communities. As a consequence of the customary American reliance on volunteer troops and citizen militia, and of the absence of mandatory conscription policies, the Union army was largely constructed through individual acts of voluntarism. Even after the federal government instituted conscription in 1863, the draft functioned primarily as an incentive to voluntarism (and the bounty systems functioned more as revenue-raising devices), rather than as compulsory means of raising troops. The numerous permissible exemptions to the draft and the prerogative, until the middle of 1864, to pay for substitutes greatly weakened the force of Union draft rules. Throughout the course of the war, the vast majority of men joined the Union forces as volunteers.[32]

When the war began, the federal government possessed neither the fiscal structure nor the administrative manpower to raise and outfit a national army. The popular distrust of a standing army instilled by the Revolutionary War had left the War Department with meager funding and only a skeletal staff. Despite temporary increases during the Seminole and Mexican wars, federal appropriations to the War Department in 1860 were at the same level as those in 1808. Policy dictated in those wars, as it would at the outset of the Civil War, that military engagements would be fought by a combination of volunteers and state militias. With the creation of the Confederacy, weak federal forces were further diminished by the departure of skilled southern officers from the regular army.[33]

The creation of a viable military force was thus heavily dependent on a broad-based mobilization of individual and local resources. Until the Lincoln administration intervened by revamping taxation policies and engaging the private market to supply the military, the burden of raising and equipping military regiments fell to state and local governments, manufacturers,

---

E. Bucklin, *In Hospital and Camp: A Woman's Record of Thrilling Incidents among the Wounded in the Late War* (Philadelphia, 1869), p. 33.

[32] Richard Franklin Bensel, *Yankee Leviathan: The Origins of Central State Authority in America, 1859–1877* (New York, 1990), pp. 85, 138–39; Carl Russell Fish, "Conscription in the Civil War," *American Historical Review* 21 (October 1915): 100–103; Fish noted that out of nearly 2.5 million enlistments, only 61,950 men were actually drafted through federal conscription laws. See also Eugene C. Murdock, *Patriotism Limited, 1862–1865: The Civil War Draft and the Bounty System* (Kent, Ohio, 1967), p. 16.

[33] Leonard D. White, *The Jacksonians: A Study in Administrative History, 1829–1861* (New York, 1954), pp. 187–205. White notes that in the decades before the war, in addition to a lean staff and poor funding, the army was plagued by resignations of officers and the demoralization of enlisted men, who deserted regularly.

and private citizens. States assumed most of the initial costs of recruitment, allotting funds to raise militias and to purchase uniforms, food, arms, and munitions. But the need to redirect private resources to military purposes required civic participation on a grand scale, and throughout the North, cities and localities assisted by staging recruitment drives to organize regiments and companies. County and city governments instituted taxes to fund their own bounties for local recruits, while communities of all sizes raised funds to support the families left behind by departing soldiers. The support offered by individual citizens was considerable; the *New York Times* reported that donations by private citizens exceeded $23 million within the first two weeks of the war.[34]

Soldiers' Aid Societies

In the context of a highly decentralized and voluntaristic mobilization of human and economic resources, middle-class women constituted a wellspring of needed labor and supplies. Anxious to convey loyalty to the Union cause and accustomed to handling the welfare needs of others, thousands of northern middle-class women reacted to the war emergency both by refocusing existing charitable organizations to meet the increased demands of military mobilization and by creating new societies devoted solely to the needs of soldiers.[35]

Many of the initiatives undertaken by women during the first weeks of the war drew on the social networks they had developed in antebellum sewing groups, church associations, and moral reform societies. They also drew on women's extensive domestic skills. It is probable that nearly every nineteenth-century northern woman had some ability to sew and, at the outbreak of the war, most were still responsible for the production of their households' clothing. While the burgeoning textile industry increasingly relieved women from the spinning of yarn and manufacture of cloth, few could afford to rely solely on ready-made clothing. Indeed, most women were regularly occupied with the cutting, sewing, and repairing of clothing.

[34] Fred Albert Shannon, *The Organization and Administration of the Union Army, 1861–1865*, 2 vols. (Gloucester, Mass., 1965), 1:15–148; Emerson David Fite, *Social and Industrial Conditions in the North during the Civil War* (New York, 1963), pp. 288–89; Hurn, *Wisconsin Women*, p. 63; David Martin Osher, "Soldier Citizens for a Disciplined Nation: Civil War Conscription and the Development of the Modern American State" (Ph.D. diss. Columbia University, 1992), pp. 113–18, 126.
[35] Robert H. Bremner, *The Public Good: Philanthropy and Welfare in the Civil War Era* (New York, 1980), pp. 74–75.

Even genteel women, who could hire the services of seamstresses (and whose husbands and fathers purchased ready-made suits), were expected to be able to sew and do needlework. Women often sewed together, gathering to share each other's company while engaged in the time-consuming task of stitching personal garments. Farm women, with less available time, came together for quilting bees, combining their labor to produce large items, sharing techniques and camaraderie. In smaller towns and villages, women formed sewing circles and "Dorcas" societies, merging work and social interaction in quasi-institutional formats.[36]

Though it was easy to modify the object of a local sewing group to serve the needs of mobilization, the war prompted women in many locales to create organizations specifically charged with aiding the federal war effort and, through a process of renaming, provided women with another means of making their patriotism visible to a larger public. The first recorded soldiers' aid society was constituted on April 15, 1861, in Bridgeport, Connecticut. In many cases, organized relief was instigated by the elite— "leading"—women in the community, such as those in Peekskill, New York, who arranged to receive contributions and prepare supplies before the first volunteers departed from town. The women of Rockdale, Pennsylvania, began war relief within days of the South's insurrection, soon extending their labors to the military hospital in nearby Philadelphia.[37]

The historical record is inherently skewed to reflect the activities of those with the resources and self-consciousness to keep accounts of their doings, or those with sufficient social stature to merit attention in contemporary narratives and regional histories. But working-class women also participated in soldier relief work: some, like their propertied counterparts, as members of local aid societies, and others as laborers hired to work in improvised workshops to produce garments from materials purchased by wealthier neighbors. Mary Marsh reported that at Henry Ward Beecher's

[36] Susan Strasser, *Never Done: A History of American Housework* (New York, 1982), pp. 123–34; Juliet A. Matthaei, *An Economic History of Women in America: Women's Work, the Sexual Division of Labor, and the Development of Capitalism* (New York, 1982), pp. 45–47. In contrast to most northern women, elite white women in the Confederacy who ventured to take on relief work found themselves hampered by a lack of domestic skills, a consequence of their reliance on slave labor; see Faust, *Mothers of Invention*, pp. 25, 77–78.

[37] William B. Weeden, *War Government, Federal and State in Massachusetts, New York, Pennsylvania, and Indiana, 1861–1865* (1906; rpt. New York, 1972), p. 126; Young, *Women and the Crisis*, pp. 67–71; Colin T. Naylor Jr., *Civil War Days in a Country Village* (Peekskill, N.Y., 1961), p. 60; Anthony F. C. Wallace, *Rockdale: The Growth of an American Village in the Early Industrial Revolution* (New York, 1978), pp. 460–64. See also Mrs. Prescott Keyes, "Soldiers Aid Society 1861–1865, Concord, Massachusetts," Alice Reynolds Keyes Papers.

Brooklyn church "a dozen sewing machines [were] hard at work ever since Sumter," allowing the wealthier women to boast that they had accomplished "heaps of work."[38]

An array of individuals, local and state governments, and independent contractors outfitted the first three-month volunteers. But in the early days of the war, and in the absence of any mandated, standardized uniform, women felt free to improvise garments of their own creation. Relying on available materials and personal tastes, army dress appeared in every sort of material, from "broadcloth to satinette." The resulting mixture of styles and colors occasionally created confusion on the battlefield. Fred Shannon found that "three regiments from the same state had no less than five distinctive colors of uniforms; blue, gray, black and white striped, dark blue with green trimmings and light blue." The fact that, in the early months of the war, gray was a favorite color among both northern and southern soldiers led to fatal cases of mistaken identity.[39]

Women determined the army's needs on a word-of-mouth basis, imitating one another in producing items they heard were most in demand. Though lint was later found to increase the potential for infection and abandoned as an application to wounds, the first months of the war saw women everywhere gathering together to scrape and unravel cloth to create lint fibers. "Inside the parlor windows the atmosphere has been very fluffy, since Sumter," reported Jane Woolsey, "with lint-making and the tearing of endless lengths of flannel and cotton bandages and cutting out of innumerable garments." Women in Canandaiga, New York, met "every day in one of the rooms of the court house . . . [to] cut out garments and make them and scrape lint and roll up bandages."[40]

The best-known item produced during the early weeks of the war, which was later deemed useless, was havelocks. These head coverings, cloth caps with material added to the back and sides, were intended to keep men protected in warm climates, but were found to make them swelter. Sarah Henshaw remembered the "havelock mania" that took hold in communities in the Midwest, some of which even formed specialized "havelock societies." In

[38] Mary B. Marsh to Sarah Watson, May 27, 1861, Marsh Papers. When George Templeton Strong's wife, Ellen Ruggles Strong, established a committee of ladies at Trinity Church to supply lint, bandages and clothing for the army, the New York lawyer urged the church vestrymen to finance the project. See Strong, Diary, May 7, 13, 14, 1861, George Templeton Strong Papers.
[39] Shannon, Union Army, 1:53–55, 80–84, 90; Wiley, Billy Yank, pp. 21–22.
[40] Young, Women and the Crisis, p. 69; Jane S. Woolsey to "Friend," in Bacon and Howland, Letters, 1:67; Richards, Village Life, p. 131.

New York, "some thirty ladies" gathered at the home of the lawyer George Templeton Strong to make "Havelocks caps" for the Seventh Regiment.[41]

A few women sought more direct means of providing needed supplies and assistance to the men they gave up to the Union army. Learning of horrid camp conditions, a dearth of nursing services, and inadequate cooking, these women took it upon themselves to carry food and clothing directly to men at the warfront. For many, the line separating the war from the homefront was blurred by the improvisational means through which the army itself was constituted, as well as the realities of a civil war fought on familiar territory at close proximity. While most women paid only brief visits, a few remained at camp, some donning uniforms and traveling with their husbands to battle. The most famous military wife to join her husband at the front was Julia Grant. Coming at General Grant's request, Julia brought their children as well.[42]

Calls to Action

Though thousands of women had taken it upon themselves to assume responsibilities for local regiments, female readers of the popular press were deluged with calls to increase the level of their support. Editors of popular women's magazines such as *The Sibyl*, *Arthur's Home Magazine*, and *Leslie's Monthly* exhorted women to become active and productive participants in the Union cause. Conservative publications placed such deeds within the customary benevolent work that middle-class women were expected to perform, while reform-minded journals argued that war-related labors constituted politicized acts against the Confederacy, some even prevailing upon their readers to disavow all slaveholders and expose traitors in their communities.[43] Local newspapers urged women to transform their households into centers of patriotic production. The *Poughkeepsie Daily Eagle* insisted that women "go to work *immediately*" to produce two hundred shirts, noting "you can do a great work, and *now is the time*." From town to town, pa-

[41] Philip Van Doren Stern, *Soldier Life in the Union and Confederate Armies* (Bloomington, Ind., 1961), p. 196; Young, *Women and the Crisis*, p. 70; Henshaw, *Our Branch*, p. 21; George Templeton Strong, *The Diary of George Templeton Strong*, ed. Allan Nevins and Milton Halsey Thomas, 4 vols. (hereafter *Diary*), vol.3, *The Civil War* (New York, 1952), p. 137 (April 29, 1861).

[42] Livermore, *Story of My Life*, p. 470; Young, *Women and the Crisis*, pp. 90, 94; William S. McFeely, *Grant: A Biography* (New York, 1982), p. 89.

[43] See Kathleen L. Endres, "The Women's Press in the Civil War: A Portrait of Patriotism, Propaganda, and Prodding," *Civil War History* 30 (March 1984): 31–53.

pers publicized women's efforts with expressed hopes that such news would prompt others to compete. A Watertown, New York, paper lauded one household of women for crafting "one of the handsomest flags" in the village. A public challenge accompanied news of a woman from a "country town" who reputedly knit one hundred pairs of mittens for the soldiers: "Can any young lady show a more patriotic record than this!"[44]

It was not long before newspapers assessed women's patriotic efforts by comparing them with the achievements of women in neighboring communities. Amid the decentered mobilization of northern resources, the race to display nationalist fervor heightened as towns and states competed to outdo each other. After Connecticut legislated new national holidays for the state, a nearby New York town praised it for "getting ahead of other states in the variety of her patriotism." When the women of Bridgewater, New York, resolved to "not be excelled in patriotism by the ladies of other towns and counties," a Utica newspaper published their resolution as a letter to the editor. Such competitive patriotism extended even to the raising of military regiments. Women of Saratoga, New York, were said to be "shaming and bribing the men into volunteering" by donating valuables to those who signed up.[45]

Whether newspaper reports reflected general anxieties about the extraordinary demands of warfare, or whether they betrayed a more specific myopia about what women were already contributing to the war effort, collectively they formed a contradictory narrative about female warwork. On the one hand, they implied that women's labors served only as expressions of a common patriotism or community pride. On the other hand, these printed announcements carried with them the premise that, in its capacity to personify national unity, women's unpaid household labor created genuine political value and, by compensating for deficiencies in army provisions, produced genuine economic benefits as well. Further, they underscored the differences between men's and women's obligations to the state. While men who volunteered for the army would be paid for their services, women's patriotic devotion was only measurable by manual labor and the free donation of homemade goods. The connection between labor and nationalism was not only brought home, it emanated from the home.

Doubtless many women were influenced by published calls for their contributions, which matched their own personal and political concerns.

[44] *Poughkeepsie Daily Eagle*, April 24, 1861, September 11, 1862; *New York Daily Reformer* (Watertown), April 27, 1861; *Poughkeepsie Daily Eagle*, February 18, 1862.
[45] *Poughkeepsie Daily Eagle*, June 17, 1862; *Utica Morning Herald*, May 25, 1861; *New York Daily Reformer*, April 22, 1861; *Poughkeepsie Daily Eagle*, September 9, 1862.

Though it is impossible to measure the extent to which women responded to public pressure or acted from their own charitable and patriotic motives, thousands assumed the task of outfitting departing troops and producing hospital supplies. Many women believed that they had clear obligations to the army and its men. Growing up on a Vermont farm, Alice Watts was occupied with an exhausting array of household tasks that suddenly mushroomed in 1862, when her mother and grandmother died within nine weeks of each other. Though she found herself at once the "boss and all hands," she still resolved to "*knit* two hours" a day and meet weekly with other women to sew for soldiers.[46]

Forming the Woman's Central Relief Association

As women in remote villages and small cities mobilized themselves to outfit troops and provide supplies, believing that their labors translated into real assistance to the war effort, stories began to surface that their energies were in fact producing an opposite effect. By rumor and hearsay, accounts of useless clothing, ill-fitting uniforms, spoiled food, and overstocked hospital supplies flowed from army camps and military hospitals back to the homefront. Despite the efforts of women who, according to Livermore, "rifled their store-rooms and preserve-closets of canned fruits and pots of jams" and packed all these together with clothing, blankets, and books, the results were dispiriting. "Baggage cars were soon flooded with fermenting sweetmeats, and broken pots of jelly. . . . Decaying fruit and vegetables, pastry and cake in a demoralized condition, badly canned meats and soups. . . were necessarily thrown away *en route*."[47]

More than the cakes stood to become demoralized. Even before such reports surfaced, the prospect that women's labors for the army might be viewed as well-meaning but feeble attempts to augment military strength worried a group of professional and upper-class New York City women. Barely a week after the firing on Fort Sumter, these women anticipated the criticisms that would be leveled at female volunteers. The absence of some system of coordination threatened to efface the considerable labors north-

---

[46] Alice Watts, quoted in Lynn A. Bonfield and Mary C. Morrison, *Roxana's Children: The Biography of a Nineteenth-Century Vermont Family* (Amherst, Mass., 1995), pp. 181–82.
[47] Livermore, *My Story of the War*, p. 122. See also Shannon, *Union Army*, 1:86–87; Wiley, *Billy Yank*, p. 22.

ern women had undertaken. They concluded that the "uprising of the women of the land" was in need of "information, direction, and guidance."[48]

At the same time, as some women sought to guarantee the impact of women's contributions, one woman in particular perceived in mobilization drives an opportunity to supervise an unprecedented female intervention in the war. Dr. Elizabeth Blackwell was most responsible for the idea of a centrally organized war relief operation. For Blackwell, the Civil War offered an opportunity to integrate personal, political, and professional goals. English by birth, reared in an antislavery household and, as she remembered, "nourished from childhood on the idea of human freedom and justice," she felt an "absorbing interest" in a war over slavery.[49] The war also represented an opportunity to make claims for other women in the field of medicine. The first woman to receive a medical degree in America, Blackwell hoped that, under her training and supervision, a corps of female nurses could be sent to military hospitals and, through their skilled work, demonstrate the professionalism and expertise that women could bring to the practice of medicine.

Long an advocate of the training of female nurses and doctors, Blackwell had begun in the 1850s to remedy women's lack of access to professional medical education. As a result of her own difficulties in finding a medical school willing to train and graduate her, she had concluded that sufficient numbers of women could become physicians only if an institution were dedicated exclusively to their education. In 1857, together with her sister, Dr. Emily Blackwell, and the financial support of radical and abolitionist New Yorkers, Blackwell founded the New York Infirmary for Women and Children, an institution that combined the training of female doctors and nurses with the care of indigent patients. Though the infirmary's board of trustees included a number of prominent male physicians, the hospital staff was composed entirely of women. Despite vigorous opposition from the larger medical community, the hospital prospered.[50]

---

[48] "The Origin, Organization, and Working of the Woman's Central Association of Relief," in USSC document no. 32, *Report concerning the Woman's Central Association of Relief* (New York, 1861), 1:1–5 (all USSC numbered documents are collected in *Documents of the U.S. Sanitary Commission*, 2 vols. [New York, 1866], hereafter cited as *Documents*).

[49] Elizabeth Blackwell, *Pioneer Work for Women* (London, 1914), p. 189.

[50] Ishbel Ross, *Child of Destiny: The Life Story of the First Woman Doctor* (New York, 1949), p. 192; Blackwell, *Pioneer Work*, p. 169; see also Regina Markell Morantz, "Feminism, Professionalism, and Germs: The Thought of Mary Putnam and Elizabeth Blackwell," *American Quarterly* 34 (Winter 1982): 459–78. After the war, the hospital became a college for training women physicians; see Young, *Women and the Crisis*, pp. 367–68.

Only two weeks into the war, Blackwell announced a meeting of the managers of the infirmary on April 25, 1861, to discuss what role the hospital staff might play in training nurses for the war. At the same time she wanted a report on the medical condition of soldiers stationed on Staten Island and a review of the voluntary activities already under way on behalf of Union recruits.[51] Blackwell invited women from many of New York's leading upper-class and Unitarian families, including Mrs. William Cullen Bryant, Mrs. Peter Cooper, and Mrs. George Schuyler and her daughter, Louisa Lee Schuyler. She also extended an invitation to the Unitarian minister Henry Whitney Bellows, who led the city's prominent All Soul's Church.[52]

The meeting's organizers published a letter the next day in the New York newspapers addressed to the women of New York, "especially. . . those already engaged in preparing against the time of wounds and sickness in the Army." Signed by "Ninety-Two of the Most Respected Ladies," the announcement offered to coordinate the efforts of existing charities and soldiers' aid societies through one organization and warned women that their lack of direct communication with government authorities about the needs of the army would cause problems. Anticipating what indeed was about to happen, the letter predicted that women engaged in voluntary war relief "are liable to waste their enthusiasm, to overlook some claims and overdo others, while they give unnecessary trouble in official quarters." The plan emphasized the collaborative nature of the work; to avoid competition among voluntary associations, no single group would be elevated above any other. The chief goal was to facilitate and intensify what the meeting had identified as the two predominant forms of female war relief contributions: the donation of "labor, skill and money," and the "offer of personal service as nurses." Henceforth both activities would be managed by a single administrative structure. To consolidate the proposals and gain citywide support for the idea, the women's letter called for a second public meeting to be held the next day at Cooper Union.[53]

On April 26, the Great Hall at Cooper Union was filled to capacity. On the platform, according to the *Tribune*, were the "wives and daughters of many of our most distinguished citizens." Among those who addressed the crowd of four thousand were Henry Bellows, Vice President Hannibal Hamlin, and a number of noted physicians (fig. 3). Before adjourning the

[51] Marjorie Barstow Greenbie, *Lincoln's Daughters of Mercy* (New York, 1944), pp. 54–56.
[52] "Origin," *Documents*, 1:6–9; Walter Donald Kring, *Henry Whitney Bellows* (Boston, 1979), p. 227.
[53] "Origin," *Documents*, 1:6–9.

An engraving from *Frank Leslie's Illustrated Newspaper* of the April 26, 1861, Cooper Union meeting of the New York City women who formed the Woman's Central Relief Association. © Collection of The New-York Historical Society.

meeting, a committee of women and men announced the formation of the Woman's Central Association of Relief. The new organization would meet the needs outlined the day before: "give organization and efficiency to the scattered efforts" already in progress; gather information on the wants of the army; establish relations with the Medical Staff of the army; create a central depot for hospital stores; and open a bureau for the examination and registration of nursing candidates. The women's association would be run with the voluntary labor of elite women, but it was to some degree a women's organization in name only. Its board of managers was composed of twelve women and twelve men, and was responsible for the selection of officers. Dr. Valentine Mott was named President and Rev. Henry Bellows Vice President of the Board of Management. Though men were given overriding authority, the association's structure provided a number of well-known, upper-class women with important positions as well. Two women, Mrs. Eliza L. Schuyler and Miss Ellen Collins, were included on the eight-member executive committee. Dr. Elizabeth Blackwell was made chair of the registration committee, which was charged with examining and registering women volunteering as nurses. Louisa Lee Schuyler was appointed corresponding secretary of the WCRA.[54]

Of all the women appointed to the new association, none would have more influence than the young Louisa Lee Schuyler. The daughter of George Schuyler and Eliza Schuyler—one of the "Ninety-Two . . . Most Respected Ladies" and herself a well-known figure in New York's reform circles—Louisa Schuyler was a member of the Dutch Hudson Valley family that traced its lineage to Alexander Hamilton and Philip Schuyler. The Schuylers were also important members of Bellows's All Soul's Church. Then twenty-four years old, Louisa Schuyler was already active in one of the philanthropic enterprises that emerged in prewar New York City, working under the auspices of the Children's Aid Society as a sewing instructor in an industrial school for immigrant children. Louisa Schuyler's appointment as corresponding secretary accorded with her mother's view that the day-to-day running of the office was best left to the "younger ladies." Schuyler worked closely with Ellen Collins, herself the daughter of a wealthy New York merchant family that was prominent in New York phil-

[54] Ibid., 1:10–17. Although the organization's formal name was the Woman's Central Association of Relief, neither the branch's leaders nor Sanitary Commission officers were consistent in their identification of the association. USSC documents sometimes shortened the name to the Woman's Central. The branch's officers most frequently referred to it as the Woman's (or, sometimes, Women's) Central Relief Association or by its initials, the WCRA; I have chosen to follow their lead.

anthropic circles. At the outset of the war, Collins was thirty-two and like Schuyler, unmarried.[55]

As the volume of women's voluntary work grew, Schuyler assumed an increasingly important role in the coordination of homefront relief to the army. Handling the correspondence between the WCRA headquarters and regional societies, she possessed a unique vantage point from which to observe female voluntarism and apprehend the homefront's approach to war relief. "She is certainly a most intelligent & energetic diligent young damsel," George Templeton Strong observed in his diary, "though not pretty at all," he felt compelled to add.[56]

Louisa Schuyler's eventual prominence in the WCRA came by default, as a result of the association's failure to maintain authority over female nurses. Despite the WCRA's initiatives and its access, in the person of Blackwell, to professional expertise, Dorothea Dix, the well-known medical reformer, acquired authority over the recruitment and training of nurses for the warfront. Though she lacked formal medical or nursing training, Dix had gained a national reputation as an advisor on the management of hospitals and the care of the insane. During her years of lobbying for federal legislation on behalf of the indigent insane, she had acquired numerous personal connections with Washington politicians. Arriving in Washington a few days after the war began, she actively sought direction over the women who volunteered to nurse soldiers, proposing to the War Department in early April the creation of an Army Nursing Corps under her leadership. Secretary of War Cameron appointed Dorothea Dix as superintendent of nursing.[57]

With Dix in authority, Elizabeth Blackwell found her position both in Washington and within the WCRA seriously undermined. Soon after she and her sister prepared guidelines for the recruitment of a nursing corps and for screening and sending female nurses to the front, they learned of the government's decision. "We are very busy as we have taken part in the work of selecting & registering women to be trained as nurses for the Army," Emily Blackwell wrote in June. Hinting at the redundancy of their

---

[55] Eliza H. Schuyler to "Sir," November 8, 1861, Box 954, United States Sanitary Commission Papers (hereafter USSC Papers); Kring, *Bellows*, pp. 140–44; Robert D. Cross, "Louisa Lee Schuyler," in *Notable American Women: 1607–1950*, ed. Edward T. James, Janet James, and Paul Boyer, 3 vols. (Cambridge, Mass., 1971; hereafter *NAW*), 3:244–45. Ellen Collins's father, Joseph, helped establish the Association for Improving the Condition of the Poor and the New York Juvenile Asylum. See Robert H. Bremner, "Ellen Collins," in *NAW*, 1:360–61.

[56] Strong, Diary, January 28, 1863, Strong Papers.

[57] Kristie R. Ross, " 'Women Are Needed Here': Northern Protestant Women as Nurses during the Civil War, 1861–1865" (Ph.D. diss., Columbia University, 1993), pp. 62–67; Young, *Women and the Crisis*, pp. 55–66.

efforts, she added, "We have given a great deal of time & labour to the work but are uncertain how valuable the result will be." The Blackwells were critical of the government's choice, considering Dix ill equipped to train or obtain professional acceptance for female nurses.[58] By November, the WCRA had sent thirty-two women to military hospitals. Once Dix was in control the WCRA severed its ties with nurse recruitment, and Dix worked alone.[59]

While the WCRA's plans for managing a nursing corps ended precipitously, its work at the homefront posted considerable successes. Able to exploit an established network of women's organizations, the women who led the WCRA expected that these groups would be sufficient to meet the demands of warwork. The association promoted greater participation in war relief and pushed for a coordinated handling of supplies, but it refrained from dictating the ways in which localities were to organize themselves and from calling for the creation of new societies. Aware that thousands of women had already rededicated their prewar benevolent and church groups to warwork and that some had even created new aid societies, the WCRA felt confident that these organizations could meet the army's demands. The association emphasized providing accurate information about army needs and assuring the efficient transport of donations from the homefront to the warfront.

The strategy worked; in response to WCRA announcements, hundreds of women mobilized neighbors, collected donations, and forwarded them to the association's office at Cooper Union. For small-town and rural women, the initiative taken by elite urban women provided an example they were anxious to emulate. "On the same day of the monster meeting of ladies at the Cooper Institute in New York," the women of the Dorcas Society of Cornwall, New York, resolved to organize themselves into the Cornwall Soldiers Aid Society and work for the duration of the war. "The response made to our appeals is grand," wrote Louisa Lee Schuyler in August 1861, "and it is a privilege to know and feel the noble spirit that animates the women of the loyal states."[60]

---

[58] Emily Blackwell to Barbara Smith Bodichon, June 1, 1861, Elizabeth Blackwell Papers. Emily Blackwell added that Dix, "without a particle of system," gained "semi-official recognition as medler general."

[59] William Quentin Maxwell, *Lincoln's Fifth Wheel: The Political History of the United States Sanitary Commission* (New York, 1956), p. 66. See also Greenbie, *Lincoln's Daughters*, pp. 62–63; Ross, " 'Women Are Needed Here.' " Eventually 9,000 women served as nurses; see Nina Bennett Smith, "The Women Who Went to War: The Union Army Nurse in the Civil War" (Ph.D. diss., Northwestern University, 1981), p. 3.

[60] Elisa Cunningham to J. S. Blatchford, August 27, 1866, Box 981, USSC Papers; Louisa L. Schuyler to Georgina M. Woolsey, August 7, 1861, in Bacon and Howland, *Letters*, 1:159. See

The preliminary work of the Woman's Central Relief Association revealed more than the potential for a mass voluntary participation for the war effort; it also hinted at the possibility of revising popular notions of female sacrifice. Suddenly, women were being flattered and appreciated by national institutions and men of power, who paid tribute to women's supposedly unique contributions and the vital part they played in supplementing the limited, and sometimes shoddy, provisions of the federal government. Here was a scenario in which unpaid female labor might be judged as expressing unqualified political commitment and producing real economic value. The exigencies of war would test the ability of the antebellum ideology of gender to dictate how women's labors were comprehended, whether they would be viewed as mere emanations of female nature or as the results of human exertion and skill.

Raised Expectations

Historically, wars have offered the politically disadvantaged opportunities to contribute to the defense of the state in return for expanded rights. African Americans, both slave and free, understood the Civil War to represent just such possibilities; by sacrificing lives and livelihoods to protect the Union, people could "earn" political and civil rights. For women, wars likewise have presented occasions to demonstrate their right to political inclusion by means of economic and personal sacrifices. While women have supported wars for immediate reasons, including the assistance of local regiments and defense of the military cause, the quid-pro-quo formula invariably emerges at war's end. During the American Revolution, colonial women organized consumers' organizations, anti-tea leagues and soldier relief societies. But despite some agitation for their inclusion in the apportionment of political rights during the writing of the Constitution, there was no reciprocity. The gendering of republican concepts of public virtue and liberty positioned women not as active citizens but as mothers of citizens, who possessed the morality necessary for producing virtuous free male citizens but were unsuited for participation in the political realm.

The Civil War portended something different. As a result of decades of agitation for women's rights, the feminist critique of women's secondary status hovered over northern society as an unanswered challenge. Wartime

also Katherine Prescott Wormeley, *The Cruel Side of War: Letters from . . . the Sanitary Commission . . .* (Boston, 1898), p. 6.

expectations for gains in women's status drew not only on the woman's rights movement but also on the experiences of those women who tried to enact the gender compromise through reform work. By the 1850s, female activists had ascertained the necessity of gaining access to legislative and political power in order to effect the changes they sought. Abandoning the tactic of moral suasion, they had moved from sending petitions to addressing legislatures directly. As Lori Ginzberg's work makes evident, women's increased responsibility for a wide range of welfare institutions and their active participation in temperance and other reform movements made their disfranchisement both more anomalous and more humiliating.[61] Moreover, the prewar decades witnessed the passage of married women's property laws which, though they may have served the larger needs of a capitalist political economy, nonetheless weakened coverture as the paradigm for the gendered distribution of political rights.[62] In both ideology and practice, the essentialist rationales for women's separate citizenship had begun to crack before the war began.

With war mobilization so dependent on voluntary civilian support, the time seemed ripe for translating women's assistance to the state into an exchange of support for full inclusion in the body politic. Though women's patriotic sentiments were cast as the natural expression of moral beings, the changing conditions of women's lives and the need for their contributions opened the way for a different reading of their wartime activities. Soon after the fighting began, a number of northerners suggested that this war might permanently alter women's status. The movement for woman's rights was effectively put on hold for the duration of the conflict, as feminists decided it was incumbent on them to demonstrate their loyalty to a state to which they were making bids for greater political access. But expressions of raised expectations came from sectors beyond the woman's rights camp. In fact, it is probable that the American Civil War was the first modern war in which masses of women participated with expectations that their homefront contributions would translate into expanded political rights.[63]

---

[61] Ginzberg, *Women and the Work of Benevolence*, pp. 98–132. See also Nancy A. Hewitt, *Women's Social Activism and Social Change: Rochester, New York, 1822–1872* (Ithaca, N. Y., 1984), pp. 160–76.

[62] That coverture persisted as the determinant of male property rights, even after passage of married women's property acts, was most evident in the ways in which the courts adjudicated the new laws. See Basch, *In the Eyes of the Law*, pp. 200–223; Reva B. Siegel, "Home as Work: The First Woman's Rights Claims concerning Wives' Household Labor, 1850–1880," *Yale Law Journal* 103 (March 1994): 1082–85.

[63] For decision by feminists to set aside their political demands for the sake of the war, see Elizabeth Cady Stanton, Susan B. Anthony, and Matilda Joslyn Gage, *History of Woman Suf-*

From the outset of the military conflict, the question of political compensation for women's assistance was in the air, palpable, alluded to in public as well as in private statements, by men as well as women. The idea that the war offered women unusual opportunities for advancement was voiced across the political and cultural spectrum. Just as the larger society cohered politically in the face of disunion, so too northern women put aside differences over feminist demands for equality in order to advance the war. In all the expressions of raised expectations lay assumptions that women would make some sort of political gain as result of their wartime sacrifices.

Politically moderate voices framed the question of the war's potential in terms of how it could advance women's development. In a volume assembled during the war, Mrs. C.B.W. Flanders conjectured that women, who had long complained of the limitations placed upon them, would find in war ample opportunities to demonstrate their capacities. While deferring to the natural order that made domestic duties women's "highest mission," Flanders argued that external forces might transform female nature and demonstrate women's aptitude for many professions. "As saleswomen, daguerrians, librarians, artistes, accountants, book-keepers, amaneunses, teachers, physicians, and indeed in most of the occupations not dependent on physical ability, females would not only prove equally desirable, but in many respects more acceptable."[64]

Feminists, who were already arguing for equality before the war, were cautiously optimistic about the war's potential for transforming women's perceived capacities and demonstrating their fitness for full citizenship. During the war years Frances Dana Gage wrote a regular series of articles for *Field Notes*, a farm journal she helped edit, which were reprinted in the feminist publication *The Mayflower*, offering detailed accounts of women's war-related activities and inserting herself in the debates such work engendered. A few months into the conflict Gage noted that "public journals are giving high praise to woman for her noble heroism, and self-sacrificing patriotism." Yet she was dismayed to find one editor taking shots at woman's

frage (Rochester, N. Y., 1881), vol. 1, *1848–1861*, p. 747, vol. 2, *1861–1876*, p. 50. For the expectations and dashed hopes of women in later wars, see Steven C. Hause, "More Minerva than Mars: The French Women's Rights Campaign and the First World War," in *Behind the Lines: Gender and the Two World Wars*, ed. Margaret Randolph Higonnet, Jane Jenson, Sonya Michel, and Margaret Collins Weitz (New Haven, 1987), pp. 99–113.
[64] Mrs. C. B. W. Flanders, "Women of the Times," in *Our Country, in Its Relations to the Past, Present, and Future, A National Book, Consisting of Original Articles in Prose and Verse, Contributed by American Writers*, ed. Mrs. Lincoln Phelps (Baltimore, Md., 1864), pp. 253–60. This volume was prepared for sale with proceeds to go to the U.S. Sanitary Commission and the U.S. Christian Commission.

rights activists by quipping that, because women finally had something to do, they had "now found that 'sphere' about which so much senseless twaddle has been expended in this nineteenth century."[65] Gage retorted that if the author would concede that "woman knows how to bound her own 'sphere,'" then "all twaddle on the subject will cease." "If in such a time as this, she has not been found wanting," she continued, "need we have any more twaddle about 'weaker vessels,' and the need of restriction to preserve her morality?"[66] By December 1861, Gage observed that "feeble women have grown strong, selfish women philanthropic, giddy women assumed labors and duties unthought of before, [and] ambitious women found opportunities for gratifying aspirations." "This," she declared, "is what war is doing for women." The bargain for women's support of the war would eventually bear fruit: "The womanhood of our whole nation is being uplifted, . . . and twenty years hence we shall see, not only what this war had done for women, but what it has done through her."[67]

Sometimes the analysis of what war might do for women was more calculating. In an 1862 article titled "The Blessings of War," the *Mayflower* concluded that "the war is demonstrating the impossibility of always excluding the woman question from politics." The article's argument was not that women's labor earned them political rights, but rather that it was giving women access to real economic clout. With the likelihood of the widespread "butchery of our adult male population" and the greater ease with which women will enter professions, women's chances for acquiring property had increased tremendously. "Property exerts influence, and influence controls politics," the magazine reminded its readers, and urged them to take advantage of the 1862 Homestead Act to acquire property of their own.[68] Gone were the clichés about women's moral power: here was a concrete, market-based conception of the term "influence." Even men outside the equal rights movement foresaw that women's wartime efforts might result in lasting changes. In 1861, a Mr. Tess wrote in *Field Notes*, "If women are so gladly welcomed into business circles in time of war, they surely will not be driven out when peace is restored."[69]

Although most women heard a consistent message about the ways in

---

[65] Editor of *Chicago Journal*, quoted in F. D. Gage, "Women and the War," *Mayflower*, August 1, 1861, p. 117. Frances Dana Gage had long been committed to abolitionism, temperance, and woman's rights and had an active career as a writer and editor before the war began. See Eugene H. Roseboom, "Frances Dana Barker Gage," in *NAW*, 2:2–4.

[66] Gage, "Women and the War."

[67] F. D. Gage, "What the War Is Doing for Women," *Mayflower*, December 15, 1861, p. 185.

[68] "The Blessings of War," *Mayflower*, July 15, 1862, p. 108.

[69] Mr. E. Y. Tess, quoted in *Mayflower*, May 15, 1861, p. 76.

which their natural abilities should serve national needs while simultane-ously elevating their own political status, some were exposed to a more crit-ical analysis of the demands being made upon them. Though the *Mayflower* acknowledged the necessity of women's participation, it was nonetheless cynical about any long-term benefits that their wartime labor might gener-ate. "The fact is, men have rather more than got their hands full with this war, and they welcome woman as a powerful and generous ally," observed the paper. Behind and subsumed in such praise, however, lay a secret agree-ment: "The contract being, on our part, that we are to do any work they give us; and on their part, that when they are done with us, they will turn us over to our former occupations, and abuse us just as handsomely as ever."[70]

It is likely that relatively few northern women heard such caustic assess-ments of their patriotic labors. But its very existence was significant, provid-ing evidence that at the very start of the war a line had been drawn in the sand around war relief work. This unambiguous critique of the inequity im-plicit in the antebellum gender compromise, together with the expressed hopes that the war might even the political playing field, suggests that at the onset of northern war mobilization, women's unpaid household labors con-stituted highly charged economic and political acts, performed under watchful eyes.

[70] Gage, "Women and the War."

2

IMPOSING "A MASCULINE DISCIPLINE": A NATIONALIST ELITE AND THE U.S. SANITARY COMMISSION

Even before the fighting began, many at the northern homefront believed the Civil War would be an event of epoch-making proportions, an upheaval with the capacity to redistribute political and economic power and transform cultural and religious institutions. While apprehensive about the radical course of military conflict, significant groups of northerners nonetheless accepted war as the means necessary to realize long-standing political and social goals. Abolitionists anticipated the destruction of southern slavery; free-soil workingmen and farmers hoped for a reversal of the decline in economic opportunities; former Whigs and Republican politicians looked for a realignment of national political power that would advance their vision of a modern industrial nation; far-sighted entrepreneurs perceived new prospects for profit, both in supplying the materials for war and in the long-range effects of a consolidated national market. For those who interpreted the war in religious terms, the impending bloodshed represented an overdue purging of the sins the nation had acquired in its pell-mell rush toward accumulation, foremost among them the sin of slavery, but also including avarice and selfishness.[1]

---

[1] Ronald Walters, *The Antislavery Appeal: American Abolitionism after 1830* (Baltimore, Md., 1978); Benjamin Quarles, *Black Abolitionists* (New York, 1969); Eric Foner, "The Causes of the

Although many Americans saw the war as an indispensable step in a march toward progress, some also expressed equally acute fears about the depths to which the country could fall while waging a violent conflict. Rebellion in one quarter might encourage rebellion in others, and the fabric of northern social life might break down by following the example of southern defiance to government rule. Writing to his sister more than a year before the war erupted, the Unitarian minister Henry Whitney Bellows confided the anxiety he felt about the "alarming & all-engrossing character of our political times," especially the "possible insecurity of life & property." "If secession & revolution should occur," he worried, it would drive people into "panic for bread & violence towards capital & order."[2] There were dangers in waging a war with revolutionary possibilities; a military conflict in which people invested expectations for sweeping changes had the potential to unleash forces that the polity might not be able to contain.

Notwithstanding these hopes and concerns about the Civil War's revolutionary potential, almost no one thought in terms of what impact military conflict might have on gender relations or ideas about the place of domesticity in a market economy. Indeed, given the numerous pronouncements during the early days of mobilization about the naturalness of women's altruism and the innocence of their patriotism, most observers preferred to cast female participation as an activity that flowed effortlessly from women's beings. But the mass entry of northern women into war preparations and their expressed desire to play a significant part in defending the Union soon generated expectations that this war could lead to a different understanding of women's household labors and political loyalties. In a society that had come to identify both middle-class status and social mobility with beliefs in sexual difference and a gendered division of labor, the occasion of creating a degendered, united public was at once liberating and destabilizing.

American Civil War: Recent Interpretations and New Directions," in Foner, *Politics and Ideology in the Age of the Civil War* (New York, 1980), pp. 15–33; Daniel Walker Howe, *The Political Culture of the American Whigs* (Chicago, 1979); Eric Foner, *Free Soil, Free Labor, Free Men: The Ideology of the Republican Party before the Civil War* (New York, 1970); John Ashworth, *Slavery, Capitalism, and Politics in the Antebellum Republic*, vol. 1, *Commerce and Compromise, 1820–1850* (Cambridge, U.K., 1995); Robert H. Abzug, *Cosmos Crumbling: American Reform and the Religious Imagination* (New York, 1994); James H. Moorhead, *American Apocalypse: Yankee Protestants and the Civil War, 1860–1869* (New Haven, 1978); James Oliver Robertson, *American Myth, American Reality* (New York, 1980).
[2] Henry Bellows to "Dearest Sister," December 12, 1860, Henry W. Bellows Papers. See also George M. Fredrickson, *The Inner Civil War: Northern Intellectuals and the Crisis of the Union* (New York, 1965), pp. 53–54.

The "Zeal of Women"

On its face, the formation of the Woman's Central Relief Association portended no fundamental changes in the character of female benevolence. The organization proposed to maximize women's voluntary efforts for the army by providing accurate information on hospital supply needs as well as access to a network of shipping depots. Though it intended to intervene in the army's medical services by recruiting and training female nurses, it embodied no overarching agenda for women's labors. Rather, it arose out of fears that, without some semblance of coordination, women's relief efforts might be squandered and subject to ridicule.

It might be argued, however, that the WCRA was the institutional expression of the potentials and pitfalls embedded in female warwork. While its impact on military conditions would depend on the individual calculations of thousands of women about aiding the army through a central agency, the organization presented a means for intensifying the visibility of female benevolence, transforming it into a patriotic force that might be felt by those in power. Here was a voluntary structure that applied women's political loyalties to their household labors in order to produce cost-free supplies for the army and allowed ordinary women to achieve a national presence in the conflict. But the WCRA also exposed the weaknesses that inhered in the unequal balance of social and economic power between the sexes in mid-nineteenth-century America. Not only did the association's female leadership feel the need to secure the presence of conservative, nonfeminist men at its meetings and on its board of directors, but it was powerless to prevent these same men from appropriating their organizational ideas and structure to serve a distinctly masculinist nationalist agenda.

In fact, the WCRA was barely in operation when Henry Whitney Bellows took steps toward creating a separate, male-run organization that would supersede it. Bellows had played an active role in the formation of the Woman's Central Relief Association, drafting its organizational structure and planning its public debut.[3] But his apparent interest in the women's association was short-lived. As he later recalled, the need for a more forceful and authoritative intervention into homefront organizing became obvious when it appeared that independent soldiers' aid societies were unwilling

---

[3] Bellows's wife wrote to their son, Russell, that planning for the "extensive society" had to be done with "great pains" to insure the "harmonious cooperation of many parties." See [Eliza Townsend] Bellows to Russ Bellows, "My Dear Son," April 28, 1861, Bellows Papers.

to "merge themselves" under the direction of one enterprise. "The local and personal jealousies which hinder all great undertakings displayed themselves," he wrote.[4]

Bellows's concerns about the "crude character" of female benevolence deepened when the War Department announced that it would not receive nurses recruited by the WCRA, an act he read to mean that the association would languish as a marginal, female charity, dismissed by the government and unknown by the public. Bellows was even more disturbed by his encounter with Dr. R. C. Satterlee, the federal army's medical purveyor in New York, who rejected any connection with the group based on his assessment that, in Bellows's words, "the sphere of the public in the work of assisting and relieving the army, was predestined to be a very small one." Satterlee worried that the "zeal of women & the activity of men assisting them" was not only "obtrusive" but "likely to grow troublesome if they did not die down." Such rebuffs, Bellows later asserted, "nearly paralyzed" his interest in soldier relief work.[5]

With these justifications in mind, Bellows set out to create the United States Sanitary Commission (USSC), a centralized, national relief agency that would coordinate all the donations of the northern homefront, assist in managing military hospitals, and advise the government on recruitment, medical, and sanitary issues. As Bellows planned it, the commission would be sanctioned by the government but privately run, thus possessing the advantage of being able to claim formal legitimacy while maintaining a healthy distance from a partisan state.

Stories about the disorganized character of female benevolence and the confusion it produced at the warfront formed the basis of a narrative about the creation of the United States Sanitary Commission that depicted the organization as the embodiment of rational benevolence. Not only was the USSC charitable in its mission to assist wounded Union soldiers, but its gesture toward northern women was itself altruistic, offering to rescue them from their own frailties and from certain defeat by powerful government forces. Bellows's private accounts of the WCRA's early failures formed part of the published raison d'être of the commission, eventually becoming absorbed into a collective postwar memory that cast women's early warwork as well-meaning but ineffectual. "Having discovered . . . the futility of carrying out the plans of the Woman's Central Association," the official USSC

[4] Henry Bellows to Charles Stillé, November 15, 1865, Bellows Papers.
[5] William Quentin Maxwell, *Lincoln's Fifth Wheel: The Political History of the United States Sanitary Commission* (New York, 1956), pp. 2–3; Bellows to Stillé, November 15, 1865, Bellows Papers.

record read, "the idea of a 'Sanitary Commission' . . . suddenly presented itself . . . as the only means of a solution of the difficulties with which the benevolent intentions of the women of the country were threatened."[6] But it is telling that Bellows discredited the WCRA when it had only just begun, proclaiming its imminent undoing as the impetus behind the establishment of a new agency. Within two weeks of the WCRA's founding, Bellows traveled to Washington where, he contended, the concept of a federally sanctioned national commission was born.[7]

Reconstructing the commission's origins at war's end, Bellows conspicuously trumpeted his own initiatives. "Having a natural taste for getting . . . near to the bottom of things," he organized an investigative tour of army camps in Washington, D.C. He departed on May 15, 1861, together with William Holme Van Buren, Elisha Harris, and Jacob Harsen, all New York City physicians prominent in sanitary reform. Bellows claimed to be visiting as emissaries of the WCRA and a group of New York hospitals, with no notion other than evaluating the government's management of military medical affairs. But, on the train somewhere between Philadelphia and Baltimore, in the midst of a discussion about the British and French experiences in the Crimea and the possibility that a high proportion of Union army recruits were unfit for service, Bellows's mind started churning. Suddenly, he recollected, the need for a wholly new coordinated, civilian intervention became apparent.[8]

"Not a Feminine Business"

Ostensibly founded to meet the medical and supply needs of the Union Army and to guide the voluntary benevolence of the people, the United States Sanitary Commission was, from the outset, burdened with complex ideological and political goals. In fashioning an extragovernmental agency to oversee homefront donations and military medical practices, Bellows was joined by other urban elite men, notably Frederick Law Olmsted and George Templeton Strong. In the decade before the war, these men had found in the social dislocations brought on by the spread of capitalist production opportunities to claim the mantel of reform from evangelical radicals and place it in the service of more conservative goals. For its founders, the commission constituted an experiment in "organized popular sympa-

[6] "Origin," *Documents*, 1:18.
[7] Henry Bellows to Charles Stillé, April 15, 1865, Bellows Papers.
[8] Ibid.

thy." The commission form, they hoped, would shield the state from contamination by partisan politics and make it more responsive to the advice of the nation's organic leaders.[9]

The efforts of elite men to manage wartime voluntarism would have far-reaching consequences, not only for their own positions as brokers between the public and the state, but also for the middle-class northern women who provided the voluntary labor for soldier relief. Though oblivious to the degree to which they were encroaching on a female domain of social authority and power, Sanitary leaders understood the body politic in gendered terms. Only days after the war broke, Bellows worried that northern society had become "effeminated" by "too luxurious & self indulgent habits"; the only solace he could find was the hope that "this bitter trial" would arouse "our manhood & womanhood."[10] Though women were summoned to serve the Union with flattery about their patriotic nature and praise for their charitable instincts, the scope of war relief threatened their relatively meager and locally based positions of social power. At stake for some women was the influence over social welfare that they had successfully arrogated to themselves under the aegis of the ideology of domesticity. At stake for all women were the gender balance of power and their ability to make claims for political and legal equality.[11]

When private largess was called into the service of politically potent purposes, when voluntarism was seized upon as the vehicle through which a new national spirit could be fostered, any claims that women made to supervise welfare or to determine their own charitable capacities were threatened. "Even the care of the sick & wounded in war is not a feminine business," Frederick Law Olmsted wrote to Bellows a few months into the war. "It must have a masculine discipline, or as a system, as a sustained & 'normal' arrangement, it must have a bad tendency."[12] Even though bourgeois women were hailed as the moral guardians of an increasingly corrupt and commercial society, when it really mattered the organization of benevolence could not be left to women.

---

[9] Stillé, *History of the United States Sanitary Commission*, p. 19.

[10] Henry Bellows to Russell Bellows, April 21, 1861, Bellows Papers.

[11] Ann Douglass suggests that Unitarians were especially vulnerable to criticism that Christianity had become too effeminized and, in response to what she calls the "feminization" of antebellum northern culture, Unitarian ministers were vocal in calling for a more aggressive, "militant masculinity." See *The Feminization of American Culture* (New York, 1977), pp. 17–23.

[12] Frederick Law Olmsted to Henry Whitney Bellows, August 16, 1861, in Frederick Law Olmsted, *The Papers of Frederick Law Olmsted*, ed. Charles E. Beveridge, 5 vols. (Baltimore, 1977–90; hereafter *FLO Papers*), vol. 4, *Defending the Union*, ed. Jane Turner Censer (Baltimore, 1986), p. 148.

Henry Whitney Bellows. Photograph by Mathew Brady. Prints and Photographs Division, Library of Congress.

Impressed by the mobilizing efforts initiated by women, the men who created the Sanitary Commission glimpsed in soldiers' aid a means for gaining social and political legitimacy on a national stage. Prior to the war, they had little occasion to scrutinize the gender relations that shaped the language and experience of class; they approached women's political and social status as something natural and self-evident. But when the war broke and their fears about class discord escalated, women's voluntarism—culturally constructed as apolitical—presented a way to advance their claims to disinterestedness. By cloaking their demands for leadership in the language of patriotism, female benevolence, and the exigencies of military crisis, Sanitary leaders believed they had found the ideal instrument for their program.

Urban Liberals

Together, Bellows, Olmsted and Strong were instrumental in providing the Sanitary Commission with a coherent ideological message and a consistent administrative style. Known to one another as leaders of major institutions in antebellum New York City, they believed themselves uniquely qualified to discipline the spontaneous patriotism of the northern populace and to disseminate their vision of a rationalized, harmonious Christian society to the entire nation. In the massive voluntarism exhibited by northern women during the early days of the war, they perceived a social base especially amenable to the guidance of prominent men that extended far beyond the reaches of New York City. The founders of the Sanitary Commission sought to harness northern women's unpaid household labor to serve grandiose personal and political goals.

Henry Whitney Bellows personifies the blending of Whig nationalism, urban institutionalism, and Unitarian rationalism that found expression in the United States Sanitary Commission. Born to a wealthy merchant family in Boston in 1814 and educated at Harvard College, he taught for several years and then attended Harvard Divinity School, where he received training rooted in the liberal Unitarian tradition. In 1839, two years after he was ordained, he became minister to the First Unitarian Church in New York City, the largest and most affluent Unitarian congregation in the nation. After overseeing the construction of an ornate building in 1855, Bellows christened it All Soul's Church and counted in his congregation important members of New York's intellectual and business communities.[13]

[13] Walter Donald Kring, *Henry Whitney Bellows* (Boston, 1979), pp. 146–65. Despite his position in New York, Bellows never relinquished his New England ties, building a retreat for his family in Walpole, N.H., in the 1850s. See also Thomas Bellows Peck, *Henry Whitney Bellows: A Biographical Sketch with Portrait* (Keene, N.H., 188-), pp. 289–92. Among All Soul's members were William Cullen Bryant, Peter Cooper, Moses H. Grinnell, James and William Bryce, Henry D. Sedgwick, and Joseph H. Choate.

Bellows's first decade in New York coincided with the explosive growth of industrial production and the influx of rural migrants and foreign immigrants to fill newly created waged jobs. The rise of an identifiable working class focused Bellows's attentions on the difficulties a democracy posed for maintaining order in a society divided by class. As he pondered solutions to the conflicts that increasingly marked urban life, he fashioned himself as a spokesman for conservative interests beyond the merchants who dominated his congregation. The New York lawyer George Templeton Strong, though himself a High-Church Episcopalian, respected Bellows's ability to dispense what he considered to be coherent, practical addresses at All Soul's. Ridiculing the tendency of other Unitarians to expound on social topics without offering practical strategies for action, he complimented Bellows for being "pleasant and instructive," and credited his "native masculine common sense" for his ability to come across as "far sounder and wiser than the great majority of his school."[14]

Bellows was more conservative than many other Unitarians; he stood firmly against the radical individualism of Ralph Waldo Emerson and the transcendentalists. Nonetheless, Bellows propagated his own version of religious activism. During the 1840s, he shared with other urban elites the belief that crime, intemperance, and even poverty itself were the consequences of a lax moral environment.[15] Rather than focus on personal renewals of faith or individual renunciations of sinful behavior, Bellows propagated a notion of Christian duty that urged the propertied classes to counter social malaise with firm religious direction and a willingness to police sources of communal immorality. He later wrote, "I had a deep persuasion that poverty about as much as crime . . . was a spiritual disorder, to be treated far more with moral tonics than with practical relief."[16]

[14] Bellows reached Unitarians far beyond All Soul's Church. In 1846 he founded the *Christian Inquirer*, a weekly paper published by the New York Unitarian Association and intended for all the middle Atlantic states. (In 1866 he renamed it the *Liberal Christian*.) In the circles of the American Unitarian Association he argued his liberal interpretation of theology. Yet even within his own congregation, Bellows sometimes provoked dissent. George Lee Schuyler, husband of Eliza and father of Louisa Lee Schuyler, disagreed with some of Bellows's political positions, and in 1854 threatened to leave the congregation. See Kring, *Bellows*, pp. 65, 139–44, 522; Strong, *Diary*, vol. 2, *The Turbulent Fifties, 1850–1859*, p. 386 (February 15, 1858).

[15] Abzug, *Cosmos Crumbling*, esp. chap. 5, on the tensions between evangelicals and Unitarians and the relationship between reform and religion in the antebellum North. See also William G. McLoughlin, *Revivals, Awakenings, and Reform: An Essay on Religion and Social Change in America, 1607–1977* (Chicago, 1978), pp. 112–13; Clifford S. Griffin, *Their Brothers' Keepers: Moral Stewardship in the United States, 1800–1865* (New Brunswick, N.J., 1960), pp. 49–53.

[16] Early in the century, Harvard Unitarianism had provided some of the key rationales for rejecting the doctrine of innate depravity and played a part in the redefinition of human nature; nonetheless, it remained at odds with evangelical Protestant sects. See Daniel Walker Howe,

The limitations of such sermonizing became evident when, during the 1849 Astor Place Riot, citizen militia fired into a crowd of working-class protesters, killing twenty-one and injuring more than one hundred people. The riot began as a popular protest against the establishment of a restricted, elite theater and the presence of a perceived antidemocratic English actor. By the time it ended, cannons were stationed in the streets of lower Manhattan as a warning to any other "mob" that all available force would be used in the interest of securing peace and private property. The Astor Place Riot revealed not only the powerful political meanings embedded in popular cultural practices but also the real potential for dangerous class conflict. As the uprising spread, Bellows pronounced it a "civil and social war" that demonstrated the perils faced when "the worst portions of our people" harbor "a secret hatred of property and property-holders" and misinterpret liberty as freedom from all authority.[17]

Yet, however much he condemned the rioters, the specter of persistent class hostility moved Bellows to revise his thinking about the sources of poverty and the ease with which the laboring classes could be managed with moral strictures. In the years following the riot he promoted the view that elites needed to become actively engaged in negotiating urban class relations and embrace a less punitive approach to workers' social life and leisure pursuits. In 1857, in a series of lectures delivered at the Lowell Institute in Boston on the "Treatment of Social Diseases" (a title he later termed "unfortunate"), Bellows proclaimed that poverty and crime could be prevented only with "general religious education," legal remedies, and the development of "self respect and self reliance." While he rehearsed older notions of the duty of the wealthy to care for the poor and cautioned against "careless charity," he now argued for the eradication of the conditions that produced pauperism. "The true view of poverty considers it as an evil to be extin-

The Unitarian Conscience: Harvard Moral Philosophy, 1805–1861 (Middletown, Conn., 1970), pp. 60–61. See also Joseph Conforti, "Edwardsians, Unitarians, and the Memory of the Great Awakening, 1800–1840," in *American Unitarianism, 1805–1865*, ed. Conrad Edick Wright (Boston, 1989), pp. 40–42; Jane H. Pease and William H. Pease, "Whose Right Hand of Fellowship? Pew and Pulpit in Shaping Church Practice," in Wright, *American Unitarianism*, pp. 181–201; Clifford E. Clark Jr., "Religious Beliefs and Social Reforms in the Gilded Age: The Case of Henry Whitney Bellows," *New England Quarterly* 43 (March 1970): 63–65; Fredrickson, *Inner Civil War*, pp. 26–27; Bellows to Stillé, November 15, 1865, Bellows Papers.

[17] Peter G. Buckley, "To the Opera House: Culture and Society in New York City, 1820–1860" (Ph.D. diss., State University of New York at Stony Brook, 1984), chap. 1; Henry Whitney Bellows, *A Sermon Occasioned by the Late Riot in New York* (New York, 1849), pp. 12–13. See also Edward K. Spann, *The New Metropolis: New York City, 1840–1857* (New York, 1981), pp. 235–41; Iver Bernstein, *The New York City Draft Riots: Their Significance for American Society and Politics in the Age of the Civil War* (New York, 1990), pp. 148–52.

guished," Bellows announced, adding in a decidedly liberal vein, "the true charity of a nation . . . lies in equal laws, social right, popular education and protective legislation." Bellows had moved a long way from the idea that poverty was at best a natural part of the social order or at worst a moral problem to a conception that acknowledged the influence of social and cultural forces. Convinced of the deleterious effects of a polarized class structure, he advocated broad-based social, political, and juridical interventions.

Employing the language of pathology to describe poverty and working-class cultural practices signaled the influence of sanitarianism on Bellows's intellectual development. A body of thought that emphasized the environmental origins of both urban epidemics and moral decay, sanitarianism appealed to elite reformers who welcomed the neutrality offered by "science" as a justification for the supervision of public spaces and private behavior. To Bellows's mind the issues of sanitary reform and social reform were one in the same. In fact, he credited the innovative nature of the Sanitary Commission plan to his prewar interest in "social science" and his extensive inquiries into the causes of "social evils and sickness." He was especially gratified by the "mental contact" he felt "with the noble Englishmen who for twenty years past have been battling so courageously for Sanitary Reform." For Bellows, the accomplishments of Florence Nightingale and the British and French Commissions in the Crimean War demonstrated the advantages of an aggressive, systematized approach to diseases, be they biological or social.[18]

By 1859, in what became known as his Divinity School Address (which directly rebuked Emerson's address of 1838), Bellows pulled together the many strands of political, social, and scientific thought that had captured his imagination during the previous decade. Introducing a "doctrine of institutions," Bellows presented liberal and decidedly Whiggish solutions to the perceived excesses of evangelical individualism and Jacksonian democracy. The route to undermining the sources of immorality, he argued, lay in creating robust social and political institutions with the power to implement "scientific" attacks on sinful behavior.[19]

[18] See John Duffy, *The Sanitarians: A History of American Public Health* (Urbana, Ill., 1990), esp. chap. 7; Bellows to Stillé, November 15, 1865, Bellows Papers.

[19] Henry Bellows to Charles Stillé, November 15, 1865, Bellows Papers; *New York Times*, February 3, 1858; Kring, *Henry Whitney Bellows*, pp. 177–78; Peck, *Bellows*, p. 292; Clark, "Religious Beliefs," pp. 66–67. Peter Buckley's use of the term "liberal intelligence" captures the interventionist and preventive proscriptions advocated by men such as Bellows; see Buckley, "To the Opera House," pp. 583–602. George Fredrickson labels these men "conservatives" because of their opposition to antebellum radical thought and their defense of institutional structures, and argues that their fear of "sweeping egalitarianism" was animated by their own status

In the aftermath of the Astor Place Riot, and armed with an activist brand of Unitarianism, Bellows and other members of the New York elite developed an approach to the problem of class division that promised to ameliorate conflict and limit popular influence. Central to their agenda was the creation of planned urban spaces and cultural institutions that would provide shared experiences and generate a permanent sense of community. In the decade before the war, New York City witnessed a host of liberal experiments aimed at remolding the working class and the relationship between the classes. From Charles Loring Brace's Children's Aid Society, which sought to inhibit a hardened "unconscious society" of poverty with a program of moral instruction and manual training for vagrants and orphans, through Frederick Law Olmsted and Calvert Vaux's design for Central Park as a location for cultivating a peaceable social order, to the opening of Peter Cooper's union of liberal education and mechanic arts, urban liberals devoted themselves to perfecting a society based on free labor. [20]

"Hurrah for Peter Cooper," Olmsted wrote to Charles Loring Brace in 1853. Olmsted's enthusiasm for Cooper's plans to create an educational union for all classes conveyed the affinity that existed among New York's elite reformers. Further, it suggested that they undertook their institutional innovations with a shared faith in their ability to elevate the character of the city's laboring people. Olmsted also applauded Brace's Children's Aid Society, and called for upper-class men to do more of the same: "get up parks, gardens, music, dancing schools, reunions which will be so attractive as force into contact the good & bad, the gentlemanly and the rowdy." Believing that private and public efforts needed to go hand in hand, he insisted that "the state ought to assist these sort of things."[21]

It was as architect-in-chief and superintendent of Central Park that Frederick Law Olmsted made his mark on the history of liberal reform in New

---

anxiety. See *Inner Civil War,* pp. 7–9, 26–27, 69–71. See also Laura Wood Roper, *FLO: A Biography of Frederick Law Olmsted* (Baltimore, Md., 1972), p. 151.

[20] Charles Loring Brace, quoted in Paul Boyer, *Urban Masses and Moral Order in America, 1820–1920* (Cambridge, Mass., 1978), p. 96; Olmsted, in *FLO Papers*, vol. 3, *Creating Central Park,* ed. Charles E. Beveridge and David Schuyler (Baltimore, 1983), pp. 9–10. Roy Rosenzweig and Elizabeth Blackmar note that New Yorkers who argued for the park believed it would be "a less repressive means of reforming the character of the city's working classes." See *The Park and the People: A History of Central Park* (Ithaca, N.Y., 1992), pp. 24–26. See also Sean Wilentz, *Chants Democratic: New York City and The Rise of the American Working Class, 1788–1850* (New York, 1984), pp. 392–93; Thomas Bender, *Toward an Urban Vision: Ideas and Institutions in Nineteenth Century America* (Baltimore, Md., 1975), pp. 138–41, 153.

[21] Frederick Law Olmsted to Charles Loring Brace, December 1, 1853, in *FLO Papers*, vol. 2, *Slavery and the South: 1852–1857,* ed. Charles Capen McLaughlin and Charles E. Beveridge (Baltimore, Md., 1981), pp. 232–36.

York City. Born in Hartford, Connecticut, he spent his early adulthood trying out a variety of occupations, including gentleman farmer, editor, and writer, before he appeared on the New York scene as the superintendent of a major public institution. His ideas about social order and progress, reflected in the design he and Calvert Vaux created for the park, mirrored those that informed the plethora of other liberal experiments of the 1850s. But Olmsted brought to the park project ideas about social order and the importance of government gained in a context far from northern urban life. During the 1850s, he traveled to the slave states in order to study the South's economy and society for a series of books that soon gained him a national reputation. As much as he admired southern "aristocrats" and the genteel society they had created for themselves, he still found himself committed to the more progressive northern approach to social development. For Olmsted, the degradation of the South was a direct consequence of the excessive individualism and the impaired sense of community that resulted from crippled government.[22]

Though confident of the superiority of northern society (and of New England communities in particular), Olmsted worried that the growing cultural differences among classes threatened to destroy the civilizing forces that bound a people together. He was contemptuous of the "rowdyism, ruffianism, want of high honorable sentiment & chivalry of the common farming & laboring people of the North." For him, the question of progress was an issue of the people's "character," and transforming human character could only be accomplished by elevating its lowest elements. "The poor need an education to refinement and taste and the mental & moral capital of gentlemen."[23] As his thinking evolved, Olmsted perceived a larger role for government than the "simple protection to capital and letting-alone to native genius and talent." This, he asserted in 1854, "is not the whole duty of Government"; even "common schools, with their common teachers, and common instruction . . . are not enough." To raise the level of civilization, the state needed to work side by side with private institutions devoted to cultural uplift.[24]

[22] Frederick Law Olmsted, "The South, Letters on the Productions, Industry and Resources of the Slave States," no. 27, New-York Daily Times, June 30, 1853, in FLO Papers, 2:172–80. Though he opposed southern ideologues who argued that slavery was necessary for the elevation of the African race, Olmsted was unwilling to support abolitionism, maintaining it was unconstitutional and an impetus for slave insurrection.

[23] Frederick Law Olmsted to Charles Loring Brace, December 1, 1853, in FLO Papers, 2:232–36.

[24] Frederick Law Olmsted, "The South," no. 46, New-York Daily Times, January 12, 1854, in FLO Papers, 2:244.

With the plan he and Vaux devised for Central Park, Olmsted hoped to demonstrate that a large park, carefully designed, expertly supervised, and open to all classes, could foster a spirit of civic pride and social cohesion that would help transform urban social relations. The moral influence exerted by rural landscape would provide the lower classes with the means of self-culture and self-improvement, he claimed, which in turn would quicken the engines of social mobility. While the wealthy New Yorkers who supported the park idea had differing agendas, some driven by a determination to regulate the public behavior of the working classes and others motivated by a desire to create an urban haven for their own class, Olmsted and Vaux's Greensward Plan incorporated aspects of both agendas.[25]

Learning of Bellows's interest in the park's progress, Olmsted invited him to view the park in order to observe for himself the "moral influence" that pastoral scenery would exert on the city's population. After surveying Central Park in the spring of 1861, Bellows agreed that he had witnessed "grand proof" of the success of directing the "foresight and liberality of concentrated powers upon democratic ideas." The purposeful design and execution of the park's ambitious plans demonstrated the possibility of applying informed management to transform the physical and moral landscape of the nineteenth-century city.[26]

For George Templeton Strong, Central Park was an important component in the complex of economic, technological, and moral innovations that made the mid-nineteenth century an "era of special development and material progress." He delighted in the "splendid march of science on earth" and envied younger generations that would "grow up with this park." If all went according to plan and, in Strong's words, did not "decompose into anarchy," the park, together with other urban institutions, "promised to make the city twenty years hence a real center of culture and civilization."[27]

A prestigious lawyer and civic leader with close ties to New York City's merchants, Strong was not professionally involved in the reform activities

[25] Olmsted, in *FLO Papers*, 3:273; Buckley, "To the Opera House," pp. 551, 585–88. As Rosenzweig and Blackmar write, "many of the gentlemen merchants who advocated a park were more concerned with serving their own needs" than with uplifting the poor. *Park and the People*, pp. 26–29, 45–50, 136–42, 240–41.

[26] Henry W. Bellows, "Cities and Parks: With Special Reference to the New York Central Park,"*Atlantic Monthly* 7 (April 1861): 416–29. Roper, *FLO*, pp. 141, 151–52. It was in his experiences with Central Park that Olmsted became both anti-party and anti-politician, views that he carried over into the commission. See Rosenzweig and Blackmar, *Park and the People*, pp. 180–90, 263–66.

[27] Strong, May 28, 1860, *Diary*, 3:30. Throughout the park's construction, Strong made a number of visits, assessing its progress and critiquing its design; see Strong, June 11 and September 2, 1859, *Diary*, 2:454, 458.

Frederick Law Olmsted, 1860. © Collection of The New-York Historical Society.

of some of his peers. Nor could he be considered liberal in his religious beliefs. Yet as a trustee of Trinity Church and Columbia University, he counted himself among the upper echelon of New York society, possessing the authority and breeding regarded as necessary for instructing others in civic behavior. Disdainful of the poor and a strident defender of the privileges of the propertied, Strong felt deeply the obligations that attended his social position. During the economically depressed 1850s, he complimented "the dealings of our 'upper class' with the poor." Noting the "readiness with which money is contributed," Strong observed that "it has become fashionable and creditable and not unusual for people to busy themselves in personal labors for the very poor."[28]

Although Strong believed in the ethic of progress so characteristic of the nineteenth century, he was also susceptible to frequent bouts of pessimism about the capacities of Americans to fulfill their historical destiny. As the sectional crisis deepened, he criticized the powerful allegiances to localities and regions that characterized antebellum American nationalism and, in emotional entries in his diary, satirized Americans' tenuous attachments to the state. "The Bird of our Country is a debilitated chicken disguised in Eagle feathers," he railed on March 11, 1861. "We have never been a nation, we are only an aggregate of communities, ready to fall apart at the first serious shock & without a centre of vigorous national life to keep us together." The next day he continued his lament: "We are a weak, divided, disgraced people, unable to maintain our national existence. We are impotent." The fragility of the American nation was embarrassing, particularly when nationalist forces were ascendant elsewhere. With a touch of melodrama, Strong declared his personal humiliation at southern secession: "I shall never go abroad. That question is settled. I should be ashamed to show my nose in the meanest corner of Europe. . . . I'm tempted to emigrate, to become a naturalized British subject and spend the rest of my days in some pleasant sea-side village in the southern counties of old Mother England. It's a pity we ever renounced our allegiance to the British Crown."[29]

---

[28] Strong was an easy ally of prominent Unitarians such as Bellows and Olmsted. One example of his extreme tolerance of Unitarians was his defense of the nomination of Wolcott Gibbs to a Professorship at Columbia University in 1854 despite strong opposition to Gibbs's Unitarian affiliation; Gibbs was rejected. Strong, January 9, February 4, and April 3, 1854, *Diary*, 2:147, 154, 165–67.

[29] Strong, March 12, 1861, *Diary*, 3:109–10.

George Templeton Strong, 1863. © Collection of The New-York Historical Society.

Secession and War

Strong was not alone in experiencing more fear than hope during the secession crisis. As the North and South moved farther apart, Bellows and Olmsted also turned their attention from the specific social problems of New York to those of the nation at large. From his pulpit at All Soul's, Bellows expanded his injunctions about religion's role in civic morality into an argument for the spiritual origins of human government. It was time for a "Christian revival of the 'State,'" he proclaimed, and "essential to the life and glory of the State" was the "sentiment of nationality." He spoke with passion about the "national life," contending that the nation, being the repository of all the history, laws, and institutions of the people, represented their collective will and thus had the right to demand their universal allegiance.[30]

Notwithstanding opinions voiced abroad that Americans would always shun a strong state, Bellows asserted that a "latent nationality" had rushed in to say "we *are* a nation." In fact, Bellows developed a creative argument for the advantages America offered over Europe for the cause of nationalism. In Europe, Bellows argued, nationalism historically competed with civil liberties; American nationalism posed no such threat. The sole problem in America was that the loyalty justly due to the national state had been stolen by localities and individual states. Indeed, the very word state was problematic. "It is unfortunate that our local governments are called States," Bellows preached to his congregation a few days after the firing on Fort Sumter. "It misleads the people by clothing these admirable organizations with a delusive seeming of sovereignty." But localism had no place in America now; "this narrow, selfish, ignorant provincial pride must be permanently humbled."[31]

Bellows's commitment to the "national life" led him to devise a version of Unionism tailored to the economic interests of his genteel constituency. "We did not as a congregation sympathize with the Abolitionists pure and

---

[30] Henry W. Bellows, *The State and the Nation—Sacred to Christian Citizens: A Sermon Preached in All Soul's Church, New York, April 21, 1861* (New York, 1861), p. 7. By 1863 Bellows likened government to a divine institution; indeed, he argued, Americans were fortunate enough to possess a state that required them to "make a religion of patriotism." See Henry W. Bellows, *Unconditional Loyalty* (New York, 1863). Bellows fits Daniel T. Rodgers's description of a Protestant "counterrevolutionary," akin to those Protestant moral philosophers who, in language reminiscent of sixteenth-century ideas of the divine right of kings, claimed that government was "divine." See Rodgers, *Contested Truths: Keywords in American Politics since Independence* (New York, 1987), pp. 116–22. See also Fredrickson, *Inner Civil War,* p. 70.
[31] Bellows, *State and the Nation,* pp. 11–13.

simple," he wrote of All Soul's Church. "We had many merchants connected by shipping lines with Southern ports, who were naturally sensitive even to the least agitation of the subject." Aware that "there were few congregations representing larger personal interests or connected so directly with commerce, banking and political affairs as ours," Bellows initially declared his opposition to any stance that might threaten the business interests of cotton merchants: "The interests of very many were in conflict with their patriotism."[32] But when war finally erupted, he pushed the city's business elites to support the Union, flattering their political views and consciences while addressing their economic fears. "I know very well," he preached, "that it is not a little more or less of domestic splendor, or personal comfort, a few more hundreds or thousands in the strong-box; a rise or fall of ten or even fifty per cent in stocks and mortgages that appalls their hearts. It is the sickening uncertainty how they are to meet their engagements; how in a totally changed state of things they are to fulfill promises made in the best faith, and to carry out large plans."[33] Capitalist interests, Bellows argued, were synonymous with the aims of the war and the defense of the Union: "Radically and truly considered, there is no conflict between moral interests of society and its material interests. What is most for the interest of piety and virtue is most for the interest of trade and commerce."[34]

But behind his public assurances about the justifications for this war, Bellows was privately cynical about the northern political groups that he thought were as responsible for the war as were southern slaveholders. In a distinctly conservative interpretation of antebellum political debates, he denounced antislavery politics; antislavery arguments, like pro-slavery ones, were merely means "used by selfish people" to attain power.[35] When the war erupted, Bellows feared that a weak federal government was threatened not so much by military failure as by the opportunity of radical abolitionists to stage their own revolution. As Bellows explained to his congregation in September 1861, the specter of abolition born of revolution was worse even

---

[32] Henry W. Bellows, *The First Congregational Church in the City of New York, A Sketch of its History and a Review of his Own Ministry* (New York, 1899), pp. 25, 28.

[33] Henry W. Bellows, *Duty and Interest Identical in the Present Crisis, A Sermon Preached in All Soul's Church, April 14, 1861* (New York, 1861), p. 11.

[34] Ibid., p. 5.

[35] Henry Bellows to Cyrus Bartol, March 1, 1861, Bellows Papers. While many Unitarian preachers were staunch opponents of slavery, Bellows tempered his criticism of the institution in order to avoid offending the commercial interests of his congregation. During most of the 1850s he navigated a careful course on slavery, opposing its extension while allowing the slaveholding states to secede. See Conrad Wright, *The Liberal Christians: Essays on American Unitarian History* (Boston, 1970), pp. 70–75.

than slavery itself: it would "risk our constitution and our union, our historic life and national identity." To abolish slavery "at a blow" was something "only fanatics and reckless enthusiasts would dare to propose." Claiming that "riddance of slavery" was the wish of "every true American heart," he cautioned against "violent, unmethodized, rapid emancipation" as the "gravest wrong we could do the slave."[36]

While he singled out political radicals as especially responsible for the war, Bellows was also troubled by the failure of most northerners to appreciate the war's moral significance. The American public appeared dangerously unprepared for the sacrifices required to defend the Union. Defeating southern political power was an empty feat without winning general allegiance to the Union and the Constitution. Even New England, with "her older & better civilization," did not know how "exposed the country at large is to anarchy."[37] Organized violence might destroy an already frail popular citizenship by exposing it to the ravages of war. Even the initial shows of patriotism and military enthusiasm did not relieve Bellows of concern about the potentially deleterious effects of warfare on a society with a weak public culture. Anticipating war in early April 1861, Bellows expressed to his friend, Cyrus Bartol, "a longing for a time of personal sacrifice" so that Americans would better appreciate their civic inheritance.[38]

Bellows's apprehensions about northern loyalties subsided after he witnessed the generosity with which people responded to the outbreak of war. The rush to take up arms and the public's energetic support of military volunteers fired his imagination about the power latent in the public will. On April 19 he wrote to his son that he had "never seen such an extraordinary manifestation of national feeling and such a revolution of public sentiment." Suddenly, the war and the forces that produced it suggested an unprecedented opportunity to tap the public spirit and remold civic culture.[39] Olmsted likewise welcomed the war as an unprecedented opportunity for stimulating nationalism. "No patriotism where no occasion for its exercise,"

[36] Henry W. Bellows, *The Valley of Decision: A Plea for Unbroken Fealty on the Part of the Loyal States to the Constitution and the Union, Despite the Offenses of the Rebel States. A Discourse Given on Occasion of the National Fast, September 26, 1861, in All Soul's Church* (New York, 1861), p. 17.
[37] Henry W. Bellows to Cyrus A. Bartol, December 12, 1860, Bellows Papers.
[38] Henry W. Bellows to Cyrus Bartol, April 12, 1861, Bellows Papers.
[39] Henry W. Bellows to Russell Bellows, April 25, 1861, Bellows Papers. Bellows continued to express his fears to friends and colleagues throughout the summer of 1861. Responding to one such missive in August of 1861, his fellow Unitarian Charles Eliot Norton assured Bellows that his fears were exaggerated; the war was sure to build national character, and "the heaviest blows will not be heavier than we need to discipline our souls to a true manliness." Charles Eliot Norton to Henry W. Bellows, August 23, 1861, Bellows Papers.

he reflected. The occasion no doubt had arrived; the challenge, in Olmsted's view, lay in the "effort to federalize sentiment" throughout the nation.[40]

In March 1861, George Templeton Strong was apprehensive about the seemingly inevitable coming of a civil war, fearful about the impact of military violence on the political fortunes of the country as well as its effects on his own personal fortunes on Wall Street. As he had for much of the preceding year, Strong took a raffish delight in ridiculing the weak nationalism of his fellow citizens. Yet as "secessionitis" spread, the unity and sense of purpose that overtook the northern public abruptly changed his perspective. "I look with awe on the national movement here in New York and through all the Free States," he wrote in his diary. "After our late discords, it seems supernatural." Reflecting on his own mercurial response to recent events, Strong concluded that "one's opinions change fast in revolutionary times."[41]

Cosmopolitan Rationalists

Despite the hopefulness Bellows felt as he watched northern mobilization drives, he found it difficult to keep old anxieties at bay. In August 1861, he confided to Eliza Schuyler, wife of George Schuyler and mother of Louisa, that the outbreak of civil war had stirred his deepest fears for American society. "I am afraid of our money-changers; afraid of our party-politicians; afraid of our whole people—so debilitating, & demoralising have been the influences of the last five and twenty years." Worrying that "our people are not used to self denial, suffering or gloom," he cautioned that "every man, woman and child must be watched," lest they fail to meet the challenges that faced them.[42]

Reflecting on the recent defeat of Union forces at the first Battle of Bull Run, Bellows prayed the rout would teach fellow northerners something about the suffering and discipline that would be needed to win this struggle for "humanity herself." But the obstacles to social cohesiveness were considerable, and none more so than the fact that, in Bellows's mind, the defense of the Union was not a compelling enough reason for most people to

---

[40] Frederick L. Olmsted, Notes, 1861, and "Plan," Private Book, Olmsted Papers.

[41] Strong, March 4, March 12, April 28, and January 31, 1861, *Diary*, 3:105, 109, 95. In an effort to stimulate patriotic sentiments, Strong reluctantly took part in a scheme of the Union Club to award a prize of $500 for a national hymn. The "absurd 'National Hymn' Committee" received bales of "patriotic hymnology," but found no acceptable song. See Strong, May 14 and June 22, 1861, *Diary*, 3:142-43, 161-63.

[42] Henry W. Bellows to Eliza H. Schuyler (Mrs. George), August 9, 1861, Bellows Papers.

tolerate a long and fierce war. The South, after all, stood for *"Separation &*
Recognition," concepts that readily arouse passion, he contended, while "We
are for Constitution, the Laws, for Liberty," the elements he thought comprised "the spirit of the 19th Century."[43]

Bellows had long agonized about the growing chasm between the nation's
regions. "We are *two* peoples in civilization, religion, temperaments, tastes,
climate," he wrote to his friend Cyrus Bartol at the end of 1860. Though
the two peoples spoke with "a common denominator," southerners were
decidedly "low-toned, uncivilized & undeveloped in moral and spiritual experience." By the time the war began, his assessment of the sections' differences had become more precise. Southerners, he remarked to Schuyler,
were irrational and "Catholic" in nature, while northerners were "cosmopolitan rationalists" and "champions of truth," arguably the weaker side
in a battle for hearts and minds but the right side all the same.[44]

While Bellows's language implied that all northerners were "cosmopolitan rationalists," the phrase more precisely described the urban, mostly
Unitarian, social leaders and professionals who formed his circle, men who
could be characterized as nationalists as much as rationalists. Bellows's use
of the term rationalists was telling, however, because it expressed a Whig
reverence for the capacity of reason to tame man's passions and for
capitalism's potential to advance social and moral development. For these
predominantly New England–bred New Yorkers, southern secession and
the challenge to the federal constitution dramatized in the starkest ways the
central drama of the nineteenth century. Ralph Waldo Emerson described
the unfolding drama as the contest to hold together "two states of civilization." At issue were not just competing labor systems, represented by the
conflict between industrial capitalism and plantation slavery, or differing
political values, expressed by the South's assertion of states' rights in defiance of constitutional federalism. Espousing a form of historical determin-
ism, cosmopolitan rationalists interpreted the Civil War as the final contest
in an evolutionary struggle between peoples in different stages of cultural
and moral progress. On one side stood the forces of modernity and nationalism, generated by the spread of industrial capitalism, marked by the rise of
a liberal and sober bourgeoisie, and removed from the radical reform sensibilities of earlier decades and eager to manage a class society through an
array of elite-led institutions. On the other side was gathered a loose collec-

[43] Ibid.
[44] Henry W. Bellows to "friend" [Cyrus Bartol], January 24, 1860, Bellows Papers; Henry W.
Bellows to Eliza H. Schuyler (Mrs. George), August 9, 1861, Bellows Papers.

tion of "rural" mentalities, inclined to religious excess, resistant to efforts at class negotiation, and loyal to the politically reactionary ideas of localism and states' rights.[45]

The nationalism of cosmopolitan rationalists was a distinct melding of religious and political ideas that corresponded closely to what Lewis Simpson calls New England nationalism. For them, the war possessed deep transformative potential. Though initially dubious about the effects that war would have on the nationalist project, Emerson was encouraged by its apparently salutary effects on the credibility of the federal government. "The country is cheerful & jocund in the belief that it has a government at last," he wrote in his journal in 1861. "What a healthy tone exists!" Bellows too gained strength from the sudden changes the war wrought in the national temperament. Both men believed the best hope for America lay in spreading the influence of nonevangelical, refined New England culture to all corners of the nation as well as the world.[46]

Cosmopolitan rationalists saw themselves as natural civic leaders for the Civil War. Events had called upon them to reinvigorate the moral complexion of the nation and give worldly meanings to the people's raw patriotic sentiments. "I am deeply & solemnly impressed with our duty," Bellows wrote to Bartol a few days before the firing on Fort Sumter. Anxious about the "maintenance of our Institutions," he saw the war as an occasion for "personal sacrifices," and hoped the nation would "pour out blood & treasure like water, to maintain the authority of the Constitution & the dignity of the Nation & the flag!"[47] Confident in their assessment of society's failings, they assumed the position of gifted visionaries, which Frederick Law Olmsted, employing Jefferson's notion, designated "a natural aristocracy." These men argued that their positions as gentlemen derived neither from any birthright nor from their relation to the market, but rather from their self-education, breeding, and defense of a moral order. Innate breeding and social prerogatives placed them above the laboring masses, who posed a

---

[45] Ralph Waldo Emerson, "American Civilization," *Atlantic Monthly* 10 (April 1862): 502–22, quoted in *"The Real War Will Never Get in the Books": Selections from Writers during the Civil War*, ed. Louis P. Masur (New York, 1993), p. 127. According to John Ashworth, "It is scarcely too much to claim that the Whig party owed its existence to the desire to challenge the populistic tendencies of the Democratic party." *Slavery, Capitalism, and Politics*, 1:297.

[46] Ralph Waldo Emerson, Journal, 1861, quoted in Masur, *"Real War,"* p. 123. See Lewis P. Simpson, *Mind and the American Civil War: A Meditation on Lost Causes* (Baton Rouge, La., 1989), pp. 33–70, for a discussion of New England nationalism as expressed by Emerson at midcentury and its shift from a culturally confined loyalty to an imperialist vision of America's mission.

[47] Henry Whitney Bellows to Cyrus Bartol, April 12, 1861, Bellows Papers.

demonstrated danger to the security of property rights, and differentiated them from business elites, who were guided by selfish economic interests. This was a war of principle, Bellows explained to his Unitarian congregation in September 1861: "Wars of principle imply persons of principle to conduct them, and methods of principle by which they are pursued."[48]

A New Nationhood

While cosmopolitan rationalists had been pondering for some time the need for greater state intervention in an industrializing and urbanizing nation, the approach of war confirmed the necessity of strengthening the federal government, at the very least for the task of mobilizing armed forces to defend itself against dismemberment or dissolution. As they had favored active state initiatives in the 1850s to supervise and ameliorate a class-divided metropolis, so they saw the role of the federal government in war as one of shoring up the forces of law against the possible radicalism that the conflict might provoke. In December 1860, Bellows conveyed to Bartol his assessment of just how "very threatening" was the state of the nation. Fearing a descent into "confusion & riotous chaos," he opined that the only hope stood in "making all possible support for the federal power."[49] Based on his acquaintance with the world views of southern planters, Olmsted had come to similar conclusions about the danger of allowing society and capital to go unrestrained. "What made these Southern gentlemen Democrats," he had explained to Charles Loring Brace, was their belief in having as little government interference in their lives as possible. "All these sort of free traders want is protection to capital," Olmsted recognized. For his part, "laissez aller" philosophy was wanting; self-interest alone was a poor guide to national health. The only way to ensure social order in a class society was to have active government intervention.[50]

In many respects the antebellum American state was distinctively weak. What one scholar has called a "sense of statelessness" pervaded a "radically decentralized" national structure that reserved only minimal power for itself and left most of the tasks of government to individual states and localities. Not surprisingly, most northerners expressed loyalty to an attenuated

[48] Frederick Law Olmsted to Oliver Wolcott Gibbs, November 5, 1862, *FLO Papers*, 4:467; Henry W. Bellows, *Valley of Decision*, p. 6. See also Howe, *Political Culture of the American Whigs*, pp. 30–34.
[49] Henry W. Bellows to Cyrus A. Bartol, December 12, 1861, Bellows Papers.
[50] Frederick Law Olmsted to Charles Loring Brace, December 1, 1853, in *FLO Papers*, 2:232–36.

national state precisely because it allowed for extensive local control and self-government.[51] To advance a new type of nationhood, it was critical to replace the narrow sense of community felt by most Americans with devotion to a structure that encompassed the entire geographical extent of the United States. Conscious of the centripetal political forces that were pushing other western nations to consolidate their political and territorial boundaries, one hope of these nationalists was to constitute an American state powerful enough to rival those taking shape in countries such as Italy and Germany. Strengthening the American state meant transforming traditional loyalties to the village, county, and individual state into a stronger attachment to a distant, federal power. It meant loosening people from their customary institutional moorings.[52]

As activists for a newly defined nation during what Eric Hobsbawm has characterized as the heyday of liberal nationalism, northern intellectuals understood the requirements for a "viable" nation to include not only the elements of unity and territory, issues clearly at stake in the Civil War, but also the capacity to produce cultural and political cohesion.[53] The process of nation building in nineteenth-century America did not involve inventing a nation from disparate linguistic or historical groups, as it did in much of Europe, but rather required generating popular political and emotional identification with a national government that, though it had maintained a symbolic presence since the Revolutionary War, exerted seemingly scant influence in people's daily lives. Although the federal government had provided enormous benefits for economic development and private interests, in the form of territorial acquisitions, protective tariffs, and internal improvements, persistent myths about American individualism and laissez-faire development all but obliterated this history, casting the federal government as indifferent to or a neutral agent of change.

For these self-appointed public leaders, the force that would transform America's political condition and raise the moral character of its citizens was

[51] Stephen Skowronek, *Building a New American State: The Expansion of National Administrative Capacities, 1877–1920* (New York, 1982), pp. 22–23. See also Fredrickson, *Inner Civil War,* pp. 44–46; Phillip S. Paludan, "The American Civil War Considered as a Crisis in Law and Order," *American Historical Review* 77 (October 1972): 1013–34; Merle Curti, *The Roots of American Loyalty* (New York, 1946), pp. 158–61; Harold M. Hyman, *A More Perfect Union: The Impact of the Civil War and Reconstruction on the Constitution* (New York, 1973), pp. 67–69.

[52] Richard Franklin Bensel characterizes the government before the war as the "self-effacing antebellum state." See *Yankee Leviathan: The Origins of Central State Authority in America, 1859–1877* (New York, 1990), p. 17.

[53] E. J. Hobsbawm, *Nations and Nationalism since 1780: Programme, Myth, Reality* (Cambridge, U.K., 1990), pp. 37–38.

an activist state guided by an intelligent and liberal class of men. The agenda of nineteenth-century modernity included empowering the institutions that could foster a cohesive society as well as a national political economy. During the secession crisis, this goal entailed moving beyond generic support of the federal government to a robust nonpartisan, nationalistic spirit among the people. If America was to create a nation state capable of holding itself together—a state able to avert future social discord, protect the interests of capital, and earn international respect—then the Union that emerged from war needed to be not only structurally sound but emotionally valuable to the people. In 1861 liberal intellectuals determined that, in order to assure the nation's destiny, it was imperative to go beyond subduing the reactionary forces of the South to assail the provincial and antistatist sentiments within the North itself. How the war was conducted would determine not only its victors but also the substance of that victory. How people defined their loyalties and what they understood the Union to represent were all-important at this critical juncture in the nation's history.

That northern war mobilization was so dependent on the voluntary labor and resources of citizens underscored both the strengths and weaknesses of the American system. Voluntarism exposed the fragility of the nation's political bonds, but at the same time presented a means for engaging the populace in a unique nationalistic experience. The stakes were high. If people employed traditional, ad hoc means to raise and support a military force, if they viewed their obligations to the state as conditional on the policies of any particular administration, and if they privileged democratic rights over military discipline in times of crisis, more than the war would be lost. By exploiting the patriotic and democratic rhetoric to which northerners had responded in the past, nationalist elites believed that they could manipulate those impulses to strengthen the federal structure and, by extension, their own authority. They presupposed the existence of common interests that cut across class, religious, and gender boundaries, which themselves could be obliterated by the exigencies of war in the name of some shared American destiny.[54]

The accumulated anxieties of cosmopolitan rationalists about class dis-

---

[54] There were striking similarities between the northern version of liberal nationalism and the more hastily constructed southern nationalism in the Confederate states. Like the northern elite, southern planters faced the problem of maintaining control over a state structure that was vulnerable to democratic demands from below. Confederate nationalists drew on local and sectional loyalties and invoked historical myths about the Revolutionary War and Manifest Destiny to gain broad appeal. See John McCardell, *The Idea of a Southern Nation: Southern Nationalists and Southern Nationalism, 1830–1860* (New York, 1979), pp. 3–6, 226–76; Anders Stephanson, *Manifest Destiny: American Expansion and the Empire of Right* (New York, 1995),

cord, social order, and the dangers of war would be assuaged by ordering the labor of women. By transforming women's charitable activities into a political program, the men who created the Sanitary Commission sought to further their own cultural ascendancy and the primacy of their nationalist ideas. Here was an opportunity to remedy the debilitating aspects of the nation's federal structure and to demonstrate the saliency of liberal solutions to the social problems produced by industrialization and democracy. But in order to accomplish this, a new centralized structure would have to supersede women's traditional bases of social power. In this context, the antebellum compromise on gender relations, having produced a separate domain of female power, posed a threat to a sweeping nationalist program. With the creation of the Sanitary Commission, women would confront the first organized appropriation by men of the privileges hitherto accorded their sex.

Means and Aims

As Americans hastened to raise a citizen army, men such as Bellows, Olmsted, and Strong observed homefront behavior with a mix of awe and worry. They watched in dismay as people organized themselves in haphazard, autonomous ways, while officials of an ill-prepared federal government stood by. At the same time, however, they deemed that popular support of the Union offered an occasion to translate provincial charitable efforts into a centralized system of army relief and to mold organic patriotism into a general devotion to the principles of law, order, and a strong state. The task ahead was difficult. The exigencies of supporting an army engaged in what was fast becoming a massive and total war precluded reliance on customary democratic structures.

Signs of excessive democracy abounded not only on the homefront but within the army itself. The practice of early recruits electing their own officers was the most forceful example of the lack of military discipline. "Our volunteer system with its elected colonels and its political major generals, is very bad," Strong noted in his diary. To these nationalists, Americans' antipathy toward authority was endemic, and discipline was the only antidote for unreasonable exercises of popular power. "This strange infatuation," wrote Charles Stillé, a Philadelphia lawyer and writer who authored the

---

chap. 2; Drew Gilpin Faust, *The Creation of Confederate Nationalism: Ideology and Identity in the Civil War South* (Baton Rouge, La., 1988), pp. 14–15.

commission's official history, "pervaded all ranks of the people, and as it seemed a foregone conclusion that discipline, such as that which existed in other armies, could not be enforced in ours, of course little effort was made to introduce it among the volunteers."[55]

Chaos in the army was clearly a problem of class, and military discipline was closely analogous to labor discipline. By the commission's own assessment, the first recruits were predominantly artisans and workers, drawn from cities and large towns, long accustomed to "independent habits," and unprepared for the rigors of military life. The potential for excessively high casualty rates resulting from undisciplined military behavior and unsanitary environments was great[56] Indeed, the problems posed by civilian recruitment and military organization mirrored and threatened to dwarf those of congested northern cities. Particularly for urban and public health reformers, the concentration of huge numbers of men in small, impoverished environments was a familiar scenario, in which epidemiological emergencies imperiled public morals.

For the commission, its success as a broker between the public and the army and as a watchdog over government military policy rested almost exclusively on its ability to impose discipline on its constituencies. After the war, Bellows alluded to this dilemma by claiming its resolution as one of the commission's most important achievements. The "service" the organization "rendered the country" by "standing between the army, as cared for by the government, and the country, which expected impossibilities" and which foolishly "proposed to take care of the army by countless State, county, and town committees," was accomplished by "defending military discipline" while at same time "pacifying the fears and representing the solicitudes of home."[57]

By force of argument, scientific data, and professional influence, the commission's founders hoped to persuade the federal government to heed their disinterested expertise over the claims of political partisans. By applying popular benevolence to a fighting army, commission leaders would demonstrate to the public the logic of rationalizing social welfare to achieve nationally determined goals. They sought to invigorate both the state and the newly imagined nation as a means for addressing the problems of an industrializing society. It fell to these "natural" leaders to assume the task of

---

[55] Strong, August 2, 1861, *Diary*, 3:174; Stillé, *History of the United States Sanitary Commission*, p. 26.
[56] Stillé, *History of the United States Sanitary Commission*, pp. 1, 21–22.
[57] Henry W. Bellows, "U.S. Sanitary Commission," in *Johnson's Universal Cyclopaedia*, ed. Frederick Barnard and Arnold Buyot (New York, 1877), p. 74.

teaching the army, the government, and the female homefront the value of discipline, sanitation, and national devotion.

Forming the United States Sanitary Commission

In early May 1861, barely two weeks after the firing on Fort Sumter, Bellows and the physicians who had traveled with him to Washington inspected the nursing situation and consulted with Dorothea Dix, who was already establishing a federally sanctioned nursing corps. Dix disapproved of the commission idea, a fact Bellows attributed to her intention to be "wholly independent."[58] The delegation interviewed Colonel Wood, the acting Surgeon General, only to find that he was equally unenthusiastic about the idea of a privately based citizen's commission. But the trip proved valuable. The men confirmed their suspicions about the inadequacies of the Medical Bureau and the need for outside, private assistance. By the time Bellows left Washington he was convinced that, as he wrote to his wife, "perhaps if I live a thousand years, I may never again have the opportunity of doing such a work as now opens."[59]

Anxious to establish their credibility with the very public they planned to organize and discipline, Bellows and his team of physicians maneuvered to gain government sanction for themselves and their ideas. Three days into the trip, they submitted a letter to the Secretary of War outlining the rationale for government sanction of an independent civilian commission to assist the War Department. Claiming to act on behalf of the Woman's Central Association of Relief, the Advisory Committee of the Boards of Physicians and Surgeons of the Hospitals of New York, and the New York Medical Association, the letter laid out their plans to advise the government on the "class of men" recruited into the army, gain appointment of one hundred nurses to army hospitals, employ and instruct a body of cooks to prepare healthful food for military volunteers, and recruit "young medical men" trained in New York hospitals to assist the army's regular medical force.[60]

Bellows claimed the right of a civilian review of the military on the grounds that the Civil War was "essentially a people's war," a democratic ex-

[58] At war's end, Bellows recalled of Dix that he and the physicians "found her then, what we always found her, wholly & most self-sacrificingly absorbed in her voluntary duties." Bellows to Stillé, November 15, 1865, Bellows Papers.
[59] Bellows to "Wife" [Eliza Bellows], May 1861, Bellows Papers.
[60] "An Address to the Secretary of War," May 18, 1861, no. 1, *Documents*, 1:1–4.

pression of a populace who volunteered to save the Union. "The hearts and minds, the bodies and souls, of the whole people and of both sexes throughout the loyal states are in it," he wrote, adding that the "rush of volunteers to arms is equaled by the enthusiasm and zeal of the women of the nation."[61] Arguing that the department no doubt would want to encourage "this noble and generous enthusiasm," he offered to regulate the "relations" of voluntary organizations with the War Department.

Despite his acknowledgment of women's part in making the war popular, Bellows's actions nonetheless represented the beginning of a process by which the Sanitary Commission appropriated control of soldier relief work from the WCRA. Less than a week later, Bellows submitted a formal request to President Lincoln and Secretary of War Simon Cameron for "official recognition and moral countenance" of a citizen-based commission. Citing the exemplary work of the commissions that accompanied the Crimean and Indian wars and cautioning against delaying action as the British had done, Bellows suggested that a commission made up of civilians from philanthropic, medical, and military fields be appointed to investigate the best ways to systematize and maximize charitable contributions to the army.[62]

The formation of the Sanitary Commission proceeded rapidly. On June 13, 1861, the same day they received presidential approval, the future commissioners issued a formal "Plan of Organization" that divided the organization into two branches, of "inquiry" and of "advice." After the inquiry committees carried out investigations of troop and camp conditions, the branch of advice would recommend measures to the War Department and "explain and enforce upon inexperienced, careless, or ignorant officials" the necessary sanitary regulations. As for the public, the plan proposed a convention, to be held in New York City, of delegates from every benevolent association in the country to receive information on the needs of the Medical Bureau and the Sanitary Commission's system of shipping goods to special depots. "Thus the organizing, methodizing, and reducing to service-

[61] Ibid.
[62] "Letter from the Acting Surgeon General to the Secretary of War," pt. 2, "Draft of Powers Asked For, May 23, 1861," no. 2, Documents, 1:4–5. During the Crimean War (1853–1856), mortality rates among soldiers who were not injured in battle were high. Poor sanitation, inadequate diet, and untrained medical practitioners were responsible for four times as many deaths as those from wounds incurred in battle. After the English government gave sanction to the British Sanitary Commission, and under the guidance of Florence Nightingale, survival rates improved dramatically. See Maxwell, Lincoln's Fifth Wheel, p. 5, and Anne Summers, Angels and Citizens: British Women as Military Nurses, 1854–1914 (London, 1988), chap. 2.

ableness the vague, disproportionate, and hap-hazard benevolence of the public, might be successfully accomplished."[63]

The hierarchy of the new commission also took shape quickly, flowing as it did from the structure of the WCRA and the network of urban reformers who stood ready to assume national roles in the military conflict. Bellows became president of the USSC, a position he held for the duration of its existence, and that entailed, according to his description, responsibility for the "unity, method and practical success" of the mission. George Templeton Strong was appointed treasurer, a post he also held throughout the commission's existence. When Frederick Law Olmsted joined the commission, it was with the belief, as he wrote to Bellows, that in such work he would find the "mission" that he was "pining to find, in this war."[64] As general secretary, Olmsted was stationed at the commission's headquarters in Washington, D.C., where he assumed responsibility for shaping its bureaucracy and for overseeing its dealings with the army. When Olmsted left the USSC in 1863, he was replaced by John Foster Jenkins, a physician from Schenectady, New York, who had worked for the commission since 1861. Dr. Elisha Harris, an original member of the team that traveled to Washington on behalf of the WCRA, served briefly as the corresponding secretary and later joined the medical committee along with the physicians Cornelius R. Agnew, William H. Van Buren, and Oliver Wolcott Gibbs. Alfred Janson Bloor, an English-born architect living in New York City, was named assistant—also known as corresponding—secretary, responsible for communicating with female-led regional branches and local aid societies on the needs of the army and for oversight of the supply depot in Washington. Frederick Newman Knapp, a Unitarian minister and first cousin of Henry Bellows, became the special relief agent in Washington, where he supervised the care of discharged soldiers, soldiers in transit, and soldiers' homes. Appointed vice president, to replace Bellows in the event of his absence, was Alexander D. Bache, a graduate of West Point, superintendent of the United States Coast Survey, and one of the founders of the National Academy of Sciences.[65] During the early months of the war the executive committee gathered every six weeks in Washington in rooms provided by the

[63] "Sanitary Commission Ordered by Secretary of War and Approved by the President," no. 2, pt. 3, *Documents*, 1:6–7; "Plan of Organization," no. 3, June 13, 1861, *Documents*, 1:1–6.
[64] Frederick L. Olmsted to Henry Whitney Bellows, June 1, 1861, in *FLO Papers*, 3:117–18. Olmsted was one of the original twenty-four directors of the WCRA, for which he made inquiries about the conditions of the army.
[65] Censer, introduction, *FLO Papers*, 4:78–110; Maxwell, *Lincoln's Fifth Wheel*, pp. 317–50.

government. As the work grew in complexity, the commission created a standing committee to oversee activities between executive meetings. The standing committee, which included Bellows, Van Buren, Gibbs, Strong, and Agnew, met five and sometimes six days a week in New York City, and was later joined by the lawyer and writer Charles Stillé.[66]

Though the membership of the Sanitary Commission expanded and shifted over the course of the war, Bellows, Olmsted, and Strong remained its most influential leaders. They were responsible for creating the USSC's elaborate bureaucratic structure, developing its strategies for dealing with government officials, and shaping the nationalistic messages issued for public consumption. Though the Sanitary Commission experience would eventually distance them from one another and even lead some to question their commitment to centralized power, the leaders never wavered in their assumptions about their class and gender prerogatives or their vision of a harmonious and powerful national culture. Throughout the war they insisted on their right to ideological authority over a nation in crisis.

Once they obtained the president's signature of approval, the commissioners wasted no time in getting operations under way. "Without powers, without pecuniary support, without any immediate sympathy even from the people," Bellows recalled, the commissioners "flung themselves upon the merits of their cause."[67] The leading order of business was the acquisition of money to hire agents in the field and cover the cost of transporting supplies to the front. They made their first appeals to those who stood to profit from decreases in soldiers' mortality, life insurance companies. In the early days of recruiting, many northern communities had obtained life insurance policies for their local volunteers, with the premiums being guaranteed by either aid societies or individuals for the duration of the war. "This Commission is now in full organization, and ready to go to work," read a notice sent to all American life insurance companies. "It wants money. It needs twenty thousand dollars in hand to proceed with vigor." The USSC argued that by reexamining army recruits and discharging those deemed poor health risks, it had established a way for companies to limit their financial risks. "Reasonable fears exist, that unless the most energetic efforts are made, one-half of our whole volunteer force may not survive the exposures of the next four months." Employing the sanitarian scenario in which epidemiological emergencies imperiled public morals, the USSC warned that

---

[66] Bellows, "U.S. Sanitary Commission," pp. 79–80; Censer, introduction, *FLO Papers*, 4:41.
[67] Bellows, "U.S. Sanitary Commission," p. 73.

the "mere presence in any country of an army extensively infected, is a cen-tre of poison to its whole people." The commission directed its next letter of solicitation to "men of wealth." Explaining that the lives of 250,000 men were in danger from dysentery, fever, and cholera, it declared that "extraor-dinary means" were required to save the army. Appealing to both partisan loyalties and class anxieties, the circular reminded Republican men that "every man lost by neglect makes a complaining family, and forms a ground of unpopularity for the war."[68]

Taking Over the WCRA

Just as important as gaining funding was the commission's object of super-seding the WCRA in its influence over soldiers' aid societies and its recog-nition among northern women. Though the Sanitary Commission had been officially recognized by the government in June, the Woman's Central Relief Association continued operating autonomously throughout the sum-mer of 1861. By September 1861, however, for reasons that were never recorded or made public, the WCRA's existence as a separate entity was ter-minated. According to the official record, the merging of the WCRA into the USSC was mutually planned and agreed upon. Despite the "closest practical relations," the report read, the WCRA, "at its own generous in-stance," was brought under Sanitary authority. "Finally, by formal vote rati-fied on both sides," the historical account noted, on September 19, 1861, "the Woman's Central was made a branch of the Sanitary Commission."[69]

Despite the respectful words that attended the merger of the two organi-zations, becoming a branch of the commission effectively stripped the WCRA of its public status and authority. In a joint agreement, the WCRA was guaranteed specific areas of autonomy and allowed to take charge of its own affairs, but it was also held responsible for its own finances and debts. After losing all of its executive decision-making powers, the WCRA's sub-committee on correspondence and supplies was the only sector to retain any of its original functions, and soon encompassed the entire work of the branch. Maintaining contact between the two organizations was left to the

[68] "To the Presidents and to the Citizens of the United States," June 21, 1861, no. 5, *Docu-ments*, 1:1–2; see Greenbie, *Lincoln's Daughters*, p. 73; "Letter to the Public, Soliciting Contri-butions," June 22, 1861, no. 7, *Documents*, 1:1–2.
[69] "The Origin, Organization, and Working of the 'Woman's Central Association of Relief,' New York," October 12, 1861, no. 32, *Documents*, 1:22.

commission's corresponding secretary, Alfred Bloor, who was charged with writing to the WCRA twice a week, "keeping it regularly informed of the wants of the army, and the expectations of the Commission from that source of supply."[70] Though members of the USSC's executive committee worked without pay, the organization paid substantial salaries to its chief officers, such as Olmsted, as well as to its agents and lecturers. Female branch leaders worked for the organization on an entirely unpaid basis.

The transformation of the Woman's Central Relief Association from an autonomous organization into a branch of the Sanitary Commission was marked by a statistical summing up of the work it had accomplished on its own. In less than seven months the WCRA had received over 30,000 hospital garments, 15,147 bedding contributions, 6,112 havelocks, and over 2,000 packages of jelly and preserves. If nothing else, the WCRA gave evidence of its existence by quantifying the substance of female warwork. Most items were forwarded to the commission's office in Washington, indicating that homefront women most likely viewed the commission, once it was in operation in June, as a reliable and efficient depot. The commission acknowledged the WCRA's central role in collecting supplies and recruiting nurses, while the various committees, headed and operated by the New York City women, were commended for their accomplishments and exhorted to continue and enlarge their work. Though Bellows admitted that "this so-called branch, was, in truth, the original seed" of the commission, the WCRA's pioneering role in mapping out the potential of a mass citizen relief effort was now in the process of being erased by the commission's determination to dictate the historical narrative of warwork.[71]

When Elizabeth Blackwell and "Ninety-Two Respected Ladies" formed the Woman's Central Relief Association, they did so believing in their prerogatives, as women, to direct social welfare and voluntary charity—a right expressed in the antebellum compromise on gender. Of course, voluntarism had long been a feature of American culture, forming part of the very self-

[70] Ibid., 1:22–23. The WCRA served as both an office for the commission and its New York base for shipments. Its relationship with the USSC served as the model for subsequently created branches, which by war's end numbered twenty-five. Most were urban and run by women. Larger branches—such as the New-England Women's Auxiliary Association, based in Boston, and the Northwestern Sanitary Commission, in Chicago—supervised the supply work of whole regions, encompassing several states. List of branches in Packet 7, Box 951, USSC Papers; Stillé *History of the United States Sanitary Commission*, p. 78.
[71] "Origin," *Documents*, 1:32–33; *First Annual Report of the Woman's Central Association of Relief, May 1, 1862* (New York, 1862), Box 993, USSC Papers.

definition of northern character. Indeed, it might be argued that voluntarism was an essential element in American notions of nationalism. In the decades before the war, middle-class women had become the backbone of northern voluntarism, an achievement that gained them the attention of powerful men but also made their positions assailable.

For cosmopolitan rationalists, women's position in charity work posed a problem. Precisely because they recognized the strength of female voluntarism and because they assumed that women's benevolence was inexhaustible, liberal reformers judged it the chief mechanism through which they would shape a new nationalism. Yet if these men were to be successful, women could not remain in control of war relief. Convinced as they were of their own fitness to guide the nation in its time of crisis, and expressing in exaggerated rhetoric their anxieties about the perils the war presented for social order and institutional life, Bellows, Olmsted, and Strong offered themselves as the organic leaders of popular benevolence. The United States Sanitary Commission was, for them, the perfect vehicle for realizing personal, political, and ideological goals. A nonpartisan agency, unbeholden to the government, and yet with wide access to the public, it was an ideal site for both forming opinion and making policy.

The wives, sisters, and daughters of elite cosmopolitan rationalists were comfortable choices to head the WCRA in its subsidiary role as a Sanitary Commission branch. But the leadership of professional women presented USSC men with potential competition for their claims to expertise. The Blackwell sisters received little support in their attempt to maintain authority over nurses' training and, once the USSC went into operation, were hastily removed from their places in the WCRA. Hostility toward female physicians had begun long before the war, nurtured by a male medical profession that felt threatened by the Blackwells' presence. In fact, Elizabeth Blackwell's own hospital was omitted from the list of institutions backing the WCRA. The evidence is scanty on the process by which the Blackwells were removed from authority, but when Elizabeth sent an English friend a copy of an early WCRA report, she revealed the bitterness surrounding their loss of leadership positions.

> We shall do much good, but you will probably not see our names for we soon found that jealousies were too intense for us to assume our true place. We would have accepted a place on the health commission which our association is endeavoring to establish in Washington, & which the government will probably appoint—but the Doctors would not permit us to come forward. In the hospital committee which you will see referred to in the report they declined

Dr. Elizabeth Blackwell, 1870s. Manuscripts Division, Library of Congress.

to allow our little hospital to be represented—& they refused to have anything
to do with the nurse education plan if the Miss Blackwells were going to engi-
neer the matter.[72]

---

[72] Elizabeth Blackwell to Barbara Smith Bodichon, June 5, 1861, Blackwell Papers.

The inability of the Blackwells to sustain their influence with the government and the New York medical establishment presaged other problems the WCRA would encounter in its dealings with Sanitary leadership. But in a larger sense, the rebuff of the Blackwells implied that the popular glorification of women's labors applied to the unpaid labor of average wives and not to the paid and skilled work of professional women. For the rest of the war the Blackwells' names never again appeared in connection with either the WCRA or the United States Sanitary Commission.[73]

[73] Years after the war, Elizabeth Cady Stanton observed that though nearly every northern woman was involved in some way with supplying the Sanitary Commission, almost none knew of Elizabeth Blackwell's pivotal role; "not a hundred of all those thousands who toiled . . . knows that to one of her own sex was the formation of the Great Sanitary due." Elizabeth Cady Stanton, Susan B. Anthony, and Matilda Joslyn Gage, *History of Woman Suffrage*, 3 vols. (New York, 1881–86), vol. 1, *1848–1861* (New York, 1881), p. 15.

3

"FOR THE 'BOYS IN BLUE' ":
ORGANIZING THE HOMEFRONT

The men who created the United States Sanitary Commission never anticipated that the greater part of their energies would be occupied by persuading northern women to participate in their project. Having witnessed the
explosion of female support for mobilization during the first days and weeks
of the war, they assumed that women would embrace a plan that promised
to maximize the impact of their benevolence. For Sanitary Commission
leaders, the key to success lay in their "wise foresight and perfect comprehension" of the gendered division of social authority in American society,
an understanding that would enable them to manipulate the nonpolitical
arena of feminized benevolence to serve their own version of nationhood.
The "most novel and striking characteristics of our American civilization,"
wrote commission historian Charles Stillé, was the fact that benevolent organizations "had been for a long time under the control and management
almost excusively of women." When the USSC "sought to make the women
of the country its agents in the vast work of supplying. . . the Government
in its care of the Army," it did so with a unique appreciation of the antebellum compromise on gender or, as Stillé phrased it, the "peculiar position
which [women] occupy in a democratic society like ours."[1]

---

[1] Stillé, *History of the United States Sanitary Commission*, pp. 170–71.

At the outset of USSC operations, the commissioners expected that their most challenging task would involve revamping an outmoded, entrenched War Department bureaucracy and advising the Medical Bureau to adopt modern sanitary and medical procedures. The commission's "great object," recalled Bellows, was to "develop, strengthen and support the regular medical and military authorities and methods." Yet by war's end, people believed the commission's "chief business" had been "the collection and distribution of voluntary supplies." "The vast proportions [relief] assumed, during the progress of the war," remarked Stillé, "were due to circumstances, which it was impossible to have foreseen from the beginning."[2]

What the men of the USSC did not foresee was the extent to which their relief scheme involved an incursion into the social prerogatives middle-class women had acquired in the decades before the war, namely dominance over the welfare needs of their communities and the labor conducted within their households. The commission, of course, was not repudiating female philanthropy; in fact, it called for greater discretionary efforts on the part of the public. But its assertion of control over the destination and uses of women's gifts carried with it the imputation that customary methods of benevolence were inadequate to winning a war, even perilous for a nascent army requiring systematic care. By declaring that a national emergency rendered unpaid female labor a form of military materiel that could legitimately be requisitioned for the war, the commission plan suffused housework and voluntarism with national political purposes. At the same time, however, by defining benevolence as a province of the state requiring the supervision of elite men, it also declared that women's control over domesticity and charity was no longer inviolate.

Making claims in the name of defending the nation for rights to the products of women's household labor was one thing; commanding that labor was another matter. Indeed, as soon as the commission postulated that women's homemade gifts were goods owed the state in a military emergency, it broached a number of potentially disruptive problems that were only dimly glimpsed in the early weeks of the war. What, in fact, was a woman's obligation to the state in wartime? What was more important for the Union cause: women's labor or women's loyalty? Did female benevolence extend past community boundaries to the nation as a whole? How could a plan that was predicated on the antebellum gender ideology—a romanticized construction that asserted women's inherent proclivities for do-

[2] Bellows, "U.S. Sanitary Commission," p. 73; Stillé, *History of the United States Sanitary Commission*, p. 166.

mesticity and charity—expect easy compliance when it erased the allocation of power that gave the gendered separation of economic responsibilities its legitimacy? By placing so much emphasis on the products of women's housework, the Sanitary Commission scheme came close to unmasking the fiction that household labor produced no market value, that it was merely a leisurely or instinctual endeavor.

The confidence with which the commissioners began their enterprise was reinforced by the early successes of the Woman's Central Relief Association. The women's organization appeared to have gained acceptance from local women's groups with relative ease. But the WCRA's structure and mode of operation differed significantly from the organization Bellows and his colleagues created. In contrast to the WCRA's willingness merely to coordinate the workings of existing charitable groups, the Sanitary Commission's nationalist vision was premised on a network of uniformly structured societies dedicated to soldier relief and answerable solely to the central agency. Intent on fostering wholly new benevolent entities, the commission devoted considerable energy to communicating with the loyal female public about the bureaucratic framework and the procedures it considered essential for maintaining competent aid societies.

Among the USSC's first messages to the female homefront was a call to form a soldiers' aid society in every village and city in the North. In order to justify such a sweeping step, it reiterated stories that women's spontaneous benevolence was creating chaos at the front by deluging the army with useless goods. Explaining to women the problems they had caused, the commission carefully couched its criticism within a sentimentalized account of the work they had already initiated: "The churches, the schools, the parlors, the bedchambers, were alive with the patriotic industry of those whose fingers could not rest while a stitch could be set, a bandage torn, for the relief of the brave soldiers." Before long, the "little circles and associations, with patriotic intent . . . were multiplying, like rings in the water, over the face of the whole country."[3] But the cumulative impact of these random efforts was problematic, for although "the stream" was in "full flow," it was guided by zeal rather than discretion. Worse still, the army was "inundated by a flood of public bounty, wasting itself where it was not wanted." Given the "immense mischief" such charitable efforts might create "if allowed to run wild," it was necessary to establish some control over these "national impulses." The commission's "purpose" was "to systematize the impulsive, disorderly, and uninformed sympathies and efforts of the women of the

[3] "Origin," no. 32, *Documents*, 1:5.

country so as to make effective . . . the generous and restless desires to help the young army."[4]

Although the commission justified its intervention in homefront relief on the grounds that women's early wartime benevolence had been effusive and disorganized, the reality was very different. While many women had taken it upon themselves to aid departing relatives and outfit local regiments, these activities were usually conducted on an ad hoc, personal, and temporary basis. In fact, by the middle of 1861, many towns were still without a soldiers' aid society. "The Spring of 1861 & nearly the whole Summer passed away, without any organized movement in this place," explained the secretary of the Fayetteville, New York, Ladies Soldiers Aid Society. Though "every loyal woman felt constantly self-reproved for her inaction" and "many sent their offerings through distant societies," the remoteness of this "small country village" inhibited a more concerted effort.[5]

Women who did not see fit to establish permanent soldiers' aid societies may not have been apathetic or inexperienced in civic affairs, for no one expected a long or exceedingly destructive war. The first call for volunteers stipulated only a three-month military term, and men rushed to volunteer in part because they shared the belief that the war would be brief. Young men raised with literary images of military heroes welcomed the opportunity to attain their own piece of historical glory.[6] One soldier remembered that, during the early days of the war, "the belief then was almost universal throughout the North that the war would amount to nothing much but a summer frolic, and would be over by the 4th of July."[7] Like the men who volunteered for military service, homefront women too assumed that violence and bloodshed would be kept to a minimum. Mrs. Bordwell from Corinovia, New York, noted that the women in her town "accepted Secretary Seward's prophecy respecting the duration of the struggle, and did not at first deem any organization necessary." (Corinovia women did not organize formally until the middle of 1862).[8] For a brief and doubtlessly triumphant conflict, local regiments could be adequately cared for by the redirected energies of existing philanthropic agencies.

Whether or not it was aware of the fragile state of homefront organizing,

[4] "Statement of the Object and Method of the Sanitary Commission—with Supplement," December 7, 1863, no. 69, Documents, 2:49; Bellows, "U.S. Sanitary Commission," p. 73.
[5] Fayetteville Ladies Soldiers Aid Society, 1866, Box 981, USSC Papers.
[6] Charles Royster, The Destructive War: William Tecumseh Sherman, Stonewall Jackson, and the Americans (New York, 1991), pp. 252–53.
[7] Leander Stillwell, The Story by a Common Soldier of Army Life in the Civil War, 1861–1865 (Erie[?], Kan., 1920), p. 9.
[8] Mrs. P. Bordwell to USSC, 1866, Box 981, USSC Papers.

the commission moved ahead with its scheme to create a network of local societies that would form a resilient infrastructure for its welfare experiment. In October 1861, it distributed 40,000 copies of a circular, composed by Frederick Law Olmsted, endorsed by President Lincoln, and addressed to the "Loyal Women of America," that spelled out the USSC plan for structuring relief and channeling supplies to the army.[9]

Taking care to address the issue of the state's role in caring for national soldiers, the letter to "Loyal Women" judiciously complimented federal officials for attending to soldiers "so soon after the breaking out of a war of this magnitude." But Olmsted also faulted "organic defects" in the government for the disorder at the front, charging that suffering and death were "partly owing to the inhumanity and knavery of various agents of government," making the need for an "intermediate agency" self-evident. Introducing itself as "a volunteer and unpaid bureau of the War Department," the commission appealed for "the gift-offerings of their own handiwork from the loyal women of the land."[10] Far from suggesting a casual approach to army welfare, Olmsted emphasized that even voluntary assistance must be administered in a disciplined fashion. "It is, therefore, suggested that societies be at once formed in every neighborhood where they are not already established, and that existing societies of suitable organization, as Dorcas Societies, Sewing Societies, Reading Clubs, and Sociables, devote themselves, for a time, to the sacred service of their country." Lest there be any misunderstanding about how extensive participation was expected to be, Olmsted alleged that "every woman in the country can, at the least, knit a pair of woolen stockings, or if, not, can purchase them." "Let there be concert on this subject," he admonished, "taking care that three or four sizes are provided."[11]

The "Loyal Women" circular assumed a condescending tone, approaching mid-nineteenth-century women as if they had no experience in benevolent work. Offering what it referred to as "simple hints," it provided detailed instructions on how to form a local soldiers' aid society, from the recruitment of neighbors to the choice of the day, hour, and location for regular meetings. The circular advised women to notify fellow

[9] The "Letter" was addressed to all "Countrywomen," though the only branch in existence was the Woman's Central Relief Association, which covered women living in New York State and parts of Connecticut, Rhode Island, Massachusetts and New Jersey. See "To the Loyal Women of America," October 1, 1861, no. 32, *Documents*, 1:35–43. Olmsted noted the number of appeals in a letter to his half-sister, Frederick Law Olmsted to Mary Olmsted, November 6, 1861, in *FLO Papers*, 4:219–22.
[10] "Loyal Women," *Documents*, 1:35–36.
[11] Ibid., 1:37–38.

townswomen through notices distributed to pastors who would then read them to their congregations. After selecting a president, secretary, treasurer, and committees on supplies and correspondence, society members were to begin preparing boxes. In a particularly pointed note, it suggested that if women felt unsure about how to proceed they should consult some gentlemen in town for advice. The implication was clear: organizational precedents set by women's groups were inadequate to carry on work of national importance.[12]

After outlining how women should organize, the appeal enumerated those articles most needed by the army, a broad and imaginative list that included items from undershirts and feather pillows to arrowroot, jellies, and checker and backgammon boards. All goods were to be "closely packed in wooden boxes, or in very strongly wrapped bales," and shipped to either the Woman's Central Relief Association in New York or in care of five male officers of the Sanitary Commission stationed around the country. WCRA or USSC workers would take charge of repacking and forwarding the boxes to assigned hospitals. In the event that women remained immune to such entreaties, the letter included a memorandum signed by the Postmaster General urging all postmasters to initiate organizations in their respective towns or, failing that, to gather contributions themselves.[13] Olmsted was proud of the letter, later expressing to his half-sister, Mary Olmsted, his hope that "there is not a hamlet in all the free West where the women are not at work."[14]

Soldiers' Aid Societies

By the time Olmsted's letter reached the homefront, popular assumptions about a brief and benign war had all but disappeared. The defeat at Bull Run in July 1861 had been sobering, provoking a shattering awareness of the fragile condition of Union forces. Stories of frightened, inexperienced soldiers running from battle revealed the ease with which ill-prepared men could be demoralized. "We are utterly and disgracefully routed, beaten, whipped," George Templeton Strong wrote upon hearing of the humiliating defeat, predicting that the day would be known thereafter as "Black

[12] Ibid., 1:39–42.
[13] The WCRA was listed as the only depot in New York City; other locations were Philadelphia, Boston, Cincinnati, Wheeling, Va., and Washington, D.C. See ibid., 1:38; "To the Post Master" (draft), October 4, 1861, Box 735, USSC Papers.
[14] Frederick Law Olmsted to Mary Olmsted, November 5, 1861, in *FLO Papers*, 4:220.

Monday." Writing to Eliza Schuyler about the urgent need for public assistance, Olmsted described the "fearful fever of cowardice" and "savage brutality" that possessed the troops after the fight. Tragic in its outcome and unsettling for those concerned with military and sanitary discipline, the Battle of Bull Run nonetheless proved fortuitous for the commission.[15]

With the public's concern about the military heightened, the "Loyal Women" letter struck a sympathetic chord. "Responding at once to the first call of the President's for help. . . . the ladies of Antwerp met and organized themselves. . . . Scarcely any opposition was manifested," wrote Mrs. Ira Abell of Antwerp, New York. The president of the Ashville, New York, Soldiers Aid Society recalled that about ten women met for their first meeting in October 1861; "our village having but few inhabitants the prospects were rather dark but we resolved to do all we could." The women of Adams, New York, gathered together "in response to the appeals" of the Sanitary Commission and "about seventy became members of the society," eventually recruiting eighty women from a town of 1,500 inhabitants. Though the women of Adams sustained a relief society for the duration of the conflict, their contributions fluctuated with the perceived needs of the troops at the front. After particularly vicious battles, the women resolved to "work day after day till boxes were filled and sent away." Few towns, however, demonstrated the staying ability of Clarence, New York; the aid society founded there in October 1861 continued steadily for the remainder of the war.[16]

While most soldiers' aid societies were formed by white, Anglo-Saxon Protestant women, the war provided almost all women with opportunities to enter benevolent work. Some women from racial and ethnic minority groups utilized the recognized importance of such work to claim social legitimacy for themselves. African American women, Jewish women, and Catholic women formed societies of their own, with names that proclaimed their identities and their difference. The Hebrew Women's Aid Society of Philadelphia reported that it corresponded with thirteen other Jewish groups in Pennsylvania alone. Lydia R. Ward of Bridgeport, Connecticut, informed WCRA officer Ellen Collins that "the colored women of this city have formed an association for the relief of their soldiers." In St. Louis,

---

[15] Strong, July 22, 1861, *Diary*, 3:169; Frederick Law Olmsted to Mrs. E. Schuyler, July 31, 1861, Box 954, USSC Papers; William L. Barney, *Flawed Victory: A New Perspective on the Civil War* (New York, 1975), p. 5.

[16] Mrs. Ira P. Abell to Blatchford, April 17, 1866; Mrs. R. Roselle Ticknor to Mr. Blatchford, April 16, 1866; Carrie Z. Webb to J. Blatchford, April 5, 1866; Mrs. Henry Rue to USSC, November 20, 1866, Box 981, USSC Papers.

though white women had created a society for black women within their own organization, the city's middle-class black women insisted on forming a group of their own. Stationed as a nurse in the Benton Barracks Hospital in St. Louis, Emily Parsons was outraged by the racist humiliations black women endured daily, especially since so many were "intelligent, colored women,—ladies in fact, many of them, well educated and wealthy." She was gratified to observe that "these colored women have got up a colored Union Society among themselves," and had successfully obtained the "right of visiting *their* soldiers in this hospital," and even the "privilege" of riding in public streetcars on Saturday.[17]

The commission's goal of reorienting women from simply donating surplus household contributions to forming an infrastructure for a centralized operation worked on a number of levels. Appearing just as women's concerns about the war's devastation were rising, the USSC's plan to channel military donations to an agency that distributed goods on a national basis offered a way of ascertaining, with some degree of accuracy, the actual needs of the army, thereby insuring the applied value of donated labor. No doubt some women were flattered by the recognition of their potential economic worth in a crisis; the exigencies of war forced influential people to acknowledge the contributions that women could make to the cause.

Once an aid society was formed, women employed an array of methods to enlist the labor of neighbors. Some followed commission instructions closely, announcing meetings in the local press or from church pulpits and holding them in public places. Others modified USSC suggestions to reach their neighbors in more effective ways. Mary Scholl of Athens, New York, recalled that "a committee of ladies was formed who canvassed our village" to raise money and supplies. A committee in Clarendon, New York, covered the town according to school districts to raise money. Appeals were most successful when conducted within the face-to-face context of village life. Finding that the first priority for relief work was raising money, women such the treasurer of the Amenia Aid Society "called from door to door"

---

[17] See Nancy A. Hewitt, *Women's Social Activism and Social Change: Rochester, New York, 1822–1872* (Ithaca, N.Y. 1984), pp. 38–43, on leadership provided by evangelical and abolitionist women in wartime Rochester, N.Y. Lori Ginzberg argues that the war attracted a new, younger generation of women into relief, who abandoned earlier traditions of reform for the more "corporate" style of professional charity. Younger, more radical abolitionist women were attracted to working with freedpeople. See *Women and the Work of Benevolence: Morality, Politics, and Class in the Nineteenth-Century United States* (New Haven, 1990), pp. 134–38. Lydia R. Ward to Ellen Collins, October 6, 1863, Box 955; Rebecca Moss to Jno. S. Blatchford, March 29, 1866, Box 980, USSC Papers; Emily Elizabeth Parson, *Memoirs of Emily Elizabeth Parson, Published for the Benefit of the Cambridge Hospital* (Boston, 1880), pp. 138–39.

collecting funds. The society in Bridgeport, Connecticut, found it necessary to "beg from door to door and try to wake up every one to a sense of the sacred duty that devolved upon us all." A number of societies charged nominal dues in order to purchase raw materials and cover shipping costs. Mrs. Simons from Beech Ridge, New York, told the commission that members were charged twenty-five cents. The German Ladies Aid Society of Buffalo sustained participation through, among other means, "the monthly dues of the members, [and] collections in churches and synagogues."[18]

The most successful means of raising needed funds was through the staging of local fairs and festivals. A long-established activity of charitable organizations, festivals attracted wide audiences and offered recreation together with attractive commodities in exchange for the public's money. Throughout the war, women staged a variety of thematic events featuring the sale of particular foods such as strawberries or ice cream, while others offered lectures and entertainment such as music and dancing. The Soldiers Aid Society of Bainbridge, New York, held masquerade parties, an oyster supper, and "sold ice cream twice" to raise almost $200 for the war effort. The German Ladies Aid Society of Buffalo reported that "by far the greater part of the revenue" they amassed derived from fairs, concerts, balls, and amusements. Women in Antwerp, New York, held a Union Jubilee after Lincoln's reelection, raising $215 through their efforts. Ashville, New York, women held "sociables to get money with which to buy cloth and other materials to work with."[19]

Through printed circulars, the commission supplied the homefront with regular bulletins on the army's needs and the items most wanting in military hospitals. Included in the circulars were instructions to produce a variety of clothing and hospital supplies, from the ill-conceived havelocks so prized in the early months of the war to bandages, shirts, drawers, and sheets.[20] Because nineteenth-century women were expected to be proficient in making patterns, cutting, and sewing clothing, many of the requests were accompanied with only abbreviated instructions, such as "short shirts made like long, only 1 yard long, and open in front," or "White or Gray Flannel Hos-

[18] Fayetteville Ladies Soldiers Aid Society, 1866; Mary Scholl to Blatchford, April 3, 1866; Mrs. Malaina Cooper to USSC, April 12, 1866; Mrs. Clara C. Reed, March 29, 1866; Mrs. E. Lewis to USSC, April 2, 1866; Mrs. A. Simmons, 1866; Mrs. Louisa Weiss, 1866, Box 981, USSC Papers.
[19] Mrs. A. McDougall, May 8, 1866; Caroline L. Hughes, April 19, 1866; Soldiers Aid Society of Bainbridge, 1866; Mrs. Louisa Weiss to USSC; Mrs. Ira P. Abell, April 17, 1866; Mrs. R. Roselle Ticknor to Mr. Blatchford, April 16, 1866; Carrie Webb to Blatchford, April 5, 1866; W. Scott Hicks to Blatchford, April 2, 1866, Box 981, USSC Papers.
[20] "To all Loyal Citizens of the United States," July 4, 1862, no. 44-2, *Documents*, 1:1–4.

pital Undershirts—two breadths flannel gusset at the neck, narrow neck-band." Articles particular to hospital requirements, however, were described with greater specificity. Thus, the commission requested quilts 7 feet by 50 inches, and long cotton and canton flannel shirts with precise measurements and details: "1 1/4 yards long; 2 breadths of unbleached cotton, 7/8 yard wide, open 9 inches at the bottom; length of Sleeve, 5/8 yard; length of Arm-hole, 12 inches; length of Band, 20 inches; open in front, to the bottom—a piece 4 inches wide lapping under—fastened with tapes."[21]

Many women came to rely on these circulars as the best means for acquiring accurate information on hospital and military supply needs, and made frequent requests for instructions, patterns, and lists of required items. "Will you also send us . . . one of your circulars, stating articles most needed, ways of making, etc."; "The ladies of this place . . . wish for directions how to make shirts & drawers the suitable sizes"; "We will make havelocks. I am very glad of the pattern you sent."[22] In New York City, the WCRA office at Cooper Union served as a clearinghouse for women seeking up-to-date information on army shortages. Abby Howland Woolsey wrote her sister Eliza that she was "going to the Cooper Union today to try and get some simple patterns for calico gowns. They advertise to supply paper patterns of garments to ladies."[23] With advice furnished by those at the warfront, women gained assurances that their labors would not be wasted and their homemade goods would be put to good use.

As the fortunes of the Union forces fluctuated, the men who led the commission identified the secret to furthering their experiment. By focusing on the humanitarian needs of soldiers suffering in particularly bloody battles, they played on the sympathies of women who might otherwise be reluctant to contribute. "No one personally familiar with the internal history of the Sanitary Commission," Corresponding Secretary Alfred Bloor wrote after the war, "would for an instant pretend that as many tens of thousands as there were millions could have been raised, if the money had been asked for in the name of the scientific and historical interests of the Commission instead of in the name of the physical needs of the 'boys in blue.' "[24] His ob-

---

[21] "Origin," *Documents*, 1:34.

[22] E. C. Sleeper to L. L. Schuyler, November 25, 1861; A. D. King, November 26, 1861; Eva M. Case to Miss Collins, June 13, 1861, Box 654, USSC Papers.

[23] Abby Howland Woolsey to Eliza Woolsey Howland, May 17, 1861, in Bacon and Howland, *Letters*, 1:76.

[24] Alfred Bloor, "Women's Work in the War. A Letter to Senator Sumner," September 1866, p. 4, Alfred J. Bloor Papers.

An allegorical rendering by Winslow Homer of female patriotic toil, complete with a large American flag, depicting elegantly dressed women gathered to make havelocks for soldiers. The American Social History Project.

servations were accurate; women throughout the North were more sensitive to reports from the warfront than they were to specific Sanitary Commission appeals. The women of Panama, New York, acknowledged: "There were many who... were urged to action only when some great Battle had been fought."[25]

The Limits of Voluntarism

"It is impossible to over-estimate the amount of consecrated work done by the loyal women of the North for the Army," Bellows wrote in 1867. "Hundreds of thousands of women probably gave all the leisure they could command, and all the money they could save and spare, to the soldiers for the whole four years and more, to the War." Written as an introduction to Brockett and Vaughan's 1867 commemorative volume, *Women's Work in the Civil War: A Record of Heroism, Patriotism, and Patience,* Bellows's words echoed the book's extravagantly romantic descriptions of women's wartime sacrifices. Readers of his essay were well aware of his role in wartime benevolence, and casting women as thoroughly committed and steadfast workers shed as favorable a light on his organization as it did on northern women.[26]

But his effusive praise betrayed an intent to conceal the actual record of homefront participation, which was less encouraging and more spasmodic. Though effective in persuading thousands to form soldiers' aid societies, the USSC's mobilization of the female homefront was far from complete, and by 1862 many towns were still without any sort of war charity organization. Bellows professed that women's work was "as systematic as it was universal," but in fact few women followed the commission's instructions closely.[27]

"Our meetings," explained the secretary of the Ellsworth, New York, aid society, "were merely 'neighborhood gatherings' of from 15 to 20 individuals." When called upon at the war's end to assess the performance of local aid societies, women frequently emphasized the disparity between their informal village organizations and the sophisticated entities advocated by the commission. The women of Cato, New York, donated food, clothing, and money in 1861 but "never had a regularly organized Society," while the Altoona Society of Pennsylvania "was conducted in a very unparliamentary style." Not only were many groups unable to recruit enough members to fill all the hierarchical posts recommended by the commission, but some considered them unnecessary. Others dispensed altogether with the idea of

[25] Mrs. J. Hoyt, 1866, Box 981, USSC Papers.
[26] Henry W. Bellows, introduction, Brockett and Vaughan, *Woman's Work*, p. 57.
[27] Ibid.

fixed meetings, favoring, as in one town, "the simple announcement from the desk in our churches that help was needed."[28]

Regardless of the forms they assumed, soldiers' aid societies were fragile entities sustained with considerable difficulty. The process of organizing neighbors, canvassing for money, buying raw materials, sewing clothing, canning food, packing boxes, and shipping them to the assigned depot required sustained time and energy, which were rarely in steady supply. "I must say," wrote one woman, "that when the call for lint and bandages was made I invited the ladies to meet at our house." Yet after successfully collecting three boxes of donations, she was unable to form a permanent society; "the interest died out with those articles." Mrs. Waters reported that the women of her Willink, New York, aid society determined soon after "the interest first evinced began to wane," that "*one half day* every week was more time than they could give." Beyond women's lack of time and resources, the distances between homes in rural areas posed additional problems. "Our obstacles were many and almost insurmountable," Mrs. M. H. France reported about the Eddy Aid Society of Pennsylvania: "Our place of meeting was very far from many of the members' homes."[29]

Forming a soldiers' aid society was a far cry from sustaining it. Although few groups were as short-lived as the Patriotic Aid Society of Dickinson Centre, New York, which lasted only five days, many were only intermittent affairs. "The maintaining of an organization of this kind is far more difficult than one would imagine," reported the secretary of the Black Creek Aid Society of New York. Attendance at meetings "grew less and less until there were but two or three who manifested any interest," and the group managed to stay together only for "a season." The women of Bloomsburg, Pennsylvania, credited a Sanitary Commission directive for their decision to organize, but "as time wore and discouragements arose, a great number wearied and fell by the way." A number of societies dispersed and reconstituted themselves over the course of the war. The women of Ashville, New York, organized themselves in October 1861, disbanded after a brief period of work, and then reconstituted a society in the summer of 1862. Even a male correspondent to the WCRA recognized that warwork imposed un-

[28] Rhoda S. Briggs, Ellsworth, N.Y., 1866; Matilda W. Shepard, April 23, 1866; J. C. Bennet, Hunts Hollow, 1866, Box 981; Charlotte L. Lewis to Jno. S. Blatchford, April 19, 1866, Box 980, USSC Papers.
[29] H. L. Boyer, March 29, 1866; Miss Clara C. Reed to J. S. Blatchford, March 29, 1866; Mrs. C. Waters, 1866; Mrs. M. H. France to Jn. Blatchford, January 2, 1867, Box 980, USSC Papers.

usual burdens on busy women; explaining in early 1864 why his wife and other women of Vernon, New Jersey, no longer sent contributions, he noted, "you have no idea what hard work those ladies found it."[30]

Though the USSC enjoyed only limited success in reforming women's charitable behavior, it was remarkably, if inadvertently, effective in stimulating correspondence from women throughout the North. From the moment the organization undertook the coordination of supply work and stretched its probing arm into the hinterland, news from the homefront poured into both national headquarters and branch offices from a female public anxious to explain its successes and failures. Women wrote unsolicited letters as well as answers to personal inquiries and, later, formal questionnaires. Stimulating a unique dialogue among the male commissioners, the female branch leaders, and themselves, northern women created an arena in which they could articulate the enormity of housework, the economic and political complexions of their communities, and the special hardships the war had imposed on their lives. Usually written to explain why they were unable to satisfy specific USSC requests, their correspondence challenged prevailing assumptions about household labor and revealed common difficulties among women in various regions. Repeatedly, women pointed to the lack of economic resources, conflicting personal and family responsibilities, and skepticism about the project's rationale as the most persistent hindrances to regular warwork. The sources of homefront resistance to Sanitary Commission entreaties were varied, but fostering sustained, voluntary labor for national purposes was clearly an unreliable and politically charged undertaking.

In industrial towns and agricultural regions alike, the commission scheme jeopardized delicately balanced economies, now under the added burdens of war. For towns such as Altoona, Pennsylvania, whose inhabitants were "mainly railroad operatives of limited means," there was the problem of enlisting working-class women to assume middle-class functions. As the Altoona Society's secretary, Charlotte Lewis, explained, little was accomplished, "there being a great scarcity of the class of women at all accustomed to act outside the home." Around the country the commission heard numerous complaints of distressed households. "A great many plead poverty," wrote Mrs. Bradfield from Hardin County, Iowa. The women of North Billerica, Massachusetts, who collected donations at the beginning of

---

[30] Mrs. L. M. Stowe, April 30, 1866; Mrs. J. E. Caldwell, April 9, 1866; Hannah J. John to Jno. S. Blatchford, April 6, 1866; Mrs. R. Roselle Ticknor to Blatchford, April 16, 1866, Box 981; C. Allen, M.D., to Miss Marshall, January 25, 1864, Box 671, USSC Papers.

the war, reported that "living became so expensive" they accomplished little more.[31]

Poor women in the WCRA region wrote to Louisa Lee Schuyler and her associates intimate, oftentimes moving, descriptions of households and local economies hard hit by the war. The head of the Dorcas Society in Lodi, New York, wrote in April 1862 that they were forwarding their last package to the commission. "And I am very sorry," she added, "but the place is a factory village and the inhabitants are mostly Hollanders and all are a laboring class of people and lately work has been scarce and Money hard to get and consequently have no funds to work with."[32] "I hardly dare now to make another specific and immediate requisition," explained a Cortland Village, New York, woman in November 1861. Though hers was "a charming rural region," farm sizes were small and the soil "only adapted to grasing." In a pointed rebuke to USSC assumptions about appealing for the "boys in blue," she elucidated the economic realities of her town's women. "We have *three* flourishing academies, no thieves or beggars, but there are not a dozen opulent individuals in the county! Nineteen out of every twenty articles I have sent to you have been made by the personal labor of people who employ no servants. . . . With such facts, in view, dear Madam, you can easily conceive why it would not be very gracious in me to cry 'another for Hector' *too* often."[33]

Notwithstanding high transportation costs and war-inflated prices for cotton and wool, it appeared that rural women were disproportionately generous contributors to the Sanitary Commission project. The women of Ellsworth, New York, may have been typical: describing themselves as "merely country people with slender purses," they regularly donated to the army.[34] In the commission's estimation, the reason that provincial areas proved more generous than did major cities such as New York was obvious: urban bourgeois women who had established their own philanthropic organizations stood to lose the most by relinquishing authority to a national organization and, as Louisa Schuyler recognized, were most likely to feel competitive with the commission. "The *love of power*, which so blinds the eyes of the city people, does not extend in the country," she wrote to Olmsted in 1863. "I feel as if I never could say enough about the noble spirit of

---

[31] Charlotte L. Lewis to Jno. S. Blatchford, April 19, 1866, Box 980; Mrs. L. M. Bradfield to Mr. Blatchford, April 19, 1866, Box 986; Eliza A. Rogers to Blatchford, April 28, 1866, Box 983, USSC Papers.

[32] A. D. Amerman to Louisa L. Schuyler, April 21, 1861, Box 655, USSC Papers.

[33] Mrs. Henry S. Randall to Louisa L. Schuyler, November 24, 1861, Box 654, USSC Papers.

[34] Rhoda S. Briggs, 1866, Box 981, USSC Papers.

self sacrifice found in these little villages. They never *see* anything & work from pure faith & principle."[35]

Moved by the sentiments of poorer women from rural locales, Schuyler nevertheless knew that the organization's well-being depended on its ability to tap the assets of wealthy men and the philanthropic capacities of upper-class women. As early as the fall of 1861, the Woman's Central Relief Association boasted of maintaining correspondence with "several hundred names of prominent ladies in different states." Eliza Schuyler routinely called upon her elite peers to sustain flagging supply work and direct their attentions to the commission. "I am engaged in writing to influential ladies," she reported to Alfred Bloor at the end of 1862, "to inform their circles, and influence them against local and partial organisations." Propertied women, after all, were "so much more easily affected by personal influences."[36]

Yet even the advantages of class could not undo the constraints posed by gender inequities in economic power; the reality was that nearly all women were dependent on their male relatives for money. After women's personal household surpluses were exhausted, contributions from individual men and local businesses sometimes constituted the only means for continuing soldier aid work. When commission agent William Hobart Hadley found people in Portsmouth, New Hampshire, expressing the "strong belief that they have done more for their soldiers than any other towns or cities in the Union," the women confided to him that such views held by the men dimmed the prospects for continuing warwork. "Their ladies assured me that they were unable to beg enough of the men to purchase materials to keep themselves in work."[37]

If women lacked influence over men in public forums, they were equally vulnerable to men's decision making power at home. Some correspondents alluded to the inequitable balance of power in nineteenth-century marriages to illuminate why their donations were not as large as they had hoped. Mrs. Delilah Allen confided to the WCRA: "My husband lacks or has not my opinions of doing for those who have fought for our country's freedom. . . . I have with my horse and carriage done much but it has been

[35] Louisa L. Schuyler to Frederick L. Olmsted, May 20, 1863, Box 955, USSC Papers. See also William Quentin Maxwell, *Lincoln's Fifth Wheel: The Political History of the United States Sanitary Commission* (New York, 1956), p. 91.
[36] Eliza H. Schuyler to F. L. Olmsted, November 8, 1861, Box 965; Eliza H. Schuyler to A. J. Bloor, December 3, 1862, Box 954, USSC Papers.
[37] See George O. Glavis to Dr. Bellows, February 7, 1863, on reliance on upper-class women to raise money; H. Hadley to H. Bellows, December 2, 1861, Box 640, USSC Papers.

to the distaste of my husband." "Politics ran high with us," Mrs. Augustus Lippincott admitted to Commissioner Blatchford at the war's end, "and Mothers and daughters were apt to work according to the opinions of Husbands & Fathers." Given the political polarization in her Hills Grove, New York, town, "there was not much harmony in regard to things relating to the war." A Bergen, New York, correspondent complained of women who "were more interested in their husbands' politics than in the suffering of soldiers," adding a special partisan rebuke for Republican women; since their men had caused the war, she reasoned, "their wives might take care of the soldiers."[38]

But the greatest constraints on women's abilities to participate in warwork were the rigors of their domestic labors. Time and again female correspondents cited household chores, childcare responsibilities, and family illnesses as the chief reasons for neglecting requests for their charity. For the majority of women, who employed no household help, housework burdens were onerous. Explaining why her neighbors failed to sustain a soldiers' aid society, Miss Denroche wrote that the few who wanted to work felt they could not do it alone and added that "some have large families of sick or young children." Sarah Bradford of Geneva, New York, informed the WCRA that she had to resign as secretary of her local aid society, "having many other cares & duties claiming my attention."[39]

These letters were extraordinary in their explication of the laborious nature of household tasks. For decades northern women had been surrounded by dictates that cast their domestic work as the antithesis of labor, indeed, as something approaching a leisurely pursuit.[40] Bellows himself had employed the language of leisure to explain how women were able to produce so much for the army during the war. But the escalating demands for the products of housework led some women to glimpse problems in cultural formulations that cast their existence as free of work. Women such as Miss Denroche used the opportunity of corresponding with the commission to delineate the realities of their household labor, possibly to acquire recognition for the otherwise invisible efforts that defined their lives: "I am shut in

[38] Mrs. Delilah Allen, February 11, 1863, Box 669; Mrs. Augustus Lippincott to Blatchford, July 2, 1866, Box 980; Mrs. Michstrussen, 1866, Box 981, USSC Papers.
[39] E. S. Denroche to Mrs. Helen W. Marshall, January 25, 1864, Box 671; Sarah H. Bradford to Mrs. Marshall, January 25, 1864, Box 671, USSC Papers.
[40] Jeanne Boydston argues that rhetoric about women's leisure constituted a central feature in what she terms the "pastoralization of housework." See *Home and Work: Housework, Wages, and the Ideology of Labor in the Early Republic* (New York, 1990), pp. 147–52.

school from 8 ½ untill 4 P.M. every day. I have all my own housekeeping to do and we have no baker here. . . . I have an acre and three quarters of land to take care of out of school and in winter all my wood to saw and split at least I had to do it until a week since I found it was injuring my health. . . . you must see I have not much leisure."[41]

Waging a national war without the federal structure and revenue to support it dramatically raised the demands for household production. What were once local surpluses were now considered by the commission, as well as by government agencies, as national resources. Many women had to set priorities for their benevolent efforts. Even in wartime, soldier relief work constituted only one of a number of charitable obligations. Whether as members of moral reform, temperance, church, or sewing groups, women attended to an array of welfare constituencies. According to Mary Ryan, "the female welfare system" of antebellum Utica, New York, included orphan asylums, "ragged schools," hospitals, the collection of donations, and charitable fairs to benefit poor families, which "surely surpassed the annual city appropriation for the poor, some $3,000."[42] In rural localities composed of complex family networks, women disbursed charity with the needs of neighbors and kin in mind. Even after the war began, women saw their primary duty as owed to village recruits and their families rather than to an unknown, albeit Union, army. This loyalty sometimes meant sending supplies directly to local regiments or saving goods to help needy families of volunteers.

The practice of ignoring Sanitary Commission circulars and sending contributions directly to the warfront was widespread. "I shall be very happy to respond to the call you make. . . but we have been fitting out a regiment from this County," Mrs. Wheeler wrote Louisa Schuyler early in the war. Eva Case informed the WCRA that when the first USSC circular arrived, the women in Vernon, New York, were occupied with their village regiment: "We are now getting woolen socks for them after those are done we will be ready to work for others." Though "nearly every household" in Ellsworth, New York, "had sent one or more of its members" to the war and "every household constantly [sent] boxes," Case conceded that most sent them to friends in the army, "which limited somewhat the contribution to the Sanitary." A few interpreted commission circulars to mean that they were being asked to work in accustomed ways. So the Comfort Club of As-

[41] Denroche to Marshall, January 25, 1864, Box 671, USSC Papers.
[42] Mary P. Ryan, *Cradle of the Middle Class: The Family in Oneida County, New York, 1790–1865* (New York, 1981), pp. 105–16, 212–18.

toria, New York, believed that the commission would defer to its authority and assign a regiment to its care for the duration of the war.[43]

While attending to community needs attested to the prerogatives women had established over social welfare, some women discerned in the Sanitary plan a means of satisfying the claims of local constituencies. Whether misreading or intentionally ignoring the commission's intentions, these women implored the organization to serve them as they saw fit. Mrs. Henry Randall of Cortland Village, New York, requested that the commission forward a box to Captain Grove's New York Company. Acknowledging that it was "a little irregular," she nonetheless explained to Schuyler that she "could not refuse the application of those who wished me to forward the box. It seems that 4 or 5 young men of Union Valley... have been ill."[44] After Mrs. Rebecca Howell prepared her own box, she placed it inside a larger one prepared by the New Village Sewing Association and politely asked the WCRA: "If there is any opportunity to send it to the persons to whom directed it would be a great satisfaction to me as they are orphans."[45] Eager to utilize an efficient system of direct transportation to hospitals and troops at the front, women employed the USSC as a conduit for their own charitable purposes, even if this blatantly contradicted the organization's philosophy.

In the most dramatic instances of homefront women enacting their obligations for charity and accountability, a number traveled alone to the warfront to distribute gifts directly to the soldiers. One woman, while claiming that her local war relief group was completely sympathetic with the commission's goals, informed the WCRA that the Hoboken society never sent boxes to the USSC: "I was ... a regular visitor in a government hospital &... it was natural, that having the opportunity, I should prefer to distribute them, under my own supervision."[46] And she was one of many. Reporting for London's *Daily Telegraph* in 1863, George Augustus Sala found "at least fifty fair dames and damsels" with the Army of the Potomac, some the wives of soldiers and military officers who were there at the request of their husbands, but others who came without invitation. Commission agent Dr. Kerlin learned in an interview with Provost Marshall General Patrick that visiting ladies were becoming increasingly intrusive in military life. "Oh! yes!," said Patrick, hoping that the doctor could clarify the problem, "about

[43] Mrs. M. E. Wheeler to Louisa Schuyler, July 12, 1861, Box 654; Eva M. Case, June 13, 1861, Box 654; Rhoda S. Briggs, 1866, Box 981; F. W. Blackwell, November 14, 1861, Box 654, USSC Papers.
[44] Mrs. Henry S. Randall to Louisa Schuyler, April 4, 1862, Box 655, USSC Papers.
[45] Mrs. R. Howell to WCRA, April 3, 1862, Box 655, USSC Papers.
[46] Isabella Stevens to Helen W. Marshall, January 25, 1864, Box 671, USSC Papers.

the female women who are coming in great numbers to the Army, with boxes, containing many of them, contraband goods; what do *you* know of them?" Though Kerlin assured him these women were not following Sanitary Commission procedures, he was probably more than a little surprised to hear from the chief of staff, General Butterfield, that such actions should not be suppressed. According to Kerlin, the General "spoke emphatically of the 'inestimable good which the Commission had exercised . . . ', but did not believe that the Commission could ever control the gifts of the people." Perhaps recognizing the importance to his enlisted men of receiving support from home, Butterfield suggested that "the little boxes were tokens of affection, for which there should always be an untrammeled passage."[47]

Those women who carried army supplies to the front enacted a sense of personal responsibility for their gifts and those of their neighbors. The vast majority, who never traveled to army hospitals but rather shipped supplies through the USSC, reminded the national organization of their need for accountability. Reprimanding the commission for not acknowledging a box the women of Watertown, New York, sent, Mrs. Fisk wrote, "I wish you would let me know so that I can satisfy the good people of those towns." After all, she advised WCRA officer Ellen Collins, "we have to take some pains to keep the ball a rolling on."[48]

Among the more troubling concerns women raised in their correspondence was the issue of whether they were being asked to carry out what was, in fact, the federal government's responsibility. Dubious about the large quantities of donations demanded of them, more than a few women suspected that the USSC was stockpiling donations while the government supplied the army, as it was supposed to do. Bellows had long anticipated a debate about the government's responsibility. "Why should the Sanitary Commission organize a systematic call upon the public, when the Govt. is under obligations & in funds liberaly supplied by the people to purchase all those things?" he asked himself in private notes. The issue of whether or not "this attempt to draw steadily from the beneficence of the public, . . . [is] likely to keep the Government on crutches" was problematic for nationalists. But Bellows felt "fearless of contradiction" in calling for popular support. The "industry of women" would be a "temporary necessity" that presented no danger of weakening the government.[49]

---

[47] George Augustus Sala, *My Diary in America in the Midst of the War,* 2 vols. (London, 1865), 1:294–95; Dr. I. N. Kerlin, "Report of Interview with Generals Hooker and Patrick," March 17, 1863, Box 757, USSC Papers.
[48] Mrs. M. Fisk to Miss Collins, January 22, 1863, WCRA, Box 655, USSC Papers.
[49] Henry Bellows, Notes, 1861, Bellows Papers.

But the question of government responsibility for the soldiers continued to plague the organization, and even led one of its founding members to resign his position. Samuel Gridley Howe, an abolitionist and a physician known for his work with the blind and deaf, decided that the idea of relying on public benevolence to strengthen the federal government was inherently flawed. Corresponding with Bellows in 1862, Howe pointed to the inconsistency of encouraging a strong state while at the same time providing enormous free public assistance to it. "You are unsound in your ideology," he wrote to Bellows; "I think you stand in the way of the action of those natural principles," which would allow government "to do its duty." Tendering his resignation, Howe announced: "I cannot bring myself to believe that it is wise to urge the people to do the government work any longer."[50]

If the USSC was to have any credibility, it was incumbent on Bellows to spread his message that women "need not fear the overdoing of this business." Mrs. Susan Crosman considered such pledges important. A member of two societies in New York, one in Sennell and another in the nearby city of Auburn, she advised Bellows in late 1861 that women in both communities "need assurance that what they send is needed and will be made a proper use of, many having already done all that they feel they can afford to."[51] Two years later Louisa Schuyler was still deflecting charges that the commission could take care of providing for the army's needs without requiring women to donate their labor. Admitting that the organization was well-stocked with money, she carefully explained to one inquiring woman that if the Sanitary Commission started using its money to buy "clothing, bedding, etc. in any quantity, the Treasury would soon be exhausted." She added that anyone who thought that the government was not doing all it could "should be *entirely dispossessed of any such idea.*"[52]

For many, of course, the issue of political responsibility came second to the needs of injured men. Though aware that she might be assuming the government's responsibility, Abby Howland was unwilling to risk denying soldiers needed goods for an abstract political principle. "Don't wait for red tape," she informed her sister Eliza, who was working in an army hospital.

[50] Howe had supported Dorothea Dix's investigations into Massachusetts asylums; he was also the husband of Julia Ward Howe, herself active in Sanitary Commission work during the war. See "Samuel Gridley Howe," *DAB*, pt. 1 (New York, 1932), 5:296–97. Howe was one of the original twelve signers of the "Plan of Organization" for the USSC submitted to Secretary of War Simon Cameron in Washington on June 13, 1861. See Stillé, *History of the United States Sanitary Commission*, pp. 533–38, appendix 4. Dr. Samuel Gridley Howe to Henry Bellows, November 5, 1862, Box 640, USSC Papers.
[51] Mrs. Susan C. Crosman to Dr. Bellows, December 13, 1861, Box 654, USSC Papers.
[52] Louisa L. Schuyler to Mrs. Chase, June 16, 1863, Box 667, USSC Papers.

"If it is mattresses, cots, pillows, spirit lamps, food, sheeting, flannel, etc. to wrap wounded men in, or what not," the family was ready to help. "You can have plenty of money, and it could not be better spent than in fitting up a hospital even if that *is* government work."[53]

The Struggle over Local Resources

Taken together, the messages from the female homefront demonstrated that mobilizing civilians into a national, centralized structure was far from easy in a society accustomed to a weak state apparatus and traditions of local political and economic networks. The Sanitary scheme called not only for relinquishing gendered control over benevolent work but for foregoing allegiances to regional and state entities as well. Commission leaders were especially concerned about people's attraction to relief agencies established by individual state governments. In the absence of federal funding, state legislatures had allocated funds to cover both mobilization and supply costs; on the very day the war broke, New York State passed legislation that provided three million dollars to recruit and equip the militia and another half-million dollars to care for 32,000 troops. State governments also empowered state-run philanthropic organizations to solicit donations from private citizens and, through agents appointed to travel to the warfront, to distribute them to state troops.[54]

In early October 1862, Olmsted confided to Bellows his fears about the competition from state-run organizations: "I regard the state agents and so do you as a great evil, as encouraging and manifesting and keeping alive a very bad and dangerous spirit." The risk to the USSC enterprise obsessed Olmsted, who wrote to Bellows again a few days later, reiterating that the "state and individual relief operations, are I fear doing us much harm." The state agencies were "very industrious" in "spreading false reports of us," he noted. "We have got to head them off," he warned; "it is not time to retrench."[55]

Olmsted's strategy was to appeal directly to northern women. In an essay

[53] Abby Howland Woolsey to Eliza Woolsey Howland, July 27, 1861, in Bacon and Howland, *Letters*, 1:137.
[54] Fred Albert Shannon, *The Organization and Administration of the Union Army, 1861–1865*, 2 vols. (Gloucester, 1965), 1:15, 23, 53; Emerson David Fite, *Social and Industrial Conditions in the North during the Civil War* (New York, 1963), p. 276.
[55] Frederick Law Olmsted to Henry Bellows, October 3 and 7, 1862, Box 951, USSC Papers.

titled "What They Have to Do Who Stay At Home," he addressed the common objections to participating in the Sanitary Commission plan. Acknowledging the "natural" desire to distribute goods to known individuals through conventional channels, Olmsted argued that the commission approach was still more "generous and efficient" than any locally organized relief agency. While he paid lip service to the notion that supplying the army was the government's obligation, he nonetheless warned his readers that the "indolent dependence on leaders and parties, have been the national sins of which this war brings the plain and direct retribution."[56]

But the central issue for Olmsted was not government responsibility or duplication of efforts. In a sweeping analysis of the political purposes of female warwork, Olmsted explained to women that the real purpose of organizing aid societies and sustaining them with "steady zeal" was for "keeping love of the Union alive through healthy, social contact, expression, and labor." Each society, he contended, "must be a centre of patriotic devotion and of the dissemination of truth favorable to patriotic devotion, radiating through communities." Charity was not an occasional activity, but a process capable of transforming those involved. In forceful terms, Olmsted rephrased the philosophy of the commission, reminding his audience of the necessity of "sacrificing local, personal, and transitory interests to the policy of the Union." "In union is strength," and "in disunion weakness and waste." "Can we not," Olmsted asked, "wholly lay aside that poor disguise of narrowness of purpose and self-conceit, which takes the name of local interest and public spirit?" The answer was critical, he argued, particularly in light of the vast need created by recent battles.[57]

While Olmsted called for total commitment to the national experiment, Louisa Schuyler approached homefront loyalties in less absolute terms. Schuyler was sensitive to the hardships that USSC directives imposed on many women. If the work was to succeed at all, then it was necessary to heed provincial interests, treat their grievances seriously, and create realistic objectives. Schuyler shared the USSC's goal but was pragmatic about the probability of reaching it: "My aim is to have a Soldiers' Aid Society tributary to the Commission, in every town & village. Of course the success could be but partial, but I should try for it." Schuyler's colleague, Ellen Collins, confessed to one woman in the WCRA region that she had revised her own expecta-

<hr />

[56] "What They Have to Do Who Stay at Home," October 21, 1862, no. 50, *Documents*, 1:1–12.
[57] Ibid., 1:7–8, 10.

tions: "For my part, I find it too much of an undertaking to attempt to *coerce* spontaneous charity into a purely formed & regular channel!"[58]

When determining how best to stimulate warwork, the WCRA learned to take its cues from the public. In June 1863, when Schuyler distributed another call to organize, she reprinted portions of Olmsted's stern letter to "Loyal Women," but also included reports of effective organizing methods invented by women in the region. Describing the technique found in New York State of having "young people" raise funds, she suggested the practice be emulated elsewhere. These "Alert Clubs," composed of "little girls and young people," should function as subsidiary societies with their own officers and should canvass towns collecting monthly subscription payments. "Where Clubs have been particularly 'on the alert,' " added Schuyler, "they have interested themselves in getting up entertainments, concerts, tableaux, strawberry parties, etc. besides the monthly subscriptions, and have materially increased the funds for the Society in this way."[59]

Responding to the severe economic pressures reported by many women, the WCRA experimented with providing raw cloth to societies in impoverished towns. The only resources local women would be expected to contribute would be their labor power. In the fall of 1862, flush with contributions from California, Schuyler recalled that "the experiment was tried. . . of furnishing Societies with materials to be made up," but the plan proved "to be impracticable owing to the heavy drain upon the Treasury."[60]

As with his 1861 "Loyal Women" letter, Olmsted's 1862 appeal to home-front women coincided with an escalation of military engagements and rising rates of disease and death. The degree to which northern enthusiasm had waned was evident in the meager response to federal calls for military volunteers. In July 1862, desperate to fortify Union forces, Lincoln called for state governors to raise 300,000 soldiers to serve for three years. When northern men were slow to respond, the government issued a call for additional troops, this time stipulating that if the new quotas were not met a conscription would be instituted. As communities faced a dreaded draft, major defeats at the Second Battle of Bull Run in late August and in Sep-

[58] Louisa L. Schuyler to Frederick Law Olmsted, December 22, 1862, Box 667; E. Collins to Mrs. Randall, November 26, 1862, Box 655, USSC Papers.
[59] The name Alert Club originated in Norwalk, Ohio. Impressed by the amount of money the town had collected, Schuyler proposed that other organizations use the name. See "Plan for the Formation of Soldier's Aid Societies," June 8, 1863, reprinted in *The Sanitary Commission Bulletin*, April 15, 1864, in *The United States Sanitary Commission Bulletin* (New York, 1866), 1:370–71 (hereafter *Bulletin*).
[60] Louisa L. Schuyler to Mrs. Chase, June 16, 1863, Box 667, USSC Papers.

tember at Antietam—the "bloodiest single day of the whole war"—heightened civilian awareness of the magnitude of military devastation.[61]

But if the deepening of the military conflict led some male citizens to resist volunteering for what had become a highly dangerous tour of service, if not certain death, setbacks on the battlefield spurred many homefront women to increase their relief efforts. News from the warfront elicited what the commission could not achieve by pleading; many women who had been reluctant to enter relief work earlier finally mobilized to provide assistance in the fall of 1862. Watching their men answer the August call for recruits, the women of Willink, New York, were "stimulated to action."[62] Jeanie Aldrich recalled that in Dewittville, New York, "a larger amount of our boys than ever before answered the call for troops, and with that call for troops, came the call for Sanitary supplies." While the women had formerly neglected commission requests, "after the 'boys' left, we began to think *we too* had an interest in the Sanitary a few decided to try what could be done."[63] The women of Deerfield, New York, first established contact with the commission in the fall of 1862, noting that previously they had divided their donations among an array of agencies. News of Union losses provided the most compelling motivation to organize. "We were incited to action," wrote the women of Stockholm, New York, "on account of the sufferings of the 60th Regiment at White Sulfphur Springs. . . many of whom were our own dear boys."[64] By the fall of 1862, the WCRA reported that 1,462 aid societies had affiliated themselves with the USSC. At no other time during the war would the WCRA count so many local organizations in its fold.[65]

Early Concessions to the Homefront

Homefront organizing proceeded haltingly, dependent on the outcomes of important battles and the vicissitudes of public sympathies. As often as women organized, they just as readily suspended their warwork, sometimes

[61] Shannon, *Union Army*, 1:259–92; Peter J. Parish, *The American Civil War* (New York, 1975), p. 189; James M. McPherson, *Ordeal by Fire: The Civil War and Reconstruction* (New York, 1982), pp. 251, 259, 285.
[62] Mrs. Wm. H. Richting, 1866, Box 981, USSC Papers.
[63] Jeanie Aldrich to John Blatchford, March 11, 1866, Box 981, USSC Papers.
[64] M. M. Greene, May 23, 1866; Lois Tucker to USSC, April 19, 1866, Box 981. For other societies that originated in fall 1862, see Mrs. A. Simmons, 1866; Bethlehem Union Relief Society, 1866; Mrs. J. E. Caldwell, April 9, 1866; Mrs. Horace Wait, 1866, Box 981, USSC Papers.
[65] *Second Semi-Annual Report of the Woman's Central Association of Relief, November 1, 1862* (New York, 1862), p. 4, Box 993, USSC Papers.

A rare photograph of a soldiers' aid society, in Springfield, Ill., c. 1863. Chicago Historical Society.

for the personal and economic reasons they so painstakingly explained to the Sanitary Commission and its branch leaders, and other times because of their ambivalence over the course of the war. Harboring doubts about the USSC plan and the place of voluntary labor in supporting a federal army, many women continued to resist commission appeals.

The organization had initiated its relationship with local women through impersonal, official announcements; circulars and public newspaper appeals constituted the bulk of the early communications. But the responses of individual women seeking direct ways to discuss the difficulties of local organizing compelled the commission to alter the manner in which it dealt with the homefront. Almost unwittingly, the commission found itself immersed in a tangle of relationships with individual women and local organizers, each writing letters or queries and all demanding replies.

Allied to its public constituency by gender and to the USSC leadership by class and ideology, the women of the WCRA assumed a special role in mediating the relationship between the commission and the homefront. WCRA officers sustained a voluminous correspondence with women in their region, made personal appeals for the formation of soldiers' aid societies, and disseminated news about supply needs. Eliza Schuyler believed that only personal missives generated the trust essential for stimulating voluntary labor, and routinely searched the names of potential participants in order to write to each one individually. After the USSC assumed the authority once exercised by the WCRA, Mrs. Schuyler offered Olmsted the benefit of her experience. Recalling the success of her method in fulfilling a particular supply order, she noted that she made "the bitter request for *more help*" in all her personal correspondence. Analyzing the efficacy of private communications, she surmised that "public appeals, through newspapers, are worth very little—we should have secured the 300 bed ticks much sooner, by writing fifty letters."[66]

For Louisa Schuyler and other WCRA officers, personal correspondence and one-to-one contact became one of the most important ways of ascertaining the state of homefront organizing. As supply work developed, the scope and frequency of the WCRA's communications with its female constituency intensified. Branch officers found this form of interchange, though taxing, emotionally rewarding. For USSC Corresponding Secretary Alfred Bloor, on the other hand, the task of giving personal attention to women's probing questions was nothing but exasperating. As he complained to one agent, homefront women proved to be surprisingly demanding clients: "I do not know whether you and others recognize how hard it is to. carry on this correspondence, from week to week and month to month, and year to year with women—the good and the bad in them always the more intense and unmanageable because they are women; how hard it is to smooth over difficulties—to hear over and over again the same complaints—to repeat over and over again the same thing made to look different in each case."[67]

The first year and a half of Sanitary Commission operations held unforeseen challenges for the organization. The effort to mobilize northern communities into trusted tributaries had evolved into a complex struggle for control over resources and labor. Least expected was that local women would emerge as critical participants in supply work. Women expressed fears about the dangers of working with a distant, elite organization, yet

---

[66] E. W. Schuyler to Frederick Law Olmsted, September 29, 1861, Olmsted Papers.
[67] Alfred J. Bloor, Report to William A. Hovey, October 18, 1864, Bloor Papers.

welcomed the efficiency of a centralized clearinghouse and distribution system. At the same time, they dismissed the national agency in favor of assisting locally raised regiments when they were convinced that in so doing they were increasing their effectiveness. And they ceased charitable work altogether when they suspected that the commission plan might be interfering with legitimate governmental responsibilities.

Challenging the Government

When Bellows wrote in his 1879 essay that the Sanitary Commission had been "born paralytic," he was thinking not about the constraints posed by the female homefront but rather about the commission's original mission merely to advise the government on military procedures. Early in the war, the USSC determined that transforming itself into an agency capable of affecting War Department policies depended on appropriating some of the authority retained by various federal officials. Thus it justified its extension into "every department, corps, camp [and] regiment," a practice that was rife with difficulties and produced relations with government officials that were strained if not hostile. For Bellows, official antagonism to Sanitary Commission interventions was attributable to "the natural jealousy and distrust of the generals and officers" of the army. But he conceded that despite occasional successes in influencing state practices, "it was in this attitude of suspicion, jealousy and check, that the Commission began, continued, and ended."[68]

The commission's decision to seek a direct role in War Department policy was precipitated by the devastating defeat at the first battle of Bull Run in July 1861. On learning of the mass defections from the line of battle, Olmsted launched a comprehensive investigation into the military and material conditions of the Union army. In a draft of a report he prepared for the Secretary of War, he enumerated a host of acute problems, from the inadequate inspection of volunteers and the failure to immunize recruits to poor sanitation and astronomical disease rates that plagued the armed forces. In Olmsted's view, much of the blame for the frightened response of the troops at Bull Run rested on recruitment drives so lax that even the "notoriously vicious and degraded" were permitted to enlist, and the failure on the part of state governors to inspect up to 58 percent of their recruits. Noting that 1,620 men had been discharged from the Army of the Potomac

[68] Bellows, "U.S. Sanitary Commission," p. 74.

in the month of October as "unfit for service," Olmsted calculated that these men had cost the government over $80,000 in wasted funds.[69]

Olmsted's public report to the government was preceded by a study he had prepared for the Sanitary Commission that contained a far more trenchant and critical analysis of the causes of defeat. His investigation into troop conditions focused the commission's attention on the relationship of preventive medical and sanitation techniques to military discipline. The lack of any semblance of military regimen was most glaring in the practice, common among early recruits, of democratically electing their own officers. After analyzing the conditions of Union troops, their training, and the process of choosing officers, Olmsted concluded that military defeats, soldiers' demoralization, and high casualty rates were directly linked to the absence of an explicit military hierarchy. Union forces were wholly unprepared for battle both physically and morally, and the federal government was to blame. The wholesale desertion of the battlefield by poorly trained volunteers demonstrated that to pursue "temperance, cleanliness, and comfort among the troops," the first "sanitary law in camp and among soldiers is *military* discipline."[70] As he confided to his wife, "there is but one Sanitary measure to be thought of now & that is discipline." The commission considered the document so damning to the government that it was never made public. The version submitted to the Secretary of War included detailed accounts of army conditions from privies to prevalent diseases, but omitted direct criticism of government practices.[71]

The data Olmsted had collected on conditions in the army set the stage for a coordinated USSC attack on the structure and personnel of the Medical Bureau of the War Department. Early in 1862, after months of tense encounters and resistance to its intrusions, the commission initiated a political assault on the department that represented much of what was reprehensible about the weak American state. Here was a federal agency burdened

[69] Draft of Olmsted's First Report to the Secretary of War, December 1861, Box 735, USSC Papers. According to the surgeon general's records, on June 30, 1861, there were 3,882 sick cases for every 1,000 soldiers, suggesting that the average soldier was ill more than once in a year's time. See Bell Irvin Wiley, *Billy Yank: The Common Soldier of the Union* (Baton Rouge, La. 1952), pp. 124–27.
[70] See "Report on the Demoralization of the Volunteers," September 5, 1861, in *FLO Papers*, 4:153–97; "A Report to the Secretary of War of the Operations of the Sanitary Commission," December 9, 1861, no. 40, *Documents*, 1:1–81; Frederick Law Olmsted to Mary Olmsted, September 7, 1861, Olmsted Papers. Olmsted's original report to the commission has not survived.
[71] Frederick L. Olmsted to Mary Perkins Olmsted, July 29, 1861, in *FLO Papers*, 4:130; Stillé, *History of the United States Sanitary Commission*, pp. 88–112; "Military Discipline," July 29, 1861, no. 20, *Documents*, 1:1–2.

with bureaucratic inertia, beholden to personal and special interests, and run by an inadequate staff wedded to archaic ideas. The commission challenged the bureau's outmoded procedures on the grounds that they directly endangered the lives of Union troops. It charged that the few doctors retained by the department were ignorant of modern military medicine and that little effort was being made to inspect hospitals, camps or recruits.

Ultimately, the attack on the Medical Bureau focused on the surgeon general himself, Dr. Clement Finley. The commissioners charged him with incompetence and an unwillingness to face emergency sanitary requirements. With Finley considered unacceptable by the commission's own corps of prominent physicians, the solution was evident. "The business before us was to kick out the Surgeon-General," Strong remarked. Bellows later explained the political challenge by invoking USSC rhetoric: "Among the *preventive* policies of the Sanitary Commission was the prevention of incompetency, inefficiency, and contracted ideas in the medical bureau."[72]

The commission's lobbying efforts succeeded in gaining the passage of a bill that reorganized the Medical Bureau. The bill, passed on April 16, 1862, increased the number of medical and nonmedical employees in the department and conferred higher rank on military physicians. It provided for more inspectors and increased requirements for sanitation reports. The bill also revised procedures for choosing a new surgeon general, opening a way for the replacement of Finley by the commission's handpicked candidate, Dr. William A. Hammond. Upon his appointment, Hammond undertook reforms to achieve USSC goals, including the examination of medical officers, the upgrading of the statistical system, and the implementation of preventive sanitary methods.[73]

For the USSC leadership, the battle to reorganize the Medical Bureau constituted nothing less than a "revolution." Not only would the revamped bureau better serve the organization's sanitary and medical agenda, but the victory represented a significant extension of its role as "advisor and friendly helper" to the federal government. "Our success is suddenly wonderfully complete," Olmsted confided to his father. "Suddenly," the Medical

[72] Dr. H. W. Bellows, "Report of the Executive Committee to the Sanitary Commission at Its Session," September 16, 1862, Box 951, USSC Papers; Maxwell, *Lincoln's Fifth Wheel*, pp. 108–15; Strong, October 23, 1861, November 27, 1861, *Diary*, 3:188, 193; Bellows, "Sanitary Commission," p. 74.
[73] Maxwell, *Lincoln's Fifth Wheel*, pp. 122–29, 135–39; Kristie R. Ross, "War and the Search for Professional Identity: USSC Physicians and Army Medical Care," paper presented at the annual meeting of the Organization of American Historians, New York, April 12, 1986.

Bureau "opens its eyes to the fact that the San. Com. is its best friend." Administrative successes brought a new confidence. In September 1862, Strong was moved to remark that "all, from the Surgeon-General down, recognize the value of what we are doing."[74]

Building Financial Strength

The commission's success in reshaping the federal war bureaucracy was mirrored by impressive fiscal achievements during its first two years of operation. Among its most important early activities was raising large cash reserves from the male public. The initial appeals made to insurance companies, businesses, and propertied men had been effective, but expenses soon outstripped donations. After only six months of operation, Strong reported that the "treasury is fast running dry." The commission needed money in order to ship and distribute household contributions to the front, pay its agents, acquire transport ships and wagons, and employ physicians. Throughout the first half of 1862 the commission issued urgent appeals, claiming that money and supplies were needed "at once, and in abundance."[75]

In the fall of 1862 Sanitary Commission fortunes changed abruptly, moving from near bankruptcy to unprecedented solvency almost overnight. Thanks to the propagandizing efforts of Bellows's friend, the Universalist preacher, Thomas Starr King, over $200,000 was sent from California to commission headquarters in just a few weeks time. By late October, money worries seemed far away. Strong remarked that the organization was "waxing fat" and California's contributions were approaching a quarter of a million dollars, while Bellows assured his colleagues that "our hold upon the purse-strings of the Nation seems fully established."[76]

The infusion of western cash did not keep USSC coffers filled for long. In the fall and winter of 1862, stores were quickly depleted by the need to care for the wounded. Since the USSC was dependent on sustained home-front enthusiasm for the war, stalemates on the battlefield posed serious problems. Beginning with the Second Battle of Bull Run in August 1862,

[74] Bellows, "Report"; Frederick L. Olmsted to "Father" [John Olmsted], April 19, 1862, Olmsted Papers; Strong, September 11, 1862, *Diary*, 3:254.

[75] Strong, December 14, 1861, *Diary*, 3:196; "To all Loyal Citizens," *Documents*, 1:1.

[76] Maxwell, *Lincoln's Fifth Wheel*, p. 188; Walter Donald Kring, *Henry Whitney Bellows* (Boston, 1979), pp. 70–72; Strong, October 23, 1862, *Diary*, 3:267; Bellows, "Report." By the war's end, Pacific coast donations reached almost $1.5 million.

Union forces had reversed their four-month string of military successes and set out on a long trail of defeats. The fighting on September 17 at Antietam Creek left over 11,000 dead and wounded. The winter was especially depressing, and nowhere more so than at Fredericksburg. On December 13, 1862, in a battle *Harper's Weekly* called a massacre that the northern people could not endure again, over 12,000 Union soldiers were killed or injured. The war in the West went no better, as Union forces retreated at Vicksburg on December 29. Many in the army were losing their ardor for the struggle, and as frustrations mounted, so did desertions. One soldier believed the defeat at Fredericksburg left most soldiers demoralized; "the whole army would run home if they had the chance." Another wrote home a few weeks before he deserted that "patriotism *played out*" with him, particularly "after the battle over the River."[77]

Military setbacks threatened the organization's ability to raise more cash. Just when the USSC was most in need of additional homefront support, many were growing ambivalent about maintaining a failing army. Assigned to tour northern towns in search of monetary aid, commission agent William Hobart Hadley found that rousing homefront enthusiasm was becoming a difficult endeavor. "I did my best," he reported to Bellows, "in trying to accomplish something valuable for the Commission but the prevailing opposition to the war and to the Administration—notwithstanding all the nominal Republicanism—and the scarcity of money combined to render money contributions almost an impossibility." Strong was equally worried, observing that, because they were "doing business on a large scale," they "must come to the end of our means before many months" unless new funding appeared.[78]

The need for greater civilian support led to a new propaganda offensive. After the battle of Antietam, Olmsted's essay "What They Have to Do Who Stay at Home" offered political rationales for why commission stores needed to be replenished regularly and abundantly. At the same time Bellows warned homefront women: "you cannot make too instant, or too generous, or too long-continued efforts." Addressing public awareness of stories of severe deprivation among the troops, he urged women to persevere. "Do not wonder. . . at the stories of neglect, of suffering, of want, you hear from soldiers and from hospitals, they may, any of them, be true." Nei-

[77] McPherson, *Ordeal by Fire*, pp. 234, 304–6, 309; *Harper's Weekly*, December 27, 1862; Parish, *American Civil War*, pp. 189, 194–97; Randall C. Jimerson, *The Private Civil War: Popular Thought during the Sectional Conflict* (Baton Rouge, La., 1988), p. 232.
[78] W. H. Hadley to Henry Bellows, December 2, 1862, Box 640, USSC Papers; Strong, December 13, 1862, *Diary*, 3:279.

ther the USSC nor the Medical Bureau was to blame. "Make the supplies in money and goods *adequate*, and you shall have no reason to complain."[79]

By January 1863 things were looking up. Whether from concern over recent casualties, fear of losing the war, or acceptance of commission appeals, women were sending supplies in greater volume. Contributions not only were arriving with a new regularity but had changed in nature from those sent at the beginning of the war. Olmsted was especially encouraged by the fact that women had moved beyond shipping surplus household goods, and were producing specific items to fill commission requests. As he reported to his friend William Henry Hurlbert, "I suppose the relative value to the contributors of goods now given is piece for piece fully tenfold greater than when, about 16 months ago, the superfluous old shirts, etc. were gathered up." Though the people's energies had fluctuated and the war had increased the cost of living, Olmsted believed a new mentality had emerged: "It was clear that certain people were taking hold of it in a different spirit; contributions became steadier and more carefully considered." In fact, he argued, "except for a short period of enthusiasm more than a year ago, contributions—household contributions, have never been as large as at present."[80]

As every decrease in money or supplies prompted the USSC to recharge its efforts to rouse the public, so each spurt in contributions was capitalized upon, lest the flow dissipate. To solidify homefront support, the commission distributed documents that detailed the accomplishments of its agents at the battlefield, and offered "testimonials" from military leaders about the lives being saved by commission stores. So readers learned that at Fredericksburg, "the steam-barge 'Elizabeth' with an efficient crew and well provided with stores, was at the Acquiz Landing when the battle commenced, and the regular corps of Inspectors and Relief Agents marching with the Army had been reinforced." USSC physician Dr. Douglas reassured homefront readers that not only did the commission "get up to our field station 5642 woollen shirts, 4439 pairs woollen drawers, 4269 pairs socks, and over 2500 towels," but these were all "liberally distributed wherever the surgeons of hospitals indicated that there was a need." "Much has been said of the demoralization of the army," he added; "I have seen no evidence of it."[81]

[79] "What They Have to Do," *Documents*, 1:1–12; "Material for Hospital Clothing," October 22, 1862, no. 54, *Documents*, 1:5. In one account of deprivation that reached the homefront, a New York surgeon accompanying a regiment during the Fredericksburg battle wrote home that two hundred of his men were without shoes. See Wiley, *Billy Yank*, p. 61.

[80] Frederick L. Olmsted to William Henry Hurlbert, January 31, 1863, in *FLO Papers*, 4:509.

[81] "What the Sanitary Commission Is Doing in the Valley of the Mississippi," February 16, 1863, no. 64, *Documents*, 2:1–31; *The United States Sanitary Commission: A Sketch of Its Purposes and Its Work* (Boston, 1863), pp. 108, 11, 114.

In the face of military disasters and rising casualty rates, the commission had reason to believe that it had established itself as a competent and effective agency. Money donations, while erratic, were often generous, and local aid societies were sending at least a portion of their donations to the national organization. Even members of the executive committee were surprised by the achievements of the first year and a half. "The success of this Sanitary Commission has been a marvel," remarked Strong in the beginning of February 1863. "Our receipts in cash up to this time are nearly $700,000 at the central office alone," and this did not include "what has been received and spent by auxiliaries, and the three or four millions' worth of stores of every sort contributed at our depots." The numbers were indeed impressive: the USSC was employing approximately 200 agents and spending at least $40,000 a month on operations. "It has become a 'big thing,' " Strong boasted, "and a considerable fact in the history of this people and of this work."[82]

After nearly two years of working to establish its reputation with the northern female public, its influence with the government, and its usefulness at the warfront, the Sanitary Commission had emerged as an impressive operation. Acting as an advisor to the government, caretaker of sick and wounded soldiers, and mediator between female charities and the army, its presence extended from village societies to army hospitals. Donations from thousands of aid societies arrived at official depots where women sorted and prepared them for shipment to military posts. In February 1863, the organization claimed to have expended over $300,000 in cash and distributed stores worth "many millions" to needy Union troops. At the warfront, it directed comprehensive investigations of troop, camp and hospital conditions. Its agents and physicians operated an elaborate battlefield relief system, implementing preventive sanitary reforms, supplying materials for vaccines, treating the sick and wounded soldiers in camps, on trains, and on specially outfitted steamers, and distributing medical tracts to both soldiers and medical staff.[83]

Though setting up the Sanitary Commission structure had required some heavy-handed measures, the results seemed worth the effort. An extensive network of soldiers' aid societies was in place and thousands of northern women appeared willing to utilize the commission's system to in-

[82] Strong, February 3, 1863, *Diary*, 3:294.
[83] "Rules of the Supply Department of the Sanitary Commission," January 27, 1863, no. 62, *Documents*, 2:1–2; "Statement of the Object and Methods of the Sanitary Commission," December 7, 1863, no. 69, *Documents*, 2:16–19. See also William Y. Thompson, "The U.S. Sanitary Commission," *Civil War History* 2 (June 1956): 54–55.

sure the impact of their labors in support of the Union. While women's contributions were irregular and their complaints many, news of war casualties served to revitalize waning energies, spurring them on to meet each new emergency. The commission had found a method not only of supporting its warfront operations but of dictating the stories about its efforts. With fiscal and bureaucratic battles behind it, the new year seemed to augur a new beginning.

4/

"A SWINDLING CONCERN": HOMEFRONT CHARGES OF CORRUPTION

In many ways, the relationship between the United States Sanitary Commission and northern women was one of competing discourses and public deceptions. Each constructed a public posture that deferred to the dominant patriotic rhetoric of the war, but at the same time obscured serious political differences and resisted direct confrontation with the other. These were hardly evenly-matched contenders for public opinion, however. The Sanitary Commission had at its disposal a private publishing house that regularly churned out official documents, public announcements, and statistics presenting its version of events, frequently accompanied by affidavits from military personnel, political officials, and men of letters who offered independent corroboration. Indeed, so effective was the commission in shaping the historical narrative of its accomplishments that later historians were hard put to find divergent renderings of events.[1]

[1] The first full history of the Sanitary Commission, though based on USSC archives, is a celebratory account that accepts that the "theoretical basis" of the organization was to "supplement deficiencies." See William Quentin Maxwell, *Lincoln's Fifth Wheel: The Political History of the United States Sanitary Commission* (New York, 1956). Allan Nevins considers the USSC a milestone in the history of American philanthropy and one of the "minor glories" of the war. See *The War for the Union*, 4 vols. (New York, 1959), vol. 3, *The Organized War, 1863–1864*, p. 317. By uncovering the political objectives of its leaders and the far-reaching changes they attempted to impose on notions of benevolence, George Fredrickson was the first historian to

From the moment of its inception, the Sanitary Commission fabricated and disseminated stories about women's patriotism and wartime labors that advanced the goals of the organization and the nationalist visions of its leaders. Not only were the commissioners' accounts of women's efforts on behalf of the army often fictionalized, they were also contradictory, changing over time to serve shifting circumstances. Sanitary Commission pronouncements moved from portraying female voluntarism as undisciplined and uncontrollable, fomenting chaos at the front, when the organization needed to justify its intervention in soldier relief, to eulogizing women's innate generosity when it sought to gain their cooperation. By the middle of the war, the organization had begun criticizing women for failing to comprehend the grave perils faced by the Union and scolding them for not meeting their responsibilities. After the war was won, the commission was effusive in its praise for women's prodigious efforts and unflagging devotion to the cause. Even when vexed by women's rationales for withholding donations or when critical of their behavior, the commission assumed a public stance of concerned paternalism, avoiding aggressive challenges to the way women managed their duties, while still insisting on its right to supervise the collection and distribution of household resources.[2]

But the Sanitary Commission's deception was labyrinthine, for its claim to being merely a safe conduit for women's natural benevolence was also an inversion of the truth. In their private correspondence, its leaders made evident their larger personal and ideological aspirations. As early as November 1861, Olmsted enlightened Charles Loring Brace on the proper place of relief work in the larger enterprise. "You are greatly mistaken if you mean that you think that the distribution of *supplies* is its 'great work,'" Olmsted explained. "It is a mere incident of its work and if it had left it alone entirely, the army would not be perceptibly weaker than it is."[3]

---

challenge the public posture of the Sanitary Commission. Yet, in the absence of an analysis of USSC communications with the homefront, Fredrickson, too, accepted the organization's claim that northern women were uniformly enthusiastic participants in the Sanitary plan. See *The Inner Civil War: Northern Intellectuals and the Crisis of the Union* (New York, 1965), pp. 98–112. Even after Fredrickson's account, some historians persisted in accepting the commission on its own terms. See Robert H. Bremner, *The Public Good: Philanthropy and Welfare in the Civil War Era* (New York, 1980).

[2] See James C. Scott, *Domination and the Arts of Resistance: Hidden Transcripts* (New Haven, 1990), pp. 1–16, for a discussion of the ways in which those in power and those who are subordinate enact public performances that respectively legitimate their claims to status and disguise their resentments. Scott argues that those in power have "public transcripts" that differ from offstage transcripts.

[3] Frederick Law Olmsted to Charles Loring Brace, November 8, 1861, in *FLO Papers*, 4:222–24.

When the war was over, Bellows boasted that the commission had deceived the public. "The Sanitary Commission was not from its inception a merely humanitarian or beneficent association," he wrote in 1879. "It necessarily took on that appearance, and its life depended upon its effective work as an almoner of the homes of the land to fathers, brothers and sons in the field." But, he now affirmed, "its projectors were men with strong political purpose, induced to take this means of giving expression to their solicitude for the national life."[4] Posing an extensive political agenda may have been a way of distancing himself from an enterprise that had not realized its full potential, but Bellows's postwar admissions also suggest the extent to which the commission had been constrained by public expectations to concentrate on soldiers' welfare. Whether intentional or not, Bellows's account expressed something of the unforeseen outcomes and thwarted ambitions that marked the USSC experiment. It also represented a last attempt to direct the historical narrative and lay claim to public memories.

Claiming the benefit of historical hindsight, Bellows explained the process by which northern women came to assume such a primary place in the commissioners' operations. According to Bellows, these politically minded men apprehended quickly that the source of potential support for a nationalist enterprise was, not the government or large social institutions, but the people: "By discovering that the people of the country had a very much higher sense of the value of the Union. . . than most of the politicians of the States . . . seemed to recognize," they concluded that the public's voluntaristic practices created the ideal setting for positioning themselves as disinterested advocates for northern patriots. Even more significant than the general loyalty of the people was the exceptional generosity of women. Because "the women of America had at least half of its patriotism in their keeping," they were receptive to supplications made in the name of nationalism. For the commissioners, northern women themselves constituted the means for advancing a new nationalism and a new polity.[5]

Bellows's postwar account, though it admitted the Sanitary Commissioners' underlying motives, was nonetheless of a piece with the confidence he and his colleagues had displayed about women's charity from the beginning of the war. They expected that female generosity would continue for the duration of the conflict, permitting the commission to draw at will on women's unpaid labor. "The good women of the country would need only

---

[4] Henry W. Bellows, *Historical Sketch of the Union League Club of New York* (New York, 1879), p. 5.
[5] Bellows, *Union League Club*, p. 5.

to see with their own eyes what is called comfort in the camp, to have their tender hearts moved to increased generosity," Bellows wrote during the war.[6] In its first public document, published in August 1861, the commission expressed "entire confidence in the good sense, the patriotism and the charitable instincts of their fellow-citizens."[7]

For their part, northern women had different stories to tell about their activities during the Civil War. Women's warwork, whether carried out on behalf of soldiers' families, homefront communities, or the Union army, was a far more complicated endeavor than that depicted by Sanitary Commission leaders. Anxious to find ways to demonstrate their patriotism and provide assistance to injured men, women undertook relief operations with the presumption that voluntary aid to soldiers was just that, voluntary. Though most middle-class women had been socialized to embrace charitable work as part of their duties, the value of such work rested on the premise that it was undertaken freely and with no constraints. But as the military conflict intensified and the commission's demands for homefront donations escalated, women confronted, some for the first time, the consequences of a set of beliefs that deemed their benevolent and patriotic acts mere extensions of their biological nature. When the war placed heavy burdens on their household economies, many became resentful of these men's assumptions about the ease with which they could continue to labor for the war. As their letters suggest, hundreds, if not thousands, of women suddenly found themselves compelled to articulate the specific content of their household tasks and to attribute precise monetary values to their homemade products. And when they became suspicious of the motives and practices of those entrusted with their gifts, northern women strove to make clear the reasoned political content of their nationalism.

But women, too, developed forms of public demeanor that disguised their true feelings. Nineteenth-century women were no more immune than men to cultural constructions of gender. The gendered discourse that construed their labor as an unproductive activity and their benevolence as a mere manifestation of instinct pervaded many women's own estimations of their abilities and framed the ways in which they explained their actions. In delineating why they rejected USSC instructions, they frequently concealed their disagreements with the national project and hid behind postures of feminine impulsiveness and inferiority. As homefront women found themselves at odds with perceived commission practices, many engaged in forth-

[6] Henry Bellows, Notes, Bellows Papers.
[7] "Origin and Objects of The Sanitary Commission," August 13, 1861, no. 22, *Documents*, 1:7.

right criticism, but invariably they did so by making the women leaders of the Woman's Central Relief Association and other branches function as their intermediaries, conveying messages they were unwilling to deliver directly. Together, established hierarchies of class and gender made provincial women reluctant to attack the elite men of the USSC directly; they were more comfortable confiding their complaints to other women, albeit not their social peers.

Because their problems with the Sanitary Commission project were rooted in widely held fictions about female nature, many northern women began to comprehend the deleterious implications of the antebellum compromise on gender. Illusions about women's nature had served the northern bourgeoisie in parceling out gendered arenas of social influence during the early decades of industrialization. True, the ideology of domesticity had lost some of its persuasiveness as the operative model of gender relations before the war, diminished by the difficulties women reformers encountered as they tried to effect legislation without political power and weakened by feminist critiques of male property and legal rights. Still, important elements of the ideology—specifically, its premises that household labor was not labor and that women were by nature charitable—had permeated northern culture as powerful truths.[8] Middle-class wives, who participated in few cash-based activities, often embraced the notion that housework and charitable work were important chiefly for their moral and social values. Moreover, the wartime notion of female patriotism had reinforced cultural perceptions of womanhood. But in a revolutionary crisis such ideas also produced contradictory effects. War made housework, always a significant component of the nation's productive wealth, more visible and appreciated, if not valued. In warwork thousands of women sensed the disjuncture between the cultural construction of their sex and the realities of their lives.

If war relief work generated circumstances that would expose some of the contradictions embedded in the antebellum compromise on gender, the men who led the Sanitary Commission had no intimation that serious prob-

---

[8] Lori Ginzberg, *Women and the Work of Benevolence: Morality, Politics, and Class in the Nineteenth-Century United States* (New Haven, 1990), see esp. chap. 4, on women's legislative reform efforts and the frustrations they encountered. Jeanne Boydston found that antebellum women expressed an understanding of the value of their housework and its importance in stretching male wages, but she also offers poignant examples of the devastating ways in which women internalized the pastoralization of their unpaid household labors. See *Home and Work: Housework, Wages, and the Ideology of Labor in the Early Republic* (New York, 1990), pp. 115–18, 142–63. For a feminist critique of the market assessment of household labor, see Reva B. Siegel, "Home as Work: The First Woman's Rights Claims concerning Wives' Household Labor, 1850–1880," *Yale Law Journal* 103 (March, 1994): 1073–135.

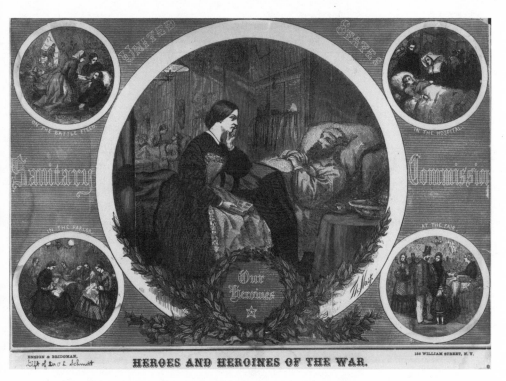

HEROES AND HEROINES OF THE WAR.

In this wood engraving produced for the Sanitary Commission, *Harper's Weekly* cartoonist Thomas Nast captured the organization's rhetoric and beliefs about the innate altruism of female patriotism. Chicago Historical Society.

lems loomed ahead. With the successes the USSC had posted in its first two years of existence—the organization of thousands of aid societies, the garnering of significant financial resources, and the restructuring of the Medical Bureau—it's leaders had reason to believe that the agency might fulfill their grandest expectations. "I have had the impression," Henry Bellows wrote to Frederick Law Olmsted in the summer of 1863, "that the telling of the History of the Sanitary Commission would afford one of the best themes for political instruction to the people, ever afforded anyone." Their experiment in centralized social welfare was sure to leave its mark on "national life." Bellows was attempting to persuade Olmsted not to resign by arguing that the commission offered the best means for disseminating their political ideas and wielding national influence. Olmsted had grown less convinced of the value of the organization and of the worth of his own services. His misgivings about the commission's effectiveness had led him to question its legitimacy as well. In his estimation, "the Sanitary Commission may continue to exist in name, but its voyage is over." Bellows's brief for the

Sanitary Commission's potential, while displaying a characteristic confidence, was nonetheless curiously obtuse. In the face of the difficulties that the female homefront encountered in meeting supply requests, he disregarded the very conditions that determined the commission's impact. He also exhibited the insularity of the commission's leaders from the shifting political opinions of the northern homefront.[9]

Bellows's optimism about the USSC's future was all the more remarkable as it occurred in the middle of 1863, when the organization faced challenges so serious they threatened its very existence. By the beginning of that year, the homefront was rife with rumors that the United States Sanitary Commission was a fraudulent operation, a ruse perpetrated by scheming men bent on deceiving the public to enrich themselves. Accusations of selfish motives and corrupt operations posed a dangerous impediment to the commission's goals of organizing the homefront and promoting its version of nationalism, as well as to its ability to obtain donations. Together with competition from a rival relief agency, opposition from the female public produced a crisis from which the organization never fully recovered.

Suspicions

It had been apparent for some time that northern women posed obstacles to the Sanitary Commission's goal of erecting a streamlined benevolent structure and generating donations on a regular basis. Their correspondence had catalogued a myriad of economic hardships, personal conflicts, and attachments to local charity channels that frustrated efforts to satisfy USSC requests. But by 1863 something else had occurred. Women were not simply describing personal or community circumstances that impeded benevolent labor, nor were they merely dismissing appeals for supplies as onerous. Rather, they had begun to question the methods and ethics of the organization itself. If the female public had hitherto been ambivalent about centralizing army relief, vague concerns now emerged as explicit suspicions that the commission was merely posing as a philanthropy, that its leaders were unprincipled and its operations corrupt.

In claiming that it was the legitimate repository for people's financial and household donations, the commission had long recognized the necessity of establishing sound credentials. One early strategy was to enlist prestigious individuals to lend their names to the money-raising effort through mem-

[9] Henry W. Bellows to Frederick L. Olmsted, August 13, 1863, Olmsted Papers; Frederick Law Olmsted to Henry Whitney Bellows, August 15, 1863, in *FLO Papers*, 4:699.

bership in its central auxiliary finance committee. Among the mercantile, industrial, and political leaders who accepted membership in the committee were Samuel Ruggles, Robert Minturn, George Opdyke, Morris Ketchum, David Hoadley, and Charles E. Strong.[10] But even men of impressive probity and high social position failed to assure some potential contributors of the commission's integrity. As early as August 1861, Alfred Bloor notified Olmsted that a man asked to contribute was told that the new organization was untrustworthy. "His informants," Bloor surmised, "must have spoken somewhat slightingly or at least distrustfully of the Commission."[11]

But precisely because propertied men had furnished enough money to assure the expansion of operations, the commission soon found itself in a bind. The richer it became the better it could execute its plan, yet the more it risked being perceived as a monopolistic entity, and the more its system of operations faced scrutiny by potential contributors. If the commission demanded more supplies while it was flush with funds, it exposed itself to charges of inefficiency or mismanagement. But if it waited until stores were depleted, it risked becoming so ineffectual at the front as to lose credibility. After sizable cash contributions started arriving from California, some members worried that these needed to be handled with special care, lest the public conclude that homemade donations had become superfluous.[12]

Of all the commissioners, perhaps none considered the issue of credibility more seriously than Olmsted. He claimed sympathy with those colleagues who felt they needed "to scrutinize our expenses more carefully and to guard against any just ground of the charge of extravagance!" or "even the appearance of careless expenditure." But Olmsted was opposed to self-flagellation. "Having thought deeply on this," he cautioned against imposing a strict regimen of accountability, reasoning that the additional bookkeeping would only increase expenses. Instead, he argued for continuance of the practice of relying on the reputations of its members. It would be one thing, he argued to Bellows, if the commissioners were "stock-brokers or church dignitaries, professional money-makers or professional philanthropists," presumably men of dubious motives. In fact, they were highminded altruists who could be trusted with the public's confidence. "They

[10] Stillé, *History of the United States Sanitary Commission*, p. 84; "Resolutions Appointing Financial Committee," June 22, 1861, no. 6, *Documents*, 1:1.

[11] Alfred J. Bloor to Frederick L. Olmsted, August 19, 1861, Bloor Papers.

[12] According to commission records, the first sum of $100,000 that arrived from California on October 14, 1862, was "more than half as much" as the organization had received up to that date, and increased monthly disbursements by almost four times. Stillé, *History of the United States Sanitary Commission*, pp. 202–4.

love not only the work," he exulted, "but they love and honor the Commission."[13] To question their status or their claims to the people's confidence was to undermine the paramount reason for serving on the commission.

While the commissioners deliberated about how to deal with expanding money reserves, the female public grew increasingly troubled about the handling of donated household supplies. Rumors about the mismanagement of women's gifts had been in circulation for some time. As early as November 1861, a letter to the editor of the *New York Times* spoke of "suspicions and doubts" and reported that "it is said" the boxes filled with homemade goods and sent to the WCRA office in New York City were not being forwarded to the army for "want of method." WCRA officers dismissed the complaint as slanderous and marked it unworthy of an official reply. But such handling of early reports no doubt heightened public concerns about the private intentions of Sanitary Commission leaders. Still confident about the patriotism latent at the female homefront, both the male commissioners and the female officers of the WCRA misunderstood the depth of homefront resistance to USSC entreaties. They also failed to anticipate the consequences of official indifference.[14]

As the Sanitary Commission's operations expanded, suspicions about a lack of oversight in its operations surfaced with greater frequency. In September 1862, one commission agent at the homefront, the Unitarian minister William Hobart Hadley, communicated to Olmsted that, wherever he traveled, "it is constantly dinned in my ears that 'the soldiers never get what is sent them.' " Hadley reported hearing preposterous charges that "the Surgeons drink up all the wine and eat up all the delicacies." In the same month, Louisa Lee Schuyler confided to Bellows that "reports of dishonest agents. . . 'selling our supplies to the soldiers'. . . have increased very much lately." She remarked that accusations about the sale of donated goods had escalated to the point that "every week we have letters from our old contributors asking us to deny it, as it is destroying the confidence of the public."[15]

Aware of the public's growing unease, the commission attempted to impose some authority over damaging stories by disseminating voluminous evidence about the valuable services it was providing to army hospitals. Many of the documents it now published included reprints of letters from army surgeons and inspectors, filled with detailed descriptions of the uses made of commission supplies. When the surgeon in charge of hospitals at

[13] Frederick L. Olmsted to Henry Bellows, Private Book, October 3, 1862, Olmsted Papers.
[14] *New York Times*, November 8, 1861, Notes from WCRA office, Box 654, USSC Papers.
[15] W. H. Hadley to Frederick L. Olmsted, September 10, 1862, Box 640; Louisa L. Schuyler to Henry Bellows, September 3, 1862, Box 642, USSC Papers.

Perryville, Kentucky, wrote of the "indispensable" aid that a commission agent had provided to his injured troops, he expressed the hope that, by knowing this, "the people will be stimulated to greater efforts to aid them in their benevolent mission." In a letter addressed to Olmsted, Dr. Brink reported that following the battle at Fredericksburg, "recently organized hospitals were visited" by Sanitary Commission agents who stocked "necessaries not provided by the medical department of the army." Indeed, he specified that the items "liberally dispensed" included "woolen shirts, drawers, and socks—blankets, lint bandages," precisely the goods northern women crafted for army hospitals. Dispatches from agents and physicians not only attested to the precise handling of donated supplies and the continuing inadequacy of government efforts but also denounced anonymous detractors and philanthropic competitors, sometimes insinuating that they were one and the same. Invariably the documents blamed inefficiencies on the War Department or those "special agents" who represented state organizations and arrived at field hospitals to tend only the wounded from their respective states. So closely did such testimonies meet the propagandistic needs of the organization that they appeared to have been prompted by Sanitary Commission officials.[16]

One of the earliest acknowledgments of specific accusations from the homefront occurred in the department that coordinated relief activities in the Midwest. In July 1862, Dr. John S. Newberry, the USSC Secretary of the Department of the West, responded to a query from the president of the Cleveland Soldiers' Aid Society, Mrs. B. Rouse, by asserting that all donations received by the commission were distributed fairly and assiduously. But Newberry also added a plea for treating negative reports with common sense. Admitting that he could not "assert positively that *every article* is honestly and wisely used to relieve the suffering of the sick in the army," he reasoned that "human nature is proverbially imperfect and it would be too much to expect that all the various persons through whose hands these stores must pass are alike pure and honest."[17]

---

[16] See James G. Hatchett to Dr. J. S. Newberry, December 16, 1862, in "Operations of the Sanitary Commission at Perryville, Ky.," October 24, 1862, no. 55, *Documents*, 1:19; Dr. Brink to Frederick Law Olmsted, December 29, 1862, in "Reports of the Operations of the Inspectors and Relief Agents . . . after the Battle of Fredericksburg, December 18, 1862," no. 57, *Documents*, 1:12.

[17] Dr. John Strong Newberry, a physician by training, was appointed associate secretary for the region between the Alleghenies and the Mississippi. Given a fair amount of autonomy for work in the Midwest—he maintained oversight of soldiers' aid societies and regional branches as well as supply and relief operations—he was still responsible for reporting and deferring to the Washington office. See Biographical Directory, in *FLO Papers*, 4:103–7; Dr. Newberry to

Mrs. Rouse remained dissatisfied, and persisted in relaying reports from returned soldiers and hospital inmates about the failure of women's donations to reach the sick and wounded. This time the commission responded more forcefully, presenting evidence of its scrupulous oversight of homefront offerings and issuing an oblique attack on the possible misdeeds of others. After months of examining the hospitals and camps throughout the Valley of the Mississippi, it claimed that "in ninety-nine cases out of a hundred, the gifts of the people transmitted through the agencies. . . of the Sanitary Commission are faithfully applied." It hastened to warn Mrs. Rouse and other doubting women that much of the public's bounty was subject to fraud precisely because it was distributed by state agents and not the national organization.[18]

The Questionnaire

With controversy about the USSC's management escalating and Sanitary Commission stores dwindling from the demands of recent battles, Louisa Lee Schuyler embarked on an ambitious project to assess the precise nature and source of doubts on the homefront. On January 13, 1863, she sent a circular to the secretaries of all the soldiers' aid societies in the WCRA region that included a series of questions about local organizational practices and public perceptions of the commission's purpose and effectiveness.

Schuyler's questionnaire to the female homefront followed an established commission strategy for amassing information. From the outset of its operations, the USSC initiated a wide range of surveys aimed at accumulating both descriptive and quantitative data. But the practice of polling political, medical, and sanitary officials, although consistent with Americans' growing predilection for statistical information, was motivated chiefly by the commission's need for numbers it could use for propagandistic purposes.[19] In July 1861, when the USSC sent a questionnaire to state governors posing detailed questions about their recruitment procedures, medical provisions, and supply systems, it did so in order to identify failures that it could later present as inherent in decentralization. As Sanitary Commission work de-

---

Mrs. B. Rouse, July 12, 1862, in appendix to "What the U.S. Sanitary Commission Is Doing in the Valley of the Mississippi," February 16, 1863, no. 64, *Documents*, 2:11.

[18] Dr. A. N. Read to President, Soldiers' Aid Society, November 5, 1862, in appendix, no. 64, *Documents*, 2:17–18.

[19] See Patricia Cline Cohen, *A Calculating People: The Spread of Numeracy in Early America* (Chicago, 1982), pp. 206–19, for history of early questionnaires and censuses.

veloped, the surveys increasingly focused on conditions at the warfront and became more elaborate. An early 1861 probe into army encampments, for example, asked respondents to describe in their own words a variety of conditions, including those of the camps' subsoils, style of tents, rules of cleanliness, and types of amusements available to the troops, while a questionnaire sent the following year sought quantifiable answers, asking camp inspectors to check off highly specific responses.[20]

But whereas Sanitary Commission inquiries probed military and government operations, the WCRA questionnaire set out to assess civilian behavior and, specifically, female voluntarism. It was probably the first time that American women were ever polled for their opinions in a survey.[21] Looking to resolve disagreements with the USSC method of distributing supplies, Schuyler designed her inquiry to elicit subjective responses rather than statistical data. In addition to questions on local charity methods and assessments of the commission's publicity, she inquired about popular feelings toward the organization, sought information on rumors in circulation, and asked for estimates of how much the project had been damaged by negative reports. Though in one sense the questionnaire represented a challenge to homefront women, calling on them to justify their ambivalence and erratic behavior, it also signified a recognition of the serious consequences of their opposition to the commission's project.

Schuyler's inquiry was hardly a dispassionate probe of public sentiment. The circular began with an account of a recent "Council" of female branch delegates held in Washington, D.C., at which women were told that the army endorsed the Sanitary Commission as "the best and safest channel" for the "gifts of the people" to the "130,000 sick and wounded soldiers now scattered among our hospitals and camps." Lest any recipient of the questionnaire had not yet heard the "federal principle" that undergirded the organization, Schuyler reiterated it: "The Commission collects supplies from all the loyal states, and distributes them to the soldiers of the United States, without distinction of State or Regiment, giving first to those who *need it most*, and *wherever the need is greatest.*"[22]

Having shaped the context for her survey by positioning the USSC as the most rational and respected war relief agency, she then asked women to comply with her inquiry "with view of obtaining such information as will

[20] "Questions Addressed to Governors of States," July 13, 1861, no. 8, *Documents*, 1:2–3; "Camp Inspection Return—Questions," no. 9, *Documents*, 1:1–5; "Camp Inspection Return—Questions," no. 19a, *Documents*, 1:1–15.
[21] Cohen, *Calculating People*, cites no surveys that included women.
[22] Circular, January 13, 1863, Box 669, USSC Papers.

lead to the furtherance of our common object." Of seven questions, four requested data about local shipping practices and the promptness of the
WCRA in acknowledging receipt of donations. But three questions dealt
specifically with public comprehension of the commission plan and the possible existence of critical reports:

1. What is the state of feeling which exists in your community in regard to the
   Commission?
2. Is the broad, federal principle, upon which it is based, thoroughly understood by the people and do they agree it is the right one?
3. What reports, if any, prejudicial to the Commission are in circulation in
   your neighborhood? And what difficulties have you to contend with?[23]

By placing seemingly neutral questions about local behavior within a generally propagandistic document about the USSC's policy and accomplishments, Schuyler effectively put those with negative reports on the
defensive.

Replies began arriving at WCRA headquarters almost immediately, and
continued over the next few months. Of the 1700 questionnaires mailed,
240 responses were returned. While it is difficult to attribute specific meanings to the fact that so many localities ignored the survey, it might suggest
that the commission's influence was less extensive than it wished. It also undercut assumptions about the willingness of northern women to feel accountable to a national agency, or perhaps to any extralocal source of
authority. Schuyler avoided comment about the vast majority of women
who did not respond, choosing to focus instead on the content of the replies
received. "The whole correspondence is most interesting," she wrote in a
WCRA publication, noting that "some of the letters are from fourteen to
sixteen pages in length, friendly, sympathetic,. . . some of them even confidential." (As they would throughout the war, homefront women positioned
female branch officers as confidants to hear their personal concerns and
opinions.)[24]

An analysis of the letters substantiates Schuyler's impression of the seri-
ousness with which respondents treated the questionnaire. Women stressed
the conscientious means they employed to provide accurate replies, some
even apologizing when they could give only subjective impressions of their

[23] Ibid.
[24] Louisa Lee Schuyler, "Report of the Corresponding Secretary of the Sub-Committee on
Correspondence and Supplies," April 1, 1863, Box 669, USSC Papers. See Brockett, *Woman's
Work*, p. 532, on number of replies.

town's mood. Jane Hardy was typical, stating cautiously that "as far as I know," the people of Ithaca were divided, some in favor of the Commission, some against, the majority indifferent. A few endeavored to handle the survey methodically and polled their towns in order to assess local biases. Mary Barton of Nichols, New York, felt confident that her community was friendly to the commission, since she had "*canvassed* the town pretty well during the last two or three weeks."[25] Other respondents, perhaps seeking sympathy from their distant colleagues in war relief, remarked that family illnesses prevented them from complying with the survey in a timely fashion. "We have had much sickness in our families and since September severe and dangerous cases," B. B. Williams confided to Schuyler. Julia Gordon apologized for the delay in her response, explaining: "I have suffered from neuralgia for the past four months and the nerves of my eyes have been so weakened by pain that I have not been able to sew, read or write during that time."[26]

But if Schuyler hoped for precise answers to specific queries, the female public again bent the commission's methods to meet its own needs. Women took this opportunity to discuss the political, economic, and psychological impact the war had on their lives and to explain why local relief work was less vigorous than the commission intended. Collectively, the letters offered a history of local relief work, and revealed the degree to which patriotism could be a tenuous and fluctuating sentiment. Aid society secretaries recounted how donations declined after Union forces failed to make substantial advances against the enemy. The women of Beekmantown, New York, having lost faith "in everything and everybody" following Union losses, stopped collecting after the winter of 1861 and, confessed Secretary McFadden, "nothing more was accomplished, until the summer of '62."[27]

In both agricultural and industrial communities, women cited their lack

---

[25] Jane Hardy to Louisa Schuyler, January 23, 1863, Box 674; Mary Barton to Louisa Schuyler, January 29, 1863, Box 669, USSC Papers. Some correspondents mistook the inquiry as another request to organize village women and forward supplies. L. L. Chapin recounted, "I took it in my hand and started out, went almost from house to house but couldn't find more than half a dozen who were willing to do anything." Mrs. O'Daniels waited to reply until she had a box to send. Cornelia Huntington joined others from East Hampton and " 'beat the bush' for money." Jason Sherman apologized for his town's lack of involvement; Lyndon, N.Y., was poor, "without a tavern, store or even a mecanicks shop in it," and when a circular requesting supplies arrived, his wife took it in hand but was able to raise only two boxes of donations. See L. L. Chapin, March 26, 1863; Mrs. A. M. O'Daniels, June 3, 1863; Cornelia Huntington to L. Schuyler, January 31, 1863; Jason Sherman, January 26, 1863, Box 669, USSC Papers.

[26] B. B. Williams to L. Schuyler, February 2, 1863; Julia A. Gordon to L. Schuyler, June 16, 1863, Box 669, USSC Papers.

[27] Mrs. S. L. McFadden to L. Schuyler, February 1863, Box 669, USSC Papers.

of resources as one of the most common reasons for their meager charitable contributions. "As this is a manufacturing place, the people are of moderate means," explained one woman. The Paterson, New Jersey, society raised thirty-three dollars each month, wrote Eliza Powers; "this amount may seem small to you but this city is a manufacturing one and we have few wealthy people." "We are a small farming community . . . with few exseption none of us with large means," wrote Mrs. Follett, and because North Pitcher, New York, was "not a wool growing community," the women there were "not supplied with flanell to bestow." Respondents repeatedly identified themselves or their constituents as poor, working people, of "medium wealth," or middling farmers; as one woman put it, "none are wealthy, none are verry poor." These writers pressed the point that their infrequent contributions reflected the painful ways in which the war was impinging on their own lives, rather than an insensitivity to suffering at the front.[28] Schuyler herself concluded that the "chief difficulty" facing soldiers' aid societies was the lack of money for cloth and other raw materials needed to make hospital supplies. Assuming that the bulk of early donations had been raised by simply forwarding surplus domestic goods, she acknowledged that "households have been gleaned of all superfluous linen and cotton, and the price of new materials is double and treble the usual rates."[29]

As the war economy impaired individual household economies, it also increased the welfare needs of local communities, leaving charitable groups struggling to balance the needs of the army with those of village residents hard-hit by the war. "There are very many things in a little village like ours which are sustained by individual contributions, and which must be kept up," explained Mary Barstow. Though she claimed continued commitment to the cause and a willingness on the part of her townswomen to "spend and be spent," she impressed upon Schuyler the strict accounting that women such as she carried out as part of their domestic labors. "While we are obliged to use the utmost care and economy to keep up our households and have something left for other purposes," Barstow pointed out, politicians in Washington were "spending millions with less consideration than we use in spending single dollars." "We are poor," declared Lucretia Brainerd, noting

[28] Hattie W. Bennett to L. Schuyler, January 23, 1863; Mrs. Eliza H. Powers to L. Schuyler, 1863; Mrs. E. A. Follett, North Pitcher, February 7, 1863; Mary D. Brooks to L. Schuyler, May 6, 1863, Box 669, USSC Papers.
[29] Louisa Lee Schuyler, 1863, Box 656; see Mrs. William W. Graves to Louisa Schuyler, February 1, 1863, Box 669, USSC Papers: "The cloth is verry dear here and seense at that there isn't wool enough raised in our town to half cloth them."

that in East Hadden, Connecticut, women were devoting their efforts to "three destitute families." That the war was dragging on far longer than originally expected posed special hardships for women unaccustomed to diverting their household resources for any length of time. Reflecting on the precise estimations required to determine the charitable needs of a community, one woman opined that "should this war continue people will make more particular calculation for this purpose than before I think."[30]

These accounts reinforced those received during the previous two years, reminding the USSC that most women functioned within households and local economies that rarely provided for anything beyond subsistence. But unlike the earlier reports, which attributed limited donations to long-standing economic problems, these often cited wartime inflation and taxes as the cause of hard times. When at the close of 1861 the federal government faced serious budgetary shortfalls, Congress passed the Legal Tender Act, which by early 1863 flooded the North with over $430 million in new money known as "greenbacks," intensifying speculation. In 1862, many northerners faced a novel form of government assessment in the form of taxes on incomes over $600; the taxes were due in June of the following year. Together, new paper money, increased speculation, and new taxes created inflationary pressures that were widely felt. Peter Parish calculates that by July 1863, as inflation intensified, "coal prices were up by a third, wood by a fifth, clothing by a similar amount." Such effects demonstrated that "wartime taxation . . . profoundly affected [the federal government's] relationship with the individual citizen."[31]

Assuming that the federal government was entitled to tax economic surpluses in order to prosecute the war and maintain the army, a number of women suggested that the Sanitary Commission's calls for voluntary contributions constituted an additional, perhaps illegitimate, tax. A letter from Pawlet, Vermont, signaled the new sentiment: "the farmers say it takes all they can make to pay their taxes and the wives feel as poor as the husbands." In the remote, "quiet agricultural district" of East Hampton, Long Island, the commission's requests appeared to mirror the intrusive arm of the state: "We only know of war by hearsay, and high prices, and bounties and all sorts of incidental taxes." Cumulatively, the economic distress imposed by the war demoralized both charitable efforts and nationalist loyalties. "The

[30] Mary L. Barstow to L. Schuyler, January 29, 1863; Lucretia L. Brainerd to L. Schuyler, February 26, 1863; Mrs. M. W. Butterfield to L. Schuyler, Eddyville, March 24, 1863, Box 669, USSC Papers.
[31] Peter J. Parish, *American Civil War* (New York, 1975), pp. 356–59, 363.

slow progress of the war, & the high prices of living & the increase of taxes all combine to depress & discourage," wrote Mrs. D. C. Squires.[32]

Notwithstanding the prolific commission literature addressing the subject of government responsibility, the responses to the questionnaire revealed a homefront still uneasy about the necessity of providing private welfare for the purpose of waging a national war. Citing the feeling that the wives of "hard toiling farmers & mechanics, feel that their husbands are to be heavily taxed for the support of the Government," a writer from Oneida, New York, stated bluntly: "We need to be convinced that ours is not government work."[33] Some women began to wonder where their political and economic loyalties properly belonged: with their town, their state, or their nation? How was a woman to know whether she was properly defending the Union or inadvertently abetting the designs of selfish elites? Indeed, Schuyler reported to her male colleagues that among the most sensitive issues raised by homefront women was where the care of the army properly belonged. "What is the govt doing? Why can't it do *all?* Why is the Sanitary Commission the best channel for the gifts of the people?" These were the questions most often put to WCRA officers, she explained to Bellows.[34]

Despite their complaints about economic hardships, many aid society secretaries characterized themselves as supporters of the USSC and were proud when they could report that the organization enjoyed respect among their townspeople. Some displayed a curious propensity to be protective of the organization's feelings and to reassure it of the people's affections. "For your encouragement, I will say that your association is gaining the confidence of the people," reported Julia Gordon. Mrs. Vorhis wrote that though "the state of feeling" in Danby, New York, was not good, the organization could take heart that at least it was "now more favorable than it was six months ago." Another woman waited until June to reply, fearful that her answer would have been "so discouraging had I replied then."[35]

But when obliged to admit existence of widespread antipathy to the Sanitary plan, women used the occasion of the questionnaire to distance them-

[32] Miss L. B. Fitch to L. Schuyler, May 18, 1863; Miss Cornelia Huntington to L. Schuyler, January 31, 1863; H. Hazettian to L. Schuyler, January 30, 1863; see also Mrs. Lydia Batty to L. Schuyler, January 29, 1863; Mrs. D. C. Squires to L. Schuyler, January 31, 1863, Box 669, USSC Papers.

[33] Mrs. S. L. Beardsley to L. Schuyler, June 23, 1863, Box 669, USSC Papers.

[34] Louisa L. Schuyler to Henry Bellows, February 24, 1863, Box 955, USSC Papers.

[35] Mrs. Julia A. Gordon, June 16, 1863; Mrs. C. L. Vorhis, January 29, 1863; Mrs. A. M. O'Daniels, June 3, 1863, Box 669, USSC Papers.

selves from dubious neighbors. The secretary of the Newark, New Jersey, society said she approached the circular "with pleasure," but admitted, "in relation to the state of the feelings in this community in regard to the Sanitary Commission, I cannot say much that is favorable." When another woman disclosed that most of the people in her wealthy town were cynical about the commission, she expressed some discomfort at having to reveal local opinion; "I know I'm not eulogizing our towns people very much— but you know you asked."[36]

Schuyler's survey elicited unsolicited information about the feelings women held toward their neighbors. Given reason to expound on the behavior of others, the questionnaire permitted some to express personal and political antagonisms on a national stage. Remarks were sometimes sarcastic, as when Jennie Vosburgh wrote that "those who take pains [to] inform themselves, entirely approve of the Federal Principle of the Comm," or when Ophelia Wait explained that the "women of the neighborhood in which I live regard the work of your noble Sanitary Commission with most perfect indifference." Harriet Ming offered her opinion that "ignorant, meddlesome people will ever find fault with your best endeavor and my experience has taught me that *silence* is the best remedy."[37]

Soldier aid work had emerged as a potentially divisive wedge in small-town associational life. While offering a way of expressing commitment to the Union cause, it also allowed national issues to intervene in community life with a new forcefulness. A number of respondents spoke explicitly of local political schisms, at times identifying the influence of peace Democrats as the source of the organization's bad press. "The difficulty we have to contend with," wrote Delilah Allen, "is want of interest and the harm done by the opposing party." "Our own immediate vicinity is very much tinctured with Copperheadism," reported another woman, while insinuating that these individuals were also the wealthiest in town. Notwithstanding efforts to present itself as a nonpartisan agency, the USSC was clearly identified with the Republican Party and its political agenda. Caroline Sherman regretfully informed Schuyler that those who had gathered "many of the evil stories in circulation" had a tendency to "treasure them with a tenacity quite becoming a miser," while others were spreading them "for the benefit of other wise-a-cres known under the polite appellation of Secessionists."

[36] Letter to Louisa Lee Schuyler, January 24, 1863, Box 674; Mrs. Lydia Batty to L. Schuyler, Easton, January 29, 1863, Box 669, USSC Papers.

[37] Jennie Vosburgh to L. Schuyler, June 30, 1863; Ophelia C. Wait to L. Schuyler, January 30, 1863; Mrs. Harriet N. Ming, January 23, 1863, Box 669, USSC Papers.

"This is a Democratic town of the Messrs Breckenridge, Stevens, and Jeff Davis persuasion," she explained, with the result that, "Soldiers Aid Societies, Relief Associations, and Sanitary Commission are left out in the cold."[38]

The results of Schuyler's questionnaire demonstrated that a good portion of the female public remained unconvinced or even unaware of the commission's benevolent creed. Whether women characterized their towns as "warm & friendly," indifferent, or even hostile appeared unrelated to the degree to which they professed understanding of the Sanitary Commission's philosophy. Thus, some respondents reported that while the commission was held in high regard, few understood the federal principle. Moreover, asserting acceptance of the principle did not necessarily alter the belief that "charity begins at home." Many localities claimed they were auxiliaries of the commission, read its publications, and communicated with its officers, yet still ignored its depots when they made donations. Mary Crosby noted that in Barrington, New York, "the more general feeling is to send to particular friends." Those cases in which comprehension of the federal principle coincided with negative feelings toward the organization suggested a decisive rejection of the Sanitary premise.[39] Even in towns that proclaimed a predominance of positive feelings toward the commission and its work, women still divided their donations among local, state, and national agencies. In many places, soldier aid work was only carried out within the most intimate and narrow of networks. As one woman explained, some people "are allways suspicious of any organization for charitable purposes and if they do not see their benefit actually applied dare not bestow."[40]

"A Swindling Concern"

The issue of whether any reports "prejudicial to the Commission" existed was rhetorical; the organization was well aware that suspicions about its

[38] Ann C. Miller to L. Schuyler, February 2, 1863; Mary L. Barstow to L. Schuyler, January 29, 1863; Delilah Allen to L. Schuyler, 1863; Mrs. Hogeboom to L. Schuyler, 1863; Caroline Sherman to L. Schuyler, January 24, 1863, Box 669, USSC Papers.
[39] B. B. Williams to L. Schuyler, February 2, 1863; Mary Crosby, January 27, 1863; see also Miss H. A. Doolittle, January 29, 1863; Mary M. Whitson, May 6, 1863; L. Villie Potter to L. Schuyler, January 28, 1863; Mrs. H. P. Green to L. Schuyler, January 26, 1863; Jennie Vosburgh to L. Schuyler, June 30, 1863, Box 669, USSC Papers.
[40] Mrs. E. A. Follett, February 7, 1863, Box 669, USSC Papers.

methods and motives were widespread. The third question in the survey went beyond the issue of rumors and sought specifics about the stories in circulation, including information on how many societies had heard them and to what degree they had undermined relief efforts. Whether Schuyler's goal was simply to understand the sources of homefront discomfort or whether she wanted to confront the homefront with the irrationality of its actions was not self-evident in the question's phrasing; it may not even have been clear to Schuyler herself.

But any attempt to ascribe authorship to malicious gossip was inherently self-defeating. By its very nature gossip offers a means of opposition or, as James Scott terms it, "disguised popular aggression," that is safe and valuable precisely because "everyone can disavow responsibility for having originated it." Even when women reported negative feelings toward the organization, they distanced themselves from such sentiments, usually attributing them to disloyal neighbors or unidentified soldiers. Furthermore, the full-blown tales that floated throughout the homefront represented a more developed form of gossip. Rumors, one twentieth-century study has found, thrive during events such as war when people perceive a lack of reliable information about actions that are crucial to their lives.[41] For most northerners the Civil War not only was a distant event, with army hospitals far removed from their own eyes, but prosecuting it seemed to undermine the very social relations and economic opportunities that had bred passions to defend the Union in the first place. Given the already palpable apprehensions about the intrusive arm of the federal government and growing evidence of the war's deleterious effects on the market, the northern female homefront was primed to embrace stories about the misappropriation of its benevolence and the corruption of its patriotism.

If the rumors constituted a means for those lacking power to express their fears about those who possessed it, the results of the questionnaire validated the existence of widespread apprehension about the motivations of Sanitary Commission leaders. Analysis of 160 letters reveals that over half of the respondents reported rumors spreading within their town, while a third stated that they personally had not heard any negative statements. Less than one-tenth categorically claimed the absence of any such stories. Not only were rumors pervasive, but most communities, no matter how remote, appeared to have received virtually identical accounts of fraud on the part of the commission. Town after town reiterated strikingly similar stories of soldiers not

[41] Scott, *Domination and the Arts of Resistance*, pp. 142, 144–45.

receiving the goods destined for them, of army patients being forced to pay for donated articles, and of unscrupulous persons lining their pockets with the value of unpaid female labor.

Suspicion of corruption and profiteering fell on any who handled soldiers' supplies. "People have gained the idea in some way," went the vague account of one woman, "that the articles in being distributed more or less, fall into hands of speculators." Most respondents, however, related stories that identified specific culprits among military and medical personnel. The correspondent from Alabama, New York, informed the WCRA that "there are reports in circulation that articles sent to the sick soldiers never reach the privates, but are appropriated by the officers . . . or hospitals." While army officers, surgeons, and nurses were frequently accused of profiting by selling USSC supplies to their patients, some respondents suspected people much closer to home. Among the many negative reports in circulation in Harmony, New York, was one that claimed "that the farmers that carted the goods to the hospitals sold them to the wounded men." One of the few accounts that claimed personal observation of fraud came from a group of women from Utica, New York, who had visited army hospitals around Washington, D.C.; it alleged that "only the officers' hospitals secure any of the delicacies forwarded, that the men suffer from want of care, from dishonesty—and faithlessness of nurses."[42]

Rumors about the misappropriation of homemade donations fell most frequently on Sanitary Commission agents, whom women held ultimately responsible for any mishandling of their gifts. One woman wrote that "a return soldier says that *every thing* is *sold* by the Commission to the patients," and as a result, the people in her town "positively *refuse* to contribute the least delicacy." The most common rumor circulating in Brookfield, New York, concerned "the general practice of all the officers of the Commission 'defrauding the people and appropriating the result thereof to themselves.' " Popular charges of greed were sometimes quite specific, as when Ophelia Wait informed Schuyler that "the common people have the impression that every thing is converted into money, *even the lint and bandages are sold for paper rags.*" For some, the stories about fraud revealed the true purpose of the USSC. "Some think the Commission a speculation," disclosed Mrs. Dales of Bloomville, New York; in Easton, New York, Mrs. Lydia Batty described neighbors who "insinuatingly talk of it being a lucra-

---

[42] Laura Savage to "My dear Miss," February 9, 1863, Louisa Lee Schuyler Papers; L. Villie Potter to L. Schuyler, January 28, 1863; Melissa Collins, January 24, 1863; Ann C. Miller to L. Schuyler, February 2, 1863; Mrs. H. P. Green to L. Schuyler, January 26, 1863, Box 669, USSC Papers.

tive business." People in Depeyester were "asserting it is a speculation," and those in Churchville called the commission "a swindling concern."[43]

The practice of attributing negative reports to others offered a means of voicing criticism and relaying detailed accusations of fraud while at the same time disowning responsibility for them. Even the most elaborate accounts of corruption were invariably reported as having been received second hand. Mrs. Proudfit reported that there were "many stories afloat prejudicial to the Commission" and claimed that these accounts hindered the work of the Argyle, New York, society. But while explicit about the charges, she was vague about their sources, recounting that "one person says: 'Such a physician . . . saw *boxes* upon *boxes* . . . which could not be forwarded,' " and "a clerk in the Department of the Interior says that he had a friend" who saw hospital storerooms in Alexandria *"loaded down* with wine, jellies, & delicacies designed for 'Our Sick & Wounded.' " Jennie Vosburgh wrote that there were many accounts of the people's gifts being "appropriated, or the value pocketed by the officers of the Com. or the officers of the Army," and that these were "wasted in hospitals by careless and irresponsible persons." But she noted that such tales came from the "mouths of those whose selfishness, indifference, or positive sympathy with the rebels, make them wish for an excuse when asked to aid in their work." "Thoroughly loyal, and unselfish persons," she asserted, were little affected by such stories.[44]

Those few correspondents who claimed some direct knowledge of corruption were especially irate about being associated with an organization that they could not defend. Delilah Allen, who first blamed political enemies and her husband's opposition for the limited support she and her group had provided, wrote again in May 1863 after spending three months at the front as a volunteer nurse. She professed to have seen with her own eyes the mishandling of supplies. Though Allen declared that she was still urging her Mecklenburg neighbors to contribute, she taunted the commission that she had "quite a supply of my own—in fruits of various kinds with jellies and wine," that she would not forward "when there is so little effort made to keep them out of the hands of the well and from the sick." "I am not alone in this feeling," she added.[45]

---

[43] Mrs. Proudfit, February 26, 1863; Caroline Sherman to L. Schuyler, January 24, 1863; Ophelia Wait to L. Schuyler, January 30, 1863; Mrs. C. Dales, February 3, 1863; Mrs. Lydia Batty to Louisa Lee Schuyler, January 29, 1863; Mrs. Alanson Tuttle, January 29, 1863; Mrs. Folney, 1863, Box 669, USSC Papers.

[44] W. E. Proudfit to L. L. Schuyler, February 26, 1863; Jennie Vosburgh to L. L. Schuyler, June 30, 1863, Box 669, USSC Papers.

[45] Delilah Allen, May 12, 1863, Box 669, USSC Papers.

Respondents not only disassociated themselves from rumors of misconduct, but they felt powerless to rebut accounts of returning Union soldiers who attested to personal knowledge of fraudulent activities. Mrs. Chapin wrote that because "there are so many reports in circulation many which we hear from returned soldiers," she could only find "half a dozen" in Antwerp willing to do anything for the war effort. Chapin claimed knowledge of "a number" of soldiers "who have returned and brought home some as many as 8 and 10 pair socks and many shirts—these same hospital shirts we make and dressing gowns, *something they never had* before." "But what makes us feel the most indignant," she continued, "is to see the soldiers coming back with these same garments we are making for the sick." Such misappropriations rendered women's benevolent labors nothing but "lost time." Remarking that this was why they felt "unwilling to do" anything more, she added: "Perhaps you can explain this if so please do."[46]

Popular apprehensions that the USSC was a money-making concern were embedded in a larger constellation of fears about the dangers of concentrated power and the rapaciousness of the market. Antebellum party politics had exploited deep-rooted anxieties about the rise of wage labor and the growth of industrial power by identifying monopolies, both political and economic, as the source of people's declining status. From Jacksonian-era fears of the monster Bank to inflammatory rhetoric in the 1850s about a conspiracy of slave owners and politicians that jeopardized workingmen's economic opportunities and political freedoms, the specter of corrupt elites loomed over the American political landscape.[47] When northern women accused the Sanitary Commission of being a "speculation," they intentionally employed a word that carried with it a critique of the machinations of the market. For them, the commission was as invisible as the market itself, a distant force that could act for good or evil but required constant vigilance if it were not to corrupt war relief.

Moreover, when women charged the commission with "swindling" them, they directly linked its behavior with the unscrupulous practices bred by market relations and embodied in the feared figure of the confidence man, who gambled away not only people's money but their good will as well.

[46] Mrs. L. L. Chapin to Louisa L. Schuyler, March 26, 1863, Box 669, USSC Papers. At the bottom of Chapin's letter were notes scrawled in pencil by someone in the WCRA office, blaming the soldiers for having accepted things when they were not in need: "This will happen with such men."

[47] See Harry Watson, *Liberty and Power: The Politics of Jacksonian America* (New York, 1990), pp. 132–71; Marvin Meyers, *The Jacksonian Persuasion: Politics and Belief* (Stanford, Calif., 1957), pp. 3–32.

Fears about confidence games and the men who plied them were expressed in many cultural forms, including literature and theater, which kept them present in popular consciousness.[48] Against this historical backdrop, the wartime actions of the federal government, especially the extensive appropriation of civil authority and the implementation of the draft, quickly ignited alarms about abuses of power. Calls for voluntary civilian participation were one thing, but conscription acts, taxes, and the expansion of federal power sparked outbreaks of intense opposition.[49]

In many ways, women's resistance to demands for their unpaid labor paralleled draft riots led by men; both constituted critiques of powerful structures overstepping their legitimate bounds of authority. For women, the authority of charitable agencies rested on an ideological construction of women's position in a democratic society and their dominion over significant portions of public social welfare. Though bourgeois women considered it their duty to donate time and labor for the benefit of others, they volunteered only when they judged such acts to be autonomous. This belief was not simply a sentimentalized reading of women's privileges and duties. Rather, it constituted an expression of the bargain women had struck in the antebellum years: they would labor in return for some measure of social control over those whom they served.

Some respondents made explicit connections between their concern about the profit motives of the commission and the larger wartime demoralization of society. When Mrs. Green informed Schuyler that people in Alfred Centre, New York, heard that all the donated goods "fall into the hands of speculators," she added: "Nor need you wonder at this lack of trust. For no time in the world's history was there ever more treachery than at the present."[50] Increasingly aware that profiteering on federal war contracts had been extensive enough to result in inadequate supplies and even deprivation among Union soldiers, some women had no difficulty identifying the fruits of war-related fortunes. In 1862 Maria Daly recorded with horror the rumor that "a saddler's wife went to Tiffany and Young's . . . and ordered the greatest quantity of pearls and diamonds and plate." Though she supported the war, Daly entertained suspicions that the Lincolns them-

---

[48] See Karen Halttunen, *Confidence Men and Painted Women: A Study of Middle-Class Culture in America, 1830–1870* (New Haven, 1982); Ann Fabian, *Card Sharps, Dream Books, and Bucket Shops: Gambling in Nineteenth-Century America* (Ithaca, N.Y., 1990).

[49] See James G. Randall, *Constitutional Problems under Lincoln* (1926; rpt. Urbana, Ill., 1951); Iver Bernstein, *The New York City Draft Riots: Their Significance for American Society and Politics in the Age of the Civil War* (New York, 1990); Fred Albert Shannon, *The Organization and Administration of the Union Army, 1861–1865*, 2 vols. (Gloucester, Mass., 1965), 1:194–243.

[50] Green to Schuyler, January 26, 1864, Box 669, USSC Papers.

selves were profiting from the war: Even "the set of china bought for the White House . . . for $1500, appeared in the bill as costing three thousand." Not only were the president and his wife wasting federal revenue on luxury items, but they were defrauding the public by charging more for the dishes than they cost, with "Mrs. Lincoln pocketing one thousand five hundred dollars."[51]

Just when ordinary citizens were being asked to impose the most severe economy on their lives, signs of extravagant waste and personal fraud, created and condoned by the state, inflamed long-standing fears about moneyed powers. It was not surprising that the commission, a relief agency based in the financial center of the capitalist economy and run by prominent men who managed to accumulate huge sums of money, became the target of suspicions. The issue facing the organization became what, if anything, it could do to rectify its public reputation. At stake was more than the maintenance of relief operations at the warfront. The national public platform that the commission's founders hoped to acquire at the beginning of the war was becoming ever more shaky. Since they had invested their aspirations for a new nationalism in their mobilization of women's labor, the leaders had to confront the female homefront. In the wake of Schuyler's questionnaire, northern women faced a more autocratic and, at times, hostile Sanitary Commission.

[51] See Shannon, *Union Army*, 1:56–71, on war contract profiteering; Daly, *Diary of a Union Lady*, pp. 192, 305 (October 24, 1862; September 25, 1864). As First Lady, Mary Todd Lincoln spent money compulsively and recklessly, in one instance purchasing over $3,000 worth of jewelry in three months; but hers was a psychological obsession and resulted in personal debt. See Mark E. Neely Jr., and R. Gerald McMurty, *The Insanity File: The Case of Mary Todd Lincoln* (Carbondale, Ill., 1986), pp. 4–5.

5

"BUMPING INTO EACH OTHER": MANAGERS, CANVASSERS, AND COMPETITION

When women accused the Sanitary Commission of exploiting unpaid household labor for personal gain, their charges echoed growing apprehensions about the expansion of the market and the centralization of state activities. To many at the northern homefront, the war's tendency to concentrate economic and political power threatened the ideals of social mobility and democracy that constituted their devotion to the Union. By the time of the Civil War, most people believed they were defending a Union that possessed a decentralized political system that was responsive to a wide exercise of democratic practices, and an economic system whose expansion westward promised to enlarge opportunities for common people. Above all, it was a Union that was contingent on the people's will.

The acts of voluntarism that sustained both army mobilization and local soldiers' aid societies underscored the singular ways in which American nationalism had developed in the decades before the war. Just as women and men organized autonomously within their villages and towns to create a Union army, so they perceived that the power of the state flowed from the margins to the center, not the other way around. They felt confidence in a governmental framework that kept significant portions of political power vested in individual states and localities, and that required people to maintain only the barest bureaucratic connection to the national state.[1] Early enthusiasm for the war, expressed through the offers of money, time, and men, was based on the belief that these contributions were uncoerced and consistent with American political traditions.

But in altering the size of the state, the war changed the relationship of the state to the people, and with it the meanings attached to their voluntarism. Waging a massive war effort precipitated a consolidation of political power, most dramatically represented by the war powers that Lincoln accrued to himself as president and, by extension, to the federal government.[2] The implementation of income taxes and the military draft signaled an unprecedented expansion of state authority over the lives of northern citizens. For a society in which voluntarism not only was a manifestation of individual will and a significant component of social life but also comprised the essence of political rights, compulsory laws and the appropriation of resources threatened to alter the meaning of the democratic system.

Wartime incursions into voluntaristic practices posed special dilemmas for northern women. Within the relatively narrow legal space allowed to women for political and civic activity in the antebellum years, women's voluntary labor had served as one of their only means of access to social power. Early military mobilization had offered many women opportunities to act on their patriotism in valued ways. Indeed, most undertook warwork with a firm sense of their prerogatives over public welfare and a desire to use their household and charitable skills to express their patriotism. But as the military conflict dragged on and the Sanitary Commission's demands escalated, women became highly sensitive to the demands being made upon them. While it was true that the shifting fortunes of Union men on the battlefields generated recurrent waves of generosity, many at the homefront greeted continued calls for their labor with increasing skepticism. As they intensified their scrutiny of the commission's operations, northern women also reevaluated the value and purposes of their unpaid labors. At issue was the degree to which warwork could be performed voluntarily, or whether, as

[1] The only regular contact most Americans had with the federal government before the war was through the local post office, in the person of the postmaster. Phillip Paludan concludes that "personal experience with self-government was of course local." See "The American Civil War Considered as a Crisis in Law and Order," *American Historical Review* 77 (October 1971): 1014–30.

[2] Lincoln interpreted his war powers to include the right to call forth militia, increase the regular army, suspend *habeas corpus*, proclaim martial law, place persons under arrest without warrant, and seize citizens' property. See James G. Randall, *Constitutional Problems under Lincoln* (1926; rpt. Urbana, Ill., 1951) pp. 36–37.

many came to feel, their donations were no longer freely given gifts but obligations owed the USSC in the name of Union.

If the majority of northern women acquiesced in the wartime expansion of state power, they nonetheless concluded that their voluntary obligations to the state should decline proportionately. With an enlarged state apparatus, there was not only less room for voluntary activity but less justification for it as well. Thus, when women linked the Sanitary Commission's calls for donations with the taxes they were now forced to bear, they made explicit their belief that they owed less to a state that demanded its share of the people's wealth through coercive means. By their actions, those women challenged the assumption of liberal leaders that older forms of female voluntarism could be marshaled to serve a newly masculinized and statist polity.[3] They also made evident that their labor and household products were theirs to own or dispense as they saw fit.

"A Sense of Duty"

For Louisa Lee Schuyler, the questionnaire represented the culmination of months of uncertain relations with homefront women. For well over a year she had received a barrage of troubled messages from those burdened by the scope of warwork. Now Schuyler had overwhelming evidence that the Sanitary Commission experiment had brought about a widespread conviction among women that they were being unfairly dispossessed of their charitable gifts. Even those sympathetic to the program longed for a form of accountability that could justify their continued affiliation. Schuyler faced the difficult task of shoring up the reputation of the commission, while at the same time addressing the anger and fear spreading among the female public.

Conclusive testimonies of homefront resistance also marked a turning point for Schuyler in her position as an officer of the USSC's dominant fe-

---

[3] Carole Pateman argues that voluntary political obligation is a fiction if political obedience is a requirement. The idea that citizens naturally feel obligations to a liberal democratic state and offer their obedience voluntarily is based on the faulty assumptions of liberal political theorists. Most liberal theorists, she argues, view political obligation as a form of "voluntarism," casting political obligation as a promise to obey. In this formulation, citizens willingly give up some political freedoms and equality in exchange for the protection of the liberal state. But Pateman points out that if one removes the "voluntarist gloss" to this formulation, the realities of state power become more transparent. See *The Problem of Political Obligation: A Critique of Liberal Theory* (Berkeley, 1979), pp. 163–78.

male branch. Schuyler had accepted the WCRA's subsidiary status, and from the outset, had applied herself to relief work with an intensity and dedication that distinguished her in the eyes of male leaders. George Templeton Strong observed that she kept long hours, working "from 10 A.M. till 3 or 4 P.M. daily" at the WCRA's Cooper Union offices, "carrying on a correspondence with some 1400 affiliated village societies, churches, clubs and societies."[4] Coming from the same social circles as the men who created the commission and sharing their political and religious ideas about the duties and privileges of urban elites, she was convinced of the rightness of the federal principle. Yet for Schuyler, relief work was above all about meeting the immediate needs of the nation's soldiers. She held none of the men's pretensions about using the USSC as a vehicle for advancing their political prestige. In day-to-day interactions with her superiors, she faced constant reminders of the differences in social power between herself and her male colleagues. As she confronted both a hostile female public and an increasingly intractable commission hierarchy, Schuyler came to embody the contradiction of using voluntary female labor to advance a nationalist program that offered women precious little in return.

Well before sending out the survey, Schuyler worked to disseminate the Sanitary Commission's message more effectively and to monitor homefront sentiments. She sustained an extensive correspondence with individual women and made personal visits to localities deemed particularly resistant to choosing the national organization over state and local agencies for their donations. Among those areas which required attention, none appeared more problematic than Connecticut. In late December 1862, Schuyler traveled around the state, lecturing on the commission's goals and urging "the necessity of *constant* contributions—not to work upon impulse but from a sense of *duty*." Upon her return, she notified Olmsted that Hartford women not only sent most of their supplies to the Connecticut state agency but also had their own "special agent" posted in Washington to handle their donations. Such news left her "feeling the necessity of a much more thorough organization throughout the field and among our auxiliaries."[5]

Learning from her aunt and fellow WCRA member, Mary Hamilton, that "Mr. Olmsted is much worried about Connecticut and wants you to go," Schuyler set out again, in early 1863, to find out why "that *rich* little state" was ignoring the USSC's pleas. The trip confirmed her belief that personal contact with regional women was extremely effective in winning

---

[4] Strong, January 28, 1863, Diary, Strong Papers.
[5] Louisa Schuyler to Frederick L. Olmsted, December 22, 1862, Box 667, USSC Papers.

converts to the commission plan. "The villages *always* want to work through the com. after the principle has been thoroughly explained," she told Olmsted, adding that his own stepmother found this to be true.

Mary Ann Olmsted exemplified the thousands of women who remained dubious about the commission's philosophy, and she compelled Olmsted to confront homefront resistance in a very personal way. In a series of letters, he presented his stepmother with precise arguments about the rationality of using the USSC as the conduit for supplies, even those destined for state soldiers. Calculating that "Connecticut Relief" and other channels she employed reached only 1500 soldiers, and that the USSC "visits every week more than 100,000 in hospitals," he posited that "if then you accept the Sanitary Commission as your only medium of administering to the wants of all the Union soldiers . . . and you give to Connecticut Relief the value of $1. for each patient they reach, and you give one tenth of that for each other man not reached by them, . . . you should send the Sanitary Commission if I am right in my hasty calculation of it 66 times as much as you do the rest."[6] Olmsted's entreaties appear to have worked. In February 1863, Mary Ann Olmsted accepted a position as an associate manager of the WCRA and began organizing the Hartford region, "devoting," she wrote Bellows, "nearly all my time, and all my energies to it." By November, she claimed to have established between twelve and sixteen soldiers' aid societies and beseeched Bellows to counter popular charges of Sanitary Commission fraud by publishing rebuttals in the Hartford paper.[7]

By the time Schuyler returned to New York, responses to the questionnaire were piling up at WCRA headquarters. "I have done nothing but read letters this whole week," she wrote to Mary Hamilton.[8] Over the next few months Schuyler studied over 235 returns and prepared an analysis of their contents. Even before she issued her report, word about the responses had spread through the executive committee. Bellows was impressed by the "answers to a series of questions addressed by Miss Schuyler to 1700 associations," commenting to Bloor that they revealed that "*our documents are read even by the women with care & pain.*"[9] The commissioners appeared less concerned about the content of the rumors, taking encouragement from women's mere willingness to reply.

Schuyler too put a positive "spin" on the results of her survey. On April 1,

[6] Frederick L. Olmsted to "Mother" [Mary Bull Olmsted], January 27, 1863, Private Book, Olmsted Papers.
[7] Mrs. John Olmsted to Henry Bellows, November 15, 1863, Box 955, USSC Papers.
[8] Louisa L. Schuyler to Mary H. Hamilton, January 30, 1863, Box 951, USSC Papers.
[9] Henry Bellows to Alfred Bloor, March 13, 1863, Box 757, USSC Papers.

Woman's Central Association of Relief officers inside the Cooper Union office (*left to right:* Mrs. William B. Rice, Louisa Lee Schuyler, Mrs. Griffith, Mrs. T. d'Oremieulx, and Ellen Collins). Museum of the City of New York.

1863, she issued a public analysis of its results, concluding that by and large the USSC was held in high regard, that most women understood the federal principle (though more did so in New York, Massachusetts, and Vermont than in Connecticut and New Jersey), and that, far from sinking into an abyss of controversy, its image was improving. "The Commission has *lived down* most of the prejudicial reports in circulation," Schuyler reported. "It is still accused of dishonesty and all other crimes," but such charges came from those "whose only motive is to undermine the confidence of the people in anything which tends to strengthen our national cause." Ignoring or misreading the meanings attached to accusations of financial fraud, Schuyler chose to interpret homefront hostility in partisan terms. Criticism of the organization was due to the "lukewarmness of the Democratic &

semi Secessionists." Fortunately, "most of our correspondents are Republicans and abolitionists," she wrote to Hamilton, adding that this was especially true among "those that are most zealous."[10]

In a published WCRA report, Schuyler presented the allegations of profiteering with little alarm. "There are always returned soldiers bringing with them stories of dishonest surgeons and nurses," she conceded, and no doubt a few of the stories were true, particularly "in so large an army as ours." But Schuyler was confident that the vast majority of the incriminating reports were false. "We have not as yet been able to trace back any of these reports to anything tangible." That few were willing to come forward and claim authorship of the rumors made their falsity obvious. Schuyler's dismissal of the very reports she had so carefully solicited placed the burden of proof on her female constituency. Even when confronted with evidence that the Sanitary Commission system was responsible for damaging deeply held ideas about charity by severing aid from the intimate bonds of sentiment, Schuyler demanded that homefront women produce evidence of their charges. "In almost every village there is the story of a returned soldier, who spent his last dollar for a pot of jelly, and then finds his mother's name on the wrapper." "But where," she demanded, "is the soldier, and what was his mother's name?"[11]

Managers and Canvassers

Together with her assessment of the survey, Schuyler reviewed some of the strategies she had undertaken to meet the public's desire for more information and greater accountability. Her most important innovation was a system of female associate managers, begun in February 1863, that established a network of women to disseminate official requests for supplies and provide the WCRA with regular reports about homefront activities. In what may have been a sign of her growing desire to identify herself as an officer of a female-led branch rather than a Sanitary Commission worker, Schuyler credited the associate manager idea to the New-England Woman's Auxiliary Association, the commission's branch in Boston. She chose not to acknowledge that as early as June 1861 the commission had appointed male

---

[10] Louisa Lee Schuyler, "Report of the Corresponding Secretary of the Sub-Committee on Correspondence and Supplies," April 1, 1863, Box 656; Schuyler to Hamilton, January 30, 1863, Box 951, USSC Papers.

[11] Schuyler, "Report."

associate managers to assist in fundraising campaigns and the formation of auxiliary associations.[12]

But if the associate manager system represented a move toward branch autonomy or perhaps female solidarity, it also underscored the class biases of WCRA women. In light of Schuyler's sympathies for the poor and middling women who, she had maintained, constituted the backbone of supply work, the new plan was also an admission that sentimental appeals to domestic founts of female benevolence had failed. No longer confident in the female public as an abstract whole, Schuyler selected managers on the basis of personal recommendations. To justify her return to familiar networks of elite women, Schuyler reasoned that the wrong choice might foster local rivalries rather than increase charity production. Hamilton concurred, warning that "in societies already established one lady might not well be placed over the others."[13] To ensure close supervision of the women appointed, Schuyler herself assumed control of the associate manager program. "Our Associate Manager correspondence is considered both friendly & confidential," she related to one candidate; "as I conduct it entirely, it has always been the greatest pleasure to me."[14]

By April 1863, Schuyler had appointed eleven women who were "going from village to village visiting and inspecting our auxiliaries, and starting new societies."[15] Each manager was responsible for coordinating the voluntary activities of her county or region—two or more managers were appointed to handle large cities—and for reporting regularly to WCRA headquarters. Among an associate manager's duties was the task of ascertaining "whether a Soldiers' Aid Society exist in every Town and Village of her section and, if so, for what they are working." If a manager found towns that were not working for the USSC, she was "to use all her influence to induce them to do so." In addition to their public functions, managers were also expected to communicate with the WCRA on a confidential basis. Indeed, Schuyler conceived of associate manager work as a delicate mixture of public relations and private spying. In response to Hamilton's concern about sparking local jealousies, Schuyler reassured her that little harm

[12] Louisa L. Schuyler to Miss Greene, January 19, 1863, Box 667, USSC Papers. By 1864, the USSC had appointed more than 500 doctors, lawyers, major-generals, judges, ministers, and leading intellectual figures such as Edward Hale, Horace Greeley, and Henry W. Longfellow as associate managers. See "Associate Members of the U.S. Sanitary Commission," March 15, 1864, no. 74, *Documents*, 2:1–22.

[13] Mary M. Hamilton to Louisa L. Schuyler, January 14, 1863, Box 669, USSC Papers.

[14] Louisa Schuyler to Mrs. T. B. Butler, June 16, 1863, Box 667, USSC Papers.

[15] Schuyler, "Report."

could result from the plan. "There will be no trouble about the Assoc. Managers," she predicted, because "no real power is delegated to them." Rather, each associate manager was "to exert all the moral influence she can in favor of the Commission and stands toward us in the capacity of a confidential correspondent."[16]

At the same time that she publicized the associate manager plan, Schuyler also announced the appointment of male canvassers: "gentlemen lecturing for us in behalf of the Commission at intervals during the last three months." In late 1862, the commission had implemented "arrangements for canvassing the country" but delegated oversight of the "travelling agents" to the female-run branches. Each of the five canvassers traveled by rail, combing the countryside and speaking in churches and public halls throughout the WCRA region. Everywhere they went they disseminated the USSC's philosophy, answered queries about the distribution of supplies and the state of military hospital care, and urged people to work for the Sanitary Commission plan. Together, female managers and male canvassers constituted human extensions of Schuyler's questionnaire.[17]

The confidential correspondence from male canvassers provided the commission and the WCRA with firsthand accounts of regional sentiments and benevolent behavior. One canvasser, Horace Howard Furness, offered his superiors rich, detailed accounts of his travels. He proudly noted that he addressed a hundred people in Hartford, Connecticut, and in Goshen, New York, he "had a capital audience of some four hundred in the church of Dr. Snodgrass." A month later he reported that "Troy was a success," for he managed to fill to capacity Dr. Kennedy's church, the largest in the city, seating twelve hundred; in Schenectady, by contrast, "the heavens frowned, [and] rain fell in torrents."[18] Nine months into his canvassing tours Furness described, with an eloquence rare among Sanitary employees, the wearisome nature of canvassing work: "I have addressed large bodies and little bodies, and nobodies and somebodies. I have spoken in Town Halls, in Concert Halls, and in Court Rooms, in Presbyterian, Methodist, Baptist, Lutheran and Episcopalian Churches, from pulpits and from judicial benches, before communion tables and baptismal fonts. Have seen before

---

[16] "The Duties of an Associate Manager," Box 667; Schuyler to Hamilton, January 30, 1863, Box 951, USSC Papers.
[17] Alfred J. Bloor to Reverend B. T. Phillips, February 10, 1863, Box 669, USSC Papers; Schuyler, "Report."
[18] Horace Howard Furness to Frederick Law Olmsted, January 29, 1863, Olmsted Papers; Horace Howard Furness to Louisa L. Schuyler, February 27, 1863, Box 680, USSC Papers.

me eyes glistening with interest and eyes drowsy with sleep. I have heard stentorian yawns and rapturous applause."[19]

Another canvasser, William Hobart Hadley, found rampant anti-Republican sentiments, which created serious obstacles for the USSC. In April 1863, he reported to Schuyler that for the first time on his trip through northern New York State he found himself at "a public house" and not "a *copperhead rumhole!*" Quipping about the influence of Democratic sympathizers, he caustically related that he had been "an hour in the most public room and probably twenty persons have been in & out, during the time, and I have not heard a curse upon 'Abe Lincoln' nor the 'baboon nigger'!"[20] By October, Hadley found almost all village societies "essentially disorganized, dissolved, indefinitely suspended, or utterly defunct." Despite promises made by local ladies to resume warwork, he doubted "that three out of twenty of them would ever move or show any signs of life again."[21]

Seeing first hand the obstacles facing those who attempted to mobilize voluntary labor, canvassers often cultivated their own techniques for overcoming resistance. Major Bush usually sought out the names of at least twenty women from the most prominent families from each district of a town and publicly appointed them as an "Executive Committee." Bush claimed great success for the method—"have organized twenty-one *Aid Societies*"—and pointed out that his audiences were both large and committed, some traveling "with their family wagons five & six miles to attend."[22] Upon returning from Connecticut, another canvasser, Reverend Tiffany, informed Schuyler that it was most important to concentrate on the smaller towns since "a great many of these are doing nothing." Noting that he successfully "started up several of them," he nonetheless cautioned that "the work will require a great deal of time, as they are very numerous."[23]

Notwithstanding the value of intimate contact with homefront communities, ineffective screening procedures and a lack of coordination plagued the canvassing effort. Furness was especially concerned with the quality of men who formed the corps of lecturers, advising Olmsted that "we should be careful whom we empower to speak for us." He provided personal assessments of his canvassing colleagues, rating Mr. Lancey a "first-rate fel-

[19] Horace Howard Furness to Frederick Law Olmsted, June 8, 1863, Olmsted Papers.
[20] W. H. Hadley to Louisa Lee Schuyler, April 11, 1863, Box 680, USSC Papers.
[21] While he struggled to mobilize women, Hadley noted that in some towns an aid society was nothing more than the labor of one woman. See W. H. Hadley to Louisa Lee Schuyler, Mannsville, N.Y., October 21, 1863, Box 680, USSC Papers.
[22] Jas. C. Bush to Louisa L. Schuyler, July 9, 1863, Box 680, USSC Papers.
[23] Rev. Francis Tiffany to Louisa Schuyler, March 13, 1863, Box 680, USSC Papers.

low" and Tiffany "a treasure," but expressing doubts about "Mr. Van S." as well as Mr. Phillips. Noting the frequent duplication of efforts, he proposed that the commission "set as many Village Evangelists at work as possible," advising them to "report weekly," but making sure "their routes be determined by one head, from whom they shall receive the boundaries of their districts." For Furness, better administration of canvassing work was critical, lest lecturers continue "bumping into each other all over the land, wasting time and strength."[24]

Schuyler concluded that canvassers should be sent only where they could be assured of some success. For the WCRA this meant concentrating on the "middle counties of the state," since the Hudson River region was so disloyal "it is almost a waste of powder to send a lecturer among them."[25] In areas designated as staunch Democratic strongholds, Bellows himself attempted to press the commission's case. In February of 1863, he traveled in the area around Albany and Hudson, calling on upstate Democrats "to increase their trust in the Government." Pleased with the results, he lamented that he did not have the time to continue his speaking tour throughout the country.[26]

The Emergence of the Christian Commission

While increased contact with homefront communities helped to stimulate donations and may have allayed some apprehensions about Sanitary Commission misconduct, reports from canvassers and associate managers revealed that a rival group had appeared to challenge their organization. Time and again, lecturers reported that the United States Christian Commission was making serious inroads in the competition for homefront contributions. Founded on November 16, 1861, under the leadership of the Philadelphia minister George H. Stuart, the Christian Commission (CC) was established by the Young Men's Christian Association to tend to the "Spiritual Good of the Soldiers in our Army."[27] During the 1850s, Stuart was the manager of the Presbyterian-led Sunday School Union, one of the many national benevolent societies started by Protestant denominations in the 1820s. Among the officers of the CC were leaders of other organizations, including the Bible Society, Temperance Union, and Tract Society,

---

[24] Furness to Olmsted, January 29, 1863.
[25] Louisa L. Schuyler to Frederick Knapp, December 28, 1863, Box 955, USSC Papers.
[26] Henry Bellows to Frederick L. Olmsted, February 11, 1863, USSC Papers.
[27] George H. Stuart, November 16, 1861, George H. Stuart Papers.

that together made up the "united front" of antebellum evangelical missions. Sensing renewed religious passion resulting from the revivals of 1857, YMCAs in a number of northern cities responded to the war by recruiting volunteer ministers to travel to the front.[28]

Though confident about the surge of religious fervor that accompanied war mobilization, the Christian Commission's system of ministering was slow to develop and generated little interest during the early years of the war. Even after the national committee of the YMCA decided to structure these "Christian efforts" into a central commission, it possessed only vague notions of strategy and purpose. The CC's official history acknowledged that "for eight or nine months after its formation it accomplished very little" and was regarded by the public "with general indifference."[29]

By January 1863, the Christian Commission had devised a workable method of operation. After moving its headquarters from New York to Philadelphia, it initiated a "delegate system" that recruited northern ministers to volunteer for six-week tours of duty at the front. Soon it was boasting of providing "direct" relief, distributing "gifts from home *in person*." By the end of the war, the CC claimed that 5,000 volunteer ministers had distributed nearly one and a half million religious tracts, all of which were donated by the American Bible Society.[30]

Actually, members of the Sanitary Commission had been receiving warnings about competition from the Christian Commission for some time. In the fall of 1862 Surgeon General Hammond cautioned Bellows that the new organization was "working against you and you ought to be on your guard." But before 1863 the Sanitary Commission paid scant attention to the other agency, regarding it as of little consequence to its own operations. The USSC adopted a public stance of cooperative goodwill and insisted that the two organizations were able to work "side by side," as the CC was assigned to aid the chaplain service of the military while the USSC assisted the medical service.[31] But as the CC's incursions into homefront benevo-

[28] Clifford S. Griffin, *Their Brothers' Keepers: Moral Stewardship in the United States, 1800–1865* (New Brunswick, N.J., 1960), pp. xi, 46–47, 248–49. The 1857 revivals began when thousands of urban businessmen, shaken by a financial panic, attended daily prayer meetings, underwent conversions, and joined churches. Lemuel Moss, *Annals of the United States Christian Commission* (Philadelphia, 1868), p. 64–68.

[29] Moss, *Annals*, pp. 100, 103, 116–22; CC work did not accelerate until late 1862, and the group's first report was not issued until 1863. See *United States Christian Commission, for the Army and Navy, Work and Incidents; First Annual Report* (Philadelphia, 1863).

[30] Moss, Annals, pp. 130, 281, 560–61.

[31] William A. Hammond to Henry Bellows, November 3, 1862, Box 955, USSC Papers; Frederick Law Olmsted, "To Each Inspector of the Sanitary Commission," December 16, 1862, reprinted in *Bulletin*, December 1, 1863, 1:87.

lence grew, the two groups began to exploit each other's weaknesses and established a pattern of confrontation that lasted for the duration of the war.

From its inception the Christian Commission distinguished itself from the USSC by its voluntary format, emphasizing that it employed only unpaid "Christian Delegates—chiefly professional men or merchants." It also stressed the fact that it distributed "moral and religious" tracts as well as hospital supplies. Like the Sanitary Commission, it claimed to aid all enlisted men, regardless of their state of origin, but it professed no purpose beyond simply tending to the physical comfort of soldiers.[32] Such assurances only served to fuel the rivalry between the two organizations. At times the acrimony became extreme, as when CC supporters charged that a California Sanitary Commission agent was earning $40,000 a year. The USSC was quick to reply that in fact it "never had an agent in California, and consequently no salaries have ever been drawn."[33]

Competition to win popular support accelerated, and by the spring of 1863 the two commissions were flooding the homefront with propagandistic tracts and pursuing alliances with local elites. Alerted by Schuyler that the CC was severely undermining USSC strength, canvassers grew increasingly sensitive about intrusions into their domains. Horace Furness, ever dramatic, declared that "the boss devil I no longer fear, his throne has been usurped by G——rge St—w—rt."[34] Wherever he traveled, Furness managed, "without mentioning it by name," to fight the CC "with a vicious fury second only to that against States Relief."[35] While on tour in Corning, New York, S. Herbert Lancey confirmed Schuyler's impression about the growth of the Christian Commission's influence; the rival group tried to recruit "a volunteer Chaplain, missionary or nurse from every town of any importance and then make use of this man's influence & efforts to secure contributors." Fired up, Lancey pledged to "leave no stone unturned in efforts to keep what belongs to us and secure what is justly ours."[36]

From the homefront, Sanitary Commission canvassers sent back accounts of CC agents invading their territories and employing ingenious techniques to win local allegiances. "Their 'plan of action' is well laid," wrote Lancey, describing how the opposition recruited local dignitaries and

[32] "Organization and Plans of the New York Christian Commission for the Army and Navy," Box 740, United States Christian Commission Papers (hereafter CC Papers).
[33] "Statement of the Object and Methods of the Sanitary Commission," December 7, 1863, no. 69, *Documents*, 2:46.
[34] Furness to Olmsted, June 8, 1863.
[35] Furness to Schuyler, February 27, 1863.
[36] S. Herbert Lancey to Louisa L. Schuyler, April 14, 1863, Box 680, USSC Papers.

then persuaded them to wield their influence over fellow townspeople. The Christian Commission deceived the public, he charged, by continually boasting of the "promptness, efficiency and extent of their work." Female associate managers also sent warnings of the "harm" caused by the CC. Mrs. Horatio Seymour, president of the Buffalo branch of the commission, informed Bloor that she managed to raise $800 in cash donations from local businessmen and that "when it is considered what efforts the CC are making this is a great success."[37] A female colleague in the Pennsylvania branch of the Sanitary Commission shared with Schuyler her idea of impeding the Christian Commission's advances by appropriating some of their message, "without exactly answering the circulars and advertisements of the Christian Commission, for we will not stoop to that; we must through the papers educate the people as to the *Christian work* which *our* Commission is doing."[38]

The Christian Commission's claim that it tended to the religious needs of soldiers undoubtedly appealed to many women, whose benevolence and organizing experiences had originated in evangelical religion. Yet the surge in the CC's popularity precisely at the moment when suspicions about the USSC peaked suggests a causal relationship. The Christian Commission offered female volunteers a means of punishing the Sanitary Commission for its alleged misdeeds and at the same time exerting some measure of control over the products of their labor. As the Sanitary Commission suffered from damaging charges about its operations, the Christian Commission evolved into a formidable competitor, capitalizing on USSC failings as well as its own pious appearance. When the CC spoke of "the offering of Christlike philanthropy," it consciously presented itself as a distinct alternative to the earth-bound and political character of the Sanitary Commission.[39]

As the Christian Commission gained in popularity, it reorganized itself into a structure capable of supplanting the USSC. A Christian Commission volunteer from Troy, New York, confided to George Stuart that while the Sanitary Commission "had pre-occupied the ground . . . with an admirable organization," he was determined to "make a new start," persuading citizens to transfer their pledges to the new organization. Aware of provincial demands for control over their own resources, Stuart made a point of reassuring a female associate from Fabius, New York, that his agency refrained

---

[37] S. Herbert Lancey to Alfred J. Bloor, April 14, 1863; S. H. L. to Alfred J. Bloor, July 7, 1863; Mrs. Emily N. Barnes to Alfred J. Bloor, April 23, 1863; Mrs. Horatio Seymour to Alfred J. Bloor, November 30, 1863, Box 955, USSC Papers.
[38] Mrs. Clara Moore to Louisa L. Schuyler, April 10, 1863, Schuyler Papers.
[39] "Organization and Plans of the New York Christian Commission," Box 740, CC Papers.

from eclipsing local charity channels. "If you consult us about sending funds, we would say unhesitatingly, send all—without delay," he wrote, but added, "There may however be some local reason for your retaining some for society use; this, of course, we would not interfere with under any circumstances." Here was a centralized organization whose approach to national welfare appeared to match that of many homefront women. Though patriotic and pro-Republican, its style was neither overtly political nor excessively nationalistic. By the spring of 1864, George Stuart boasted to Secretary of War Stanton that "the tide seems turning strong at the very sources of influence in our favor."[40]

Ironically, the success of the Christian Commission depended in large part on its appropriation of tried and true USSC methods. Initially limited to dispensing religious tracts and tending to the spiritual needs of soldiers, it soon expanded its operations to include the collection and distribution of household donations. "It has *entered our field*," Bellows informed Newberry in August 1863, explaining that the Christian Commission was "collecting money and supplies in a way that seriously interferes with our resources."[41] Before long, Sanitary Commission members recognized that, despite the rival group's claims to dispense only religious matter, the officers of the Christian Commission "*do* wish their agents to distribute supplies; and they are now attempting to raise one million of dollars to carry on their largely increased work."[42]

In fact, the explosive growth of CC activities was accompanied by a major reversal in its charity methods. The original scheme of equipping volunteers with wagons of donated religious tracts as well as some food and clothing had proved ineffective, and in 1863 the agency adopted a system of paid agents to bolster its hands-on, voluntary method. It divided the armies into units and placed an agent in charge of each. These general field agents, with annual salaries that ranged between $480 and $840, were to provide regular oversight of the nearly two thousand volunteer "delegates," who were only required to be on hand for approximately six weeks.[43]

Sanitary Commission leaders had long defended the economy and effi-

[40] Harvey J. King to George Stuart, March 12, 1864, Box 740; George H. Stuart to Mrs. Harriet Webster, September 15, 1864, Box 739; CC Papers; Griffin, *Their Brothers' Keepers*, p. 249; George Stuart to Hon. Edwin M. Stanton, April 30, 1864, Box 739, CC Papers.

[41] Henry Bellows to Dr. Newberry, August 10, 1863, Box 955, USSC Papers.

[42] Joseph Parrish to Henry Bellows, November 22, 1864, Box 955, USSC Papers.

[43] The use of paid agents in religious organizations had precedents in the antebellum Bible, tract and missionary societies. During the 1820s, the Home Missionary Society hired ministers at $400 annually to settle new regions and organize churches. In the 1840s, the Tract Society employed colporteurs (both ministers and laymen) at $150 to $200 annually to sell religious

ciency of paid employees, asserting that only by employing qualified men could they ensure expert work. Invariably, USSC propaganda insisted that "this system of paid agents does not exclude the advantage of having in the work disinterestedness and religious earnestness."[44] In attacking its rival, the USSC argued that the so-called voluntary agents of the Christian Commission were, in reality, costlier to northern communities. Bereft of their ministers, who were on leave to the Christian Commission, localities were compelled to pay replacement ministers, while those who were absent continued to draw their usual salaries. The CC's decision to add paid employees to its rolls attested to its vastly expanded work at the warfront and to the ineffectiveness of its system of relying on revolving volunteer agents. The magnitude of the Civil War and the destruction it wrought rendered older benevolent methods inadequate, especially if the goal was to gain organizational visibility on a national stage.

Though the Christian Commission capitulated to a system of paid agents, real differences remained in the ways the two commissions carried out cash payments. The Sanitary Commission paid all its agents, including the hundreds distributing goods to army hospitals, while the CC continued to maintain a predominantly volunteer force in the field. Further, the salaries of USSC officers, ranging from $1,500 to $4,000 annually, were exorbitantly high, providing employees with distinctly upper-class incomes.[45] In contrast, the average wage of manufacturing workers in 1860 was $297 a year, while privates in the Union army received, during most years of the war, only $156 annually. In late 1864, CC propaganda attacked the USSC on the grounds that Bellows received $4,000 a year while even "the most humble agent" earned $30 a week, and that of $7 million received from the people, the Sanitary Commission had spent $1 million on salaries.[46]

---

materials. Other organizations used combinations of unpaid and paid staff. See Griffin, *Their Brothers' Keepers*, pp. 67, 90–95, 249–50, 304.

[44] "Paid and Unpaid Agents," "The Two Commissions—Comparative Economy," *Bulletin*, January 15, 1864, 3:941–44.

[45] Olmsted accepted the offer of $2,000 a year for the position of general secretary, though it was less than he had earned on the Central Park project, and he and his wife worried about managing on that salary. See Mary Cleveland Olmsted to John Olmsted, October 11, 1861, Olmsted Papers; Frederick Law Olmsted to Mary Perkins Olmsted, July 2, 1861, in *FLO Papers*, 4:125-26.

[46] Salaries for top officers in tract and antislavery societies were comparable to those of the USSC, in the 1830s ranging from $900 to $2,000. Griffin, *Their Brothers' Keepers*, pp. 75–76; Clarence D. Long, *Wages and Earnings in the United States, 1860–1890* (Princeton, N.J., 1960), p. 14. Wages for privates were $13 a month until May 1, 1864, when they were raised to $16 a month. See Bell Irvin Wiley, *Billy Yank: The Common Soldier of the Union* (Baton Rouge, La., 1952), p. 49; S. H. Hester to Marshall, January 25, 1864, Box 671, USSC Papers.

Public awareness of USSC incomes must have been especially damaging. Though the Sanitary Commission made cogent arguments for the necessity of paid agents in the field, they probably persuaded few northerners of the necessity of such high salaries for its officers and employees.[47] Significantly, there were no popular objections to the CC's new policy of paying agents, suggesting that rejection of the Sanitary Commission extended beyond the question of paying agents to conduct benevolent work. It may be that few people were aware of the CC's shift in policy and were unconvinced by USSC propaganda. But people may have been less concerned about the payment of a few employees at the front than about the number and remuneration of paid agents.

While turns in public loyalty were usually attributed to the deviousness of Christian Commission missionaries, USSC officers were aware that some northerners chose between the two groups on the basis of discernible differences in religious sensibilities. Charles Stillé was incensed that rejection of the USSC was based on the "assertion that we are a set of heathen, as contra-distinguished from a body assuming the monopoly of all the 'Christian' virtues." He complained to Schuyler:

> I do wish we could have something of the same catholicity of feeling in regard to religious matters in this country we [are] all striving to cherish in reference to those of a political character. It seems true that the very word 'Christian' is used by many as a pretext to seduce large numbers of people to pursue most unchristian-like conduct. . . . All ideas of fitness, practiced usefulness, efficiency or of anything else essential to the success of the object in view are wholly ignored, when some vague, musty notion arises in the mind that a 'Christian' mode of doing it has been suggested which must necessarily be the best.

"How reason with such fools!" Stillé concluded his harangue.[48]

The identification of sectarian purposes—associating the Sanitary Commission with the rationalist Unitarianism of Bellows's church and the Christian Commission with the more conservative denominations of Congregationalism and Presbyterianism—pointed to a serious deficiency in the USSC's nationalist rhetoric. Support of the conspicuously religious Christian Commission implied a reaction against the spread of the urban, anti-orthodox Christianity of the Sanitary Commission leadership. For many

---

[47] S. H. Hester to Mrs. Moore, December 31, 1864, Box 640, USSC Papers.
[48] Charles Stillé to Louisa Schuyler, April 16, 1863, Schuyler Papers.

nineteenth-century Americans, Unitarianism projected an image of a rigid, elite religion that sought to replace spirituality with intellectualism. Especially for women living in the "burned-over" districts of the WCRA region, once the site of fervent religious revivals, the Sanitary Commission's evident irreligiosity or its connection to an analytical, dispassionate religion may have been particularly discomforting.[49]

The shift of allegiances from the USSC to the CC also reflected the hopes of many women that the more religious, more conservative agency would provide greater assurances against fraud and mishaps. While touring New York State on behalf of the WCRA, Bloor found that even associate managers were divided over which organization to support. When he learned that their representative from Syracuse solicited contributions in the name of the Sanitary Commission when "in reality" she placed "the larger portion of her receipts in the hands of the Christian Commission," he surmised "that similar practices exist elsewhere." While many northerners attached political, class, and cultural differences to the two organizations, one USSC lecturer concluded that people were simply bewildered by the profusion of competing agencies using similar names; there was, he wrote, "a prevailing & spreading confusion in the minds of the steady workers . . . growing from the name 'Commission.' "[50]

The USSC Response

The organizational successes of the Christian Commission led some USSC leaders to concede that their competitor might indeed be surpassing their own organization in meeting both army needs and public expectations. Blatchford confided to Olmsted that in Boston the CC's ability to amass

---

[49] See William G. McLoughlin, *Revivals, Awakenings, and Reform: An Essay on Religion and Social Change in America, 1607–1977* (Chicago, 1978), pp. 100–122, and James H. Moorhead, *American Apocalypse: Yankee Protestants and the Civil War, 1860–1869* (New Haven, 1978), p. 65, on conflict between Unitarianism and conservative churches. For historical background on conservative role of Presbyterians in New York, see Whitney R. Cross, *The Burned-Over District: The Social and Intellectual History of Enthusiastic Religion in Western New York* (New York, 1950), pp. 46–47, 259–64. A precedent of evangelical strength was not the sole determinant of the CC's success. The New-England Women's Auxiliary Association reported that competition between the commissions was "paralyzing activity everywhere in New England." Quoted in Lori D. Ginzberg, *Women and the Work of Benevolence: Morality, Politics, and Class in the Nineteenth-Century United States* (New Haven, 1990), p. 163.

[50] Alfred J. Bloor to Frederick Knapp, September 9, 1864, Bloor Papers; Dr. Van Ingen to Frederick Knapp, February 15, 1863, Box 955, USSC Papers.

large contributions was a result of their "meeting a popular want."[51] Mrs. John Olmsted informed Bellows that she was repeatedly confronted with reports emanating from the front that the "CC went to every bedside, were *first* on every battlefield."[52]

For its part, the Christian Commission understood that its growing popularity depended on exploiting the USSC's bad fortunes to its advantage. To the female public it emphasized its strategy of giving individualized attention to needy soldiers, accompanying marching troops with wagons of supplies, and waiting in camp with refreshments for those returning from battle. Writing to a newspaper in Allegheny, New York, Chairman Stuart reiterated that his organization "distributes *entirely* by personal delegates" and that donations were distributed "*in all cases*, directly to the men."[53]

In contrast, the Sanitary Commission seemed to be drowning in its own elaborate structure. Touring the warfront to inspect relief operations, Bloor was dismayed by the USSC's "singularly meagre and inefficient" method of attending the sick aboard ships and the disproportionate presence of Christian Commission workers among the troops. Writing to Frederick Knapp, he admitted seeing "nothing to indicate that such an institution as the Sanitary Commission had any existence," while witnessing two "well stocked" CC wagons accompanying the troops "every step of the way" and providing a "refreshing lemon for the half-sick who could not drink." Sanitary Commission agents, Bloor lamented, "never *accompany* these weary trains."[54]

Taking their cues from such reports, both USSC and WCRA leaders considered new ways to combat the Christian Commission's influence. Louisa Schuyler held the CC responsible for the decline in the Sanitary Commission's fortunes, remarking in a letter to the standing committee that accusations that the USSC was partisan, sectarian, and corrupt were absent before the competing agency appeared on the scene. As 1863 drew to a close she called for an all-out propaganda offensive to counteract CC influence. Similarly, Bloor proposed that the way to combat the growing success of the Christian Commission was "by an immediate, wise, and thorough system of lecturing and missionary teaching—a system of what may be called parochial visitation." Observing the effectiveness of CC appeals in

[51] Jno. Blatchford to Frederick L. Olmsted, July 15, 1863, Box 955, USSC Papers.
[52] Mrs. John Olmsted to Henry W. Bellows, November 15, 1863, Box 955, USSC Papers.
[53] George H. Stuart to Editor, *Angelica Reporter*, September 12, 1864, Box 739, CC Papers.
[54] Alfred J. Bloor to Frederick Knapp, July 19, 1864, Bloor Papers.

urban newspapers, Olmsted suggested mimicking their technique, calculating that an investment of $1,000 worth of advertising would yield $100,000 worth of supplies.[55]

"The Popular Verdict"

Behind the Sanitary Commission's efforts to devise new strategies lay a deeper sense that it had failed to communicate its nationalist message to the public. Private misgivings about the enterprise began to surface within the ranks. Olmsted was particularly disheartened, confiding to Bellows that he could not help seeing the entire endeavor as "a monstrous humbug." Contrary to its original purposes, "the Commission hasn't made the people liberal," and even seemed to do more to "hinder than it does to promote supplies to the sick and wounded." He was depressed by thoughts that in its obsessive attention to details and statistics, the commission had lost sight of its loftier purposes. Its pride that "the people have given 5000 barrels of potatoes to the Army" was misplaced, according to Olmsted, because the organization had not answered the critical questions: "Would not they have done it and would they not have got to the Army if it had not been for the Sanitary Commission?" "The whole question," he argued, was what the commission did with those potatoes, and whether there was any means of accounting for their distribution. Without such answers, it was arguable that the commission was fraudulent in offering the people guarantees about the destination of their supplies when, in fact, it may have had no means of doing so.[56]

To Bellows's mind, neither the encroachments by the Christian Commission nor the accusations of fraud were the fault of his organization. Rather, the public had displayed a failure of nerve and an overwhelming lack of vision. All the same, people's refusal to respond to the nationally defined needs of the USSC boded ill for the future. By the end of the summer of 1863, success seemed more remote than ever, and Bellows was bitter over the difficulty of spreading the Sanitary Commission's message. "If at this period of the war," he wrote to Dr. Newberry, "our plan & its advantages

[55] Louisa L. Schuyler to Standing Committee of the Sanitary Commission, December 9, 1863, Box 667; Bloor to Knapp, September 9, 1864; Frederick Law Olmsted to the Executive Committee, July 9, 1864, Box 955, USSC Papers. See also J. C. Blatchford to Frederick Olmsted on publishing more USSC reports in newspapers to combat CC influence around Boston, July 15, 1863, Box 955, USSC Papers.
[56] Frederick L. Olmsted to Henry Bellows, Private Book; Olmsted to Bellows, May 25, 1863, Olmsted Papers.

are not understood & appreciated—it is in vain to argue! We must submit to the popular verdict—however unjust."[57]

Unencumbered by grandiose personal and political goals for relief work, Louisa Schuyler held fast to the altruistic meanings she attached to the organization's mission. When she was not attributing blame to the Christian Commission or Democratic partisans, she turned to self-criticism. With her goal for the commission—the "patriotic education of the people"—always in mind, she blamed herself for not working harder to reach the public. "Where I have failed I think," she confided to Olmsted, "has been in letting this want of sympathy in my ideal of the work discourage me."[58] She resisted uncovering deeper meanings behind the organization's woes, and decided that this was a moment to redouble efforts and blanket the homefront with enough propaganda and personal appeals to break down any resistance. Alfred Bloor worried about Schuyler's strategies and warned her not to make any "urgent appeals." While not desiring the public to become "too lax," he cautioned against maintaining "people's philanthropic and patriotic energies all the time at their utmost tension." Schuyler complied, informing Mrs. Chase from Providence that the commission no longer "conscientiously, make[s] 'urgent appeals' after every battle" but instead wants "them to feel that they are to work *steadily* . . . to give two or three hours every week."[59]

Though Schuyler was determined to win the contest for public opinion, she continued to worry about the results of the questionnaire, and throughout the summer and fall of 1863 she pressed vigorously for verification of slanderous reports. She asked the associate manager, Mrs. Henry Randall, for example, to provide her with the name of a surgeon implicated in charges of fraud, to find out "from what hospital or regiment he comes—the nature of the complaints." With knowledge about the rumors' origins there was a chance that "perhaps they can be rectified." Notwithstanding her expressed willingness to combat all charges, even Schuyler appeared somewhat resigned to the commission's diminished prestige.[60]

The question of whether and to what extent corruption existed within commission ranks persisted for the rest of the war. It was not inconceivable that agents had found ways of abusing the system for personal gain. The commission's method of distribution was certainly vulnerable; millions of dollar's worth of supplies shipped around the country, passing through hun-

[57] Bellows to Newberry, August 10, 1863.
[58] Louisa L. Schuyler to Frederick L. Olmsted, September 1, 1863, Olmsted Papers.
[59] Alfred Bloor to Louisa Schuyler, May 29, 1863, Box 669; Louisa L. Schuyler to Mrs. Chase, June 16, 1863, Box 667, USSC Papers.
[60] Louisa L. Schuyler to Mrs. Henry S. Randall, June 4, 1863, Box 667, USSC Papers.

dreds of different hands, must have provided many temptations. It is not difficult to imagine that some degree of corruption involving supplies existed. Yet the scores of reports filed by field agents, physicians, nurses, and private citizens suggested that a good proportion, if not most, of the donated goods were shipped and delivered to Union troops as promised. While taking the accusations seriously, the organization never publicly acknowledged any profiteering. But the anguished correspondence among officials lends credence to the notion that, at least in the top echelon, the USSC was not about profit.

Stories of misappropriated donations spoke to a tangle of economic and political anxieties that had intensified in the decades before the war and exploded with new force during the conflict. The spread of the capitalist market, which changed the dynamics of human relations and turned so many encounters into potential transactions of profit and loss, had bred considerable suspicions about the intentions of strangers. Although most antebellum women had a wide range of encounters with the market, the wartime demand for the products of their household labor elevated their positions as economic actors with something to lose. War profiteering had produced a conspicuous rise in extravagant spending and garish displays of wealth, demonstrating that unscrupulous people were all too willing to exploit the needs of desperate soldiers to accumulate vast fortunes. In the "age of shoddy"—the journalistic epithet for war profiteering—this atmosphere of greed and recklessness made people wary of those who claimed to serve the interests of the Union.[61]

In many ways the Sanitary Commission mirrored the wartime centralizing processes of the federal government and the market. Based in New York and identified with that city's growing economic preeminence (heightened by both the wartime market and government actions), the organization's founders represented those who benefited most from these economic trends. To the degree that northern state formation was fueled more by private market forces than by central state control, Sanitary Commission leaders—private men of significant wealth or social standing—were ready symbols for the dangers of private forces. They were especially vulnerable to criticism of concentrated power and runaway greed.[62]

[61] See Peter J. Parish, *American Civil War* (New York, 1975), pp. 364–65; Mark W. Summers, *The Plundering Generation: Corruption and the Crisis of the Union, 1849–1861* (New York, 1987), esp. chap. 17.
[62] New York's position as the nation's financial center grew markedly during the war years. Though government decisions—including the impact of the transfer of funds from border states to the metropolis and the reliance of the Treasury department on New York bond

But if women were apprehensive about a centralized organization assuming control of their donations, they should have held the same suspicions about the rival Christian Commission. Instead, they focused their criticism on the USSC, charging not only that some articles were pilfered and sold but that the entire organization was a fraudulent charity. The Christian Commission escaped such charges, in no small part because it could hide behind the veil of religious purpose. In contrast to such avowed intentions, the Sanitary Commission was highly visible as an institution created by wealthy New York professionals, Unitarian ministers, and reformers, who identified themselves with the Republican Party, and it insisted that the public accept not only its method of war relief but also its message about the superiority of national structures. Even if they were unaware of the long-range political goals of urban liberals, women nonetheless sensed a conflict of values and disparate patriotic purposes between themselves and the Sanitary Commission leadership. Accusing the organization of corruption was a viable rhetorical tool for expressing popular opposition to felt coercion. Abandoning the Sanitary Commission's relief system for that of its Christian rival seemed to northern women a way to oversee the uses made of their unpaid labor and to preserve the meanings they attached to their patriotism and their benevolence.

---

traders—were not intended to strengthen the city's economic role, the war inhibited the development of alternative financial centers. See Richard Franklin Bensel, *Yankee Leviathan: The Origins of Central State Authority in America, 1859–1877* (New York, 1990), pp. 253–54.

6

"HALF-SAVAGE INDIVIDUALISM": THE USSC CONFRONTS THE FEMALE PUBLIC

The Sanitary Commission learned a bitter lesson in 1863. The assumption that the elite status of its leadership would provide unassailable legitimacy for a radical program of national education proved to be illusory. At the same time, its goal of promoting patriotic sentiments by guiding an obedient populace into an experiment in centralized charity was collapsing. The commission's insistence that northern women abandon their traditional philanthropic channels and participate in a national structure heightened women's awareness of the value of their domestic labors. It also sharpened their suspicions about the patriotism of Sanitary Commission elites.

Indeed, it seemed that the USSC's very presence provoked critiques of concentrated power that might otherwise have been absent. The accusations of fraud by homefront women, together with the reports filed by male canvassers, confirmed widespread anxiety about the distant, elite-led welfare agency. In a larger sense, the corruption charges articulated the popular perception that an implicit contract between the commission and the female public had been abrogated. Women's indignation at USSC leaders reflected a sense of betrayal: that by not treating their gifts with integrity, the organization had debased their acts of political obligation and devotion.

The commissioners failed to appreciate the dangers of manipulating the voluntaristic practices and popular patriotism that shaped northern national identities. When they tampered with customary channels of charity and disregarded the expressed wishes of homefront women, they opened themselves to the charge of cynically using the people's good will to subvert the type of society contributors valued. By exploiting the people's voluntarism, they threatened loyalties that, although identified with the nation as a whole, were nonetheless rooted in locally based customs.

"The Education of a Nation"

The failure of Sanitary Commission men to understand the political and social meanings embedded in voluntaristic practices compounded their isolation from women. As the commissioners reconstructed the purposes of female benevolence, they also politicized this activity, which led them to misunderstand the cues emanating from the homefront. Rather than take seriously the demoralizing impact of fears about fraud and stories of corruption, Bellows and his colleagues interpreted popular rejection of the federal principle as evidence of a separatist spirit, embodied either as sympathy with Copperheadism or as a provincial mentality. In an even more self-destructive vein, they treated criticisms of their organization as personal assaults by an ungrateful public that refused to appreciate their goal of disciplining soldier welfare efforts.

Bellows's lack of faith in the ability of people to choose their social leaders wisely was matched by an arrogant faith in his own convictions. "It is of the first importance that the enthusiasm of our people should bear its full fruit in this war," he mused to himself in 1861, "and this it cannot do, unless it be properly guided."[1] For Bellows, inculcating new beliefs about social order and public welfare was always a worthy goal, and by the second year of the war, he acknowledged the enormity of the commission's program. "We are just *beginning* the education of a Nation," he wrote to Olmsted in the summer of 1863. "Our people don't know what it costs to keep an *old* country a-going; what *Society* is worth, and by what care and sacrifices it is to be maintained." Though his purposes never wavered, his confidence in the people's potential weakened. Characterizing local benevolent traditions and female resistance as popular misrule, he chastised his public for not appreciating the higher sentiments of nationalism. Despite the best efforts of the best men, the shape of American loyalties was lamen-

[1] Henry Whitney Bellows, Notes, 1861, Box 638, USSC Papers.

table: "The great Christian idea of solidarity, mutual membership, and of the gain made by *community* over the *half-savage individualism* which constitutes an American's idea of liberty, has got into only a score of heads in the whole country."[2]

Though Sanitary Commission officers tended to dismiss the negative results of Schuyler's questionnaire, they nonetheless acknowledged, albeit obliquely, that the goal of transforming northern towns into loyal outposts, prepared to respond to all appeals for donations, was an ambitious and risky undertaking. They had been naive about the ease with which women would relinquish the products of voluntary labor to a self-appointed, elite group. They had failed to recognize the degree to which the USSC project constituted an incursion into customary female prerogatives over household production. The numerous stories of mismanagement moved women to defend their established dominion and to insist on administering social welfare according to community dictates and custom.

No longer able to rely on the prestige of its members or sustained enthusiasm for the war effort, the commission, from the middle of 1863 until the end of the war, engaged in a struggle to reassert its authority over war relief and lay the groundwork for a postwar role. As it devised new procedures to protect donated supplies and broadcast such measures to the public, it also shifted the tone of its communications with northern women, moving from solicitous appeals to female generosity and patriotism to angry attacks on the weakness of women's nationalism.

By viewing public criticisms as personal attacks, the Sanitary Commission became vulnerable to problems within its own ranks. Disagreements over how to address public anxieties sapped personal energies, while attempts to impose bureaucratic discipline damaged working relationships. As Stillé later acknowledged, the "force of sectional pride and independence" and what he characterized as the "truly American love of multiplying local associations" would have easily undone the commission had it not managed to accumulate huge cash reserves and alter its modus operandi. "Coaxing and compromising and humoring did wonders to bring about unity and co-operation," he wrote.[3]

---

[2] Henry Whitney Bellows to Frederick Law Olmsted, August 13, 1863, Olmsted Papers. Olmsted had expressed similar views to his mother, explaining that he did not "expect [or] want a short war," as "we are at the beginning of our work" to achieve the end of slavery and the "the supremacy of the laws of the Union." See Frederick Law Olmsted to Mary Bull Olmsted, May 22, 1863, in *FLO Papers*, 4:624.
[3] Stillé, *History of the Sanitary Commission*, p. 205.

Investigating Rumors

The task of rectifying the Sanitary Commission's public image and consolidating its past accomplishments proved to be formidable. The very process of appeasing the public's demand for accountability risked new charges of the irresponsible use of women's charity. New forms of bureaucratic oversight required additional personnel and increased operating expenses, while the elaboration of regulations created added burdens for those assigned to administer them. The possibility that the cure might be worse than the disease heightened with each increase in organizational discipline. Responding to suggestions from Alfred Bloor on improving communiqués to the public, Bellows sensed the danger inherent in their practices; "please write. . . at any time, in regard to. . . any matter throwing light on the office," he implored. "We do not intend to lose ourselves in methodical darkness."[4]

Despite apprehensions about excessive bureaucratic control, in 1863 the commission invented a host of procedures designed to improve the security of supplies and the effectiveness of its distribution system. At the same time, it stepped up propaganda campaigns to combat damaging rumors. Though such attempts attest to an element of responsiveness, these were managerial solutions to deep-rooted dissatisfactions that offered little in the way of a real reconciliation with the female public. To the degree that the commission remained wedded to its hierarchical structure, it displayed a distinct inability to comprehend the issues that underlay popular suspicions. Evidence of such obstinacy was apparent in the way the organization explained itself to the public. In response to accusations that it might be nothing better than a "soulless corporation," the commission boasted of its "thorough business method." Replying to criticisms that it failed to exhibit adequate sympathy for the wounded, it insisted that "strict rules and regulations, and compulsory and inevitable conformity to them, are the conditions of the largest good to the largest number."[5] Methodical darkness seemed close at hand.

[4] Henry W. Bellows to Alfred J. Bloor, March 12, 1863, Letterbook, Bloor Papers.
[5] In analyzing the responses to her questionnaire, Louisa Lee Schuyler had expressed gratitude that the USSC was no longer attacked as a "soulless corp." See "Report of Corresponding Secretary of the Sub-Committee on Correspondence & Supplies," April 1, 1863, Box 669, USSC Papers; "Why does the Sanitary Commission Need So Much Money?" *Bulletin*, January 15, 1864, 1:163; "The Sanitary Commission and the Medical Department," *Bulletin*, March 15, 1864, 1:293.

The Sanitary Commission first tackled the rumors by launching an internal probe into some of the more egregious stories of profiteering. Ever mindful of the propaganda opportunities offered by new initiatives, it announced the hiring of "special detective agents" to oversee the work of employees and field inspectors in the army. Not surprisingly, it reported that "in no one case" were the detectives able to confirm a story of the misappropriation of stores.[6] In a detailed account of one of its investigations, Bellows announced that the charge that had "been flying all over New England . . . that the Sanitary Commission stores of lint and bandages had found their way into the hands of the paper makers" was fraudulent. Though it appeared that a paper maker in Connecticut said that he had purchased lint from a person claiming to be a Sanitary Commission agent, Bellows declared it was not true: "We followed up the story from paper mill to paper mill, but all in vain."[7]

Yet, one especially damaging rumor—that the commission had sold 5,000 pairs of donated socks to the army—illustrates the gulf between the organization's penchant for simple efficiency and the moral economy applied by the female public to its handcrafted donations. A secret inquiry revealed that socks were indeed sold to the government and that the money received was to be spent replacing the supplies, which would then be distributed at no cost to soldiers as originally intended.[8] To justify these decisions, Bellows provided homefront readers with a dramatic account of soldiers suffering with "naked and half-frozen feet" who were offered the socks at 35 cents a pair when the quartermaster's supply had run dry. Since the commission could be "temporarily" spared, he argued, it "lent" the socks to the quartermaster, from whom soldiers could purchase them.[9]

Privately, Bellows admitted that he was relieved to learn "that our agents

[6] "Statement of the Object and Methods of the Sanitary Commission," December 7, 1863, no. 69, *Documents*, 2:25.

[7] Henry Whitney Bellows, "To the Committee on Supplies of the Woman's Central Relief Association, At New York," May 7, 1863, Box 993; see also *Second Annual Report of the Woman's Central Association of Relief, May 1, 1863* (New York, 1863), Box 993, USSC Papers. Bellows may have reported truthfully about the lint inquiry, but one of Schuyler's respondents cited the story as the reason her townspeople refused to contribute to the Commission. See Schuyler, "Report."

[8] *Second Annual Report.*

[9] Bellows, "To the Committee." Because the government lacked the funds to furnish recruits with sufficient clothing, in 1861 the Secretary of War told state governors that while "clothing is sometimes issued to volunteers," soldiers were expected to purchase their own garments from a monthly clothing allowance of $42 a year, which was issued in addition to their pay. The government usually purchased articles from private contractors to sell to soldiers. Why it bought from the Sanitary Commission is unknown. Given the frequent shortages that plagued the department, however, the commission may have presented a ready supply in an emergency.

do not sell stockings." But he warned his colleagues that such transactions could cause "a great deal of trouble," especially when socks "go into the hands of soldiers, who pay for them & then write all over the country that they are wearing boughten socks with our own San. Com. mark upon them."[10] That the sock incident occurred without Bellows's prior knowledge suggests that similar actions probably transpired unbeknownst to the members of the executive committee. But even more telling of the commission's travails was the judgment that buying mass-produced socks to replace the handmade donations would placate its female constituency. No doubt such explanations only fueled women's suspicions about the commission's concept of charity.

Though publicly the Sanitary Commission proclaimed the integrity of its system, privately it put in place new procedures intended to head off the possibility of future scandals. Instructions to field agents now included explicit rules prohibiting the sale of stores. "No Agent of the Commission is allowed to sell anything whatever, even though his own private property, to officers or soldiers of the National Army, or to other persons in Government employ," one directive read.[11] Because most of the corruption charges centered on activities in military hospitals, the commission determined that by increasing the presence of agents among both surgeons and arriving troops, it could improve assessments of army supply needs and prevent surpluses from accumulating. Accordingly, Olmsted created the Field Relief Corps, a group of paid agents who would take responsibility for commission wagon trains accompanying the army's Ambulance Corps and distribute stores directly to medical officers. The six "educated gentlemen" who composed the corps reported that they were well-received by military physicians. Though one military chaplain observed that the agents "work for little or no pay," the commission claimed that field service was considered to be such attractive employment that "numerous applications [were] made for admission."[12]

Yet the establishment of the Field Relief Corps illustrated the flaws inherent in the commission's approach to structural reform. The intent was to improve communication lines with hospital officials in order to dispense aid more effectively. But by placing an additional intermediary between do-

---

See Fred Albert Shannon, *The Organization and Administration of the Union Army 1861–1865*, 2 vols. (Gloucester, 1965), 1:53, 99.

[10] Henry Whitney Bellows to John F. Jenkins, March 23, 1863, Box 955, USSC Papers.

[11] "Extract from Minutes of Standing Committee," July 8, 1864, no. 81, *Documents*, 2:3.

[12] "Account of the Field Relief Corps of the USSC," September 19, 1863, no. 72, *Documents*, 2:5.

nated supplies and the soldiers, and thus creating another point at which corruption might occur, it only aggravated the potential for the misappropriation of supplies. In light of the public's growing regard for the Christian Commission, a procedure that placed another obstacle in the way of direct contact with suffering soldiers gave some credence to charges that the Sanitary Commission was hardhearted. Undaunted by such prospects, the commission defended the new system on the grounds that "it prevents interference with hospital discipline."[13]

The USSC was not wholly invulnerable to comparisons with the Christian Commission; nor was it above imitating the competition. In 1864 it organized teams of volunteer divinity students, clergymen, and professionals into an Auxiliary Relief Corps. These unpaid "gentlemen" signed on for four-month terms during which they acted as nurses, attending the wounded with "milk punch wagons," lemonade, and food.[14] Recruiting ministers to attend individually to soldiers' comforts constituted an acknowledgment of the advantage of utilizing those with overt religious connections and whose work appeared as pure charity.

Internal Defections

Notwithstanding the Sanitary Commission's attempts to remedy its failings through new initiatives and procedural changes, the conflict with the female public permanently damaged the confidence of many of its officers. While they concurred with the importance of sustaining the work for the duration of the war, the commissioners disagreed among themselves about the possibility of extending their influence in any coherent, effective manner. Unnerved by the disclosures of negative public opinion, they questioned their commitment to the organization. Concerned about the potential damage to their reputations as a result of continuing in prominent commission posts, a number of officers and agents reevaluated their decisions to postpone personal careers during the national conflict.

The most dramatic departure was that of Frederick Law Olmsted in the summer of 1863. Ostensibly resigning in order to accept a position as superintendent of the Mariposa company, a western gold mining concern, Olm-

---

[13] Ibid.
[14] *Bulletin*, July 1, August 15, and September 15, 1864, 2:532, 620–23, 678–79. See also Stillé, *History of the Sanitary Commission*, pp. 275–79, in which he explains how the corps was organized in a military fashion, "formed in squads or companies of six, each under the charge of a captain."

sted presented the commercial offer as a way out of his personal indebtedness and his differences with Sanitary Commission administration. But even before alternative employment was in sight, Olmsted had secretly tried to reinstate himself in the Central Park project. Writing early in 1863 to Calvert Vaux, he confided a willingness to "drop the Sanitary Commission instantly" if he could be assured of a position in the Park's management.[15]

In addition to being exhausted and broke, Olmsted was at odds with his colleagues. Throughout his tenure, he had insisted on the necessity of a centralized administration with complete authority over all affiliated groups. Thus, when the commission attempted to placate the rebellious Western Commission in Cincinnati with a share of funds and autonomy over regional affairs, Olmsted felt that a fatal concession had been made to the spirit of states' rights. His attempts to pursue his job in an authoritarian manner brought him into direct conflict with executive committee members. Disapproving of the extensive power he had appropriated to himself, they pared down his official responsibilities. Olmsted felt his hands were tied. He refused to yield to the commission's extreme sensitivity over its public image, believing that his ability to employ people or to circumvent bureaucratic procedures when needed was more important than deferring to popular apprehensions.[16]

By 1863 Olmsted confided to Bellows that he had a "constantly increasing dissatisfaction with the arrangements of the Commission."[17] In one particularly unnerving incident, Olmsted learned that the commission had claimed it did not have enough lemons to send to desperate soldiers in the East (and Dr. Newberry reported he had found none in the West), while at that moment it had in New York "what was equal to fifty thousand boxes of lemons on its hands." When the shortage was made public, the New York City Metropolitan Police force sent fifty boxes of lemons to Vicksburg, which demonstrated to Olmsted how seriously the commission was failing in its stated mission. Olmsted blamed the embarrassment both on the commission's overly-elaborate structure and on inept agents at the warfront. But he was disgusted and despondent, describing his work for the organization as "hateful." When the commission behaved as a "lying, cheating, humbugging, swindling, assuming, pretentious 'organization,' "

[15] Frederick L. Olmsted to Calvert Vaux, February 16, 1863, Olmsted Papers.
[16] Laura Wood Roper, *FLO: A Biography of Frederick Law Olmsted* (Baltimore, 1972), pp. 225–26; Jane Turner Censer, introduction, *FLO Papers*, 4:56–57.
[17] Frederick Law Olmsted to Henry W. Bellows, May 20, 1863, Olmsted Papers. See also Edwin L. Godkin to Frederick L. Olmsted, May 9, 1863, Olmsted Papers, on Olmsted's "pitching into the Commission in an irreverent manner."

he wrote to Bellows, he was at a loss as to what good his presence could effect.[18] He was anxious to leave, and the offer from the Mariposa company was the break he sought.

Bellows attempted to dissuade Olmsted by appealing to his patriotism and his suitability for public work. "At this special juncture in our National life," he wrote Olmsted, "I have the gravest objections to your taking yourself out of the centre of affairs." Tactfully acknowledging the attraction of a commercial offer, Bellows nonetheless attacked the crassness of mere monetary considerations and warned his colleague that there would not be "many Central Parks or Sanitary Commissions . . . if Wall Street's 'down-with-the-dosh' were the only sound rhetoric." Professing sympathy with Olmsted's desire for financial security, Bellows nevertheless offered the opinion: "You never will be rich, and I am inclined to think you never ought to be." For Bellows, Olmsted's departure would be "the final stroke of misfortune" to befall the commission.[19]

Olmsted's reply was frank and unequivocal. Agreeing that he possessed exceptional knowledge and skill that would be useful to the nation, Olmsted pointed out that after having spent two years in Washington, D.C., he had, in fact, wielded precious little influence. With characteristic exaggeration, Olmsted proclaimed his work on the commission "a complete failure," and rationalized that a well-paid commercial position offered him the possibility of acquiring the personal fortune that would make him a respected man. "My books, my views, my practical suggestions are better known in the British Parliament and by French & German political economists than by anyone in or having influence upon our own government." If he succeeded in returning from California with $50,000 in his pocket, "people—capitalists & men controlling capital would have some real confidence in my practical sagacity, in my judgment of matters of business," he reasoned. In the end, Olmsted remained undeterred by his friend's appeal; "my interest in the Sanitary Commission has ceased," he told Bellows bluntly.[20]

Bellows attempted one last time to change Olmsted's mind by challenging his conclusion that the USSC had failed. To Bellows, organizational set-

[18] See Frederick Law Olmsted to Henry Whitney Bellows, July 25, 1863, in *FLO Papers*, 4:74.
[19] Henry W. Bellows to Frederick L. Olmsted, August 13, 1863, Olmsted Papers.
[20] Frederick L. Olmsted to Henry Bellows, August 16, 1863, Box, 641, USSC Papers. The Mariposa venture was a fiasco. Olmsted not only lost his own investments but was unable to collect over $11,000 owed him from his salary. By August 1865, still mired in the failing company, he expressed longings for the USSC, commenting that "it is the place where my affections lie." Olmsted quoted in Roper, *FLO*, pp. 275–76, 281.

backs were explained by the fact that the "war has been vaster, the army ten times larger, the whole field immensely broader than I contemplated." Conceding that the commission had been unable to secure a monopoly on relief during the war, Bellows blamed the government for not supporting the commissioners in "any of the exclusive pretensions we started with." The fault, he maintained, did not lie with the Sanitary Commission.[21]

Bellows lost the argument. For Olmsted, the combination of administrative frustrations and personal anxieties far outweighed his colleague's entreaties. He left his position as general secretary in September 1863. Word of his resignation shocked and saddened his colleagues. Upon hearing the news, Schuyler wrote to Olmsted that "it has taken every atom of life out of the work today."[22]

Olmsted's departure dramatized the deep frustrations engendered by commission work. His rationales for leaving, like Bellows's arguments for his staying, revealed the extent to which those commanding the organization failed to transform female warwork. Though the men who created the commission expected all who worked for it to conform to a bureaucratic ideal, they themselves were contemptuous of it. By attempting to impose grandiose political and ideological goals on a charity organization, they erected an unviable and cumbersome artifice incapable of attaining even its immediate, material goals.

Ultimately, the Sanitary Commission was unable to stimulate the personal loyalties necessary for sustaining intense, often unpopular work. At the same time, it was incapable of constructing the type of impersonal, thorough-going bureaucracy that might have been more impervious to the actions of any individual personality.[23] In some ways, the commission resembled a political movement or party attempting to use a structured machinery to wield political and educational influence more than it did a bureaucratic organization. The formula for organizational success was overly dependent on the vagaries of voluntary labor and on government backing. Lacking both, the members felt enveloped by a system they neither chose to create nor considered worth defending.

As the Sanitary Commission's operations became more conflict-ridden,

[21] Henry W. Bellows to Frederick L. Olmsted, August 18, 1863, Olmsted Papers.
[22] Louisa L. Schuyler to Frederick L. Olmsted, August 26, 1863, Olmsted Papers. See also Katherine P. Wormeley to Frederick L. Olmsted, September 2, 1863, Olmsted papers, on disappointment over his departure and worry over the USSC's future.
[23] See Peter M. Blau, "Weber's Theory of Bureaucracy," in *Max Weber*, ed. Dennis Wrong (Englewood Cliffs, N.J., 1970), p. 141.

its employees felt more pressured. Carrying out organizational goals in the face of overt public hostility and outside competition invariably heightened internal tensions. Correspondence among employees conveyed pent-up hostilities about the work as well as critical evaluations of the efforts of coworkers. Some felt overworked and undercompensated. The Christian Commission's insinuations about paid charity agents made others highly self-conscious about earning a living from benevolent work. Frederick Knapp rejected an increase in salary because, as he put it, "I do not want to and not willing to lay aside money out of my salary in this work."[24] John Newberry turned down an income of $3,000 and returned to his former rate of $2,000 because of the overwhelming "evidence from a great number of sources that high salaries are doing a great injury in the minds of many good men, and impairing the influence of the Commission."[25]

As the organization was losing ground in the struggle for popular loyalty and uncertainty about the Sanitary Commission's project was increasing, officers and employees began scrutinizing each other's behavior. As early as April 1863, Commissioner Agnew confided to Olmsted that the commission's reputation was failing because "of the bad character of so many of our employees." Observing that a number of agents were inferior to those of the Christian Commission, he added that the men "have been a fearful load for us to carry and should have been discharged months ago."[26] Dr. Joseph Parrish was particularly sensitive to the claims made by the CC of having superior agents, and advised Bellows that "we need to surpass this. Must sift out less than ideal men—keep only best in business ability or Christian excellence."[27] The tensions of meeting the Christian Commission's challenge gradually took a toll on relationships between officers as well. In late 1864, Bellows confided to his son that "jealousies have sprung up among our chief officers Jenkins & Knapp & Collins in my absence which have created much pain & given me serious anxiety."[28] There was little tolerance for dissent or dissatisfaction.

The great experiment was losing its soul, its passion, its vigor. In his own way, each of the commissioners expressed the realization that the work was failing. Along with ever more strident lashings-out at the Christian Commission, Democratic sympathizers, and military leaders, the commissioners also blamed themselves. They had miscalculated the nature of relief work

---

[24] Frederick N. Knapp to Henry Bellows, September 16, 1863, Box 641, USSC Papers.
[25] J. S. Newberry to George T. Strong, May 11, 1863, Box 636, USSC Papers.
[26] C. R. Agnew to Frederick L. Olmsted, April 24, 1863, Olmsted Papers.
[27] Joseph Parrish to Henry W. Bellows, November 22, 1864, Box 955, USSC Papers.
[28] Henry Bellows to "Son" [Russell Bellows], November 13, 1864, Bellows Papers.

and misread their public. As Frederick Knapp concluded: " 'the tone and drift' of the Sanitary Commission seem to [be] downward."[29]

The Union League Club

Though the commissioners were willing to admit some of the failings of their enterprise, and even to recognize that the organization might hamper their political ambitions, they were not ready to abandon the war as a vehicle for their nationalist aims. As they became more cognizant of popular resistance to their operations and nationalist rhetoric, they began to contemplate other means of spreading their message and influence. As Bellows later wrote, the commission's "intensely national" agenda had engendered considerable popular resentment: "Its own movements were embarrassed by the jealousy of States toward each other, and towards the National Government." In Bellows's postwar version of history, the commissioners prided themselves on their continued indifference to public hostility. "They would yield nothing to the intense feeling of State and local pride... which sought to create differences in the administration of their resources." But the necessity of separating overt support for the Republican party from the commission's aid activities became increasingly evident. Being of "one mind and one heart," the commissioners set out to create an exclusively political organization that would advance their broader partisan and propaganda aims. In February 1863 they formed the Union League Club of New York City.[30]

Inspired by the formation of a Union League Club in Philadelphia, Commissioner Wolcott Gibbs suggested the idea of a "patriotic club" to his colleagues. Receiving enthusiastic support from Bellows, Olmsted, and Strong, Gibbs composed a circular describing their intention of establishing a club, "the objects of which shall be to cultivate a profound national devotion ... to strengthen a love and respect for the Union, and discourage whatever tends to give undue prominence to purely local interests." Though imitative of the Philadelphia organization, the New York Union League Club remained distinct from the larger Union League movement that had spread through northern cities. Considering themselves members of a "hereditary natural aristocracy," endowed with special power to guide the public in attaining the proper nationalistic spirit, they presented themselves as private men devoted to promoting nationalist aims.

[29] Frederick Knapp to Henry Bellows, September 6, 1864, Box 951, USSC Papers.
[30] Bellows, *Union League Club*, pp. 5–7.

But if it posed as an independent organization founded by a cross-section of leading Republicans, New York's Union League Club was, as Bellows later acknowledged, "the child of the United States Sanitary Commission."[31] Its founders envisioned the club as select, private, and governed by secrecy; more importantly, they would guard its identification with the Sanitary Commission closely. Dr. Van Buren, for one, worried about the commissioners being associated with an overtly political, patriotic organization, fearing it might create dissension within the commission's ranks.[32] In considering how the new organization should function, Olmsted suggested to Gibbs that its leadership needed to be separated from association with the Sanitary Commission. "The Club should be as a Club quiet," Olmsted confided, "and as little as possible known by people not its members."[33]

When the club formally opened in May 1863, it had recruited 350 members, many from New York's merchant class. By the end of the war it claimed 800 members. Along with holding receptions for politicians and dignitaries, club members traveled to Washington to act as a lobby for pro-war interests. During the New York City draft riots, the Union League Club actively supported local and federal police in "crushing the rioters" and raised three "Negro regiments" to demonstrate support of federal war policy and hostility to the defiant white laboring class. In 1864, the club formed the Loyal Publication Society, which disseminated political tracts against Peace Democrats and patriotic literature designed for enlisted soldiers as well as the donating public.[34]

Schuyler's Leadership

Unlike her male colleagues, who were profoundly disheartened by the defection of soldiers' aid societies from the Sanitary Commission fold, Louisa Lee Schuyler interpreted homefront behavior as an occasion to renew her personal commitment to relief work. She did not conflate accusations about the commission with personal life choices, nor did she construe such criticisms as attacks on her integrity. For Schuyler, the Sanitary Commission's

[31] Ibid., pp. 5, 20–22; Frank L. Klement, *Dark Lanterns: Secret Political Societies, Conspiracies, and Treason Trials in the Civil War* (Baton Rouge, La., 1984), pp. 41–42.
[32] Paul Renard Migliore, "The Business of Union: The New York Business Community and the Civil War" (Ph.D. diss., Columbia University, 1975), pp. 180–81.
[33] Olmsted letter quoted in Bellows, *Union League Club*, p. 15.
[34] Bellows, *Union League Club*, pp. 53–62; Migliore, "Business of Union," pp. 182–200; Iver Bernstein, *The New York City Draft Riots: Their Significance for American Society and Politics in the Age of the Civil War* (New York, 1990), pp. 129–31, 157–61.

chief shortcoming was its failure thoroughly to communicate the inherent logic of its welfare premise, a logic she never questioned. Rather than retreat from the public limelight or resort to any sort of soul searching, Schuyler decided to forge ahead with a program to reform the bureaucracy and redesign propaganda strategies. Publicly, Schuyler displayed a resolute confidence in the organization and its system of auxiliary societies. In her published analysis of the questionnaire, she concluded that negative rumors were caused either by malicious gossip or by a grave deficiency in the commission's communications network.[35]

Privately, Schuyler was less confident about the organization's rectitude. As early as September 1862, she expressed concern about the rumors of corruption, confiding to Bellows that "where there is so much smoke there must be some fire," and suggesting that each large city open a public office where "every soldier who has been swindled can have his complaint registered & investigated."[36] But by the summer of 1863 she favored a massive publicity effort and an intensive canvassing campaign to overcome public doubts. The problem, she had concluded, lay less in the possibility of real corruption than in the misperceptions of the female public. Her own investigations into homefront rumors demonstrated that women needed to feel that they were part of the war effort and that their labors were not wasted.[37] The key to remedying the commission's plight was to reduce women's isolation from the central organization and the war.

Yet the process of shoring up the commission as a vehicle for the people's nationalism and philanthropy also underscored Schuyler's contradictory position vis-à-vis her male colleagues and her female constituency. Linked to the commissioners by class, religion, and a shared belief in the right and responsibility of elites to direct social welfare, she was still an unpaid female volunteer. She demonstrated some comprehension of the challenges faced by women in soldiers' aid societies, and was more mindful than her male colleagues of the time demands of household chores and the rigors of benevolent work. Though she never consciously articulated the duality of her position, Schuyler struggled to reconcile the demands of homefront women for greater accountability with the commission's insistence on streamlined efficiency. Her strategy, while mirroring in many ways the male

[35] Louisa Lee Schuyler, "Report of Corresponding Secretary of the Sub-Committee on Correspondence & Supplies," April 1, 1863, Box 669, USSC Papers.
[36] Louisa L. Schuyler to Henry Bellows, September 3, 1862, Box 642, USSC Papers.
[37] For responses to Schuyler's private investigations into homefront rumors, see Mrs. Susan S. Rogers to Louisa L. Schuyler, July 25, 1863; Susan Rogers to Miss Stevens, November 30, 1863, Box 671, USSC Papers.

commissioners' preoccupation with information and method, also discarded particularly repugnant rules and invented new ones to accord with female-dictated and local welfare customs.

In some instances, Schuyler demonstrated an almost steely determination to forge ahead with the USSC agenda. She intensified her injunctions to associate managers, calling on them to devote more energy to their assigned duties, to maintain regular contact with WCRA officers, and to push for greater homefront compliance. "Try & impress upon all that this work is not a temporary one," she wrote to the manager in Providence, Rhode Island. "After the war is over the time for beginning to think of it as such may come. . . . but now we must go ahead and keep at it & put all idea of stopping out of sight & mind."[38] She also kept a close watch on the organizing status of towns in the WCRA region and used this knowledge to implore associates to apply greater pressure to weak localities. Thus, she informed the manager from Albany County, New York, that of a total of thirty-nine post offices she counted a mere eight contributors, and she reminded Mrs. Mather, the Broome County, New York, manager, that only five villages had sent donations out of a total of forty-five towns under her jurisdiction.[39]

Yet at other moments, Schuyler exhibited uncharacteristic flexibility, permitting women to depart from established methods when it seemed the only means for sustaining support. In these moments, she seemed willing to disregard commission tenets in order to preserve warwork itself. While she urged greater regional mobilization, her instructions for organizing also included concessions to local charity practices: "We never attempt to get these village societies to pledge themselves to send entirely to the Commission," she advised one associate manager, remarking, "This they will not do."[40]

The *Bulletin*

As Schuyler expanded her contacts with homefront representatives, she also urged the commission to enlarge its role as a source of military and supply information. To provincial women who worried about the condition of Union troops and felt isolated from the daily events of the war, USSC circulars represented an important supplement to scanty newspaper accounts

---

[38] Louisa L. Schuyler to Mrs. Chase, June 16, 1863, Box 667, USSC Papers.
[39] Louisa L. Schuyler to Mrs. E. W. Barnes, June 4, 1863; Louisa Schuyler to Mrs. Henry Mather, June 11, 1863, Box 667, USSC Papers.
[40] Louisa L. Schuyler to Mrs. Henry S. Randall, June 4, 1863; L. Schuyler to Barnes, June 4, 1863, Box 667, USSC Papers.

Louisa Lee Schuyler. Oil portrait by Leon Bonnat, c. 1879 © Collection of The New-York Historical Society.

of military conditions. Schuyler had learned from both canvassers and women themselves that "the extent of our influence is in direct proportion to the amount & character of the correspondence and publications emanating from the office."[41]

[41] Louisa L. Schuyler to Frederick Knapp, December 28, 1863, Box 955, USSC Papers.

Having concluded that the irregular and officious nature of commission publications undermined relations with the female public, Schuyler promoted the idea of a regular paper that would disseminate commission-related war news and agents' reports from hospitals and camps in an accessible format. Such a publication would satisfy the wishes of homefront contributors to be kept informed about the state of their army and, at the same time, address the knotty problem of organizational accountability. In the fall of 1863 she exhorted Bellows to endorse the newspaper. "As to the *desirableness* of it—I can only Judge from the States of N.Y., Conn. Rhode Island and parts of Mass. & New Jersey, with whose Soldier's aid Societies I have been in constant correspondence for the past two & a half years." If the "thirst for information" from those areas was any indication, Schuyler argued, "I think there can be no doubt as to the desirableness of issuing such a paper."[42]

Schuyler envisioned a popular, well-written magazine that would offer lively articles on military ventures and sanitary conditions. She suggested that every issue include general news about the commission's work at the front; reports from military hospitals; a column titled "Notes on Nursing" (she suggested Elizabeth Blackwell as its author); information on soldiers' homes, pensions, bounties, and back pay; and correspondence from homefront branches. She believed "great writers" such as those found in the *Atlantic Monthly* would welcome the opportunity to reach thousands of households. And, "while carefully avoiding anything political," she recommended that "a good strong influence might be exerted in favor of the Union, & as a stimulant to patriotism."[43]

The first issue of the *Sanitary Commission Bulletin*, which appeared on November 1, 1863, attempted to strike a populist note by insisting that "those who furnish the money and supplies . . . have a right to more frequent and full accounts of what becomes of their charity." Published twice a month, and circulated among affiliated aid societies, associate members, and Union troops, the *Bulletin* signaled a new attempt to control the public narrative of the Commission and generate documentary evidence that would shape its historical record.[44]

[42] Louisa L. Schuyler to Henry W. Bellows, September 28, 1863, Box 955, USSC Papers.
[43] Ibid. Schuyler suggested Henry Longfellow, Oliver W. Holmes, and Nathaniel Hawthorne as contributors. See Louisa L. Schuyler to Henry Bellows, September 30, 1863, Box 955. Bellows discussed the outline of a newspaper with Bloor in March 1863. He agreed about "the importance of posting the Ladies in the freshest & most piquant incidents in our experience," and suggested having Mrs. Kirkland edit it, but added "a younger person & a man would be better." Henry W. Bellows to Alfred Bloor, March 12, 1863, Box 757, USSC Papers.
[44] *Bulletin*, November 1, 1863, 1:1.

Yet while the *Bulletin* appeared to represent a concession to public demands, it also stood as a new vehicle for wielding class authority. Employing a distinctly coercive tone, the first issue declared that because the commission met its responsibilities, it had the right to expect more explicit commitments from its auxiliaries. Announcing that the homefront needed to be inspired "anew," the editors placed any women with complaints on the defensive. "We have warned them from the first that they were enlisted for the war; that their industry and self-sacrifice would be taxed to the utmost," the first article began. Moreover, the work needed enlargement. "Ten thousand such noble women are not enough"; it required the support of "a hundred thousand; yes, five hundred thousand other women of similar views and feelings, before our supplies can be accumulated in adequate quantities."[45]

Ostensibly, the *Bulletin* offered the USSC new space to publicize its ideology, "its matured opinions in regard to the only safe and wise means of applying the gifts of the people to the relief of the army." The publication would stimulate female generosity and provide information to soldiers' families on such things as bounties, furloughs, and burials. In addition, it would demonstrate to "our moneyed men and institutions of wealth" that the commission was not "hampered by the want of abundant pecuniary resources."[46] Along with regular appeals for homefront support, the *Bulletin* would provide reports from agents on hospital conditions, prisoners of war, preventive sanitary techniques, supply needs, and information on acquiring soldiers' back pay and pensions.

If Schuyler had intended to provide a readable and useful publication tailored to the needs of homefront women, the *Bulletin* fell far short of the mark. Issue after issue contained long, dreary expositions on such subjects as the surgeon general's "Treatise on Hygiene," the health of the British Army, and the army classification of wounds. Rather than offering popularly written pieces by experienced writers, the *Bulletin* reprinted the elaborate rules governing its staff, written in formal, bureaucratic language. With the exception of occasional reports from Schuyler on WCRA affairs and a "Notes on Nursing" column (written not by the controversial Dr. Blackwell but by the celebrated Florence Nightingale), most of the *Bulletin's* articles were neither authored by nor directed to women.[47]

By the middle of 1864 disagreements over the *Bulletin* raged throughout

[45] Ibid.
[46] Ibid.
[47] Ibid., 1:30; November 15, 1863, 1:45; January 1, 1864, 1:140.

the organization, with female branch leaders claiming that women at the homefront found the publication obscure and irrelevant to their concerns and male commissioners defending it as a sound and balanced appeal to its many audiences. Curiously, given the commissioners' fractious response to Schuyler's questionnaire, they nonetheless followed her example, determining that before implementing any changes it was best to assess public opinion by means of a survey. Suspecting that he knew where the problems lay, Bloor sent a short questionnaire to branch officers to determine how many of their female correspondents desired "more information of a personal character, and less of a statistical nature."[48]

After querying associate managers in the WCRA territory, Schuyler informed Bloor that the paper was read extensively and with interest, particularly by those in the most remote areas. Observing that the "country people take more interest in the Com, are the hardest workers, & the most diligent readers," Schuyler noted that their most frequent criticism was that the articles were "too long." Complaints varied according to the type of economy within which particular women operated. "Those coming from manufacturing & commercial centres," and who were fluent in the language of the market economy, showed a predilection for precise data on cost efficiency. They speak of the "statistics, of articles telling how the money is spent, & showing the nature & extent of every department . . . as being of especial value to them," Schuyler observed. On the other hand, women from agricultural regions seemed more interested in reading detailed accounts about the personal impact of their labor; "letters . . . which represent the country villages" asked for descriptions of those scenes that "can make them realize the war ever more fully & the consequent importance of their work."[49]

Noting the particular difficulty of communicating the realities of warfare, Schuyler suggested that the paper needed "a little more anecdote, as that brings us into nearer sympathy with the soldier." After furnishing some ideas for improving it, including a full listing of pension agencies and short articles on directions for treating soldiers' wounds at home, she added that she "reserve[d] the right of saying all sorts of 'critical' things about the *Bulletin* in the future, as I have in the past." But if Schuyler avoided extensive criticism of the publication, her fellow WCRA officer Ellen Collins wrote to the commission with a contradictory assessment; "if I understand Miss Schuyler, the

[48] Alfred Bloor to Louisa Lee Schuyler, July 23, 1864, Box 954, USSC Papers.
[49] Louisa L. Schuyler to Alfred J. Bloor, September 26, 1864, Box 954, USSC Papers.

returns from ass. managers would indicate that they have found it interesting & valuable. My own impression had been rather unfavorable."[50]

Just as with Schuyler's questionnaire about homefront rumors, the commission used information it gathered from homefront women against them. The USSC's stated desire to meet public needs was disingenuous; all information was to serve the organization and help it fend off further attacks. When affiliated women criticized the *Bulletin* for being "too heavy" and "too much occupied with business reports and scientific matter," the commission rejected any proposal for revisions. It defended the format, explaining that the publication was intended to serve diverse audiences, including military physicians and the "money-giving public," and that catering only to the "sensibilities and affections of the homes" threatened the organization's broader goals.[51]

The Sanitary Commission was becoming weary of the resistant female public. From its perspective, the *Bulletin* more than adequately met women's need to know the destination and uses of their charity. Those who continued to cast aspersions on the organization were guilty of not reading the voluminous material it issued. Ignoring claims that the *Bulletin* was eminently unreadable, the commission became defiant. "It is easier and far pleasanter to sit and listen to chit-chat of somebody who denounces or slanders it, than to sit down and wade through what it has to say for itself in its publications," the *Bulletin* announced on April 1, 1864. "We have ourselves, more than once, listened to accusations against it from persons on whose table piles of the *Bulletin* were lying, at that moment, untouched."[52]

If the commission had initially responded to public complaints and criticism with a show of concern and an apparent willingness to improve distribution methods, it now responded with a degree of animosity. Less than a year after Schuyler's questionnaire, the commission announced that it resented the "spirit of cavilling and carping" emanating from the northern public.[53] When administrative treatments proved incapable of stemming the tide of popular resistance, the organization lost interest in debating the merits of its approach.

[50] Ibid. See also Louisa L. Schuyler to Joseph Parrish, September 28, 1864, Box 954; Ellen Collins to Joseph Parrish, October 1, 1864, Box 965, USSC Papers.
[51] *Bulletin*, February 1, 1864, 1:194; for other criticisms of the *Bulletin* see Mrs. Benjamin Douglas to Louisa Schuyler, November 1, 1864, Box 677, USSC Papers. Even after the war Schuyler planned to survey associate managers about the publication and solicit suggestions for improvement. See draft of questionnaire, July 30, 1865, Schuyler Papers.
[52] *Bulletin*, April 1, 1864, 1:322–33.
[53] Ibid., 1:322.

Calls for Branch Autonomy

The commission's refusal to reform the *Bulletin* represented to female branch leaders its growing propensity to make high-handed and autocratic decisions. As the commission hardened its stance toward aid societies and the public in general, the WCRA and other female-led branches felt increasingly at odds with the parent organization. Their limited decision making powers and the inability to effect practical reforms led many branch officers far from New York City to respond to public disaffection by seeking greater institutional independence. Geographic and social proximity to provincial communities provided these women with a special vantage point from which to gauge changing sentiments. By 1864, many branch leaders viewed the commission's attempts to dominate the mobilization and management of aid societies as encroachments on their own abilities to raise supplies and money to run branch operations.

Across the North, branch leaders parlayed their intimacy with the female homefront into claims for institutional autonomy, and issued directives that allowed for less than total commitment to a centralized plan. Success sometimes meant subverting Sanitary Commission directives, reinforcing informal ties among regional women, and sponsoring independent activities, including charity fairs, local fund-raising efforts, and acceptance of competing benevolent agencies. Calls for more branch autonomy challenged the philosophy of centralization and nationalism espoused by the commission. By the end of 1863, the impact of homefront skepticism and USSC intransigence began to shift the balance of power between branches and the commission.

For the WCRA, the first and most prestigious branch, strains in an already fragile relationship escalated, exacerbated by the personal and social ties that bound many of the women to the male commission leadership. In some ways, the initial responses of the Sanitary Commission and the Woman's Central Relief Association to the rumors of corruption had been similar. Both favored tighter organizational control and improved communication with the donating public. Neither perceived the organization's failures as inherent in the commission's nationalistic agenda or its rhetoric. Yet in deciding how to respond to the personal and political needs of the female public, the USSC and the WCRA arrived at divergent conclusions. Whereas the commission assumed that stricter administrative control would be sufficient to quiet fears about corruption, the WCRA recognized the importance of delegating responsibilities among subordinates and balancing the needs of army hospitals with those of northern communities.

For Louisa Lee Schuyler, the rift between the USSC and its female-led branches was especially corrosive. The WCRA stood in a capacity different from other Sanitary Commission branches. While it carried out the functions of the branches—managing the collection of supplies from local aid societies and receiving, sorting, and repacking donations for shipment to designated depots—its prestige as the first branch, its headquarters in New York City, and its oversight of a broad geographical area in the Northeast endowed it with a special status. Within the commission bureaucracy, responsibility for overseeing the management of the aid women provided fell to Corresponding Secretary Bloor, who conducted correspondence with the branches. Schuyler worked closely with Bloor, conferring on itineraries for canvassers and appeals to female associate managers as well as the preparation of circulars for public distribution. But precisely because the organizational and personal relationships between the male officers and WCRA women were close, the issue of where particular responsibilities lay became troublesome. For Schuyler, demands for greater branch autonomy threatened personal and social ties that transcended the commission and the war.

Unlike the USSC, which was able to keep operations such as the medical corps independent of public support, the WCRA's entire existence depended on its role as a trustworthy confidant of the women in its region. Any evidence that it was plagued with the same mismanagement and waste as the commission posed a serious threat. Sensitive to these issues, Schuyler began to assert herself more forcefully with her colleagues, warning them not to overstep their bureaucratic boundaries. In one instance, she informed Bloor that they needed to avoid reproducing each other's efforts, especially in distributing publications. Bloor agreed: "it would be a great waste for us to duplicate your issues, or you to duplicate ours." Even more damaging than squandering funds, he conceded, such a practice "would produce an impression of irregularity, extravagance and unbusiness-like habits on the part of the senders, among the receivers."[54]

Despite such seemingly cordial communications about coordinating procedures, after nearly three years of coexistence the bureaucratic compromise between the commission and the woman's association was breaking down. Beyond the problem of overlapping roles lay the new issue of how the WCRA should respond to the changing welfare needs of enlisted men.

[54] Alfred J. Bloor to Louisa L. Schuyler, May 29, 1863, Box 669, USSC Papers.

Female associates had convinced Schuyler that the commission was ignoring important opportunities to leave its mark on the growing field of soldier relief. Faced with numerous requests for assistance in dealing with the military bureaucracy, she concluded that the WCRA should enlarge its operations.

In a bold and unprecedented move, Schuyler decided to seek a redefinition of the WCRA's relationship to the USSC. In October 1863, Schuyler submitted a "Motion for Reorganization of WCRA." Citing the creation of the USSC in June 1861 as the most significant event in WCRA history, she explained how the women's organization had been effectively stripped of its power to train and send nurses and to purchase those goods that were not contributed "in sufficient quantity." Bellows's successful bid to appropriate the governance of female warwork not only had removed women from the decision-making process, it contradicted the WCRA's coordination of soldier relief activities. The WCRA's forced move into a secondary role placed it in a bureaucratic stranglehold, leaving little or no room for female initiative.

Though the ascendancy of the USSC had left the WCRA with only a small part of its original mandate, it maintained its responsibility for raising its own funds. Once just a "Sub-Committee," the work of "Correspondence & Supplies" had become the mainstay of WCRA work. To remedy the branch's truncated role, Schuyler's reorganization plan stipulated that the WCRA's executive committee be empowered to "devise ways & means for improving & increasing the usefulness of the Association." It called for the establishment of a special relief committee to "extend to invalid & discharged soldiers sympathy, aid and advice." To reinforce its enlarged special relief work, she proposed the creation of a "visiting committee" composed of women who would offer assistance to invalid soldiers in their homes or in hospitals.[55]

In the months that followed her call for reorganization, Schuyler exhibited an increased self-assurance, pressuring male commissioners to reevaluate policy and approve her plan. She pointed out to Frederick Knapp that by providing local aid societies with raw materials purchased at wholesale prices the commission could undercut "the double profits of country dealers." Drawing on her extensive WCRA correspondence, she asserted the

[55] Louisa L. Schuyler to Dr. Valentine Mott, October 1, 1863, Box 955, USSC Papers. The WCRA was already carrying out special relief on an informal basis, assisting returning soldiers in finding clothing, transportation, and lodging in New York City. *Bulletin*, November 15, 1863, 1:49; "Report of Special Committee upon Reorganization of WCRA, 'Articles of Reorganization,'" November 5, 1863, Box 955, USSC Papers.

public's desire to see the commission exploit its close proximity to Union troops by devoting special attention to the "soldier relatives and friends" of affiliated women. Schuyler was persuaded that abandoning one tenet of the federal principle—that the commission cares impartially for soldiers on the basis of need, regardless of where they come from—would increase the group's effectiveness, and argued that such small concessions would yield large returns in positive feelings toward the organization.[56]

In advocating an expansion of special relief services, Schuyler cited the numerous proposals her branch received from women offering to give personalized attention to wounded soldiers. She also cited the success of the WCRA's hospital directory system, which maintained a list of the names of those in military hospitals. The WCRA office was frequently besieged by women seeking information about sick relatives in army hospitals. What would it take, she asked rhetorically, "to spare a half hour to cheer those who are anxious and despondent, or to listen to the story of 'how the battle was fought.' " If the Christian Commission was profiting from the popular perception that the USSC was preoccupied with the physical rather than emotional condition of the soldiers, then it was incumbent upon the USSC to display similar levels of compassion.[57]

Schuyler's arguments proved successful. Without a formal announcement or public circular, the commission acceded to her reorganization plan. The WCRA expanded its operations to include relief for returning soldiers and visiting committees to assess soldiers' needs.[58]

The Woman's Council

Louisa Schuyler's new assertiveness came at an inauspicious moment for the Sanitary Commission. With household donations down, the USSC was relying heavily on monetary contributions to purchase supplies needed at the front; these supplies, in turn, were being distributed by an increasingly topheavy cadre of employees who required ever more supervision. Faced with the challenge of maintaining its presence at army hospitals, the commission viewed any major organizational deviation as a threat to its operations. Nonetheless, in the light of the growing ineffectiveness of central direction, the opening for regional initiatives was considerable, and other branch

[56] Louisa L. Schuyler to Frederick Knapp, December 28, 1863, Box 955, USSC Papers.
[57] Ibid.
[58] See *Third Annual Report of the Woman's Central Association of Relief, May 1, 1864* (New York, 1864), Box 993, USSC Papers, on visiting committees and special relief.

women throughout the North moved in to claim the authority they believed they deserved and could best execute.

By the end of 1863, homefront organization was in shambles. Soldiers' aid societies that were not disaffected or rebellious were tired or broke. Though one associate manager cited "no complaints of the Commission for some time," she nevertheless determined that the societies under her purview suffered from a more general malaise: "The trouble seems rather, lack of money, lack of time, or the right kind of energetic determined women to carry the matter through."[59] Contributions of handmade goods had been low for some time. Throughout 1863 the WCRA reported that receipts of donations had "diminished greatly" from the levels reached in 1862. Schuyler had expected that her bureaucratic innovations—assigning associate managers to oversee local voluntarism and providing free transportation for supplies—would revive warwork and relieve some of the financial burdens assumed by small villages. But by the end of the year, the results were paltry. In a conspicuous departure from her customarily sympathetic tone, Schuyler berated her constituency for its lack of commitment. "There are few loyal members of a community . . . who cannot give their twenty, or at least ten, cents a month . . . there are few women who are unable *if they want to,* to give two hours of their time every week to the sewing society."[60] On February 1, 1864, the WCRA reported that during the previous nine months contributions of bedding and clothing were "only half as much monthly as last year."[61]

If women were growing uneasy about demands for more aid at the front, they were at the same time redefining war relief work to concentrate on the needs of returning soldiers. Across the country, female branch leaders became inundated with requests for assistance to soldiers that extended beyond military hospitals and troop stations. Injured and indigent soldier-citizens were being discharged and released to homefront communities in regular waves; many needed assistance in finding employment and housing, and others required long-term hospitalization.

In the context of growing demands for services to veterans and for increasing branch autonomy, the Sanitary Commission acted to head off any further deterioration of its system and authority. Perhaps taking its cue from the women themselves, who had made clear their desire for face-to-

[59] Miss Jane L. Hardy to Miss Angelina Post, Ithaca, N.Y., October 24, 1864, Box 677, USSC Papers.
[60] *Second Annual Report,* p. 4; *Third Semi-Annual Report of the Woman's Central Association of Relief, November 1, 1863* (New York, 1863), pp. 6–7, Box 993, USSC Papers.
[61] "Treasury of Sanitary Commission Report," February 1, 1864, Box 669, USSC Papers.

face contact, it decided to convene a meeting of women delegates. It invited representatives from the WCRA, other branches, and local aid societies to the commission headquarters in Washington, D.C., to discuss women's work and the efficacy of recent changes in communications and the supply system. In preparation for the meeting, the USSC asked each woman delegate to compile a list of subjects she considered important for discussion.

In a letter to Frederick Knapp, Schuyler summarized some of the dispatches she received, underscoring the anxiety numerous women experienced as a result of lengthy delays in receiving government pensions. Soldiers' families were being forced to wait up to fifteen months to receive the money due them, she reported, and they wanted to know if "govt congress [is] going to do anything about it?" Women also wanted to know more about the commission's plans for disabled soldiers. As the associate secretary of special relief in the East, Knapp was in a unique position to tell Schuyler if his experience "show[s] that these men are taken care of by their own townspeople, or will it be necessary to establish permanent 'homes' for them?"[62] To prepare for the convention, Schuyler gathered statistics on her branch's achievements. The efforts of the previous year yielded mixed results. Although 133 new societies had been added to the 415 existing societies in the WCRA region and thirty-two female associate managers had been hired, the Christian Commission was still making serious inroads into USSC strength. And the war was far from over.[63]

On January 15, 1864, sixty-five representatives from eastern and western branches, as well as individual women, such as Dorothea Dix, "distinguished for their activity in the public service," attended the Sanitary Commission's Woman's Council in Washington, D.C. The WCRA alone had twelve delegates in attendance. The agenda was clearly outlined. The USSC was anxious for feedback on its latest propaganda efforts, including appraisals of the system of associate managers, the influence of canvassing agents, and the reception of the *Bulletin*. In return, the women wanted to know about the cost efficiency of the organization, the expense of printing, and the security precautions taken in transporting supplies to the front.[64]

Bellows opened the Woman's Council with a speech that provided few surprises; he lectured the women on current methods of providing medical relief for the troops and reviewed the commission's bureaucratic structure. To demonstrate the type of commitment he expected from his audience of

---

[62] Louisa L. Schuyler to Frederick Knapp, January 14, 1864, Box 951, USSC Papers.
[63] WCRA, Notes, January 1, 1864, Box 951, USSC Papers.
[64] *Bulletin*, February 1, 1864, 1:193.

unpaid volunteers, Bellows impressed upon them that the members of the standing committee sacrificed three to five hours a day for the commission and enjoyed each other's company "more than that of anyone else—except their wives and children." Insisting that the "first duty" of the commission was to prevent sickness, he defended the employment of eighty surgeons by the USSC, the medical tracts distributed among them, and the 200 agents, who carried out a vast system of sanitary inspections. He preempted any discussion of the system of paid agents by insisting that attempts at using volunteer agents routinely failed; "instead of helpers they were very apt to become nuisances."[65]

Envisioning the meeting as a way of pulling female branches back into the fold, the commissioners offered women delegates opportunities to talk with officers, examine USSC headquarters, and see firsthand the range of its endeavors. In a carefully orchestrated itinerary, they escorted female delegates to local soldiers' homes and lodges, storehouses, and hospitals. They listened to their questions and recorded their responses. But once again, the commission's best-laid plans were foiled by the uses women made of them. In the end, the Woman's Council served primarily to cement contacts among women delegates and provide validation for autonomous branch pursuits. Gathered together in one place, delegates learned that other branches had hit upon identical methods to promote warwork, adopting techniques that softened the rigidity of commission directives. Abby May announced that the Boston branch decided not to solicit monetary contributions from rural areas and small villages, leaving these locales to use whatever funds they had to purchase materials. The same decision had been reached by Schuyler earlier in the year.[66]

Officially, the commission declared the council a triumph and professed that its innovations were enjoying wide support among women. The system of regional associate managers had produced quantifiable results, with counties assigned managers yielding "three times the amount of supplies" as those with none. This work, the commission acknowledged, resulted from the efforts of women who wrote up to seven letters to one town or personally visited, as in the case of one manager, "forty different towns." Even

[65] "Memoranda of the Proceedings of the Women's Council," Washington, D.C., January 18, 19, 20, 1864, Box 951, USSC Papers. As with the WCRA, Sanitary Commission officers were not consistent in the way they recorded the words "woman" and "women," in this case, referring to the 1864 Woman's Council as the Women's Council.
[66] Ibid. After comparing the correspondence of the WCRA with that of the New-England Women's Auxiliary Association, Schuyler found that both groups wrote informal and friendly, rather than "business-like," letters to local women.

"nests of copperheadism" were vulnerable to such persistent campaigns. Admitting the existence of strong disagreements about the *Bulletin's* format, the commission nevertheless contended that it had persuaded the women that its multiple functions precluded tailoring the publication specifically to women.[67]

In contrast, the most Schuyler could claim for the meeting was that women "came away feeling richer for having seen and known each other."[68] In its single procedural innovation, the meeting announced a plan for county councils: smaller, more frequent meetings that would draw together representatives of village aid societies every three or six months. It also suggested that associate managers convene their own councils from time to time.[69]

Like the *Bulletin*, the Woman's Council demonstrated the inability of the Sanitary Commission to establish a meaningful dialogue with its female constituency. Once more the commission assumed that merely flattering women or listening to their complaints was enough to quiet criticism. Although most female branch officers maintained their positions for the duration of the war and cooperated whenever possible with the commission plan, by the time they had shown up in Washington, D.C., many had already taken bold steps to assert greater control over soldier relief work in their regions. Whether they cloaked their efforts in the altruistic language of benevolence or the lofty ideal of patriotism, these women sensed that the war was undercutting rather than enhancing their social and political visibility. If the commission was proving unsatisfactory as the venue for their benevolent and patriotic goals, they would have to strike out on their own. The crude selfishness that Bellows blamed for the public's weak nationalism was not so much the result of any rampant individualism as it was a sign of the serious inequities that marked northern society. Neither the commission nor the war was able to bridge the regional, class, and gender divisions that defined the American polity.

[67] *Bulletin*, February 1, 1864, 1:194–95.
[68] *Third Annual Report*, p. 5.
[69] Brockett and Vaughan, *Woman's Work in the Civil War*, pp. 534–35.

7

"FAIR MANIA": BRANCH AUTONOMY AND LOCAL CIVIC PRIDE

There was no more stark demonstration of the female-led branches' desire to assume independence from the commission than the fairs they produced during the last two and a half years of the war. As Louisa Schuyler pushed for a realignment of the relationship between the headquarters and the WCRA and pursued ways of tailoring national relief needs to the realities of local welfare commitments, other female branch leaders sought ways to achieve greater institutional and fiscal autonomy from the New York–based commission. Although in most towns and cities, both male and female civic leaders organized sanitary fairs, these events were initiated by northern women and drew upon feminine forms of antebellum benevolence and reform. In adopting the traditional charity fair to raise funds for soldier relief, women across the homefront reclaimed control over their benevolent labors and the means through which they made their patriotism public.

The first fair was the inspiration of the two most prominent women of the Chicago branch, known as the Northwestern Sanitary Commission. In the fall of 1863, Mary Livermore and Jane C. Hoge proposed a large-scale fair to raise $25,000 to support branch expenses and assist the USSC.[1] The

[1] Jane Hoge had years of experience in church and reform organizations before the Civil War. In 1858, she founded the Home for the Friendless to serve poor widows and children. After two of her sons enlisted, she cared for the sick of one regiment at Camp Douglas in Chicago. Together with Mary Livermore, she began working for the Northwestern Sanitary Commis-

idea of a charity fair was nothing new. In the decades before the Civil War, fairs were employed by benevolent organizations and reform movements to raise funds and mobilize public support. In 1851 women from upstate New York held a Grand Anti-Slavery Festival to raise money for a coalition of abolitionist organizations.[2]

During the early years of the Civil War, fairs were among numerous events held in northern communities to benefit departing soldiers. "Every city, town and village had its fair, festival, party, picnic, excursion, concert and regular subscription fund," recalled Livermore.[3] In fact, the women of the Northwestern Sanitary Commission were not the first in Chicago to plan a sanitary fair. According to Livermore, Chicago children "from nine to sixteen years of age" were "seized with a veritable sanitary-fair mania" during the summer of 1863, holding bazaars on the lawns of their middle-class homes and collecting an impressive $300 on behalf of the commission.[4]

For northern women living far away from the war's battles as well as from the centers of political and social power, fairs were an especially appealing medium for demonstrating political allegiances and charitable skills. Sanitary fairs offered women highly public venues for raising large sums of money, a sure means for claiming public attention. Though Livermore claimed that one of the chief purposes of the Northwestern Fair was to "reveal the worth" and legitimate the claims of the Sanitary Commission, she was nonetheless explicit that it was planned and executed by women, "receiving no assistance from men." By the time she penned a memoir of her wartime experiences, Livermore had little interest in reigniting old feuds with USSC leaders. But she still stressed that the Chicago fair offered her and other women visibility for the management and execution of a major event. "The great fairs that followed were the work of men as well as of women, from their very incipiency," she wrote, "but this fair was the work of women."[5]

Both Livermore and Hoge were struck by the degree to which their

---

sion, which organized in the fall of 1861. The two women also served as agents for Dorothea Dix, recruiting women for hospital duty in the West, touring military hospitals in Illinois and Missouri to investigate reports of Sanitary fraud, and traveling to the warfront to visit Grant's army and care for injured soldiers. See Wayne C. Temple, "Jane Currie Blaikie Hoge," in *NAW*, 2:199–201.

[2] Nancy A. Hewitt, *Women's Social Activism and Social Change: Rochester, New York, 1822–1872* (Ithaca, 1984), pp. 150–51.

[3] Livermore, *My Story of the War*, p. 409.

[4] Ibid., pp. 152–53. Livermore reported that rural children also became involved in this "fair mania," sending small contributions accompanied by personal letters (p. 154).

[5] Ibid., pp. 411–13.

project provoked ridicule and fear among Sanitary Commission men and local politicians. While the commissioners "languidly approved" of their plans, Livermore remembered that they "laughed incredulously" at the suggestion that the fair would raise $25,000. As this first fair was "an experiment," wrote Livermore, and "pre-eminently an enterprise of women, . . . the city of Chicago regarded it with indifference, and the gentlemen members of the Commission barely tolerated it." Hoge concurred, remarking that because "it was emphatically 'The Women's Fair,' " male peers "shook their heads and prophesied failure."[6] What began as a fund-raising tactic soon had become a symbol for branch independence.

Undeterred, the women mounted a campaign to muster popular support and enthusiasm. Envisioning a gargantuan event with the participation of businesses, farms, and individuals from Chicago and its environs, they organized "fair meetings" throughout the region to raise money and collect artifacts, and publicized the upcoming event in local newspapers. Livermore and Hoge personally corresponded with governors, congressmen, military officers, clergymen, and teachers, whose support they considered necessary to ensure success. But no appeals were as numerous or as earnest as those addressed to women of the region. In one instance, the organizers shipped from their offices "seventeen bushels of mail matter" relating to fair preparations.[7]

Fair organizers "ransacked" neighboring towns for any salable item, while mechanics and manufacturers sent everything from barrels of cologne to refined coal oil. The women ordered special buildings constructed to house the exhibits and sale booths, and persuaded the railroads to run excursion trains at low prices to bring in rural crowds.[8] Their strategies worked. Indeed, as Livermore noted, branch efforts were so impressive that eventually "even men became inoculated with the fair mania," coming forward to donate money and merchandise and assisting the women in their work.[9]

In October 1863, the Northwestern Sanitary Fair opened with considerable fanfare. A three-mile procession of military companies, country women, farmers in wagons laden with agricultural goods, and carriages of children singing "John Brown's Body" wended its way through Chicago's streets. With courts, post offices, public schools, banks, and even the Board

[6] Ibid.; Jane C. [Blaikie] Hoge, *The Boys in Blue; or Heroes of the 'Rank and File'* (New York, 1867), pp. 333–34.
[7] Livermore, *My Story of the War*, p. 413.
[8] Ibid., pp. 415–16, 429.
[9] Ibid., pp. 412–17. See also Henshaw, *Our Branch*, p. 210.

of Trade closed in honor of the inaugural ceremonies, the entire city stood ready to become part of the spectacle. For two weeks "the multitude came and went," while the newspapers provided daily coverage of the fair's progress, invariably reading political meanings into each public display of excitement. Noting the "bands of music playing patriotic airs, bands of young men and women singing patriotic songs, groups of children singing their cheerful and loyal school songs," the Chicago *Tribune* proclaimed it was "a grand, sublime protest, on behalf of the people against the poltroons and traitors who were enemies to the government, and opposed to the war."[10]

Financially, the Northwestern Sanitary Fair was an unqualified success, far exceeding its original goal by raising over $100,000. Both the city of Chicago and the Sanitary Commission were swayed by the spectacle and the financial boon it provided to their coffers.[11] And though it grabbed the attention of the city for days, engaging Chicagoans in a consuming frenzy in the name of soldier relief, the Northwestern Fair never lost its identification with women. Nowhere did the female managers make their ownership of the event as visible as in the closing ceremonies. Attended by young female waiters dressed in patriotic costumes "of their own devising," Livermore and Hoge hosted the festivities. Significantly, the featured speaker was Anna Dickinson, a twenty-year-old feminist. This "second Joan of Arc," as Livermore called her, gave a series of lectures that kept "an immense audience spell-bound."[12]

Impressed with the fiscal and public relations benefits of the Chicago fair, women in Cleveland, Boston, Pittsburgh, and St. Louis quickly followed suit, drawing up plans for their own regional events. Though all called themselves "Sanitary" fairs and donated much of the money raised to the commission's central office, each was organized and run by committees composed of local civic leaders. These large urban fairs resembled one another in the types of goods collected for sale and in the historical tableaux and war memorabilia they offered for consumption.[13] But while the Chicago and subsequent fairs impressed Sanitary Commission leaders as effective fundraising schemes, their popularity also posed serious problems

[10] Chicago *Tribune*, October 28, 1863, quoted in Livermore, *My Story of the War*, p. 419.
[11] Henshaw, *Our Branch*, pp. 215–18; Livermore, *My Story of the War*, p. 455; "The Great Northwestern Sanitary Fair," *Bulletin*, December 1, 1863, 1:65–71.
[12] Livermore, *My Story of the War*, pp. 446–47.
[13] Robert H. Bremner, *The Public Good: Philanthropy and Welfare in the Civil War Era* (New York, 1980), pp. 63–64. A number of fair committees persuaded President Lincoln to donate drafts of his Emancipation Proclamation and Gettysburg address for auction. Lincoln's addresses had already attained the status of war relics.

for the parent organization. If not adequately controlled, such outpourings of homefront generosity directed through local organizations threatened to divert attention from the commission's own supply network. The fairs also jeopardized the disciplined charitable habits that the commission had tried to instill in the female public. Even more problematic was the fact that such independent activities accentuated the growing strength of the female-led branches.

Given the existing public confusion about the relationship between the central organization and its regional branches, the commission went to great lengths to assert that the vast sums collected by the sanitary fairs did nothing to aid the central treasury.[14] In one public document, Bellows warned that the extensive press coverage of the fairs had led people to assume that the commission was awash in new money when, in fact, it was in great need of contributions from the public. Acknowledging that the money raised from these ventures might "relieve the Central Treasury partially from the necessity of buying," he hastened to add that they contributed "nothing to the general work of the Commission." Indeed, pointedly belittling branch initiatives, Bellows concluded that "these great Fairs have not, strictly speaking, been conducted in the interest of the Sanitary Commission of the United States."[15]

The Metropolitan Fair

The fairs' momentum was unstoppable. Ever ready to take the public's pulse, the commissioners concluded that exploiting the concept to their own advantage was easier than trying to quell fair fever. No sooner had the Chicago fair closed its doors than the Sanitary Commission announced plans to sponsor a fair of its own in New York City. Recognizing the symbolic benefit of making women the visible organizers of fairs, and hoping to delegate to others the unpaid labor required by such an event, Sanitary Commission officers tried to enlist the women of the WCRA to assume responsibility for the USSC fair. In November 1863, Bloor wrote to Ellen Collins urging WCRA officers to consider organizing something in New York. "It's not only that such a Fair . . . brings a great deal of grist to the Commission's mill," he argued; "it is incalculable what a vast amount of good is done to the National cause."[16] But the WCRA women were un-

[14] *Bulletin*, January 15, 1864, 1:161–63.
[15] "Supplement" to no. 69, December 28, 1863, *Documents*, 2:2–3.
[16] Alfred J. Bloor to Ellen Collins, November 10, 1863, Box 656, USSC Papers.

moved by such appeals. Already sensitive about being treated simply as an extension of the organization they had founded, and concerned about the long-range impact of the fairs on regular relief work, they declined to participate in the commission's New York fair.

Still considering such charity functions the proper purview of women, and in this case wanting to feature names that were recognizable to New York's propertied classes, the commissioners turned to their wives and female relatives, as well as to the wives of fellow Union League Club members, to head the women's committee of what came to be called the Metropolitan Fair. They appointed Mrs. Hamilton Fish as president, George Strong's wife, Ellen, as treasurer, and Agnew's sister-in-law, Miss Cavendish Nash, as assistant secretary. The "Ladies Committee" which also included such prominent figures as Mrs. John Jacob Astor, Mrs. Francis Leiber, Mrs. Alexander Hamilton, Mrs. Morris Ketchum, and Mrs. August Belmont, was in charge of coordinating the thousands of items donated to the fair's departments, organizing specialized stalls, and supervising the necessary voluntary labor.[17]

Though structurally similar to previous fairs, the Metropolitan Fair represented a break with its predecessors. For one thing, the Sanitary Commission had organized this event to serve the parent organization rather than a branch. In typical commission style, it sought to maximize the cosmopolitan temper of the fair not only by involving the city's major financial and businesses interests and its leading artistic and literary institutions but also by creating companion fair committees in London, Paris, and Rome, imbuing this fair with an international status to which no other could aspire.[18] But the most significant way in which the Metropolitan Fair deviated structurally from the previous fairs was its management by elite men. While two hundred women were selected for their "taste, energy and talents" to head the various committees, a group of three hundred men was appointed to handle all the business dealings for the Metropolitan Fair, "matters which ladies could not be expected to deal with."[19]

Officially the men, "representing the business heads of the various industrial, commercial, trading, locomotive, financial and charitable interests of

[17] *New York Tribune*, April 4, 1864; Strong, April 4, 1864, *Diary*, 3:424. The wives of some commissioners had participated in other USSC work. Eliza Bellows and Ellen Strong were among twelve women who traveled (with servants) on commission hospital ships in May 1862. See Henry Bellows to wife, May 8, 1862, Bellows Papers; Strong, May 5, 1862, *Diary*, 3:223–24.
[18] Notes in Strong, *Diary*, 3:417.
[19] Strong, April 1, 1864, Diary, Strong Papers.

the metropolis," were to abide by the wishes of the women.[20] But tensions flared regularly between the male and female committees. Strong concluded—in no small part because of his wife's role on the women's committee—that the men were great impediments to the smooth running of the affair. After a heated controversy over the inclusion of games of chance at the fair, the Ladies Committee agreed to a ban on lotteries or raffles. But Mrs. Hamilton Fish was indignant that the women were the targets of "fanatical attacks from men," who blamed them for "debunking the public morals & corrupting the public virtue," and directed Bellows to announce the decision to ban gambling succinctly and without editorial comment.[21] When the women petitioned for a large geographical area to house the fair, the men objected. "The ladies have failed to convince their inert and stupid masculine colleagues," Strong wrote in his diary, "that the Fair will be a disastrous failure and a disgrace to New York without at least four times the area yet secured for it." According to Strong the women "were despondent," and when he heard that they were prepared to advertise in the local papers that "the Metropolitan Fair was given up and would not come off at all" he suggested they first appeal for redress to the commission's standing committee, "which expressly reserved the right to decide between the two committees, male and female." But arbitration accomplished little; only after the women's committee appealed directly to the mayor did it secure an agreement for the construction of a large building in Union Square.[22]

Disagreements between the men and women running the fair persisted. A few weeks after the fairgrounds debate, Strong observed that "the quantity of gossip, intrigue, and personal pique that grows out of the Fair and its hundred committees is stupendous and terrible." The "executive he-committee" was again attempting to appropriate the authority of the women, this time over whether to charge admission. Shocked at "this piece of insolent, monied dirtiness," Strong attacked the men as mere parvenus, "without substantial culture and refinement," "whose bank accounts are all they can rely on for social position." As far as the commissioners were concerned, Strong was convinced that, like himself, "the husbands and brothers will, of course, side with [the ladies]."[23] Ironically, while members of the

[20] *Bulletin*, December 15, 1863, 1:98–99.
[21] Mrs. Hamilton Fish to H. W. Bellows, February 19, 1864, Box 641, USSC Papers.
[22] Strong, March 8, 1864, *Diary*, 3:412–13. Strong may have taken undue credit for resolving the crisis, as Miss Nash wrote to him that the ladies' committee "beg to leave to appeal to the higher court" for a decision on the issue of space allotment for the fair. See C. Nash to Geo. T. Strong, March 7, 1864, Box 951–52, USSC Papers.
[23] Strong, March 28, 1864, and April 2, 1864, *Diary*, 3:419–20, 423–24.

commission's standing committee invariably agreed with their female peers working on the fair, the incompatibility of the male and female fair committees mirrored many of the conflicts that Sanitary Commission men had experienced with the female branch leaders. Whether the issue was the politicized content of war relief work or the way in which charitable labors now commanded public respect, it was evident that once again women's dominance of benevolence was being called into question by powerful men.

Notwithstanding the conflicts that surrounded its preparation, the Metropolitan Fair emerged with a form that reflected both the class perspective of its managers and the political tenor of the commission. Though a short-lived event, it imitated the other cross-class cultural experiments created by New York's liberal intelligentsia in the decade before the war. Just as Peter Cooper had envisioned an institution that would bind together the city's antagonistic class interests, and Frederick Law Olmsted and Calvert Vaux had envisioned Central Park as a staging ground for the better classes and the masses to share in democratic urban leisure, so the Metropolitan Fair advanced a harmonious rendition of industrial, urban life and a romanticized vision of the Union.

The New York fair, its planners explained, was not to be "a mere fancy fair on a large scale," but a visual and theatrical event with explicit nationalist goals. Setting out their scheme for a citywide event that would uplift the poor while not degrading the elite, they described their intention of producing something that "must be democratic, but not vulgar; elegant, but not exclusive; fashionable, but not frivolous; popular, but not mediocre."[24] The public was expected to consume more than the articles for sale; it was also to absorb a vision of a diverse, multi-class, peaceable culture, efficiently run by the city's ruling elites. Accordingly, when the fair's managers planned a daily newspaper to run for the duration of the fair, they decided that instead of expanding the press's coverage of each day's events the *Spirit of the Fair* would be a "paper of rare literary excellence." Day after day the paper served up sentimental poetry, patriotic stories, and personal testimonials about military life, seemingly politically innocuous and far removed from the daily life of New Yorkers at the homefront.[25]

But the goal of providing a cohesive ideological message took on special political content in a city deeply divided about federal war policies. Occurring less than a year after the New York City draft riots of the summer of

[24] "The Metropolitan Fair," *Bulletin*, February 1, 1984, 2:201.
[25] *Spirit of the Fair*, New York, no. 2, April 6, 1864, p. 15. New York papers gave the fair substantial coverage; the New York *Herald* even published a special fair supplement for each day of the event.

1863, the fair offered New York's upper classes a way of reasserting their social authority over the city's population. More than any other event during the war, the draft riots dramatized the deep social and economic cleavages within northern society. To the city's immigrant white laboring classes, hard-hit by declining wages and long fearful that the demands of abolitionists would lead to bitter job competition with a flood of newly freed slaves, the passage of the Emancipation Proclamation signaled the Republican party's disregard of their interests. Indeed, the riots constituted a rejection by many in the white working class of the city's elite leadership and the social order it promoted.[26]

With elite New Yorkers still nervous about the prospect of public disorder, the fair's leaders concluded that if the power of persuasion failed to ensure a consensus, other means of imposing order were necessary. Anticipating that the partisan, upper-class message of the fair might be sufficiently overt to incite opposition, the commission consulted with city police and fire departments about, as Strong put it, "the fearful possibility of fire, panic, and slaughter." Strong himself arranged for an earthen embankment to be constructed at the base of the fair building to prevent "any malignant, devilish Copperhead or sympathizer from poking a little lump of cotton or of rags, saturated with camphene, under the floor."[27]

When the Metropolitan Fair opened its doors on April 4, 1864, the city's attention was riveted to the mammoth event. Mayor George Opdyke proclaimed the fair's opening day a holiday and suspended all city business. The *New York Tribune* described the "eager thousands" who waited amid buildings that "blossomed with bunting" while, as "the Stars and Stripes streamed in the bright sunshine," the streets were festooned with "the many-hued uniforms of the military." The opening ceremonies offered a respectable blend of patriotism and religion, beginning with a choir singing the Star Spangled Banner, an opening prayer, and an Army Hymn.[28] Ten thousand troops were assembled on the fair grounds for a grand military

[26] Disproportionately vulnerable to a draft law that permitted wealthier citizens to purchase substitutes for themselves, workers viewed the imposition of conscription as a class-based assault by Republican Party leaders. See Iver Bernstein, *The New York City Draft Riots: Their Significance for American Society and Politics in the Age of the Civil War* (New York, 1990); Emerson David Fite, *Social and Industrial Conditions in the North during the Civil War* (New York, 1963), p. 276. In a gesture of defiance to working-class resistance, the WCRA kept its Cooper Union office open during the riots. See Ellen Collins to Alfred Bloor, July 21, 1863, Box 955, USSC Papers.

[27] Strong, April 2, 1864, *Diary*, 3:423.

[28] *New York Tribune*, April 4 and 5, 1864.

parade.[29] Inside the fair buildings, New York's propertied classes had an opportunity to present themselves as both patriotic and powerful. The *Evening Express* described those who "thronged the Palace Garden Building" as "the most prominent of our merchant princes with their wives and daughters, our literati and artists, the fashion and beauty of the great Metropolis of the Union."[30] Strong was delighted to see "well-dressed people" among "showy decorations."[31]

But the symbolism for the audience extended beyond nationalistic gestures and revealed the particular gender dynamics of this sanitary fair. In striking contrast to the Northwestern Fair, the women of the executive committee of the New York fair were barred from the inaugural proceedings; the men had refused them places on the platform. Though the Ladies' Committee was symbolically presented with the "contents" of the Fair, Mr. Joseph H. Choate was chosen to respond "in behalf of the Ladies Committee." Strong recorded that the women were mortified by their exclusion, many "almost tearful about it."[32]

Over the next three weeks, between 10,000 and 30,000 visitors crowded into the fair's two custom-built structures on Fourteenth Street and Union Square.[33] People either purchased season tickets or paid separately for each entrance and special event. But the ticket prices—fifty cents at the entrance and twenty-five cents for special departments—limited access to the most comfortable classes. Both the *Times* and the *Tribune* noted the predominance of "well-dressed persons" and private carriages lining all the nearby streets. While acknowledging the crush of patrons, they cautioned that such high prices—two dollars if one wanted to see everything—were counterproductive. The political and ideological value of the commission lay in its ability to bring home "a sense of the stern realities of the battlefield." Thus, it behooved its leaders to admit the working public to purchase some souvenir or "non-luxury" item to stimulate a united "popular sympathy," while also helping to fill the commission's coffers. Great international fairs, observed the *New York Times*, usually set aside certain days each week for lower ticket prices.[34] Nonetheless, only a few days after the fair opened, the

---

[29] *New York Times*, April 4, 1864, Box 1003, USSC Papers.
[30] *Evening Express*, April 5, 1864, Box 1003, USSC Papers.
[31] Strong, April 6, 1864, *Diary*, 3:425.
[32] *Spirit of the Fair*, April 6, 1864, p. 12; Strong, April 4, 1864, *Diary*, 3:424.
[33] *A Record of the Metropolitan Fair, Held in Aid of the United States Sanitary Commission, New York, April 1864* (New York, 1867), p. 187.
[34] *New York Tribune*, April 9, 1864; *New York Times*, April 12, 17, 1864.

managers raised the admission price to one dollar, claiming the need to alleviate crowding. Alfred Bloor even proposed charging two or three dollars, noting that "it will be crowded even at a high price," while reminding his colleagues that at the Boston fair, the "real purchasers" were let in before the opening hour.[35]

Inside the fair buildings, New Yorkers were presented with an extensive array of articles, from carriages, furniture, soaps, dry goods, boats, and machinery to sewing machines, hats, and lingerie (fig. 13). Donations from regional merchants, farmers, artisans, and individuals formed the bulk of the commodities available.[36] The *World* delighted in pointing out that normal market behavior did not apply in a charity market, where the goal was to sell or spend as much as possible. "Fair ladies, who have passed their lives in tormenting shopmen and shopwomen, become shopwomen themselves," the paper quipped; "for a brief space thrift is pronounced odious by common consent." There were thematic displays such as the Knickerbocker Kitchen, fitted in colonial style, a replica of Mathew Brady's photographic gallery, featuring "portraits of Generals, groups of sailors" and "among the finest portraits of General and Mrs. McClellan," and stalls labeled the Machinery Department, Arms and Trophies, Lingerie Department, House Furnishings Department, Mathematical and Nautical Instruments, and Indian Rubber Goods. The fair also provided services ranging from restaurants to a library. Each stand, organized according to trade, business, or theme, was ornately decorated, most overflowing with evergreens and flowers.[37]

Departments with historical and patriotic themes were especially popular. In their own way, each contributed to an overarching narrative about American nationhood, offering visitors an ennobling view of the Union, justified in its military excursions and gaining in prestige around the world. In one arena, women in colonial attire impersonated the characters in a Washington Irving story. The Indian Department, designed as a wigwam, with "walls hung with skins of the buffalo, bear & dear antelop," and com-

[35] Alfred J. Bloor to Dr. J. Jenkins, December 20, 1863, Box 951, USSC Papers.
[36] "Metropolitan Fair," *Bulletin*, February 1, 1864, 2:202–3.
[37] *World*, April 9, 1864, p. 4; *New York Herald*, April 4, 1864; *New York Times*, April 5, 1864; *New York Tribune*, April 4, 1864. Mathew Brady's New York gallery was among the most popular cultural sites in the city; its photographs of famous Americans drew the famous and anonymous alike. Alan Trachtenberg offers a nuanced reading of Mathew Brady's popular *Gallery of Illustrious Americans* (published in 1850), a group of photographs of twelve political leaders chosen for their strong nationalist positions, each accompanied by an ennobling biography. Trachtenberg also writes that the war photographs taken by Brady and others were produced for consumption by a homefront anxious to find heroic meanings in visual images as well as a way of experiencing military conflict. See *Reading American Photographs: Images as History, Mathew Brady to Walker Evans* (New York, 1989), chaps. 2, 3.

"Grand Hall of the Fair Building, Fourteenth Street," *Harper's Weekly*, April 12, 1864. Prints and Photographs Division, Library of Congress.

plete with dancing Iroquois warriors, was presented as the legitimate booty seized by United States Army officers in battles with tribes. The Art Department, created from the "private collections of some of New York's wealthiest citizens" as well as many of its artists, was billed as a "monument to the wealth, magnificence, and progress in art for the greatest city of the Western Continent," a testament to the advance of American culture for a constituency grappling with a sense of national inferiority.[38]

In keeping with the Commission's ambition to represent itself as the engine of wartime voluntarism, the Metropolitan Fair included demonstrations of how people who were themselves the objects of charity seized the spirit of war relief. After procuring articles from a number of the city's asylums, including the Deaf and Dumb Asylum, the Blind Asylum, and the State Lunatic Asylum, and displaying the handiwork of their inmates, the fair committee proudly pointed to the fact that charity gave to charity. Children from the Home for the Friendless made thirty packs of lamplighters, and young girls from the Church Mission School contributed a doll complete with a wardrobe of clothing. Who could question the value of institutions that trained the indigent to conform not only to the labor discipline of industrial society but to its welfare ideology as well?[39]

What most clearly set this fair apart from those presented by female branches was its elaborate, romanticized representation of women and their labor. In the center of the main building, standing symbolically like a shrine, was the Floral Temple, a tableau vivant of northern patriotism represented by women engaged in pastoral pursuits. While not officially labeled as one of the tableaux vivants offered at the fair, the Floral Temple borrowed the popular antebellum cultural form of placing human beings in poses on stage to imitate paintings, statues, or scenes from fiction. Tableaux vivants had achieved wide popularity in New York theaters during the 1830s and 1840s. By the 1850s middle-class audiences were increasingly drawn to creating tableaux with patriotic themes, eschewing the more eroticized fare favored by the working class.[40]

Though the *Evening Post* noted that the wives of elite Republicans, such as Mrs. Albert Gallatin and Mrs. Carl Schurz, were accorded prime locations at the Floral Temple, the *New York Tribune* emphasized that what stood out at "this magic place," "rich in arches and deep alcoves" and

[38] *New York Tribune*, April 4, 1864; *Spirit of the Fair*, April 9, 1864, p. 52; Daly, April 5, 1864, *Diary of a Union Lady*, pp. 286–87.
[39] *Spirit of the Fair*, April 16, 1864, p. 123.
[40] For history of tableaux vivants, see Robert C. Allen, *Horrible Prettiness: Burlesque and American Culture* (Chapel Hill, N.C., 1991), pp. 92–94.

adorned with everything from rare flowers to tropical birds, was "a score of bright-eyed beauties" (fig. 14). In this overtly sexualized composition, young women, obviously chosen for their physical charms, were on view "weaving bouquets, arranging baskets, and dispensing their treasures" with "a fascinating force that added to the fragrance of the blossoms [and] fairly overcame all who ventured within the influence of their magic circle."[41]

The Floral Temple's rustic and sensual depiction of a "naturally" generous woman not only echoed the antebellum image of bourgeois womanhood but also reinforced the broader romanticization of women that marked northern war mobilization and patriotic discourse. Just as northern soldiers frequently conflated their loyalty to the Union with devotion to their mothers and their lovers, so the Commission drew on available cultural imagery of the nonpolitical, benevolent, and domesticated female to represent national loyalty in its purest form.[42] Here was woman literally portrayed as an extension of nature: beautiful, scented, and bearing earth's bounties. The Floral Temple tableau embodied the antebellum ideology about the non-economic value of domestic production, and underscored the equation of female handiwork with expressions of love and moral refinement. Its sentimentalized depiction of women contrasted sharply not only with the strenuous work of branch women and their overburdened provincial associates but also with the realities of women's everyday lives.

Yet even the Metropolitan Fair could not maintain a universalizing message about womanhood, for in the midst of lavish tributes to a mythic female nature, real women were exhibiting economic behavior quite at odds with this constructed fantasy. On April 7, fair detectives arrested two women for pickpocketing on the grounds. The *New York Daily News* reported that the women were "exploring the pockets of some ladies who were purchasing tickets." In a stunning, public form of penance, the arrested women were paraded around the fair wearing placards bearing the word "Pickpocket"; according to one newspaper, this humiliating display "constituted one of the liveliest features of the immense exhibition." Though they "elicited the sympathy of many of the ladies," who "hesitated to believe that the prisoner could be a professional thief," the detectives announced that these criminals were well known, having engaged in "thieving from their childhood."[43] Three days earlier, Strong recorded in his diary

---

[41] *Evening Post*, April 6, 1964, Box 1003, USSC Paper; *New York Tribune*, April 5, 1864.
[42] For the importance of "domestic imagery" in the sustenance of northern soldiers at the front, see Reid Mitchell, *The Vacant Chair: The Northern Soldier Leaves Home* (New York, 1993).
[43] *New York Daily News*, April 7, 1864. The *New York Tribune*, April 7, 1864, identified the women as Reilley, Catherine Sweeny, and Mary Kelley, noting that Reilley was "an old thief."

"Floral Department of the Great Fair," *Harper's Weekly*, April 16, 1864. Prints and Photographs Division, Library of Congress.

that police were much in evidence at the fair and on April 4 had caught four or five pickpockets (he did not note whether they were male or female) and "marched them backward and forward through the building with placards round their necks, defining their vocation in large capitals." Strong thoroughly enjoyed the "goodly spectacle" but noted that many of the Fair's women were upset about it, calling the episode " 'painful' and 'cruel' and 'humiliating.' "[44] Whether these accounts described the same arrests or different ones, it was evident that the female fair executives gained no pleasure from seeing poor women shamed in public. Though they shared the class position of their husbands and male relatives, these elite women did not share the perspective of upper-class men who felt entitled to use the fair to reinforce lessons about property rights—indeed, for whom the fair was a spectacle about the political value of property.

Other women quietly but visibly dissented from the fair's imposition of a unified portrayal of northern womanhood. A week into the event, the New York *World* reported that young women who operated the stalls were discarding the plain black dresses that someone in charge had evidently mandated as official fair attire. Though the editors of the *World* recognized that the uniform had probably been instituted to provide visual harmony and reduce competition, they were delighted that the women, in "covert acts," were dispensing with this "piece of prudery" and wearing more elegant dresses of their own choosing. Bending over backwards not to appear lascivious in their joy at the women's new clothing, the editors claimed they did not mean "to intimate that the ladies are mere toys to make a pretty appearance," but argued that the women were acting in a "progressive" mode and that it would not help the fair "to place old and ugly women at the tables."[45]

The New York fair was a huge financial success. Bourgeois New Yorkers, accepting both the charitable and patriotic messages of the event, enthusiastically participated in a unique consumption experience. After only two days the fair raised close to $700,000 dollars, and in May 1864, a check for one million dollars was sent to the Commission's treasury.[46] To Strong, the fair's impressive fiscal achievement signified not only a popular endorsement of the commission but also a marked shift in the organization's prestige. "Who

[44] Strong, April 4, 1864, Diary, 3:424.
[45] *World*, April 12, 1864.
[46] Strong, April 6, 1863, Diary, Strong Papers; "Results of the Fair," *Bulletin*, May 15, 1864, 2:429. More money trickled in later, as donations from Europe and late sales were collected. The final total was approximately $1,183,000.

dreamed two years ago, last June," he remarked to himself, "that the poor little Sanitary Commission would ever make such a noise in the world?"[47]

Whether the fair successfully bolstered the commission's public image, however, remained unclear. For other New Yorkers, the lavish, lucrative event reinforced suspicions about the class-based purposes of the commission. Though she traveled in the same social circles as the fair's coordinators, Maria Daly was cynical about the motives of her peers, remarking sarcastically that "it is the apotheosis of fashionable and cheap patriotism."[48] To women such as the Woolseys, immersed in the daily rigors of soldier relief work both at home and in army hospitals, the attention devoted to the fair's preparation seemed at best misplaced. Writing to her cousins, Jane and Georgina, Harriet Woolsey deplored the competitive displays of wealth associated with the fair: "New York is really in a disgusting state of fashionable excitement; nothing is talked of, or thought of or dreamed of, but the big Metropolitan Fair! Mrs. Parker has her thousand dollar tea-sets to dispose of; Kate Hunt, her two hundred dollar curtains; Mrs. Schermerhorn, her elegant watches; and Mrs. Somebody else, the beautiful jewelry sent from Rome for the Sanitary Commission."[49]

The New York *Herald* echoed the suspicions of many observers when it claimed that, among all the fairs held around the country, "one-third of the receipts [were] stolen by managers, or entirely misappropriated." Following the Metropolitan Fair, the paper claimed to "see men now living in grand houses, riding in splendid carriages, and indulging in all sorts of extravagant displays, who, before their connection with those sanitary fairs, were obscure people." "All these fairs," the *Herald* concluded, "have proved to be grand schemes of robbery from beginning to end."[50]

The Impact of the Fairs

The Metropolitan Fair not only represented an effort by the commission to upstage the female-led branches in producing a major patriotic event as well as a means for raising money, it also became the standard for future urban sanitary fairs. Even before the New York fair opened its doors, men and women in Philadelphia paid close attention to its plans, determined to stage

[47] Strong, April 6, 1864, *Diary*, 3:427.
[48] Daly, April 3, 1864, *Diary of a Union Lady*, p. 286.
[49] Harriet R. Woolsey to J. and G., March 1864, in Bacon and Howland, *Letters*, 2:570.
[50] Quoted in James Dawson Burn, *Three Years among the Working-Classes in the United States during the War* (London, 1865), pp. 239–40.

their own event that would rival it in both spectacle and financial gain. In fact, Philadelphia's Great Central Fair, held between June 7 and June 28 of 1864, was second only to the Metropolitan Fair in size and in the amount of money it raised for the organization, over a million dollars. Like the New York event, the Philadelphia fair was conducted by the city's elite, organized in parallel male and female committees that likewise experienced considerable tensions. And when Philadelphia businessmen took over the fair's management, some women determined that they would no longer support the fair with their own labor.[51]

The promotion of the Metropolitan Fair as an event produced by the central organization did not settle the question of the effects that sanitary fairs had on the larger Sanitary Commission project. Despite the economic success of the New York fair, the commission continued to lament the impact of fairs on homefront consciousness and commitment. Sanitary fairs, it appeared, undermined the credibility of demands for additional material donations. The early fairs, though adding to the central treasury, increased the financial independence of individual branches and threatened to dampen efforts to stimulate voluntary labor. Even plans for the Metropolitan Fair, sponsored wholly by the commission, offered little relief. Only a few weeks before the New York fair opened, John Foster Jenkins reported that "the three principal depots at Boston, New York and Philadelphia, are now nearly empty, and the prospect of their speedy replenishment . . . is not good." He blamed the "diverting influence of present and project[ed] Fairs."[52]

Channeling most fair proceeds to the central treasury failed to rectify the problem. In May of 1864, the *Bulletin* announced that the fairs "resulted in loss rather than in gain to the Sanitary Commission." Indeed, "far from assuring its future," the events "have placed it in some peril." The public exaggerated the financial proceeds of the fairs, the commission asserted, claiming that its records showed that the value of donated supplies far exceeded the revenue that fairs yielded. Supplied with money rather than finished products, the commission was compelled to purchase the supplies it needed at increasingly inflated prices.[53]

---

[51] See J. Matthew Gallman, *Mastering Wartime: A Social History of Philadelphia during the Civil War* (New York, 1990), pp. 146–62, for a detailed discussion of the planning and execution of the Philadelphia Great Central Fair.

[52] "Survey of the Field," *Bulletin*, March 15, 1864, 1:292.

[53] "The Effects of the Fairs on Our Funds," *Bulletin*, May 15, 1864, 2:417–18. According to one estimate, the fairs cumulatively raised $4,392,980.92, of which $2,736,868.84 went directly into the USSC treasury. See William Y. Thompson, "The U.S. Sanitary Commission," *Civil War History* 2 (June 1956): 57. Despite such sums, the Sanitary Commission men never recon-

Ever since rumors of corruption had cast suspicion on the commission's operations, the organization seemed bent on positioning itself as financially beleaguered, misunderstood by the public, and abandoned by the women it courted so assiduously. Yet the Sanitary Commission's claims that the fairs injured its financial health and institutional strength were belied by personal communications. On February 8, 1864, in a letter to Henry Ward Beecher that included a summary of facts regarding commission coffers which he intended to made public in the next *Bulletin*, Bellows admitted that commission branches had sent to the parent organization some seven million dollars worth of "domestic-made Hospital Garments" according "to a nice estimate of their *value*." While Bellows was compelled to give concrete value to the products of unpaid household labor, he wanted it made known that during the first two years these gifts derived from "*home-superfluities*." Now that homes had exhausted all of their surpluses, the branches relied on the money raised in "these great Fairs" to buy materials for hospital clothing. In what appeared a reversal of the commission's position that it was most interested in the labor and donations of homefront women, Bellows lamented that "the supplies come to us, but *not* the money."[54]

Such concerns about the diversion of funds may have been one factor that impelled Sanitary Commission officers to launch a fair of their own. But their attempts to portray the commission as bereft of cash were disingenuous. The organization relied heavily on large contributions from California, and, though it was operating at a deficit, future fairs had already pledged money to the parent organization. Only a week after Bellows's letter to Beecher, Strong noted that they expected to make up the deficit in their operating expenses from money that would be raised by the Brooklyn and Metropolitan events. By March, Mr. A. A. Low informed Bellows that the executive committee of the Brooklyn and Long Island fair was sending $300,000 in cash as "the first installment of the Fair held in this City for its aid." Low acknowledged that the USSC had allowed the Brooklyn managers to retain the balance of $100,000 "for the purpose of having it accounted from time to time to the Commission in the shape of supplies, to be rapidly furnished through the agency of our Woman's Relief Association." Furthermore, on April 23, 1864, Strong noted receipt of $80,000

---

ciled themselves to the fair phenomenon. Although in his official USSC history Charles Stillé detailed the amount of money the fairs provided the parent organization, he dismissed the events by writing that "the history of these 'Sanitary Fairs' as they were commonly called, need not be repeated here." See *History of the United States Sanitary Commission*, p. 483.

[54] Henry Whitney Bellows to Henry W. Beecher, February 8, 1864, Bellows Papers.

from the Albany Sanitary Fair, and mentioned that $15,000 would be returned to the "Albanians for their local work in getting up and forwarding supplies."[55]

The Woman's Central Relief Association also inferred a negative impact from the fairs. Schuyler was reluctant to castigate the efforts of so many women on behalf of the soldiers, yet she declared that one reason women in her region were less active in sending donations was that so many were in a "society [that] has been working for the Fair to be held at Buffalo, or Rochester, or Elmira, or Binghamton, or Albany, or Poughkeepsie, or Yonkers, or Brooklyn or New York, or in its own village." The "Fair epidemic," she judged, "has swept no state so thoroughly as the state of New York."[56]

Accounts of fairs within the WCRA region recorded the intense activity required for planning and staging the events. Once the women of Poughkeepsie and Dutchess County decided to hold a large fair, all hands were called out. "Preparations went on vigorously through the town. Schools gave Concerts, Soirees, and Tableaux . . . Ladies engaged popular lecturers at their own expense." The Poughkeepsie fair's most popular area was the "Old Room," featuring women dressed in colonial attire serving tea, while "the aborigines were represented by an Indian girl in full costume." The local press hailed the fair as a great success, with net proceeds of over $15,000.[57]

Sanitary fairs offered women ways of expressing not only national patriotism but also local civic pride; preparations were invariably made with one eye on neighboring fairs. The Brooklyn and Long Island fair was, to its creators, "the first great act of self-assertion ever made by the City of Brooklyn."[58] Unlike the routines of Sanitary Commission work that generated conflict and confusion, the fairs were unifying acts, offering citizens a sense

[55] Strong recorded in his diary that California was sending huge sums and had pledged $25,000 a month for 1864. Though monthly expenses during 1863 averaged $48,000 a month, he appeared confident that fair proceeds would reduce treasury deficits, noting that cash subscriptions for the Brooklyn fair, scheduled to open the following week, already amounted to $125,000. See Strong, February 17, 1864, *Diary*, 3:406; A. A. Low to Henry Whitney Bellows, March 28, 1864, Box 951–952, USSC Papers; Strong, April 23, 1864, *Diary*, 3:432.

[56] *Third Annual Report*, pp. 7–8, Box 993; Schuyler reported to the WCRA Board that for the month of March 1864, "the attention of their correspondents [was] primarily engaged with the Fairs." See Schuyler, "Report of Sub-Committee on Correspondence, Board Meeting," April 1, 1864, Box 954, USSC Papers.

[57] *Report of the Dutchess County & Poughkeepsie Sanitary Fair Held at Sanitary Hall in the City of Poughkeepsie, from March 15, to March 19, 1864* (Poughkeepsie, N. Y., 1864); *Poughkeepsie Daily Eagle*, March 9, 18, 21, and 29, 1864.

[58] *History of the Brooklyn and Long Island Fair, February 22, 1864* (Brooklyn, N. Y., 1864), p. 5.

of social cohesiveness that they especially appreciated during wartime. The sponsors of the Albany Sanitary Fair proclaimed it "the most important epochs of the history our city and vicinity," for never before "has any undertaking met with so general a support and so unanimous a feeling."[59] To the women of Watertown, New York, the decision over whether to contribute to the Albany fair or stage one of their own became a topic of public debate. "The question is one of some importance to our citizens," reported the local paper, not only in terms of raising contributions but "in point of reputation as a patriotic people."[60]

To Schuyler, the fairs were antithetical to the type of patriotic, voluntary labor she tried so diligently to cultivate. Reliable and sufficient donations required consistent work habits; women were to labor steadily, little by little, developing long-term commitments to benevolence. Not only were the fairs "spasmodic efforts of intense excitement" that ran counter to a "regular routine," but the money from these later fairs went to the central treasury, leaving the WCRA's storehouses "so empty."[61] In the end, the Woman's Central Relief Association had little option but to ignore the fairs and concentrate on other strategies. WCRA officer Angelina Post, noting that the fairs resulted in "comparatively small" receipts of donated goods, resolved that "what we need now is that the loyal women should again turn their attention to making the garments and their comforts which are so greatly required in our hospitals."[62]

Even the WCRA misunderstood the importance that local women attached to the exercise of control over their voluntary labor. The fairs, particularly those held in towns and small cities, provided a sense of accomplishment markedly absent from the tedious labor of preparing packages for a far-away war. As local women made choices about the type of charity work they were willing to engage in, they also made explicit their assessments of the overall efficacy of raising cash over producing homemade articles of clothing. In a society that readily recognized economic value in cash terms, it was not surprising that so many women were attracted to a means of attributing bona fide worth to their labor.

Moreover, the fairs represented a rejection of the notion that efficiency was best achieved through centralization. What Stillé later depicted as the

---

[59] *Canteen*, February 22, 1864, Box 1011, USSC Papers. *The Canteen* was published by the organizers of the Albany fair, an event that included the cities of Troy and Schenectady.
[60] *New York Daily Reformer*, January 19, 1864, p. 3.
[61] *Third Annual Report*, May 1, 1864, pp. 7–8, Box 993, USSC Papers.
[62] Angelina Post to Mrs. Powers, 1864, Angelina Post Papers.

"desperate efforts to throw off the yoke" of the commission by the "already half-independent Branches" applied not only to the relationship between the branches and the main organization but also to that between local women and branch leaders at the WCRA.[63] In the staging of local fairs, hundreds of women retreated not only from the overreaching arm of the Sanitary Commission but from the intrusiveness of the WCRA as well.

The female-run branches were, in the end, only able to slow, but not to reverse the female public's retreat from the national charity experiment. Northern women reclaimed some of the authority over voluntary work they had previously relinquished. Numerous soldiers' aid societies returned to the practice of directing homemade supplies to state agencies and local regiments. And in the final show of independence, women organized sanitary fairs as an autonomous means of raising contributions for the soldiers' welfare. Just as the commissioners themselves hoped the war would offer a national platform for their political agenda, so women who launched regional and local fairs recognized the value of public, charitable events as a means of increasing both their local social authority and their political presence. As the USSC came under increasing attack, the opportunity that the war presented for a new national cohesiveness dissolved.

With the Metropolitan Fair, the Sanitary Commission successfully positioned itself, at least for a moment, as the leading and perhaps most powerful wartime charity. The fair raised enormous sums of money and proved itself to be a prestigious event with few rivals. It was ironic, however, that the one fair run by the USSC chose a name that revealed none of its origins. Either out of fear of reigniting suspicions about the motives of commission officers or because nearly all the other fairs had appropriated the term "Sanitary" in their titles, the Sanitary Commission was left bereft of its own imprimatur. The "Metropolitan" fair was just that, the fair in the metropolis, the commission's base and the center of the nation's financial and cultural power. Meanwhile, all along the periphery, events known as "Sanitary" fairs represented an ongoing redefinition of soldier relief work that highlighted the decentralized, local, and female sources of social welfare.

---

[63] Stillé, *United States Sanitary Commission*, p. 205.

8

"IT IS A PEOPLE'S WAR": THE USSC RETREATS

"National affairs are all bright," Bellows wrote to Olmsted in February of 1864; "the South is collapsing too evidently for doubt." Bellows was elated by the spate of northern victories in the final months of 1863 and the early weeks of 1864; Union forces, it appeared, were finally winning the war. From the Sanitary Commission's perspective, the turnaround in military fortunes came none too soon. Just as the commission began waging a concerted action against the possible collapse of its relief network, the Union's final offensive against the South lifted northern homefront morale, sparking renewed interest in the army's welfare. It seemed that what the organization could not accomplish by building a liberal constituency committed to a judicious benevolence and a dispassionate nationalism, violent military encounters would. "It is a people's war," Bellows bemoaned; "they have been driven by instincts & passions rather than by reasonings."[1] Louisa Schuyler was also optimistic about the capacity of victories on the battlefield to stimulate charitable energies and rescue the ailing organization. But in contrast to Bellows's cynicism, she demonstrated more faith in the rational calculations the female public made about the usefulness of its labors.

---

[1] Henry Bellows to Frederick L. Olmsted, February 12, 1864, Box 951, USSC Papers.

"The battles do our work for us," she acknowledged, "speaking more broadly to the hearts & heads of the people than [Committees] on [Correspondence] can."[2]

By the spring of 1864, the disparate northern armies had been brought together under a coordinated command to subdue the Confederacy. As Grant assumed direction over five armies, the campaign depended on Meade's Army of the Potomac in Virginia and Sherman's army, organized into three separate groups under Thomas, McPherson, and Schofield, which was undertaking the long, difficult Atlanta campaign.[3] This massive push through the South produced lengthy and costly confrontations, forcing the USSC to provide aid on an unprecedented scale and placing heavy burdens on its finances and staff. In the month of May alone, the commission spent over $260,000 purchasing stores, as compared to $90,000 for July 1863.[4] "We are working on a very large scale in aid of Grant's army," Strong recorded in his diary. The USSC was spending $650 a day for steamers, barges, and schooners to transport supplies and, he noted, was "manning fifty or sixty wagons with four- and six-horse teams and employing from 150 to 200 relief agents (all to some extent skilled laborers), and twice as many teamsters, servants, and contrabands."[5]

Disbursing huge sums of money made Treasurer Strong uneasy, particularly with memories of sharp public criticism still ringing in his head. "I foresee a fearful time at hand of newspaper queries—'What has become of all this money?'—that may irritate me to suicide," he wrote on May 21, 1864. "No matter," he sneered, "if the money have been so used as to help save the country." Six weeks later, after visiting General Grant at the warfront and inspecting USSC operations near Petersburg, Strong renewed his faith in the importance of relief efforts and concluded that "the work of the Sanitary Commission . . . may materially influence the result of the campaign and the destiny of the country." As he figured it, "Fifty thousand pounds of anti-scorbutics issued daily to an army that has begun to shew symptoms of scurvy, . . . are no insignificant contribution."[6]

[2] Louisa Lee Schuyler, June 8, 1864, Schuyler Papers.
[3] James M. McPherson, *Ordeal By Fire: The Civil War and Reconstruction* (New York, 1982), pp. 345, 410–12, 429, 436.
[4] Theodore W. Dwight, "Case and Opinion," 1864, no. 85, *Documents*, 2:4.
[5] Strong, May 21, 1864, *Diary*, 3:450.
[6] Strong, May 21 and July 8, 1864, *Diary*, 3:450, 465.

The Homefront Disorganized

While the Sanitary Commission's usefulness on the frontlines was legitimated by the intensified military assault, its position with the female homefront was still precarious. The recent string of sanitary fairs had damaged the credibility of continued appeals for donations, while the bureaucratic wrangles between the female-led branches and the national office left little energy to attend to the disintegrating system of soldiers' aid societies. Worse still, charges that the commission was a speculative operation persisted. Together with ongoing competition among relief organizations, the enduring skepticism on the part of the public worried officials as they determined how best to aid the army in its new offensive.[7]

Vague impressions about disarray at the homefront became depressingly concrete when a WCRA survey, conducted in January 1864, found that disorganization abounded in its region and that many soldiers' aid societies had fallen on hard times. Isabella Stevens reported from Hoboken, New Jersey, that the society there "was in abeyance," and cited the "great preponderance of foreigners" in the city. Mrs. H. Evans of Hales Eddy, New York, wrote that "the society here died long since," adding, "It was small and poor always." "Our society has not been in operation for a few months past, for want of funds to purchase materials to work," explained the representative from Bolton, Connecticut. Other respondents blamed heightened political opposition to the war and the Republican party for low levels of welfare activity, remarking that their communities were "entirely of the Copperhead persuasion" or "decidedly Coppery."[8]

Not surprisingly, more and more women cited the impact of the wartime economy as the reason for their limited participation in soldier relief work. Rather than describing the humble nature of agricultural communities or the working-class character of industrial towns, as they had in the early years of the war, by 1864 female correspondents increasingly identified wartime economic difficulties as the source of their material woes. Anecdotal accounts of dwindling resources reflected real changes in north-

[7] See S. H. Hester to Mrs. Moore, December 31, 1864, Box 640, USSC Papers.
[8] Isabella Stevens to Helen W. Marshall, January 25, 1864; Mrs. H. Evans to Helen Marshall, January 28, 1864; J. A. Ruggles to Helen W. Marshall, January 25, 1864; C. Allen to Miss Marshall, January 25. 1864; J. A. Ruggles to Marshall, January 25, 1864, Box 671, USSC Papers.

ern buying power; according to one estimate, between 1864 and 1866 food prices in urban areas increased approximately 70 percent above prewar levels.[9]

In response to a questionnaire the commission distributed after the war, women emphasized the economic hardships they faced in the later years of the conflict. Harriet Pierce from Nantucket, Massachusetts, explained that the "principal discouragement" her group met in soliciting aid was "the inability of our towns people to make considerable contributions, in consequence of a general decay of business." The women of North Billerica, Massachusetts, managed to collect $80 at the beginning of the war, but in the last year "living became so expensive," in the words of Eliza Rogers, that "few families were interested" in sustaining the work. Enumerating the many obstacles that faced women in Berlin, Iowa, Mrs. Bradfield informed the commission that her area was "not very wealthy" and "a great many plead poverty."[10] Commission statistics confirmed the dispiriting accounts sent by female correspondents. During the early months of 1864, receipts of homemade contributions continued to fall.[11]

Making matters worse, the Christian Commission continued to make inroads into Sanitary Commission strongholds. Having set a goal of raising one million dollars for 1865, it stepped up publicity campaigns to appeal directly to disaffected USSC workers, a strategy that yielded considerable success.[12] Women in Adams, New York, stopped sending donations to the Sanitary Commission in the spring of 1864, discovering in the Christian Commission "something new."[13] When, in July 1864, a CC delegate lectured the town of Cincinnatus, New York, the loyalties of its once-cohesive soldiers' aid society fractured. That the CC spokesman was a minister "created intense excitement of course," related J. C. Kingsley. Though he surmised that "as in every town there were a great many . . . who were willing for any excuse to keep their pockets shut," he nonetheless pointed to the chronic problem of the USSC's religious identity and made clear that

[9] Patrick O'Brien, *The Economic Effects of the American Civil War* (London, 1988), p. 53.
[10] Harriet Pierce to Mr. Blatchford, April 23, 1866, Box 983; Eliza A. Rogers to Blatchford, April 28, 1866, Box 983; Mrs. L. M. Bradfield to Mr. Blatchford, April 19, 1866, Box 986, USSC Papers.
[11] Louisa Lee Schuyler, "Report of Sub-Committee on Correspondence," April 1, 1864, Box 954, USSC Papers.
[12] William Quentin Maxwell, *Lincoln's Fifth Wheel: The Political History of the United States Sanitary Commission* (New York, 1956), p. 266.
[13] Carrie Webb to Blatchford, April 5, 1866, Box 981, USSC Papers.

some "left us because there were Unitarians connected with the Sanitary Commission."[14]

Given the number of aid societies that divided their donations among private and government agencies, the impact on Sanitary Commission coffers of any decrease in total welfare activity was pronounced. "There were few steady working societies in my district," wrote Mrs. Saunders of Newburgh, New York, at the war's end; even then "some of those work wholly & some in part for the Christian Commission—some for particular reg[imen]ts." Though in "little hamlets-about" donations were gathered from time to time, these were "sent through regular organizations in their vicinity." Boasting that a "great deal has been sent to regts outside of our society," Saunders admitted that "there is much less of that than formerly."[15]

Apart from defections to the Christian Commission camp, the final year and a half of the war was marked by women's growing weariness of both the work and military conflict. "As the dreary months dragged on and the war seemed endless," recalled Caroline Hughes, "many became discouraged." Though the women of Fayetteville, New York, had pledged to work for the duration of the war, in the last year their interest "began to flag," and attendance at meetings as well as donations became "merely spasmodic." The associate manager of Ithaca, New York, disclosed in late 1864 that while she no longer heard "complaints" about the commission, the towns in her area contributed very little. "The trouble," Jane Hardy speculated, "seems rather, lack of money, lack of time, or the right kind of energetic, determined women to carry the matter through." In Hardy's judgment, among those aid societies that "commenced earliest" and "best" there was "generally stamina" to stay the course. Still trying as late as October 1864, to offer the USSC some encouragement, she wrote that, "in several of the villages, they are organizing for the winter, hoping to accomplish somewhat more than they have."[16]

---

[14] J. C. Kingsley, April 3, 1866, Box 981, USSC Papers. The issue of USSC religious identification dogged the organization until the end of the war. In 1865, Knapp received a letter from a chaplain with the 27th Michigan Volunteers, noting the widespread belief that the USSC was "binding itself to Unitarians" and trying to "spread their tracts & views." "I wish I had the documents to show how large a majority of the managers of the San. Com. are not Unitarians," he wrote Knapp, asking if he possessed any such evidence. See S. S. Hunting to Knapp, January 23, 1865, Box 955, USSC Papers.

[15] Mrs. E. W. Saunders, November 8, 1864, Box 677, USSC Papers.

[16] Caroline L. Hughes to John Blatchford, April 19, 1866, Box 981; Fayetteville Ladies Soldiers Aid Society, 1866, Box 981; Jane L. Hardy to Miss A. Post, October 24, 1864, Box 677, USSC Papers.

This sense of exhaustion was tied to the long, destructive nature of the Civil War. Unlike peacetime charitable labor, which was expended within the confines of a community and delivered on a face-to-face basis, warwork demanded that women contribute to anonymous Americans without seeing the consequences of their labors. Perhaps even more important, warwork produced few measurable or verifiable improvements; soldiers were still dying and, with no peace in sight, women were losing momentum.

Searching for explanations for waning receipts, the men and women of the Sanitary Commission responded in what had become characteristically divergent ways, with male officers blaming events and people outside of their control and WCRA women looking inward to identify where they had personally failed. In November 1864, Bellows informed his son that the "people are getting somewhat tired of the large demands made upon them." Ever more pessimistic, he presumed that this new state of affairs would undoubtedly be exploited by the Christian Commission, which was "cutting extensively into our constituency."[17] John Foster Jenkins, now general secretary of the commission, judged that the fairs continued to exert a negative impact, and confided to Bellows at the end of April 1864 that he was "growing somewhat more apprehensive lest the rural districts satisfied as to our great wealth, should give us over." "The falling off of supplies in kind" was considerable, Jenkins advised, and placed in jeopardy all other USSC endeavors.[18] For WCRA officer Mrs. John Swett, however, the problem lay not with the public but with Sanitary Commission policy and branch initiatives. Even Schuyler's reorganization plan did little to stem the steady falling off of receipts. The idea of providing aid societies with raw materials at wholesale prices "worked well," Swett acknowledged, "but did not meet the demands [made] upon the [association] by the San. Com."[19]

Despite the escalating needs of the army, the organization backed away from trying to rouse homefront support. Convinced that whatever support it garnered would be generated more by news from the warfront than by formal appeals, it launched no new campaigns for donations. While continuing to inform northerners of the vast medical aid it was providing at the front, it no longer heralded important bureaucratic and military innova-

[17] Henry W. Bellows to "dear Boy" [Russell Bellows], November 13, 1864, Bellows Papers.
[18] J. Foster Jenkins to Henry Bellows, April 30, 1864, Box 640, USSC Papers. Jenkins began his service as an inspector at the front and later became associate secretary for the East. He resigned briefly in 1863 but soon returned to replace Olmsted as general secretary. See Censer, introduction, *FLO Papers*, 4:99–101.
[19] Mrs. John A. Swett, May 5, 1864, Box 954, USSC Papers.

tions. Nor did it spend much time publicly debating the advantages of its system over others. It still sought contributions of money and household products, but it now tailored its requests to meet the demands of recent battles.

Schuyler's Final Offensive

As the male commissioners distanced themselves from the problems at the homefront, Louisa Schuyler and other female branch leaders felt an urgency to support the intensive military campaigns with renewed promotional efforts. In the spring of 1864, the WCRA dispatched canvassers to organize the unorganized and to rally those whose commitments had deteriorated. Whether because homefront women were ready for appeals to put aside other concerns and focus on recent victories, or because agents had honed their lecturing and publicity techniques, this canvassing campaign yielded considerable triumphs. Major Bush, the WCRA's lone canvasser at the outset of the campaign, was surprisingly successful, mobilizing some women for the first time. "Tuesday eve, April 26th, '64 Major Bush lectured here upon the work before the Sanitary Commission after which a committee of ladies was appointed to assist," recorded the women of Exeter, New York. Women in Coventry, New York, responded to his appeals and organized a new society in June 1864. Bush registered organizational victories even after the military hopes of early spring disintegrated into a midsummer stalemate. In October 1864, Mrs. Mason informed the WCRA that the community of Hamilton, New York, had been doing precious little, "but since Major Bush's visit, the ladies have begun with renewed vigor."[20]

Bush's accomplishments impressed Schuyler, who reported to Joseph Parrish that "the ladies write that he has done good service in stimulating societies in their sections." "He is the only lecturer now assigned to us," she noted; "I wish there were more."[21] Schuyler followed the canvassing cam-

---

[20] Jannette G. Palmer, Schuyler's Lake, Oswego Co., 1866, Box 981, USSC Papers. James McPherson notes that by July, "the hopes of May for a quick victory had been drowned in the sorrows of 100,000 Northern battle casualties." See *Ordeal by Fire*, p. 436. Mrs. S. C. Mason to Miss Post, October 28, 1864, Box 677, USSC Papers. For other accounts of renewed activity resulting from canvasser appeals, see Mary A. Pratt, 1866; M. C. Warren, Coventry; Mrs. J. W. Smedley, March 8, 1866; L. Gould, April 8, 1864; M. M. Greene, May 23, 1866; Miss S. C. Beebe, 1866, Box 981, USSC Papers.

[21] Louisa L. Schuyler to J. Parrish, October 6, 1864, Box 954, USSC Papers. Bush's methods, while successful, must have been unorthodox, as Parrish considered him "irregular" and in need of being "better harnessed." See J. Parrish to Louisa L. Schuyler, November 26, 1864, Box 669, USSC Papers.

paign closely, treating the mobilization of new societies as seriously as if the war had just begun. As late as spring 1865 she was still urging the commission to send more lecturers into the WCRA region. Pressing her ideas on Parrish, she asserted that "there can be no doubt as to the *value* of a thorough canvass of our field. If you wish to stimulate the sending of supplies it is *the thing* to do." "Of course," she pointed out, "everything depends upon the character of the agents sent."[22]

Schuyler succeeded in gaining more lecturers for the WCRA region. One of these men, D. W. Evans, conducted extensive tours of upstate New York in 1865. Evans's trips revealed that the wariness of northern women was difficult to dispel, even when the war seemed almost won. Indeed, three years into the war he found towns still unsure about the merits of forming an aid society, reporting that the people of Union Mills, New York, for example, "could not be hurried." "They take time to deliberate," he advised; "you will hear from them in due time." Evans remained steadfast in his mission, "inspired by the conviction," as he put it, "that the San. Com. rests on principles half a century ahead of [the] C.C."[23] His faith in the commission's liberal agenda may have been commendable, but it was doubtful that many at the homefront saw it quite that way. In fact, it was likely that women who organized in the final year of the war did so either as a consequence of the personal appeals of Sanitary Commission lecturers or from a sense that the Union army was facing decisive military encounters. This last public relations campaign posted impressive gains. Between March 1864, and June 1865, canvassers delivered 369 lectures, and the WCRA reported that 138 new societies had formed, raising the total in its region to 813.[24]

Canvassing was only one of the approaches Schuyler wanted to employ at this stage in the war. In December 1864, in a move that revived some of her original hopes for the *Bulletin*, she suggested recruiting "the very best oratorical talent which our country affords" to combat the erroneous ideas afloat about the commission. Schuyler had in mind such well-known lecturers as Henry Ward Beecher, who had extensive experience on the antebellum lyceum circuit and to whom she planned to offer what she thought was his "usual charge of a hundred dollars." To her thinking, men who had no official connection to the USSC might have better results than can-

[22] Louisa L. Schuyler to Dr. J. Parrish, April 10, 1865, Box 667, USSC Papers.

[23] D. W. Evans to Miss A. Post, May 1, 1865; D. W. Evans to A. Post, April 4, 1865; D. W. Evans to Miss C. Nash, May 11, 1865, Box 680, USSC Papers.

[24] *Fourth Annual and Final Report of the W.C.A. of R, July 7, 1865* (New York, 1865), p. 8, Box 993, USSC Papers.

vassers in countering impressions that the organization was "partisan" and unprincipled.[25]

Schuyler's management of canvassers and her suggestions to the USSC's standing committee represented one more sign—in addition to the bureaucratic restructuring she had implemented the year before and the WCRA's refusal to participate in the Metropolitan Fair—of the more aggressive posture she assumed with her male colleagues. The rumors of corruption and mismanagement had caused a shift in her behavior, if not her thinking. Not only did she refrain from defending the commission at every turn, she decided that the ability of local women to sabotage relief plans called for stronger branch management of homefront affairs. Where once she deferred to the men who led the USSC, she increasingly asserted her own voice about relief policies.

But preserving her changes in branch-commission relations required constant vigilance. Only a year after she won approval for the WCRA's reorganization, Schuyler found herself engaged in a feud with Parrish over instructions he had given to her associate managers, and reminded him that while the commission had ultimate authority over its branches, the WCRA was still independent, "retaining full power to conduct its own affairs." Associate managers "have never received any directions except from ourselves," Schuyler admonished him. Parrish defended his actions by claiming that other branches were not as efficient as the WCRA and that he needed to know the exact amount the USSC could expect to collect from any particular area.[26]

No matter how much her male colleagues might have stymied her endeavors, the real test of Schuyler's leadership rested with the homefront, and there too she continued to meet with resistance. Resolved to bring wayward localities back into the fold, she called a convention of WCRA associates. On November 16, 1864, 213 women, representing 92 aid societies, met at Cooper Union and listened to speeches from Bellows and Knapp, among others, on the workings of specific Sanitary Commission depart-

---

[25] Louisa L. Schuyler to Standing Committee of the Sanitary Commission, December 9, 1864, Box 667, USSC Papers. Henry Ward Beecher was one of the most successful and savvy lecturers on the mid-nineteenth-century circuit. By 1852 he had already hired an agent to handle his bookings, and by 1856 he had been offered as much as $250 to deliver a lecture in Chicago. Whether Schuyler knew she was offering less than Beecher could command, hoping he would accept it for the sake of the Union cause, is not clear; she was well aware of his enormous popularity and "marketability." See Carl Bode, *The American Lyceum* (Carbondale, Ill., 1956), p. 196.
[26] Louisa L. Schuyler to Dr. J. Parrish, December 6, 1864, Box 667; J. Parrish to Louisa L. Schuyler, November 26, 1864, Box 669, USSC Papers.

ments. Like the Woman's Council of 1863, the WCRA meeting served chiefly to solidify personal relationships among delegates and effected little change in homefront participation.[27] Inspired by the meeting to mobilize her town as a Sanitary Commission affiliate, the delegate from Poughkeepsie, New York, returned home only to find "the old American spirit of independence too strong" to overcome. Explaining the refusal of her townswomen to forward their contributions to the commission, Julia Crosby begged Schuyler not to consider them "a very unmanageable & obstinate set of women," but to remember they were all working for the same cause.[28]

Internal Dissension

Schuyler was not alone in trying to generate homefront loyalty late into the war. Even as the commission retreated from major propaganda efforts, one officer pursued his own tactics for stimulating voluntarism and bolstering the organization's prestige. In May 1864, Alfred Bloor traveled to the military lines to "pick up such scenes and incidents, . . . as might in their narration prove interesting to and effective with, that portion of the public, especially the women, who are interested in such work." Stationed with the Army of the Potomac, he wrote a series of letters to female correspondents, ostensibly to satisfy the women's desires for information on hospital conditions, military camps, and the work of USSC agents. But Bloor's letters, which were reprinted as an official USSC document, were calculated incursions into the public debate over soldier welfare and the Sanitary Commission's expediency. From a camp near Spottsylvania, Virginia, he portrayed the "kitchen and feeding lodge of the Commission, whence [the wounded] were without trouble constantly supplied with hot coffee and beef-tea, iced water and lemonade, milk punch, wines and stimulants, farina, and whatever else in the way of prepared sustenance was needed."[29]

[27] *Bulletin,* December 15, 1864, 3:874–86; *New York Times,* November 16, 1864; see letters to Ellen Collins, Box 673, USSC Papers, on those women who could not attend. For Schuyler the convention underscored the importance of keeping homefront workers in constant touch with the commission's activities. The meeting, she explained, "made plain to us . . . [that] *information* in regard to the work and wants of the Sanitary Commission is the one thing needed to bind the hearts of our people to [the] work." Such information, moreover, was only effective when conveyed within a network of personal relationships. See Louisa Lee Schuyler, "WCRA Lecturers—No. II," December 2, 1864, Box 669, USSC Papers.

[28] Julia N. Crosby to Louisa L. Schuyler, December 1, 1864, Box 673, USSC Papers.

[29] Alfred J. Bloor, "Letters from the Army of the Potomac, Written during the Month of May, 1864," no. 80, *Documents,* 2:17.

Bloor's published reports revealed none of his private disappointments at seeing the "singularly meagre and inefficient" USSC method of attending the sick aboard ships. Nor did they include any of his concerns about the superior techniques of the Christian Commission agents, who personally accompanied soldiers on marches, while USSC agents remained in hospital and transport posts.[30] In the end Bloor's report appeared as yet another self-serving narrative, a style that had become characteristic of the Sanitary Commission.

But if Bloor was disappointed by practices at the warfront, a trip through the homefront was even more disheartening. In the fall of 1864, with guidance from Schuyler, he toured New York, New England, and Canada, meeting with branch officers and associate managers to assess USSC strength in the WCRA region. In city after city, women informed him of the growing attraction of the Christian Commission and a pervasive mistrust of the Sanitary Commission. While many indicated that they objected to the commission on "religious grounds," Bloor believed that the rival group had succeeded by exploiting the idea that the USSC was too corporate in style and dispassionate in tone. The chief complaint seemed to be that the Sanitary Commission "is much governed by professional ideas . . . in regard to its administration as a business organization, [and] to its humanity as a medical one." "I hear much of this in my journey," he remarked.[31]

In a confidential letter to Frederick Knapp, Bloor elaborated on what he viewed as a widespread repudiation of USSC principles and methods. He described women who used their positions as official Sanitary Commission representatives to forward donations to the Christian Commission and state agencies. Bloor surmised that rival agents "have so worked their two strong points of not paying salaries and of reaching each soldier patient in person . . . that the public mind has become trained . . . into a tacit or avowed admission of the superior claims." Most damaging of all was the fact that "the patriotic purposes of the Sanitary Commission were in reality an objection to it among these people."[32]

With women making explicit critiques of the USSC's nationalist aims, Bloor had no choice but to place his hopes for continued donations in the demands created by the war itself. "I believe from what I saw and heard, that—however high prices may become—just as long as the war lasts, cloth-

[30] Alfred J. Bloor to Frederick Knapp, July 19, 1864, Bloor Papers.
[31] Alfred J. Bloor to Frederick N. Knapp, September 9, 1864, Bloor Papers.
[32] Ibid.

Sanitary Commission wagons leaving Washington for the front in the last days of the war. Prints and Photographs Division, Library of Congress.

ing and food will be prepared in abundance by the loyal women of the country." But perhaps because he had sustained contact with numerous female representatives, he also came to understand something about the reasons behind women's acts of charity. These were not simply emanations of women's nature, but calculated decisions to play an active role in the national crisis. "Women of all classes, from the richest and best placed to those who are quite poor and obscure," sought participation in the effort to sustain the nation, Bloor told Knapp. "They can not fight, but nevertheless they like to feel that they, as well as the men, are of some importance to the State."[33]

Whether such support would find its way to the Sanitary Commission was still unclear. Based on his many conversations with homefront women, Bloor was convinced of the need to cultivate as many individual relationships with female associate managers as possible. Analyzing the commission's track record with different strategies, Bloor submitted that

[33] Ibid.

"printed documents and circulars are good for the dispersion of information" but that "manuscript letters are much better." "Public lecturing" was fine, "but far best of all is face to face talk between two or three persons." "This seems to be understood by the shrewd business men who control the springs of the Christian Commission," Bloor added. "The only way" for the USSC to stave off the further advances by the CC was by "an immediate, wise and thorough system of lecturing and missionary teaching," which he called "parochial visitation."[34] Bloor, who had once complained so melodramatically about his dealings with women and was still upset with their apparent fickleness, had come to appreciate women's importance to the commission's project. In October 1864, in a letter to William Hovey, who was newly assigned to aid him in handling correspondence and overseeing supplies, Bloor reminded Hovey that the commission depended first and foremost on the women of the country. The commission was "upheld" by the "Loyal American Public," he proclaimed, and "the moving Power in that Public is the Women."[35]

Bloor's tour of the homefront caused more stir than he anticipated. By suggesting that the Sanitary Commission become more responsive to the concerns of women, he unwittingly jeopardized his position as an organizational spokesman. His deference to the unpaid sector of the commission hierarchy, his willingness to take the women at their word, and his readiness to criticize official procedures set him apart from an organization enveloped in its own propaganda. But Bloor remained steadfast, asserting that whatever the consequences of his actions he was, in the end, "responsible to my own conscience." Strong interpreted Bloor's "insolence and insubordination" as retribution for not receiving a higher salary and longer furloughs.[36] Bloor was indignant at charges that he was "hypercritical" and "discontented" and genuinely puzzled as to why the commission rejected the truth.[37] Upon his return, Bloor found both Jenkins and Knapp unsupportive of his labors, even to the point of declining to reimburse him for his expenses. His appeals to Strong succeeded in obtaining the disputed funds, amounting to $138.97, but little else.[38]

To the standing committee, Bloor's disapproval of official USSC policy made his commission untenable, and at the beginning of October 1864 he

[34] Ibid.
[35] Alfred J. Bloor to William A. Hovey, October 18, 1864, Bloor Papers.
[36] Strong, September 19, 1864, *Diary*, 3:490.
[37] Bloor to Knapp, September 9, 1864, Bloor Papers.
[38] Alfred J. Bloor to George T. Strong, October 11, 1864; George T. Strong to Alfred J. Bloor, October 18, 1864; Alfred J. Bloor to George T. Strong, October 25, 1864, Bloor Papers.

was dismissed from his post. Retelling the series of events that led to his departure, Bloor noted that committee members demanded that he "retract and apologize for expressions . . . of the habitual dislike of the Administration of the Comm. to hear disagreeable truths." Bloor considered the demand "unjust," and his refusal to comply sealed his fate. In a letter to another aggrieved employee, Bloor claimed that only his sense of duty to the commission and the Union had kept him so long at the job. "If I had followed my personal interests," he remarked, "I would have resigned as soon as Mr. Olmsted did."[39] Female branch leaders and associate managers with whom he had long corresponded reacted to Bloor's departure with surprise and sadness. From Buffalo, Mrs. Seymour wrote Bloor that she was grateful for the "uniform courtesy, candor and promptness with which you have always responded to our enquiries." Abby May of the Boston branch reported that the news "surprised and pained us all."[40]

Bloor's dismissal took place against a backdrop of increased discord within the commission. In early 1864 Bellows temporarily left the New York office to fill the vacancy left by the death of Thomas Starr King, chief organizer for the commission in California. Upon his return, he found debilitating "jealousies" among his chief officers and learned that the "New York and Washington offices are not on smooth and confiding terms." The Washington headquarters still had not recovered from Olmsted's departure, and John Foster Jenkins, who replaced him as general secretary, was himself ready to resign. Jenkins reported to his colleagues that he felt overwhelmed by the work and inadequate to the task. Making matters worse, Jenkins quarreled regularly with Frederick Knapp, who had recently been promoted to associate secretary of the Eastern Department in Washington, and the rivalry between the two men left the commission's base at the warfront in shambles.[41]

To some degree, the men who left the organization could be accused of trying to impose their individual will on what was intended to be a con-

<hr>

[39] A. J. Bloor, "Extracts from a Letter," July 8, 1865, Bloor Papers. Bloor was replaced by William Hovey and Joseph Parrish, who divided his tasks. A. J. Bloor, "To Each Supply Correspondent of Principal Eastern Branches," October 31, 1864, Bloor Papers.

[40] Frederick N. Knapp to Standing Committee, October 15, 1864, Box 636, USSC Papers; Mrs. H. Seymour to A. J. Bloor, October 11, 1864; Abby W. May, October 17, 1864, Bloor Papers. See also Ellen Collins to Alfred Bloor, December 19, 1864; Jane C. Hoge to Alfred Bloor, October 22, 1864, Bloor Papers.

[41] Maxwell, *Lincoln's Fifth Wheel*, p. 226; Strong, September 16, 1864, *Diary*, 3:487. The standing committee requested Jenkins's resignation in 1865; Knapp's duties were reduced, and J. S. Blatchford was brought in from Boston to replace Jenkins and run the Washington office. Maxwell, *Lincoln's Fifth Wheel*, p. 265; Strong, September 13, 1864 and April 20, 1865, *Diary*, 3:486, 590.

certed, bureaucratic effort. But disagreements about management and direction reflected more than idiosyncratic personalities; they revealed some of the fundamental problems inherent in the Sanitary Commission project. Once again the commission's structure proved too fragile to withstand the pressures exerted by conflicts over voluntary relief work. Though they left for different reasons, Bloor and Olmsted found USSC rules inconsistent and out of touch with the realities of the homefront and the warfront, respectively. Olmsted had wanted more authority accorded to himself and more control exerted over wayward commission affiliates, particularly the Western Sanitary Commission.[42] Bloor advised listening more closely to female workers at home, recognizing their need for a voice in soldier relief. Just as the popular rumors forced the commission into a dilemma over how to respond without undermining the entire operation, so internal dissent and private criticism drained it of organizational strength.

The final year of the war saw the commissioners withdraw from attempts to secure a national audience for their liberal agenda. Popular hostility was a constant nuisance, reminding the commission of its ever-tenuous hold over supply lines, while dismissals and resignations took their toll on internal motivation. Faced with military slaughter on a grand scale, the organization narrowed its sights to serve the army and keep money and donations flowing for its medical operations. Like the northern citizenry, USSC leaders found in the military actions of the last eighteen months the needed impetus to keep going. But, despite their grandiose hopes, the commissioners had grown to see their work less as an inspiring opportunity than as a lackluster duty. Nowhere was the impact of homefront resistance more evident than in the internal debates over the postwar care of disabled soldiers. As the war drew to a close, the question of whether to implement a national welfare system for men damaged by the war weighed heavily on commissioners' minds.

The Problem of Disabled Soldiers

While the USSC may have been losing the battle for the hearts and minds of homefront women, it was still deeply engaged with the medical repercussions of the war which, given the continual stream of discharged soldiers

---

[42] The Western Sanitary Commission, based in St. Louis, was founded to aid soldiers in Missouri, and throughout the war attempted to maintain its independence from the central organization. See Censer, introduction, *FLO Papers*, 4:34.

from the front, were increasingly invading civilian life. As the war intensified, thousands of men left service permanently damaged by their military experience. Though the commission was founded to meet the medical and supply needs of soldiers recuperating in army hospitals, the length and severity of the war soon presented it with another social problem—the long-term care of disabled soldiers—that mirrored its original concern about the social upheaval consequent on military conflict. Well before the end of the war, Sanitary Commission agents at the front recognized that their work might need to expand in order to address the reintegration of these men into civil society. Did they represent a threat to the social order? Who would care for them? Should the nation construct hospitals devoted to maintaining men who had sacrificed their health and well-being for its maintenance? Should the commission assume responsibility for the design and management of such institutions?

When the time came to act on behalf of disabled veterans, it would not have been surprising if the commissioners had welcomed direct involvement. Union men disabled in combat possessed powerful symbolic capital that liberal elites could exploit in the name of a consensual nationalism. These men also posed some of the same social dangers upon their exit from the army as they had when they volunteered. The care of discharged, injured soldiers was certainly an arena in which disciplined charity might be displaced by overly indulgent attention to individuals. In fact, the commissioners worried that "Soldiers' Homes might prove lurking-places for malingerers and deserters." The objective, as Sanitary Commission officers saw it, was to resolve the "delicate problem" of "how to relieve the soldier without at the same time impairing his sense of duty."[43] If America followed the lead of European nations and created government-supported institutions, the maintenance of veterans would not require incessant propaganda work to garner public support. More important, it would not depend on the voluntary labor of thousands of women.

Yet when the commissioners, who at the outset of the war had claimed to know how to organize and discipline mass populations, examined the issue of disabled soldiers, their views were tempered by their experiences with the northern female public. Without a deep wellspring of patriotic loyalty to tap, their public stewardship over veterans offered precious few personal rewards. Nowhere was the commissioners' retreat from the national stage as transparent or as revealing as it was in their approach to the problem of disabled veterans.

[43] Stillé, *History of the United States Sanitary Commission*, pp. 296–97.

Early Proposals

From the earliest months of the war, a number of Sanitary Commission officers recognized that providing food, clothing, and medical care to regiments at the front represented just one aspect of soldier welfare. With early regiments serving only three-month tours, there was a constant exodus of men who had witnessed battle, were injured, and needed assistance to return home. In June 1862, Olmsted was already looking beyond the commission's routine hospital and field relief work to consider services for discharged soldiers. Olmsted worried not only about the challenges that veterans posed for civilian charities but also the political hazards that loomed ahead if they were not cared for adequately. "The ground work before the Commission yet to be entered upon," he wrote to Bellows, "is the nationalization of the care of the invalids of the war, guarding them from humiliation and fostering among them the spirit of independence and self support." Characteristically, Olmsted thought in terms of highly structured, hierarchical solutions to social problems, and proposed recruiting injured veterans into a "National Invalid Corps of the Sanitary Commission," whose members would be "uniformed and numbered" and employed in suitable urban occupations. "One legged men can collect fares and take tickets and keep tally," he reasoned, while "one armed men can run errands, carry telegraphic messages, watch against fires and ring alarm bells." Providing clothing for the invalid corps could be easily handled by women acting in the same capacities as they had during the war. "We should keep up our ladies—Women's Relief Associations and get them to furnish the clothing for instance," Olmsted suggested. Anticipating popular resistance to any centralized veterans' program, he warned Bellows that the commission's first duty was to "head off by a concerted movement all provincial poorhouse arrangements," and to do so "adroitly" and "cunningly."[44]

Bellows too believed that assisting mustered-out soldiers constituted both a social need and an opportunity. In August 1862, in a letter to Boston associate manager, Stephen G. Perkins (published and made available only to "fore-looking men"), he predicted that "not less than a hundred thousand men, of impaired vigor, maimed, or broken in body and spirit, will be thrown on the country." Apart from the enormous demands for special relief services, the social consequences of military service were grim. "Add to this a tide of another hundred thousand men, demoralized for civil life by

[44] Frederick L. Olmsted to Henry W. Bellows, June 22, 1862, Box 641, USSC Papers.

military habits," Bellows speculated, "and it is easy to see what a trial to the order, industry, and security of society, and what a burden to its already strained resources, there is in store for us."[45]

Bellows's document on discharged soldiers was contradictory: on the one hand, it disavowed any intention of interfering with the "natural laws" of the market and individual habits of "self-help"; on the other, it announced that the commission had already deemed the problem worthy of its attention. Barring foolish attempts by individual states to overcompensate and indulge incapacitated soldiers in a network of state institutions, Bellows hoped that a national pension law would be sufficient to allow localities to absorb and employ their own men. For those few—"the large body of foreigners, the reckless, and unrelated"—who were still unable to eke out an existence by honest labor, a system of "National Institutions" might be in order. But before formulating proposals for the structure of such institutions, he reported that Perkins had been commissioned to scrutinize European military pension and invalid systems and prepare a report for the commission. If the prospect of hundreds of thousands of invalid and indigent young men descending on northern cities was frightening, it also represented another occasion for the expert management of national affairs.[46]

After a lengthy trip abroad inspecting European veteran institutions, Perkins submitted his report, which the commission made available to its male associate managers. Foreign systems of care for invalid soldiers were gravely deficient, Perkins determined, particularly in failing to provide any "civil occupation" for the veteran. The results were all too evident in institutions such as the Hôtel des Invalides in Paris, where patients routinely spent their time drinking alcohol. Drafting suggestions for Pension and Hospital Laws, Perkins emphasized the importance of providing all disabled veterans with government pensions and the widows and orphans of deceased soldiers with some allowances. For those without means of support, he suggested that the federal government establish "an invalid-industrial village" in every state, where up to one hundred unmarried men would be provided with suitable employment and be "paid wages according to the value of their labor," which would be turned over in return for government care.[47]

---

[45] "Provision for Disabled Soldiers—Letter to S. G. Perkins," August 15, 1862, no. 49, Documents, 1:1–2.
[46] Ibid.
[47] Stephen H. Perkins, "Report on the Pension Systems and Invalid Hospitals of France, Prussia, Austria, Russia and Italy," May 22, 1863, no. 67, Documents, 2:11–19.

While the commissioners appeared anxious to develop an organizational position on the care of veterans, they were reluctant to take on another ambitious venture. For one thing, the war was still going on and the headquarters in Washington was handling the immediate needs of discharged soldiers. For another, their experiences with soldier relief had made them cautious about exploiting soldiers' welfare for political influence. Perkins's findings appeared structured to defend any position the commission might choose—large national institutions were probably untenable, yet some sort of decentralized system of care for single men might be in order.

Special Relief and Soldiers' Homes

The issue of disabled veterans divided the leadership, separating those who believed they had a responsibility and a right to impose themselves on the national scene from those who concluded that the war had outlived its usefulness for their personal objectives. More than anyone else, Frederick Knapp, Bellows's cousin and the organization's sole special relief agent in 1861, pulled the Sanitary Commission into debates about the welfare problems posed by demobilization. Officially charged with aiding soldiers traveling to and from the front, he found many discharged soldiers virtually abandoned by their regiments in Washington, where they were in need of medicine, clothing, and bureaucratic help.[48] On his own initiative, Knapp extended aid to such men. Before long, the USSC boasted of numerous special relief agents who, along with providing services for those in transit to the front, also attended to the financial and medical needs of "soldiers honorably discharged from service or dismissed from general hospitals."[49]

Pressing for an expansion of special relief services, Knapp kept the impressive record of his department in front of the standing committee. "Previously to our helping them," he recounted to the central office, "some poor discharged soldiers had been waiting in this place many days and weeks trying to collect the means to get home." Still others were too ill to travel and required medical assistance. Setting up a "Lodge" near the paymaster's office and providing food, clothing, and money to the soldiers represented funds well spent. Beyond all else, the work alleviated untold

[48] "First Report, Aid and Comfort given by the San. Com. to Sick Soldiers Passing through Washington," September 23, 1861, no. 35, *Documents*, 1:1–12; S. Newberry, *The U.S. Sanitary Commission in the Valley of the Mississippi* (Cleveland, Ohio, 1871), pp. 333–34.
[49] Henry W. Bellows, "The U.S. Sanitary Commission," pp. 76–77.

"mental anxiety."[50] As Knapp's system developed, agents routinely aided veterans in filing papers at government claim offices, gave direct handouts to those without means of returning to their homes, and rescued those who had been "induced by evil companions to remain behind," seeing to it that they did indeed go home.[51]

Special relief services soon grew to include a cluster of refuges improvised to meet the needs of the diverse constituencies affected by demobilization. The "Home" on Capitol Street in Washington served as the headquarters of special relief, providing shelter for tens of thousands of soldiers returning to northern villages and cities. Over time, it enlarged its operations, increasing the number of beds from 140 in 1862 to 320 in 1863, and setting up a separate hospital building to treat those soldiers too weak or ill to travel. In January 1862, the USSC founded two nurses' homes, one in Washington and one in Annapolis, that accommodated nurses on their way to military hospitals. For women who journeyed to Washington to assist male relatives, the commission established a Home for Soldiers' Wives and Mothers, where soldiers' families, "in nearly every case without money," found temporary shelter. In addition to the main soldiers' home, the commission also maintained a number of smaller "lodges" in Washington and throughout the South that provided a soldier with "food, lodging, assistance in correcting his papers, aid in looking up his claims, help in obtaining his pension and his bounty." The special relief service also boasted a claim agency, a pension agency, and a back-pay agency.[52]

The care of soldiers, their families, and injured veterans was never just a warfront issue. Throughout the war years, homefront women informed branch leaders and commission officers that they considered the care of local soldiers' families a salient component of their wartime responsibili-

---

[50] "Third Report concerning the Aid and Comfort given by the Sanitary Commission to Sick Soldiers Passing through Washington," March 21, 1862, no. 39, *Documents*, 1:1–5.

[51] "Fourth Report concerning Aid and Comfort given by the Sanitary Commission to Sick Soldiers Passing through Washington," December 15, 1862, no. 59a, *Documents*, 1:1–3.

[52] "Fifth Report concerning Aid and Comfort given by the Sanitary Commission to Sick and Invalid Soldiers," October 1, 1863, no. 77, *Documents*, 2:1–21; *Bulletin*, April 15, 1864, 1:367; *The United States Sanitary Commission: A Sketch of Its Purposes and Its Work* (Boston, 1863), pp. 222–25; *The Sanitary Commission of the United States Army: A Succinct Narrative of its Works and Purposes* (New York, 1864), p. 231. Charles Stillé wrote that the "soldiers' Home" that Knapp created became the headquarters of the Special Relief Service in Washington. The Commission set up similar stations on the route to the Army of the Potomac, and "the same work was performed under the auspices of the Commission at Louisville, at Nashville, at Memphis, at New Orleans." See *History of the U.S. Sanitary Commission*, pp. 290–94.

ties.[53] Special relief itself expanded into the homefront with temporary way-stations and homes, administered either by female-led branches or itinerant relief agents. In New York City, the WCRA helped soldiers with immediate provisions of clothing and transportation and, when necessary, directed them to institutions such as the privately funded New England Rooms or the state-run New York Soldiers' Relief Association for extended care.[54] Anticipating the growing need for services for returning soldiers, Schuyler had provided for the enlargement of homefront special relief in her reorganization plan for the WCRA. Reminiscent of the "visiting" practices of early nineteenth-century moral reform societies, WCRA women, beginning in 1864, regularly visited the tenements of impoverished veterans applying for aid to determine the legitimacy of their claims.[55] In many northern communities, Sanitary Commission branches and local soldiers' aid societies administered their own homes for discharged soldiers. The Buffalo branch constructed the Soldiers' Rest and treated thousands of "friendless" soldiers, many on their way to the West. In 1862, the women of Elmira, New York, set up a way station and, with a contribution of $2,000 from the state of New York, assisted men traveling north. By 1864 the USSC boasted twenty-five affiliated homes and lodges; by the end of the war, the number had reached forty.[56]

Like the aid societies themselves, local soldiers' homes soon became contested sites for competing welfare groups as well as for individual women who used them to accommodate personal needs. After a visit to Buffalo, Bloor suspected that both the Christian Commission and a state-run relief

---

[53] For extended discussion of the impact of the Civil War on soldiers' families and the response of the federal government, see Megan J. McClintock, "Civil War Pensions and the Reconstruction of Union Families," *Journal of American History* 83 (September 1996): 456–80.

[54] The New England Soldiers' Relief Association was located at 194 Broadway, because "of convenience to routes of travel of disabled soldiers," and was supplied with goods from local benevolent and soldiers' aid societies; Bellows sat on its board. See *Report of the Superintendent of the New England Soldiers' Relief Association, December 1862. Founded by Sons of New England resident in New York, April 3, 1862* (New York, 1862); "Fifth Report," no. 77, *Documents*, 2:3–4.

[55] See C. K. Griffen, Report of Special Relief, February 1864, Box 955, USSC papers, on women who requested that men assume some of the visiting responsibilities because tenements were "not always in respectable parts of the city." For the practice of "visiting ladies" in early moral reform societies, see Christine Stansell, *City of Women: Sex and Class in New York, 1789–1860* (New York, 1986), pp. 64–68; Keith Melder, "Ladies Bountiful: Organized Women's Benevolence in Early Nineteenth-Century America," in *Women's Experience in America: An Historical Anthology*, ed. Esther Katz and Anita Rapone (New Brunswick, N.J., 1980), p. 102.

[56] Newberry, *Commission in the Valley*, pp. 414–18; *Bulletin*, February 1, 1864, 1:209; Henry W. Bellows to Thomas Starr King, February 12, 1864, Box 951, USSC Papers; Maxwell, *Lincoln's Fifth Wheel*, p. 306.

organization were "obtaining a foothold" in the management of the Buffalo home. In Portland, Maine, the WCRA associate manager informed him that the local soldiers' home had "passed into the hands of the Christian Commission and of a local organization."[57] From Buffalo, Mrs. Seymour alerted the commission to still other uses of homes in her region; she observed that women were traveling around the country "looking after vagabond husbands and using the *Homes* as hotels on the route."[58]

The Sanitaria Idea

While the Commission's special relief department facilitated the continual redeployment and demobilization of the Union army, Knapp was concerned that the organization was not addressing the issue of veterans' care as forcefully as it should. His experience with discharged soldiers and his close proximity to the military afforded him a special vantage point from which to consider the problems associated with demobilization, and he worried that the return of hundreds of thousands of young military men to civilian life at war's end could prove disastrous. In September 1864, he commenced a long correspondence with his colleagues about what intervention the USSC should make. For him, the question was not just one of charity. Rather, the social needs of discharged soldiers offered an unparalleled opportunity to project the commission once more into the forefront of social welfare and the management of class relations.

In language that recalled the original objectives of the founders, Knapp offered Bellows an analysis of why the commission was losing precious ground. "It does not keep up with the movements of the day," he wrote Bellows. "It *is not comprehensive* enough, and *bold* enough. . . . The Sanitary Commission is gradually *losing* its *scientific character.*" The opportunity to become an "Established Institution" appeared to be losing out to the day-to-day problems that beset soldier relief. He attributed the recent successes of the Christian Commission to the fact that the Sanitary Commission had failed to broaden "its sphere of action" or to "make itself known . . . as the most effective agency for providing for the wants of soldiers." More serious still, the social identity of Sanitary leaders had evidently compromised the organization's claim to being a truly national structure. Indeed, the specific class and urban character of the USSC had undermined its claims to represent nationalism as an ideology. Noting the "feeling growing throughout

---

[57] Alfred J. Bloor to Frederick N. Knapp, September 9, 1864, Bloor Papers.
[58] Mrs. H. Seymour to J. A. Anderson, January 24, 1865, Box 952, USSC Papers.

the country, that this is not so much a *'United States Sanitary Commission'* as a *'New York'* Commission," Knapp suggested that the standing committee include men from other states even if they could not attend meetings.[59]

For Knapp, the organization had demonstrated its malaise most starkly in its failure to act on recommendations for concerted intervention in veteran care. One idea was to transform the Sanitary Commission into a postwar claim agency that would provide immediate assistance to discharged soldiers, paralleling in some ways the provisions of the Civil War pension law. In Knapp's view, the claim agency could be "so wide reaching & generous . . . it would give aid . . . to every soldier."[60]

Even more serious was the commission's apparent refusal to take seriously his proposal to build a comprehensive system of "Sanitaria" for disabled soldiers. "Sanitaria" was Knapp's term for a formidable complex of institutions that would create domesticated, free laborers out of formerly rough and wild soldiers. His hope was to go beyond merely warehousing discharged soldiers to shape their moral development and industrial futures. As Knapp described them, sanitaria would combine "the best methods of . . . the *Asylum*, the *School*, the *Work-shop*, and the *Home* all in one, for these waiting men." The ideas behind sanitaria were organic to *"the times,"* he reasoned, and naturally *"forced themselves* upon the attention of the Commission." It was incumbent upon the USSC to recognize that its responsibilities "to *nurture* and to *lead* public sentiment in this direction of humane and patriotic exertion" operated not merely for the duration of the war but were "reaching *far beyond* this war." "The Commission," he argued, "is a body which ought to be both *respected* and *feared.*"[61]

Sanitary Intervention

Knapp was not alone in fearing the social impact of demobilization. As the war drew to a close, the northern press repeatedly voiced anxiety over the potential upheaval posed by the rapid, massive discharge of soldiers. The North, after all, faced the return of over one million men to civilian life. Secretary of War Stanton devised a system for the orderly disbandment of the army, utilizing existing military organization to insure each man's his-

[59] Frederick Knapp to Henry W. Bellows, September 6, 1864, Box 951, USSC Papers (underlined in original).

[60] Ibid. For a discussion of the early and extensive Civil War pension system, see Theda Skocpol, *Protecting Soldiers and Mothers: The Political Origins of Social Policy in the United States* (Cambridge, Mass., 1992), pp. 102–15.

[61] Knapp to Bellows, September 6, 1864, Box 951, USSC Papers (underlined in original).

tory was recorded and his payroll registered. For the most part, demobilization proceeded peacefully and quickly. The few instances of spontaneous violence, as when the First Vermont Heavy Artillery rioted in New York City and again in Troy on its way home, failed to spark larger uprisings. Contemporary observers, as well as later chroniclers, were struck by the relative ease with which the Union army disbanded and returned home.[62]

But before the final verdict was in, and before a popular consensus emerged that determined that their families would provide the best "homes" for discharged soldiers, descriptions of destitute, starving men returning from the front frightened many. Accounts of "maimed and battered veterans" grinding hand-organs on the street prompted private contributions of shelter and money. Cities and towns alike were faced with secondary welfare needs created by the war. In early 1864, the *New York Times* estimated that in New York City one thousand children of soldiers were forced to seek lodging in the crowded Soldier's Child's Refuge.[63]

Knapp was at a loss to explain why his colleagues chose to ignore a social danger so many others perceived as imminent. But Knapp's perspective on the commission's capacities was shaped by a circumscribed knowledge of war relief. Having spent most of the war in Washington managing troops, supplies, and special relief, he experienced none of the wrangling with the female public that had demoralized his New York-based colleagues. For Knapp, the pressing issue for Sanitary Commission leaders had been and still was one of class relations. In January 1865, he wrote Bellows again, impressing upon him the serious consequences that might result from neglecting the state of affairs at the front. "Our statistics, taken at Lodge No. 4 Sanitary Commission (where all the discharged men of the Eastern Armies present themselves) and my own *eyes*, resting daily on these men helpless or half helpless from disease or wounds, tell me that . . . there will be, in the aggregate, a vast amount of *suffering*, & *poverty* & *toil* among these men . . . unless some wise provisions is made for them now, while the sympathies of the people are all alive." Knapp implored Bellows to look to the future and judge the potential for disorder. *"Five years after* the struggle is over . . . there will be far less thought and sympathy waiting at every corner, as it now is, to meet a disabled soldier," he predicted. "We shall get *accustomed* to

[62] Dixon Wecter, *When Johnny Comes Marching Home* (Cambridge, Mass., 1944), p. 144; Ida M. Tarbell, "Disbanding the Union Army," *McClure's Magazine* (March 1901): 400–412; Allan Nevins, "A Major Result of the Civil War," *Civil War History* 5 (September 1959): 239–50.

[63] Edward Winslow Martin [J. Dabney MacCabe], *The Secrets of the Great City . . .* (Philadelphia, 1868), p. 470; *New York Times*, November 11, 1864; "The Homeless Children of our Soldiers," *New York Times*, February 9, 1864.

it—and communities will accept the fact & pressure of a larger number of these disabled men among them, struggling for a livelihood, just as they accept the fact of the vast mass of *permanent poverty* in their midst."[64]

How seriously the Sanitary Commission ever considered the sanitaria idea is difficult to assess. Sensing the public's concerns for disabled soldiers, it discussed the idea in its publications early in 1864. While not repudiating the concept, the organization made a point of reminding its readers of all the work it was presently doing for returning soldiers. In the "temporary homes, lodges, and rests, of which there are about thirty already in existence," it was feeding and lodging some four thousand soldiers a day. With such experience under its belt, the commission proclaimed itself "more thoroughly conversant with the wants and habits of disabled men, and with the means of supplying them, than any other organization in the land."[65] In March 1864, the standing committee announced that it had appointed a subcommittee to research material "upon which to base action in establishing 'Sanitaria.' " If it deemed the plan feasible, the subcommittee was authorized to set up "experimental Sanitaria for certain classes of disabled soldiers."[66]

While Knapp's suggestions for veteran relief measures made little headway, his persistent entreaties began to irritate his colleagues, giving some a reason to attack his position in the organization. Standing committee members charged that, though effective as the special relief agent, Knapp was ignoring his other duties in Washington. Claiming to have been particularly dismayed about his excessive purchases of supplies, Strong recorded that by September he, Agnew, and Jenkins were convinced that they "must throw Knapp over." In essence, Knapp concurred, requesting that he be charged solely with handling special relief. The committee compromised. It refused Knapp's request to establish a separate bureau of special relief, but appointed him general superintendent of special relief and relieved him of other responsibilities.[67]

Repudiating Centralization

After investigating the potential disorder of demobilization, the Sanitary Commission rejected a leadership role in veterans' care and shied away

---

[64] Frederick N. Knapp to Henry W. Bellows, January 17, 1865, Box 641, USSC Papers.
[65] *Bulletin*, March 15, 1864, 2:1074.
[66] "Plan of Executive Organization of the U.S. Sanitary Commission and Rules for Its Executive Service," December 16, 1864, no. 86, *Documents*, 2:233–34.
[67] Strong, September 13, 1864 and January 14, 1865, *Diary*, 3:486, 543.

from supporting the creation of national asylums. Drawing on a question-naire sent by Knapp to military personnel and civilians involved in special relief, Bellows concluded that very few men—probably only 150 in New York City—would require extensive care. Cautioning against making wholly dependent men "a separate class" and a "public show," he worried about creating a prominent reminder of their wartime sacrifices. Estimating that probably only 2000 men nationwide were in need of some public care and that most of them were Irish and German immigrants—"We doubt if 2 per cent would turn out Americans!"—Bellows concluded that these men would be absorbed into agricultural communities. "It would be idle . . . and a wicked waste of money and time, and wisdom, to make permanent provision." In what appeared a reversal of his position on centralized welfare, Bellows urged localities to pick up the burden of veterans' relief, since public charities operating on the local level were more than sufficient to care for the "small per centage of homeless and friendless incurables." By the end of 1865, he announced that most disabled men were "the objects of a proud and tender domestic or neighborly care" and had been "withdrawn from public view, as it is desirable they should be." Bellows had come full circle; now he was quick to praise the benefits of community-controlled philanthropy and the independent initiatives of women. Rather than advocating the establishment of federal homes for veterans, Bellows deemed the feminized private "home" the only suitable site for the long-term care of the nation's defenders.[68]

Though rejecting the idea of a large system of national institutions, Bellows was hesitant to relinquish completely a Sanitary Commission presence

[68] "Provision Required for the Relief and Support of Disabled Soldiers and Sailors," December 15, 1865, no. 95, *Documents*, 2:4–13. Despite Bellows's assertion that a crisis had been averted, demobilization did result in social problems. Even with the wartime expansion of the economy, Union army veterans exacerbated a growing labor surplus. The war had stimulated inflation more than production, and most industries grew at slower rates during the conflict than they did either before or after the war. In cities like New York, foreign immigration—often encouraged by employers to keep wages depressed—had mushroomed in the last three years of the war, adding to labor competition. See David Montgomery, *Beyond Equality: Labor and the Radical Republicans, 1862–1872* (New York, 1967), pp. 3–8; Emerson David Fite, *Social and Industrial Conditions in the North during the Civil War* (New York, 1963), pp. 190–96. The inability of the economy to absorb veterans was evident by social indices such as criminal arrests, which increased sharply immediately following the war. Prisons began to fill up with men who had been, in the words of one penitentiary official, "incapacitated and demoralized by an apprenticeship to the trade of war." In the summer of 1865, the New York State Inebriate Asylum reported a sharp increase in alcoholism, which it linked to the effects of the war. See *Report of Eastern Penitentiary of Pennsylvania*, quoted in Edith Abbott, "The Civil War and the Crime Wave of 1865–70," *Social Service Review* 1 (June 1927): 228; "New York State Inebriate Asylum," *Nation*, August 31, 1865, p. 273.

in veteran welfare services. In published documents, he assured the home-front that the commission was fulfilling its responsibilities in the numerous soldiers' homes and lodges it maintained. Commission homes incorporated few of Knapp's concepts, however. The USSC's New York City Lincoln Home followed the regimented model of antebellum asylums. Discipline was of paramount concern, as was rigorous record keeping. The superintendent, who was responsible to an examining committee composed of members of the standing committee of the Sanitary Commission, was charged with canvassing the city, including Blackwell's Island (the site of New York City's almshouse), in search of disabled soldiers who might need assistance and be unaware of its existence.[69] When the Lincoln Home opened in May of 1865, 365 men—many Irish, most single, and most laborers—registered for occupancy.[70]

Bellows even accepted an invitation to head a state-run soldiers' institution. Upon learning of the growing demand for shelter, fifty New York civic and business leaders signed a petition in 1864 requesting the establishment of a state institution. In New York City alone, the petition noted, there were at least 1,000 disabled, homeless veterans, while the needs throughout the state were undoubtedly larger.[71] In August 1865, a committee for the proposed home invited USSC officers to serve as trustees. Strong, Stillé, and Gibbs declined; Van Buren and Agnew did not reply. Bellows alone accepted, and he became chairman of the executive committee of the Home for Disabled Soldiers, which was formally incorporated in January 1866.[72]

---

[69] Frederick Knapp to Dr. J. Foster Jenkins, "Working Plan for the 'Lincoln Home,' " March 4, 1865, Box 641, USSC Papers. See David J. Rothman, *The Discovery of the Asylum: Social Order and Disorder in the New Republic* (Boston, 1971), pp. 138–54.

[70] "Minutes of the Executive Committee, Lincoln Home, May 14, 1865–March 10, 1866," esp. entries for June 7, 1865, and February 2, 1866; "Applications for Admission into Lincoln Home, May 22, 1865–May 26, 1866," Box 725, USSC Papers.

[71] Col. Vincent Colyer to Mr. Andrew Warner, May 30, 1865, Home for Disabled Soldiers Papers (hereafter HDS Papers). "Petition for Permanent Home for the Soldiers," New York, December 17, 1863; signees included William Cullen Bryant, Theodore Roosevelt, Charles Daly, and Frank Moore.

[72] "An Act to Incorporate the Home for Disabled Soldiers, January 24, 1865," HDS Papers. Bellows's commitment to the Home for Disabled Soldiers was calculated to serve the propaganda needs of the USSC. Borrowing from Knapp's proposals, Bellows suggested the creation of a "self-supporting Asylum on a Farm in the neighborhood of New York, on hired land . . . where industrial pursuits could be introduced." While seemingly constructive, his was a cynical move to gain public sanction. The "experiment," he admitted, would mainly serve to "shut the mouths of the gainsayers who captiously complained that New York was doing nothing for Soldiers." The home's trustees, in doubt as to how to proceed, agreed to seek "a healthy site in a rural district of this state." See "Minutes, Board of Trustees of the Home for Disabled Soldiers," February 8, 1866; Andrew Warner to John P. Crosby, August 16, 1865; Frederic de Peyster to James Lenox, January 29, 1866, HDS Papers.

• • •

Rather than risking another failed venture in nationalizing welfare or wasting resources on what was deemed an unimportant dependent population, the Sanitary Commission under Bellows's direction repudiated a leadership role in the care of veterans. It rejected the idea of permanent "military asylums" in favor of the national pension system, and urged Congress to allot a minimum of $5 million to establish provisions for soldiers' families.[73] In retreating from the issue of veteran welfare, the commission revealed not only the toll taken by the years spent negotiating with the female public but also its estimation of the small political capital to be gained by means of disabled veterans.

Most of all, the USSC's stance on veterans' services represented its leaders' assumption that women should voluntarily provide the material and emotional resources needed to care for the nation's defenders. Once again, women's unpaid household labor would produce social value that could serve the interests of cosmopolitan rationalists. Having determined that veterans requiring long-term care were numerically insignificant and of no value politically, the commissioners resolved to leave them "friendless," confident that sentimentalized forms of feminine care would suffice to protect society from any dangers they might pose.

Just as the commissioners had resigned themselves to rely on public concern about the war's final military offensives for the continuance of army relief, so they concluded that popular affections for disabled veterans could supplant any organized intervention into the long-term care of soldiers. The homes of northern women, once castigated as the sources of disorganized charity and inefficient labor, were reinscribed as essential sites of social order and political stability. Sanitary Commission men were on the defensive. The female public's sustained critique of the patriotic and economic motivations of cosmopolitan rationalists made any new bid for political leadership unsound. The commission experiment had unwittingly exposed the contradictions of the antebellum compromise on gender; the notion that women's acceptance of a secondary political status afforded them primary status in the arena of social welfare unraveled in the course of warwork. As the war drew to a close, it seemed that whatever breach had occurred in the nineteenth-century gender compromise had to be repaired. Once more situating women in a compensatory position, as valuable to the nation for their voluntary charity and sentimental labors, the war might leave the gender balance of power unshaken.

[73] "Provision," *Documents*, 2:17.

9

"BECOMING HISTORY": APPRAISING FEMALE WARWORK

The question of a postwar presence was far from most commissioners' minds when the war finally ended. While USSC officers continued to discuss ways in which they might influence demobilization, they increasingly looked forward to returning to their prewar careers or pursuing new interests. Given the unexpectedly conflictual nature of the Sanitary Commission's operations, its leaders welcomed a future free from their wartime responsibilities. Where they had once regarded the war as an opportunity to gain authority for their ideas about class management and the value to the state of nonpartisan expertise, they now felt defeated by the crises they and the war had generated. While they disagreed among themselves on how quickly the commission should close down its operations, most were ready to abandon the project and move on.[1]

Even before the military conflict was over, Bellows began to distance himself from the Sanitary Commission, putting his energies into plans for reorganizing the Unitarian church and for transforming the Union League Club into a vehicle for municipal civil service reform.[2] Writing to his son,

---

[1] Strong observed that Bellows favored a more gradual closing, while he, Agnew, Binney, and Stillé wanted a "more expeditious and less costly process." See Strong, July 13, 1865, *Diary*, vol. 4, *The Post-War Years, 1865–1875*, p. 20.
[2] Disturbed by the parochial condition of Unitarianism and the theological divide between its conservative and radical factions, Bellows spearheaded a plan to spread Unitarian doctrine

Russell, in December 1864, he revealed his desire to concentrate on his "ministerial and strictly religious work," if only he "could wholly lay down my Commission work & office." Two months later he complained to Russell that USSC affairs had become "so methodical and unambitious" that he was satisfied to do the minimum necessary and felt a "painful pleasure" at seeing the "dismantling of the great work of the land." To his wife, Bellows confided that the war's closing "releases me from external cares and responsibilities & gives me such hopes of new interim life, parish usefulness, & domestic happiness." Years later, Bellows recalled his commission days more regretfully, expressing concern that he might "never recover the vigour I then squandered."[3]

George Templeton Strong was equally anxious for the commission to wind up its operations. "Thank God the time for the Sanitary Commission's release and disembodiment seems so near at hand at last!" he exclaimed on June 19, 1865. The standing committee had just met and decided "to draw in our tentacles, dismiss agents, close relief stations, curtail work and expenditure everywhere and at once."[4] For years to come, Strong would reiterate that he had suffered personally and financially—being, as he phrased it, "professionally demoralized"—for having served on the commission.[5] Olmsted, mired in the financially strapped Mariposa company in San Francisco, claimed still to feel the deleterious effects of his wartime labors. His assignment in Washington had made him "over wrought and over-strained," he

---

throughout the country. In April 1865, he convened a national conference at which 385 delegates representing 225 Unitarian churches agreed to pledge funds to support missionary work. See Walter Donald Kring, *Henry Whitney Bellows* (Boston, 1979), p. 306; Conrad Wright, *The Liberal Christians: Essays on American Unitarian History* (Boston, 1970), pp. 314–20. Under Bellows's leadership, the Union League Club in 1865 passed a resolution to pursue the passage of civil service reforms. See Bellows, *Union League Club*, pp. 85, 191; Paul Renard Migliore, "The Business of Union: The New York Business Community and the Civil War" (Ph.D. diss., Columbia University, 1975), pp. 410–16; Morton Keller, *Affairs of State: Public Life in Late Nineteenth-Century America* (Cambridge, Mass., 1977), pp. 115–17.

[3] Henry Bellows to "Son" [Russell Bellows], December 12, 1864, and February 12, 1865; Henry Bellows to "Wife" [Eliza Bellows], 1865, Bellows Papers; Bellows, January 22, 1869, quoted in William Quentin Maxwell, *Lincoln's Fifth Wheel: The Political History of the United States Sanitary Commission* (New York, 1956), p. 286.

[4] Strong, June 19, 1865, *Diary*, 4:10. The commission continued to operate for years after the war, dispensing special relief (according to Strong, 16,000 men were still unsettled at the end of 1866, and the USSC processed them at the rate of 1,200 a month) and publishing reports on military hygiene. See Strong, December 28, 1866, and May 4, 1867, *Diary*, 4:116, 134. Strong complained of the inability "to get our affairs closed" as late as November 1, 1867. See *Diary*, 4:159. He recorded that the commission had its accounts ready for final examination by the auxiliary finance committee in November 1870, but still was trying to close up shop in November 1873. See Strong, November 1870 and November 25, 1873, *Diary*, 4:329, 503.

[5] Strong, December 13, 1872, *Diary*, 4:462.

complained to Knapp in 1865; nearly two years later, he continued to suffer "the weakness of the unstringing of certain faculties and talents that were too long, severely and steadily bent."[6]

As the war drew to an end, Louisa Lee Schuyler supervised the closing of the WCRA's office at Cooper Union and made plans to travel to Europe with her father and brothers. Expecting to stay abroad for at least a year, she was ambivalent about creating such a sharp rupture with her four years of warwork. "I am sorry too, to leave the country just now," she wrote to Angelina Post; "there seems so much to do." She did not lack opportunities to work. Bellows was trying to recruit her to join him in the plans he was laying for the Unitarian church. Schuyler had already engaged a number of female friends in discussions about organizing care for soldiers' families in New York. She even thought of "forming a new Society," hoping to forge it "from as many of our old members, as could be got together." Yet, notwithstanding her vow "not to work in the driving way we have been" but in a "reasonable" way that would allow for "other life than a *one-ideaed* one," even Louisa Schuyler was too exhausted to bring a new project to life. She sailed to Europe in November 1865, leaving Post in charge of the remaining tasks.[7]

Constructing History

Though they might have felt weary and bitter about their wartime experiences, the men who led the Sanitary Commission were not ready to abandon the work without ensuring that they had a hand in shaping the historical record and public reputation of their organization. As they wound up official operations at the front, they pledged to "be diligent in gathering and arranging material for a final report."[8] So important was this work that the standing committee agreed to fund a historical volume "at any expense which may be required." Strong noted in his diary that among the duties to which the committee attended in its final meetings was the selection of someone to write the commission's history.[9]

Louisa Lee Schuyler also felt strongly about the need to create a history

[6] Frederick Law Olmsted to Frederick Newman Knapp, April 9, 1865, in *FLO Papers*, vol. 5, *The California Frontier: 1863–1865*, ed. Victoria Post Ranney (Baltimore, 1990), p. 349.
[7] Louisa Schuyler to Angie Post, August 2, 1865; Louisa Schuyler to Angie Post, November 8, 1865, Schuyler Papers.
[8] Strong, June 19, 1865, *Diary*, 4:10.
[9] Stillé, *History of the United States Sanitary Commission*, pp. iii; Strong, July 13, 1865, *Diary*, 4:20.

of the Sanitary Commission's accomplishments. Ever conscious that the needs of the public rarely matched those of the organization, she suggested separate volumes on field relief, special relief, the collection of supplies (which would include the work of the branches, fairs, and "homework"), and claim agencies and bureaus of employment, each tailored to a specific audience. Most important would be the "popular history," a single volume that "will be read everywhere" and "ought to go into every public library in the country." In a private letter to Bellows, Schuyler urged the men to choose "someone who understands the whole work thoroughly, can grasp its magnitude, & can present the spirit of the work." Comprehending the need for some distance from the war, she cautioned that "this volume should not be written for two or three years."[10]

Even before Schuyler penned her letter, the commissioners had already chosen Charles Janeway Stillé to author the official history. Stillé was, in Strong's words, "a man of leisure and culture," the most salient qualifications for the task. A member of the USSC's standing committee since 1864, he had made his wartime name by writing the 1863 Loyal Publication pamphlet *How a Free People Conduct a Long War*, which argued for unified popular support in the face of military setbacks as well as for the necessity of strict military discipline. The commission distributed it by the hundreds of thousands at both the homefront and the warfront.[11]

Stillé's final text, *History of the Sanitary Commission* (which was published in 1866, less than a year after it was commissioned), opened with a statement on behalf of the commission, announcing its firm intention to educate the public of the "truth of its theory, and the practical success of its methods." Hoping to strike a popular note by underscoring the people's patriotism, it claimed that "never has there been an instance in History such as that presented in this country during the late war, in which everything that was accomplished, good or bad, was due to the impulse of popular ideas."[12] Mindful of this chance to interpret the cataclysmic events Americans had just experienced, Stillé structured his account as a primer on what could be accomplished by partnerships between private citizens and the government. At the same time, he offered criticisms of the government's policies in order

---

[10] Louisa Lee Schuyler to Henry W. Bellows, July 26, 1865, Box 642. In August 1865, the archives of the USSC were collected in New York, and a historical bureau was created. See J. Parrish to H. W. Bellows, August 3, 1865, Box 642, USSC Papers.

[11] Strong, July 13, 1865, *Diary*, 4:20; Censer, introduction, *FLO Papers*, 4:41; Charles J. Stillé, *How a Free People Conduct a Long War*, Loyal Publication Society, no. 13 (New York, 1863), pp. 1–16.

[12] Stillé, *History of the U.S. Sanitary Commission*, pp. v, 17–19.

that "future generations" might "avoid the errors of the present." Notwith-standing the self-promoting and overheated language of Stillé's history, a tone of bitterness was all too evident; responsibility for the commission's wartime difficulties was placed squarely on the shoulders of others.[13] Col-lecting data for his volume, Stillé asked his colleagues to provide personal accounts of their experiences with the organization. In a long, detailed let-ter, Bellows traced his memories about the origins of the commission, pro-ducing the stories about the failure of Elizabeth Blackwell's women's association and the need for masculine intervention that would be retold long after the war was over.[14]

But while the commissioners planned the end of their own patriotic labors and looked to posterity, they were disinclined to release the female homefront either from their oversight or from voluntary service to the state. Following an assessment of the aid that the Sanitary Commission continued to dispense, especially in helping soldiers collect back pay and pensions (which continued for months after the fighting ended), Bellows re-vived some of Olmsted's ideas when he asked women to maintain their aid organizations in order to supplement federal veteran welfare services. Ap-parently, such female benevolence posed no risk of upsetting the natural mechanisms of the market that would reabsorb veterans into the work force. Invoking the gendered rhetoric of the domestic ideology, Bellows summoned women—the "natural guardians of the soldiers"—to remain ready to work "for an indefinite period," reasoning that they could effort-lessly redirect their labors to assist veterans from their communities to find employment and avoid the "evils and temptations" of civilian society. Equally important, women's groups could also serve as propaganda chan-nels, "communicating with the people, from time to time, upon such topics as concern the continued welfare of returned soldiers."[15]

Joseph Parrish offered some proposals of his own for expanding home-front operations during the transition to a peacetime society. Canvassers, many of them lecturing until the last days of the war and still in the field, could serve the commission as propaganda agents, he reckoned. "They should be ministers who are stationed in considerable Inns," where they could "control the local press, and exert in social circles, as in their public ministrations, a large influence." If USSC claim agencies were established in most of the towns and cities of the WCRA region, Parrish thought that

[13] Ibid. pp. v–vi.
[14] See Henry W. Bellows to Charles Stillé, November 15, 1865, Bellows Papers.
[15] Henry W. Bellows and Jno. S. Blatchford, "To the Branches and Aid Societies . . . ," May 15, 1865, reprinted in *Bulletin*, June 1, 1865, 3:1203–5.

these, together with canvassers, could "secure the attention at least of the people to the work of the Commission." By July 1865, as funding for official claim work dried up, Parrish proposed that women volunteer to serve as agents. "Are there not assoc. managers & others throughout your department," he queried Schuyler, "who can act efficient as claim agents for the next three months?" Writing to Bellows of his ideas, Parrish expressed sentimental admiration for the "womanhood of America" and the "spirit & purpose that has animated their work." Reflecting on the "sorrows and weeps" of women who had to "sunder the ties that have bound them in a fellowship of toil & trial" and abandon the work that "elevated themselves" and "dignified the nation," he had a heartfelt solution: "Let us have three more months of this earnest work."[16]

Sanitary Commission officers had hit upon a pared-down formula for nation-building, one still guided by elite management but no longer requiring direct intervention. Warwork apparently sufficed as a training ground for patriotic labors; homefront women could go on as dutiful unpaid workers, spreading the Sanitary Commission's message, for their own good as well as that of the nation. After years of battling the female homefront for its support and its confidence, the commissioners assumed that those who remained in the USSC fold were loyal participants and could be trusted to carry on whatever the leaders were themselves disinclined to do. In a sense, they were admitting that women and canvassers, operating on a local level, would probably have more success than they would in creating a positive Sanitary Commission presence.

Promoting his new credo of decentralized welfare provision and once more invoking the sanctity of the home, Bellows advised USSC affiliates to convey the idea that "it is a disgrace to a town to allow its own soldiers or its widowed and orphaned families to look beyond its own limits for support." He still insisted on a discerning approach to benevolence and cautioned against indulging unemployed soldiers who took to the streets with hat in hand: "Public, shameless beggary from door to door and in the street is every way corrupting," he wrote in the *Bulletin*. But Bellows also sounded the alarm against the dangers of centralization and implored his constituency to aid in undoing the concentration of political power that had occurred during the war. A former Whig, Bellows now preached, "That government is best which governs least," adding that "that state of society is

---

[16] Joseph Parrish to Louisa L. Schuyler, July 15, 1865, Box 669, USSC Papers. Though the standing committee accepted Parrish's canvasser plan, no evidence exists to suggest that it actually went into operation. Joseph Parrish to USSC, May 4, 1865; J. Parrish to H. W. Bellows, May 8, 1865, Box 642, USSC Papers.

freest and happiest which embodies least of its humanity, mercy, and philanthropy in governmental charities." Assuming a traditional nineteenth-century liberal stance, the architect of one of the largest federally sanctioned charities deplored the "habit of dependence on the Government machinery [which] has not only centralized, but bureaucratized our motions."[17]

If the male commissioners were largely relieved by the termination of warwork, female branch officers experienced considerable ambivalence about letting go of their jobs. For those who staffed the WCRA and other commission branches, news of peace was bittersweet. They were grateful that the military conflict and the suffering of so many northern families had ended. At the same time, however, many were depressed, even frightened, lest the conclusion of the war and the termination of relief activities signify a complete rupture with the meaningful work and leadership positions they had carved out of wartime benevolence. Unlike their male colleagues, women officers had no professions to which they could return.

"Aching Hearts"

The women who staffed local soldiers' aid societies also felt ambivalent about the meaning of peace for their lives. Undoubtedly many of those who had been worn down by the unceasing demands for their household products were pleased to return to customary familial and community duties. But at the same time, numerous women expressed regret at losing the sense of importance that the war had bestowed on them. Warwork had allowed them to gain a novel feeling of national usefulness and community prominence. For these women, the war's end meant losing the most economically and politically valuable work they had ever performed.

Hoping to avoid unnecessary confusion during the disbanding of local aid societies, Schuyler tried to provide authoritative direction and support. Flooded with inquiries about how and when the societies should dissolve, she advised Ellen Collins to give women a common closing date, some three months after the war ended, when they would simultaneously cease work.[18]

"The war is over," Collins began her circular to soldiers' aid societies. "We promised you that the U.S. Sanitary Commission would let you know, at the earliest possible moment, when our work might conscientiously be brought to a close. The accompanying circular fixes the 4th of July next as

[17] "The Future," *Bulletin*, July 1, 1865, 3:1218.
[18] Louisa Schuyler to Ellen Collins, May 4, 1865, Box 954, USSC Papers.

that date." Incorporating some of the ideas that had been discussed at headquarters about women's extended usefulness, the WCRA circular suggested that affiliated groups consider staying organized in order to attend to the problems of returning soldiers. It did not, however, go so far as to ask women to step in as claim agents. Here again, the WCRA walked a fine line between loyalty to the commission and sensitivity to its constituency.[19]

No sooner had they received notification that they were free to terminate their relief efforts than many women, by now accustomed to communicating with those in distant headquarters, expressed deep ties to their WCRA advisors and ambivalence about the ending of relief operations. Each wrestled with the contradictions that accompanied the war's end. "I rejoice with you that the necessity for further effort . . . has nearly ceased," wrote the associate manager of Norwich, Connecticut, "yet I shall miss the pleasant correspondence." "My connection with many earnest women has been so pleasant," wrote another manager, that "I am sorry to pen my last letter in this cause." Reluctant to discontinue their work, some decided to maintain their local organizations to meet other welfare needs. "We are quietly looking after disabled soldiers and their families," reported the Hartford association, "[and] have reserved a goodly amount of clothing for our Soldier's Home." "No doubt," wrote another associate, "other objects of Charity will call upon us."[20]

Schuyler was overwhelmed by the women's intimate expressions of affection. "Those last letters," she exclaimed to Post, "hundreds and hundreds of them—so full of feeling so sad at the breaking up of their intercourse with us. . . . They send their love, they want our photographs, they want us to advise them what to do next. . . . It is almost impossible to read over those letters without crying or choking rather for me." "I knew we cared for them," Schuyler continued; "I thought they cared for us. But we never really knew it, and the extent of it until now." Many women refused to stop the flow of donations. "Our people are magnificent," Schuyler declared, noting that boxes "poured in all through the last week."[21] Moved to reciprocate, Schuyler addressed her audience in her last circular: "It is with aching hearts that we read over these last, most precious letters from you. They are

[19] Ellen Collins, "Circular," May 23, 1865, Box 667, USSC Papers.
[20] "To Miss Nash," July 3, 1865, Box 678; C. P. Letchworth to Miss Nash, July 4, 1865, Box 678; S. Cowen to Louisa Schuyler, July 22, 1865, Box 673; C. D. Mitchell to Louisa Schuyler, July 19, 1865, Box 679, USSC Papers.
[21] Louisa Schuyler to "Angie" [Angelina Post], July 11, 1865, Schuyler Papers. See Louisa Lee Schuyler, "Woman's Central Association of Relief—No. XII," July 8, 1865, reprinted in *Bulletin*, August 1, 1865, 3:1269–72, noting numerous boxes arriving in July, 1865.

too personal, too sacred, to be quoted or to be answered here. We want you to know how dependent we have been upon your sympathy and encouragement throughout our work. Don't forget us."[22]

Northern women's articulations of patriotism and benevolent commitments during the closing weeks of the war stood in sharp contrast to the contentious years the USSC spent trying to reorient women's traditional charity methods. Were women making a complete about-face and admitting their support of the Sanitary Commission's philosophy and centralization? Were these correspondents different women from those who had charged the organization with unscrupulous philanthropic methods? A good many of the letters the WCRA received were, in fact, written by associate managers, highly motivated women who had been carefully chosen to serve the hierarchy and its goals. The other letter writers were probably not the same women who had previously communicated serious discontent with the organization's structure and goals.

Yet given the number of letters to which Schuyler referred, we must also assume that many of the correspondents were among those women who, earlier in the war, had admitted to major difficulties in organizing their localities. These women were not so much sorry at ceasing to produce for war relief as they were regretful to relinquish their relationships with WCRA women. After all, they referred not to the years of strife or to the labor they had expended but rather to the personal bonds they felt with their metropolitan colleagues and the pain involved in severing those ties. Communicating with women officers, local representatives felt free to express emotions ranging from deference to love.

Affixing Value

In stark contrast to the tender messages homefront women volunteered to female branch leaders at war's end, they communicated with the commission only in response to formal requests and then with a tone of defiance. When asked by the USSC to sum up their wartime experiences, women preferred to recall the intricacies of the work, difficulties and all. In the spring of 1866, the Sanitary Commission distributed a questionnaire, framed as a letter to all local aid societies from John Blatchford (who replaced Jenkins as general secretary), asking them to describe the origin of their societies, the amount they contributed during the war, and how those

[22] *Fourth Annual and Final Report of the Woman's Central Association of Relief, July 4, 1865,* p. 16, Box 993, USSC Papers.

contributions were raised and distributed.[23] In contrast to the letters they sent to the WCRA, the responses to this questionnaire expressed little devotion to the parent organization or regret at having to end warwork. Only a few respondents, such as Martha Griffith of Fluranna, New York, sent in replies "with mingled feelings of joy and regret," grateful for the ending of the war and of slavery but mourning "the breaking up of our intercourse and the severing [of] ties whose strength we scarcely knew until now."[24]

Most women offered straightforward, sometimes acerbic accounts of their years of warwork, unadorned by affectionate greetings. "Our obstacles were many and almost insurmountable," wrote Mrs. M. H. France about the Eddy Aid Society in Pennsylvania. Noting that "many were very poor," and "more than half of the husbands . . . were in the army," she stressed that the women "struggled on, thinking by day of the far away soldier fights, breathing out, as it were, his very life blood . . . and dreaming all night how to stint our short allowances more and more in order to send supplies."[25] Dutifully trying to provide the solicited information, they were either self-effacing about their labor or defensive about their accomplishments.

Though no doubt accustomed to the Sanitary Commission's elaborate questionnaires, the respondents professed to have been unprepared for the attention paid to local experiences a year after the war had ended. In part because the information was being collected for publication in the commission's official histories, some women felt compelled to assume a modest pose about their wartime activities. Mrs. H. Chafee noted that for the people of Boston, New York, "the call that brought the people together was nothing special a few Loyal women feeling deeply the privations our noble sons and brothers must. . . endure." Clara Reed explained that "the work done by our Aid Society" in Amenia Union, with its "scattered country population" of four hundred people, is "insignificant when compared with that of others." "Our society was not large," wrote the representative from Arcadia, New York, "but we did what we could, at least a few of us." Annie Overacker of Rochelle, Illinois, instructed Blatchford that her society was "so small" and provided "so little aid" that it "need not be noticed." These women seemed especially unable to view their local accomplishments as of national historical importance. Humbly stating that her people were "merely country people" with "slender purses," Rhoda Briggs informed the commission that their meetings were "merely 'neighborhood

[23] Blatchford, "Reports of Aid Societies," March, 1866, Box 981, USSC Papers.
[24] Miss Martha Griffith to [John] Blatchford, March 26, 1866, Box 981, USSC Papers.
[25] Mrs. M. H. France to Jno. Blatchford, January 2, 1867, Box 980, USSC Papers.

gatherings.' " The secretary of the Dickinson Centre society wrote, "we have done so little comparatively speaking, I should prefer to remain silent."[26]

Apparently, few of the respondents expected such an intensive inquiry into the methods they employed in their philanthropic work. A number appeared puzzled about the weight the organization placed on what they considered relatively unimportant aspects of their labor. Given the commission's instrumentality in mobilizing societies and its penchant for statistical calculations, it is surprising that Mrs. Roselle Ticknor, of Ashville, New York, "did not expect to be called upon for anything of this kind" and did not think it necessary "to keep an account of what we were doing." The women of Bridgeport, New York, thought that "all that was necessary was to work. . . not thinking that if that end was obtained, the way in which we worked would be of any importance." Matilda Shepard reported that for the women of Cato, New York, "it was not at first thought a matter of importance that we should keep a record of what we were doing." When Hannah John revealed that Bloomsburg, Pennsylvania, women never kept strict accounts of their society, she explained that they never foresaw that such records might form part of a postwar record; they had not looked "forward at that time, to their becoming History." These statements demonstrated the distance that separated the metropolitan commission's concept of voluntarism from that held by women in its provincial outposts.[27] The reports may have pointed to an inability on the part of women to see themselves as historical actors. But they also suggest another form of resistance to commission prerogatives. Since nineteenth-century women in their diaries and journals frequently recorded in minute detail the work they accomplished each day, the claim that they had no way of counting up and reporting on their labors seems disingenuous.

The chasm between women's estimation of their war relief work and that of the Sanitary Commission appears in a different light when one analyzes how some women responded to the questions about the financial worth of their donations. Despite the commission's apparent desire to accord women's labors economic value, women were reluctant to fall into the trap

[26] Mrs. H. A. Chafee to Blatchford, 1866; Clara C. Reed to J. S. Blatchford, March 29, 1866; Miss Helen Roberts to Blatchford, March 24, 1866, Box 981; Mrs. Annie M. Overacker to Blatchford, May 28, 1866, Box 986; Rhoda S. Briggs, 1866; Mrs. L. M. Stowe, April 30, 1866, Box 981, USSC Papers.

[27] Mrs. R. Roselle Ticknor, April 9, 1866; Mrs. E. Lewis to Blatchford, April 2, 1866; Matilda W. Shepard to John Blatchford, April 23, 1866; (see also Mrs. Benj. Smith, September 8, 1866; Lensey Davis, March 29, 1866, Box 981); Hannah J. John to Jno. S. Blatchford, April 6, 1866, Box 980, USSC Papers.

of giving valuation only to the monies they may have forwarded. Instead, they tried to place monetary values on the household products they donated. "We forwarded no money," explained Charlotte Lewis from Altoona, Pennsylvania, but they had sent "a great many boxes of clothing, bedding, bandages, pads, canned and dried fruits." Anne Church was stymied by the task in front of her and lamented that she did not know "exactly what value to affix to our small efforts." Helen Roberts of Arcadia, New York, approached the issue of value by reminding the commission of the speculation of which it was accused. No sooner were the women in her town "all busily engaged" in sewing garments than someone would inform them that military officers always appropriated women's donations and that what they refused would "be sold for twice their value" to wounded soldiers.[28]

A number of women resented being asked to quantify the value of their household products, preferring to list the number of different items forwarded and letting the organization calculate their worth. Most assumed that when the questionnaire asked for the "amount contributed," it was referring to cash amounts; what else had a precise value attached to it? So the women from Antwerp, New York, recorded down to the penny the amount of cash they sent to the commission and other relief agencies. But few discussed the issue of monetary amounts without mentioning the work that produced contributions in kind. "As to money," reported Amelia Pritchard, the Concord, Massachusetts, aid society "gladly received money from concerts or entertainments," but she emphasized that "our chief reliance has been upon direct contributions." Although Nantucket, Massachusetts, women never prevailed over the rumors of mishandling of supplies, they never stopped their labors. "All praise to our . . . knitters and sewers and other tireless labors," Harriet Pierce intoned, reminding the commission of the unnamed workers who labored for its cause.[29]

Though they wrestled with the difficulties of the task, a number of women attempted to place a market value on their workmanship. Mrs. J. E. Caldwell wrote that the Black Creek Aid Society sent "articles to the amount of $80.00." Mrs. Hicks, after listing the sources of the $620 that Bristol, New York, women raised for the commission and other agencies, noted that her society "contributed nearly or quite as much in the way of dried fruit, clothing, . . . etc. as in money." Julia Hoag reported that al-

[28] Charlotte L. Lewis to Jno. S. Blatchford, April 19, 1866, Box 980; Anne E. Church, West Falls, New York, April 13, 1866; Helen Roberts to Mr. Blatchford, March 24, 1866, Box 981, USSC Papers.
[29] Amelia M. Pritchard to John S. Blatchford, May 7, 1866; Harriet Pierce to Mr. Blatchford, April 23, 1866, Box 983, USSC Papers.

though the women of Coxsackie, New York, never had a local organization they still sent "about $100 in value to the Albany Bazaar." A. F. Fostin made clear that the women from the Wolcott, New York, aid society "sent no money" but that "in hospital supplies we estimate our contributions at not less than one thousand dollars." A few women gave dollar values for the goods their societies donated. J. Spoffard from Brocketts Bridge, New York, calculated that her society had sent goods worth $756.78; such a specific figure probably represented the cost of the raw materials and not the market value of homemade products. None made clearer the value that women's labor added to raw materials than Mrs. Waters, who noted that her society raised $440.67, "which has been more than trebled in value by buying material and making into garments!!"[30]

The inclination on the part of local women to place less value on organizational methods than on sincere intentions and to prize home production more highly than cash contributions highlighted the tensions that hindered their relationship with the Commission. At midcentury, most women understood that their household labor produced economic value. Even if many women were unfamiliar with feminist arguments to accord women rights in their property and household labor, they nonetheless expressed an oppositional position about the sources and purposes of voluntary labor. The dollar value of contributions was of less significance than the quantity and quality of items donated. That they did not see the necessity of recording all their meetings does not imply that they treated warwork casually. The impact of rumors of corruption and the desire to follow donations to the point of distribution emphasized the importance that women attached to the products of their unpaid labor. As Hannah Abbey of Lancaster, New York, explained, even after a few women in her town formed a society and received material from the Buffalo Commission to make clothing, they concluded that "there was no use of working when we did not know where it was going."[31]

For those who took seriously their patriotic duty and, in the words of one woman, tried to "arouse the latent sympathy lying dormant in the bosoms of those who were inactive," the important thing was the needs of the

[30] See Mrs. Ira P. Abell to Mr. Blatchford, April 17, 1866; Mrs. G. Paulding, April 14, 1866; Mrs. J. P. Stebbins, 1866; Mrs. C. E. Chatham, May 27, 1866; Clara C. Reed to Blatchford, March 29, 1866; Susan A. Ayer, 1866; Mrs. J. E. Caldwell, April 9, 1866; W. Scott Hicks, March 16, 1866; Julia S. Hoag, 1866; A. F. Fostin, 1866; J. Spoffard, May 1866; Mrs. C. Waters, Box 981, USSC Papers.
[31] Hannah Abbey to Mr. Blatchford, March 29, 1866, Box 981, USSC Papers.

army.[32] These postwar accounts confirmed what the Sanitary Commission had learned earlier in the war. Many aid societies divided their contributions, sending some to the commission and the rest through a variety of agencies and individuals, a process that hedged against the lost impact of their efforts. The women of Cornwall, New York, may have been the most ambitious in meting out their donations as widely as possible. As Elisa Cunningham explained: "Our supplies were sent some direct to Washington to friends who personally distributed them in hospitals, some through the Sanitary and Christian commissions, some to the field, some to a hospital at Fort Monroe, some to individual soldiers in hospitals and some to sick ones who had returned."[33]

No matter how thorough the commission's questionnaire, it could not elicit a fair estimation of either women's loyalty or their sacrifices. Female patriotism was not to be measured simply by tallying the garments and dried fruits they prepared or the money they raised at strawberry festivals and charity bazaars. In war, the state had demanded of women the gift of their men. "Our town has not lacked in patriotism," wrote a woman from Evans Centre in Erie County, New York. "We sent our Fathers, Husbands, Sons & Brothers to help fill the army," explained the proud Mrs. David Fuller. "As a community," wrote the respondent from Lisle Centre, New York, "we have given blood & treasure to the cause, our brothers, sons, husbands, & lovers left us—& returned in many cases—with shattered limbs, ruined health, the effect of many marches, southern prisons, etc. etc." "I am content I have done what I could," concluded J. E. Livermore.[34]

Contradictions of Warwork

A year after the war ended, Alfred Bloor, who had paid a large personal price for catering to homefront needs, made public his assessment that northern women had been instrumental to the organization's accomplishments. Having been immersed in the "stimulation & collection of supplies" for "one of the noblest volunteer organizations on record," Bloor understood that the strength behind the commission enterprise was voluntary female labor.[35]

[32] Phebe M. Ellinwood, 1866, Box 981, USSC Papers.
[33] Elisa Cunningham, 1866, Box 981, USSC Papers.
[34] Mrs. David Fuller, July 9, 1866; J. E. Livermore, July 10, 1866, Box 981, USSC Papers.
[35] Alfred J. Bloor letter, July 8, 1865, Bloor Papers.

So impressed was Bloor with women's talent for carrying out the methodical relief work of the Sanitary Commission that he volunteered to publicize an account of their accomplishments. In a dispute with Charles Sumner about remarks the Senator had made about feminine deficiencies, Bloor expounded on the scope of women's war philanthropy. Bloor disagreed with the implication in Sumner's speech, "Art in the National Capital," that women's intellectual capacities and cultural talents were naturally inferior to those of men. Women's proclivity for systematic philanthropic labor was best seen in comparison with the general lack of such ability among men, who in the early days of the war had assumed the task of supply work with dismal results. "Though entering it at first *con amore*," he wrote, men soon "began to look at it, after the sixty days allotted for the war had elapsed, as a troublesome, time-taking, sentimental excrescence, outside of real money-making business; and left it as (probably unpaid) overwork to subordinates." Rather than assume that the lack of compensation drove men away, Bloor admonished his readers to admit that the nature of ongoing charity work was a problem for men; women were better qualified for such work. Despite his essentialist assumptions about women's benevolent natures, Bloor combined this assessment with the claim that women's warwork earned them political rights: "The signs of the times . . . plainly indicate, according to the best qualified observers, that the enfranchisement of women will soon emerge . . . into the more immediately practical field of politics and legislation." Assuming that Sumner would have a role in "whatever movement may stir the van of national progress," Bloor offered his testimony as one who was "an appreciative observer of a certain class of *à propos* facts . . . from the best stand-point that has existed."[36]

To demonstrate the basis for his claim, Bloor described the vast, complicated relief work that northern women carried out during the war. "The supplies," he explained, "amounting in aggregate value to many millions of dollars—some fifteen millions I should name as a rough estimate . . . — were almost universally collected, assorted, despatched, and re-collected, re-assorted, and re-despatched, by women, representing with great impartiality, every grade of society in the Republic."[37]

This $15-million figure, which was repeated in numerous documents, highlighted the paradox inherent in the Civil War concept of female patriotism as well as the Sanitary Commission's scheme of exploiting women's un-

[36] Alfred Bloor, "Women's Work in the War: A Letter to Senator Sumner," September 18, 1866, pp. 1–2, 6–7, Bloor Papers.
[37] Ibid, p. 2.

paid labor for political ends. It also revealed something of the impact of the war on the antebellum compromise on gender. The Sanitary Commission, having sought voluntary support from the female public, found itself accountable to that public and, in response to charges of corruption, was forced to demonstrate its integrity through careful bookkeeping. In order to quantify its presence at the homefront and its impact on the warfront, it had to equate women's household labor with monetary values. By noting the cash equivalent of female donations, the organization implicitly accepted the superior valuation of labor expressed in money terms; at the same time, it acknowledged the ease with which society could place a cash value on women's household products.

Stressing the naturalness of women's labor and the simplicity of their patriotism led USSC leaders into an intractable contradiction. They had created a giant philanthropic operation, whose size stirred deep-rooted, republican fears about the inevitable corruption bred by concentrations of power. Assuming that domestic labor was not quantifiable and that women had little interest in accountability, the commissioners set themselves up for accusations of fraud and embezzlement. When compelled to give a cash equivalent to homefront donations, they not only recognized the value of unpaid labor but even reversed established verities about women's political capacities.

Bloor printed and distributed his letter to Sumner under the title "Women's Work in the War." Sumner replied, confessing in a short note that the information about women's contributions took him "by surprise," suggesting that public awareness of the extent of female wartime activities may not have been widespread. Bloor received another response to his published letter, this one from the woman who was instrumental in organizing northern women into a coordinated national war relief project. Dr. Elizabeth Blackwell appreciated Bloor's praise, yet expressed concern lest women's achievements be forgotten so soon after the conflict ceased. Thanking him "in behalf of women, for the liberal and just sentiments you have expressed," she implored him to make the document public.[38]

The WCRA Closes Its Doors

The summer following the declaration of peace was filled with ceremonial tasks that formally severed the WCRA's ties both with the Sanitary Com-

---

[38] Charles Sumner to Alfred J. Bloor, November 17, 1866; Elizabeth Blackwell to A. J. Bloor, November 24, 1866; both reprinted in "Women's Work," p. 7, Bloor Papers.

mission and with the female homefront. The WCRA convened its last meeting on July 7, 1865. In addition to its own officers, Bellows, Blatchford, and female associate managers who "came from far & wide," the WCRA also invited the Blackwell sisters to attend this final function of the organization they had founded. Bellows presided, reading reports of the commission's latest activities, notifying the audience of the historical work recently undertaken, and giving his "valedictory" to all the USSC branches. In his farewell speech, he complimented the WCRA women on their contributions to the war effort, and especially for serving as a model for other branches. Like the women of local aid societies who were unwilling to claim credit for their contributions, Schuyler felt unsure of the value of her own labors. Recounting Bellows's "very impersonal" speech to Post, she was self-effacing in her assessment of the branch's impact on the war: "I don't think [the WCRA] has had much influence, do you?"[39]

To ease the separation of provincial societies from branch headquarters and provide some material acknowledgment of the work homefront women had performed, the WCRA authorized the production of ceremonial plaques and photographs, lasting keepsakes of the war experience that would provide symbolic recognition of women's labors. Schuyler designed each souvenir to include concrete evidence of women's contributions. For the aid societies, she decided on a "sort of 'Diploma' " —"a copper-plate engraving with vignettes"—that, she anticipated, would offer a public reward for women's achievements, "something for them to have framed, & hung in their public libraries." Acknowledging the more personal ties to associate managers, Schuyler planned to give each "a photograph of the exterior of No. 11 Cooper Union, with boxes marked to go away." And for the volunteers who worked at the New York office, she decided on "photographs of the interior of the room—where they have worked for so long & so well."[40] While undoubtedly pleased with the official WCRA photographs, many women desired more personal reminders of their wartime relationships. Associate managers initiated photograph exchanges among themselves and with individual WCRA officers. Schuyler too requested portraits of her coworkers (fig. 16).[41]

Winding up affairs at the WCRA office took some time. There was much

[39] Bellows to "Wife" [Eliza Bellows], July 1865, Bellows Papers; Schuyler to Post, July 11, 1865, Schuyler Papers.

[40] Schuyler to Post, July 11, 1865.

[41] One correspondent wrote to Post: "May I not ask as an additional and especial favor that you will send me yours after your return? I should prize it highly." M. Brooks to Angelina Post, September 25, 1865, Post Papers.

This photograph of the exterior of the Cooper Union office of the Woman's Central Relief Association may have been the one Louisa Lee Schuyler reproduced as a momento for associate managers. Museum of the City of New York.

to do, contacting associates and collecting and sorting organizational records. Schuyler scrupulously and personally attended to each of the correspondences established over the years of the war, writing to "every Associate Manager, every ex-associate, [and] to the other Branches." She assumed responsibility for the association's archives, desiring to "put all our . . . papers in perfect order—pasting them in books."[42] The commission had requested that all branch records be forwarded to its historical office for use in creating the official histories of the organization. Though she firmly declined to author the history of the WCRA, Schuyler nevertheless took an active interest in the commission's historical work.

After weeks of exhausting packing and tedious paperwork, WCRA women were ready to close the Cooper Union office in mid-September. For Schuyler, the "dying hours of our dear W.C.R.A.," were moments filled with sadness and reflection. "The last hour . . . I had there alone," she confided to Angie Post; "It was good to be alone too. Just then & there." The last day was hectic: "the floor was covered with old papers, the bins had been taken down." Then "there was nothing more to do." "By a sort of tacit consent" the women in the office "never mentioned the words 'last day,' " as these had been "marked years, the four we had spent together, in that dear old room." Though Schuyler's feelings occasionally ran to sentimental excess, they nonetheless ran deep. "I waited to see the last cover put on the last box, the little flags taken down, & lastly, the window-curtain removed. Then I walked home. Not sadness, or regret—those were not the feelings, only the deepest gratitude to God for having been permitted to see that work through & to do what I could for it from the beginning to the end."[43]

As she left for Europe, Louisa Schuyler was more than tired. The sense of fatigue she expressed during the last days at the Cooper Union office signaled the onset of a serious psychological collapse. The stress and intensity of the work she had carried out depleted her for years to come. "I broke down at the end of the war," she acknowledged many years later, "as so many others did." After seven years of "health-hunting," mostly spent abroad, she returned to New York City in 1871 anxious to immerse herself once more in philanthropic work.[44]

Feeling stronger, Schuyler started to keep a journal, noting in her first entry that she regretted she had not kept one during the war. "I did jot down a few notes, memoranda of the day's doings . . . during the last year" of the war, she wrote, "and when I occasionally look over those two little books, they bring back much vivid memories, such intense living at that

[42] Schuyler to Post, July 11, 1865.
[43] Louisa Schuyler to Angie Post, October 1, 1865, Schuyler Papers.
[44] Louisa Lee Schuyler, *Forty-Three Years Ago: or the Early Days of the State Charities Aid Association, 1872–1915: An Address, February 25, 1915* (New York, 1915), p. 5; Robert D. Cross, "Louisa Lee Schuyler," in *NAW*, 3:245.

time." Sitting at her old WCRA desk, which she purchased after the war, beneath photographs of colleagues, Schuyler felt the need for a diary in part because she did not "write as easily now as I did when thirty letters a day were turned off." Presumably intending to record her activities in a future project, she confessed that "anything I may write about this work can never interest me as one or two pages about the war would."[45]

[45] Louisa Lee Schuyler, Diary, October 7, 1871, Louisa Lee Schuyler Papers, Library of Congress.

CONCLUSION: "THE LESSONS OF WAR"

"No national recognition has been accorded the grand women who did faithful service in the late war; no national honors nor profitable offices bestowed on them."

Elizabeth Cady Stanton, Susan B. Anthony,
and Matilda Joslyn Gage, 1881.

In their *History of Woman Suffrage*, three of the leading feminists of the nineteenth century wrote: "The lessons of war were not lost on the women of this nation; through varied forms of suffering and humiliation, they learned that they had an equal interest with man in the administration of the Government." Among the special humiliations the authors had in mind were the usurpation of the Woman's Central Relief Association by the Sanitary Commission and the dismissal of Elizabeth Blackwell from the organization she had created. But the indignation expressed by Elizabeth Cady Stanton, Susan B. Anthony, and Matilda Joslyn Gage went far beyond the slights of the United States Sanitary Commission.[1]

As they watched male allies from the abolitionist movement turn their backs on woman's rights to elevate black suffrage as the overriding political goal of Reconstruction, feminists sensed a growing wave of antifeminist feeling. When the Civil War began, woman's rights' activists had publicly put aside their own political agendas to devote themselves to the defense of the Union, believing that such actions would be rewarded at war's end. Yet despite their sacrifices and those of thousands of northern women, expecta-

---

[1] Elizabeth Cady Stanton, Susan B. Anthony, and Matilda Joslyn Gage, *History of Woman Suffrage*, 3 vols. (New York, 1881), vol. 2, *1861–1876*, p. 88.

tions that women's support of the state would translate into full inclusion in the polity soon dissipated. Once women were excluded from the widening of suffrage in the Fourteenth and Fifteenth Amendments, these feminist leaders began charting a separatist strategy to advance female political rights.[2]

While prominent leaders of the woman's rights movement determined after the war that rewriting federal and state constitutions represented the most important avenue for women's liberation, another form of feminism emerged in the postwar years that identified the devaluation of women's unpaid household labors as the gravest obstacle to gender equality. The rise of what Dolores Hayden terms "material feminism" signaled an important development in American feminist thought, which linked the economic exploitation of women's work in the privatized home to their lack of access to political rights. For thirty years after the war, material feminists challenged the idea of gender-specific labor as well as the architectural isolation of women within privatized homes where their labor was invisible. They concluded that only by compensating women's domestic labors and by socializing household tasks—from housework to childcare—in cooperative arrangements could they dismantle the barriers that separated household economies from the larger political economy, and thus open the way for women to participate in civil society on terms equal with men.[3]

The critiques made by material feminists suggest that whatever intellectual or political equilibrium had been achieved by the compromise on gendered spheres during the early decades of industrial capitalism no longer held by the end of the Civil War. While the demand for remunerating housework had its antecedents in antebellum feminists' arguments for a "joint property claim," which informed their advocacy of married women's property acts, the postwar growth of a feminist movement devoted to attributing economic value to unpaid household labor is intriguing in the context of the wartime crisis that emerged over the economic value of homemade products and the political significance of domestic labors. That women active in war relief, such as Mary Livermore, were at the forefront of this movement is especially significant.[4]

[2] Ellen Carol DuBois, *Feminism and Suffrage: The Emergence of an Independent Women's Movement in America, 1848–1869* (Ithaca, N.Y., 1978), pp. 58–64.

[3] Dolores Hayden, *The Grand Domestic Revolution: A History of Feminist Designs for American Homes, Neighborhoods, and Cities* (Cambridge, Mass., 1981), pp. 3–6.

[4] Livermore's first experiment with industrialized housekeeping occurred during the war when, bereft of servants who left the city to replace men on farms, she and fifty other middle-class women created a cooperative laundry to do their own wash. Hayden writes that even more influential for Livermore's ideas about cooperative schemes was the work she and Jane

The possible connections between the Civil War crisis of domesticity and the growth of material feminism and the new initiatives of political feminists lay buried in the correspondence between the Sanitary Commission and the northern female public. They were also obscured by the impressive postwar careers of some female branch leaders. For activists such as Mary Livermore and Ellen Collins, warwork provided a new appreciation for how much women could accomplish collectively. The process of organizing local aid societies, attending military hospitals, and staging sanitary fairs gave them the self-confidence and administrative experience that they applied to work with the freedpeople, urban charities, and the suffrage movement after the war.[5]

While some elite women moved easily into postwar careers, Louisa Lee Schuyler found the transition from war relief into a meaningful career more difficult. It took her seven years to recover from the serious mental collapse she suffered at war's end. When she returned to New York City in 1871, she resolved to find a new field for her energies and voluntary labor. Recalling the advice of her family doctor, who had suggested that elite women should interest themselves in the poor who were lying in public hospitals (and aware that her Episcopal cousins were already visiting patients in St. Luke's hospital), Schuyler decided to devote herself to assisting the poor in New York City by advising and inspecting state charitable institutions. Assuming that "men of the world" would resist her plans, she sought counsel from her former Sanitary Commission colleagues. Bellows confirmed her fears when he told her that while "it was a thing to be done," the "difficulties were so great." Determined to confront what she termed a "wall of apathy," she sought the advice of Olmsted, who took her ideas more seriously and "then, for three hours, went at it, with pencil & paper & diagrams." The session with Olmsted was like a tonic for Schuyler: "It was delightfully exciting. I

Hoge accomplished in shipping massive quantities of fruits and vegetables to Grant's army. Livermore joined the suffrage movement immediately after the war, and as editor of the *Woman's Journal* she consistently argued the case for women's economic independence and shared gender responsibility for household tasks. See Hayden, *Grand Domestic Revolution*, pp. 115–31.

[5] At war's end, Ellen Collins turned her attentions to aiding the freedpeople. Under the auspices of the New York National Freedmen's Relief Association, she inspected schools for blacks in Virginia. In 1870 under the auspices of the New York Board of Charities she began visiting public charitable institutions in New York. In the late nineteenth century, she became known as a landlord for the poor. In Cherry Hill, on the Lower East Side of Manhattan, she applied her inheritance to purchase and renovate three tenement houses, intending to demonstrate that private interests could house the poor in decent conditions with reasonable profit. See Robert H. Bremner, "Ellen Collins," in *NAW,* 1:360–61.

felt like my old self again—brain alive & responsive. It was all play-work, the answers came so easily."[6]

Schuyler developed a plan reminiscent of the original scheme of the Sanitary Commission, in which elite men and women, organized into volunteer visiting committees, would inspect county hospitals, state hospitals, poorhouses and almshouses, and offer advice to a larger body, the State Charities Aid Association, that would be empowered to implement specific remedies and draft state legislation. Schuyler herself drafted the by-laws of the association, secured its legislation, and convened a group of New York women to form a visiting committee for "Bellevue and other hospitals."[7] Thus she had embarked on the work that would occupy her for the next half century. As part of her mission, and in league with many former WCRA workers, including Mrs. William Preston Griffin, Mrs. d'Oremieulx, Abby Howland Woolsey, and Ellen Collins, Schuyler was instrumental in establishing the Bellevue Training School for Nurses.[8] For Schuyler and other upper-class women, Sanitary Commission work generated new ideas and opened opportunities they may have never otherwise obtained.

Generalizing from the careers of the leaders of female branches, historical accounts of the impact of the Civil War frequently have asserted that the Sanitary Commission experience was a generally empowering one that gave women hands-on experience in associational work which they translated into feminist organizing after the war.[9] But for thousands of northern women with little access to urban institutions or feminist organizations, and yet skilled in both household production and local benevolent activities, it could be argued that warwork did not so much give them valuable experience as distort the significance of that experience. While soldier relief work offered

[6] Schuyler, October 7, 9, and 18, 1871, Diary, Schuyler Papers, Library of Congress.

[7] William R. Brock, *Investigation and Responsibility: Public Responsibility in the United States, 1865–1900* (Cambridge, U.K., 1984), p. 103. The State Charities Aid Association was formally established in 1872.

[8] Elizabeth Christophers Hobson, *Recollections of a Happy Life* (New York, 1916), pp. 79–80, 89–96, 109. On the board of managers was Mrs. David Lane, who organized the Metropolitan Fair, and among the physicians who lent their support was C. R. Agnew; Schuyler, *Forty-Three Years Ago*, pp. 6–11,15. Like the Sanitary Commission, Schuyler's committees constituted private advisors to government agencies. Committee members were chosen on the basis of their rank and stake in society. "We are to 'aid' the State," Schuyler advised, "as a volunteer body of citizens, asking nothing for ourselves . . . beyond the legal 'right of entrance.' "

[9] Among the histories that suggest such a wartime legacy, see Mari Jo Buhle, *Women and American Socialism, 1870–1920* (Urbana, Ill., 1981); Sheila M. Rothman, *Woman's Proper Place: A History of Changing Ideas and Practices, 1870 to the Present* (New York, 1978); James et al., introduction, *NAW*, 1: xiii.

many women at the northern homefront a sense of purpose and inclusion in the national crisis, it also demonstrated that their unpaid household labor was too readily devalued, at best as utilitarian and at worst as instinctual. Moreover, despite the abundance of female-run benevolent organizations in the prewar decades, men in power considered them poor training for work of national political importance. Autonomously organized soldiers' aid societies were unsatisfactory solutions to real public welfare needs, and even professional women like the Blackwell sisters were unsuitable to run a national organization. The message was straightforward: when it really mattered, social welfare and civic morality needed to be guided by men.

Although, as Stanton, Anthony, and Gage observed, there was no political quid pro quo for women's contributions to the nation's military defense, recognition of female patriotic toil was abundant in postwar popular culture. Commemorative volumes, most notably Frank Moore's *Women of the War: Their Heroism and Self-Sacrifice* and L. P. Brockett and Mary C. Vaughan's *Woman's Work in the Civil War: A Record of Heroism, Patriotism and Patience*, which appeared in 1866 and 1867 respectively, were extensive chronicles by and about the accomplishments of individual women and the female-led branches. Charles J. Stillé's 1866 *History of the United States Sanitary Commission* also included tributes to the sacrifices and patriotism of women who participated in the relief effort. If these sentimentalized chronicles of real women too often mirrored mythic narratives of generic female self-sacrifice, they nonetheless represented attempts at according women's labors public recognition.

Whether ordinary women desired such visibility was questionable. Jane Ellen Schultz found that Frank Moore received letters from husbands and parents warning him not to include their female relatives in his compendium. Some of the women themselves asked Moore to omit their names from his roster. Moore met with the same self-effacing stances among female respondents that the commission had encountered with its final questionnaire. Perhaps it was fitting that women who actually resembled these narratives' characterizations of noble, self-sacrificing women were reluctant to publicize their stories. Whether shamed by others about their right to recognition or concerned about being singled out from what they viewed as a collective enterprise, these women did not feel empowered by their wartime labors. As a result, some northern women furthered the erasure of their work from the historical record.[10]

---

[10] Jane Ellen Schultz, "Women at the Front: Gender and Genre in Literature of the American Civil War" (Ph.D. diss., University of Michigan, 1988), pp. 26–29.

If postwar praise for female warwork was sometimes effusive, it was also shortlived. Only two years after he coauthored a tribute to women's abilities, Linus Brockett wrote an antisuffrage polemic that was unequivocal in its condemnation of feminist claims to political equality. Brockett based his argument—not only against female suffrage but also against universal manhood suffrage—on the notion that political rights should be situated not with the individual but within the household (precisely the argument that drove material feminists to demand the creation of feminist homes). Among his many arguments, Brockett invoked the war to demonstrate the consequences of female political participation. Southern women, he claimed, while they did not vote, became "so absorbed in the political questions at issue, and entered into them with such a violent spirit," that those who had once been the "most gentle and amiable of their sex" became "almost fiendish." Castigating southern women for unfeminine behavior was common among northern journalists in the immediate postwar years. Yet Nina Silber observes that singling out southern women for rebuke should not be read as a sectional or partisan action; rather, concerns about southern manliness and womanliness represented displaced anxieties about gender relations throughout the nation.[11]

Fittingly, Brockett concluded his volume with a reprint of an essay by Catharine Beecher, "Something for Women better than the Ballot." Writing after the passage of the Fifteenth Amendment, Beecher acknowledged that "there is something essentially wrong in the present condition of women," but continued to resist feminist claims for the vote. All she could offer women as a remedy for their disadvantaged social status was a reiteration of her earlier criticisms of female socialization and a call for respectable employment for women all classes.[12]

The ideology that portrayed women's household labor as leisure and women's political feelings as instinctual did not come apart during the military struggle. The Civil War, a conflict of such enormous proportions, requiring massive mobilization of civilian labor and resources, seemed poised to effect a radical transformation in the assessment of women's work and political consciousness. That it failed to do so hints not only at the strength of the wage theory of labor value but also at the magnitude of the threat

---

[11] L. P. Brockett, M.D., *Woman: Her Rights, Wrongs, Privileges, and Responsibilities* (1869; rpt. Plainview, N.J., 1976), pp. 261–64, 284–86. The word "fiendish" was frequently used in descriptions of southern women's patriotism. See Nina Silber, *The Romance of Reunion: Northerners and the South, 1865–1900* (Chapel Hill, 1993), pp. 28–29.

[12] Catharine E. Beecher, "Something for Women Better than the Ballot," in Brockett, *Woman*, pp. 393-412.

that women's equality posed to nineteenth-century American society. If beliefs about the gender division of labor and women's innate differences from men did not fall away during the war, the antebellum compromise on gender nonetheless suffered a major blow. Relief work demonstrated that women's sphere was too permeable to protect feminized arenas of social authority. Moreover, women's wartime participation in soldier relief work raised the political awareness of thousands of women. It also produced something of a backlash. That women were excluded from the postwar extension of suffrage points to the limited consequences that even a revolutionary struggle had for the nineteenth-century gender system.

For some predominantly elite women, the process of fashioning an acceptable philosophy of political obligation during the war led them to glimpse the possibilities of a more balanced gender system and the rudiments of female citizenship. Those individual women who discovered through their warwork a desire for continued public service demonstrated a resistance to ideas about conventional gender spheres in the postwar years. As they carved out positions for themselves as leaders of charitable organizations, these women discarded the language of sentimentality and disinterestedness in favor of a discourse that stressed social prerogative and organization.[13] Though some postwar feminists would employ arguments about women's natural moral superiority to advance their cause, the source of feminist strength after the Civil War came from the development of social theories to justify equality between the sexes and the rights of women to the value of their labor. A number of postwar feminists questioned not only the precepts of the ideology of domesticity but also the belief that the state was a source of protection or justice. These women chose "science," not political theory, to construct a degendered alternative to liberal versions of political and economic authority, an alternative that stressed symmetry, cooperation, and what they termed "universal humanity."[14]

In their conflict with the Sanitary Commission, thousands of women crystallized their political sentiments for the Union and an alternative version of female patriotism. Their nationalistic feelings were equal to those of

[13] Lori Ginzberg argues that the shift in rhetoric about female benevolence represented the triumph of a conservative, masculine version of philanthropy which united elite women and men in espousing the virtues of corporatism and scientific charity. See *Women and the Work of Benevolence: Morality, Politics, and Class in the Nineteenth-Century United States* (New Haven, 1990), pp. 172–73, 193–213.
[14] William Leach, *True Love and Perfect Union: The Feminist Reform of Sex and Society* (New York, 1980), pp. 6–13. Leach singles out Abby May, an officer of the Boston branch of the Sanitary Commission, as one feminist who articulated the view of the state as a province of male power, writing in 1869 that "the state has proven itself void of all positive worth."

men, inspired by similar political concerns for the future of the nation. Their obligations to the state must be recognized as donations of labor that created real value and constituted authentic assistance to the national cause. In the end, northern women implicitly challenged the tenets of the ideology of gender spheres by stripping away some of its sentimental veneer and rendering clearer its fictitious underpinnings.

Perhaps it was more than women's exclusion from the Fourteenth and Fifteenth amendments that gave new vitality to the nineteenth-century suffrage movement. Perhaps it was an understanding gained by women during the war that they were not so different from men in their political sentiments or physical abilities, that platitudes about women's charitable nature would not suffice to acknowledge the economic constraints under which they created value and, finally, that difference was more of an obstacle than a path to social power. Perhaps the Civil War crisis of domesticity was the necessary precondition for a revitalized and enduring feminist movement.

BIBLIOGRAPHY

Manuscript Collections

Alger Family Papers, Schlesinger Library, Radcliffe College, Cambridge, Mass.
Henry W. Bellows Papers, Massachusetts Historical Society, Boston.
Elizabeth Blackwell Papers, Columbia University, New York.
Alfred Janson Bloor Papers, New-York Historical Society, New York.
Mary S. Chapman Papers, Columbia University, New York.
Caroline Dunstan Papers, New York Public Library, New York.
Sidney Howard Gay Papers, Columbia University, New York.
Helen Grinnell Papers, New York Public Library, New York
Mary Hawley Papers, New-York Historical Society, New York.
Helen Marcia Hart Papers, Schlesinger Library, Radcliffe College, Cambridge, Mass.
Home for Disabled Soldiers Papers, New-York Historical Society, New York.
Harriet Steward Judd Papers, New York Public Library, New York.
Alice Reynolds Keyes Papers, Schlesinger Library, Radcliffe College, Cambridge, Mass.
John A. Logan Family Papers, Library of Congress, Washington, D.C.
Mary B. Marsh Papers, Schlesinger Library, Radcliffe College, Cambridge, Mass.
Frederick Law Olmsted Papers, Library of Congress, Washington, D.C.
Angelina Post Papers, New-York Historical Society, New York.
Sarah Alden Ripley Papers, Schlesinger Library, Radcliffe College, Cambridge, Mass.
Louisa Lee Schuyler Papers, Library of Congress, Washington, D.C.
Louisa Lee Schuyler Papers, New-York Historical Society, New York.
George Templeton Strong Papers, Columbia University, New York.
George H. Stuart Papers, Library of Congress, Washington D.C.
United States Christian Commission Papers, National Archives, Washington, D.C.
United States Sanitary Commission Papers, New York Public Library, New York.

Commission Histories, Reports, Bulletins, Documents

History of the Brooklyn and Long Island Fair, February 22, 1864. Brooklyn, N.Y.: "The Union" Steam Presses, 1864.

Moss, Lemuel. *Annals of the United States Christian Commission.* Philadelphia: J. B. Lippincott, 1868.

Newberry, J. S. *The U.S. Sanitary Commission in the Valley of the Mississippi.* Cleveland, Ohio: Fairbanks, Benedict, 1871.

A Record of the Metropolitan Fair, Held in Aid of the United States Sanitary Commission, New York, April 1864. New York: Hurd and Houghton, 1867.

Report of the Dutchess County & Poughkeepsie Sanitary Fair Held at Sanitary Hall in the City of Poughkeepsie, from March 15, to March 19, 1864. Poughkeepsie, N.Y.: Platt and Simon, 1864.

The Sanitary Commission of the United States Army: A Succinct Narrative of Its Works and Purposes. New York: n.p., 1864.

The Spirit of the Fair. New York: John F. Trow, April 4–April 23, 1864.

Stillé, Charles J. *History of the United States Sanitary Commission: Being the General Report of Its Work during the War of the Rebellion.* Philadelphia: J. B. Lippincott, 1866.

United States Christian Commission, for the Army and Navy, Work and Incidents; First Annual Report. Philadelphia: USCC, February 1863.

United States Sanitary Commission. *The United States Sanitary Commission Bulletin.* 3 vols. New York: n.p., 1866.

——. *Documents of the U.S. Sanitary Commission.* 2 vols. New York, 1866.

The United States Sanitary Commission: A Sketch of Its Purposes and Its Work. Boston: Little, Brown, 1863.

Woman's Central Association of Relief. *First Annual Report of the Woman's Central Association of Relief, May 1, 1862.* New York: Wm. C. Bryant, 1862.

——. *Second Semi-Annual Report of the Woman's Central Association of Relief, November 1, 1862.* New York: Baker and Godwin, 1862.

——. *Second Annual Report of the Woman's Central Association of Relief, May 1, 1863.* New York: William S. Dorr, 1863.

——. *Third Semi-Annual Report of Woman's Central Association of Relief, November 1, 1863.* New York: Baker and Godwin, 1863.

——. *Third Annual Report of the Woman's Central Association of Relief, May 1, 1864.* New York: Sanford, Harroun, 1864.

——. *Fourth Annual and Final Report of the Woman's Central Association of Relief, July 4, 1865.* New York: Sanford, Harroun, 1865.

Other Primary Sources

Alcott, Louisa May. *The Journals of Louisa May Alcott.* Edited by Joel Myerson and Daniel Shealy. Boston: Little, Brown, 1989.

Bacon, G. W., and E. W. Howland. *Letters of a Family during the War for the Union, 1861–1865.* 2 vols. New York: Bacon and Howland, 1899.

Beecher, Catharine E. *A Treatise on Domestic Economy for the Use of Young Ladies at Home and at School.* Revised edition. New York: Harpers and Brothers, 1854.

Bellows, Henry W. "Cities and Parks: With Special Reference to the New York Central Park." *Atlantic Monthly* 7 (April 1861): 416–29.

——. *Duty and Interest Identical in the Present Crisis, A Sermon Preached in All Soul's Church, April 14, 1861.* New York: Wynkoop, Hallenbeck and Thomas, 1861.

——. *The First Congregational Church in the City of New York, A Sketch of Its History and a Review of His Own Ministry.* New York: Church of All Souls, 1899.

——. *Historical Sketch of the Union League Club of New York*. New York: Club House, 1879.

——. *A Sermon Occasioned by the Late Riot in New York*. New York: C. S. Francis, 1849.

——. *The State and the Nation—Sacred to Christian Citizens: A Sermon Preached in All Soul's Church, New York, April 21, 1861*. New York: James Miller, 1861.

——. *Unconditional Loyalty*. New York: Anson D. F. Randolf, 1863.

——. "U.S. Sanitary Commission." In *Johnson's Universal Cyclopaedia*, pp. 73–81. Edited by Frederick Barnard and Arnold Buyot. New York: Alvin J. Johnson and Sons, 1877.

——. *The Valley of Decision: A Plea for Unbroken Fealty on the Part of the Loyal States to the Constitution and the Union, Despite the Offenses of the Rebel States. A Discourse Given on Occasion of the National Fast, September 26, 1861, in All Soul's Church*. New York: H. B. Price, 1861.

Blackwell, Elizabeth. *Pioneer Work for Women*. London: J. M. Dent and Sons Ltd., 1914.

Brockett, L. P., M.D. *Woman: Her Rights, Wrongs, Privileges, and Responsibilities*. 1869. Reprint. Plainview, N.J.: Books for Libraries Press, 1976.

Brockett, L. P., and Mary C. Vaughan. *Woman's Work in the Civil War: A Record of Heroism, Patriotism and Patience*. With an Introduction by Henry W. Bellows, D.D. Philadelphia: Zeigler, McCurdy, 1867.

Bucklin, Sophronia E. *In Hospital and Camp: A Woman's Record of Thrilling Incidents among the Wounded in the Late War*. Philadelphia: John E. Potter, 1869.

Burn, James Dawson. *Three Years among the Working-Classes in the United States during the War*. London: Smith, Elder, 1865.

Child, Lydia Maria. *Lydia Maria Child: Selected Letters, 1817–1880*. Edited by Milton Meltzer and Patricia Holland. Amherst: University of Massachusetts Press, 1982.

Collis, Septima M. *A Woman's War Record, 1861–1865*. New York: G. P. Putnam's Sons, 1889.

Cormany, Rachel, and Samuel Cormany. *The Cormany Diaries: A Northern Family in the Civil War*. Edited by James C. Mohr. Pittsburgh, Pa.: University of Pittsburgh Press, 1982.

Cott, Nancy F., Jeanne Boydston, Anne Braude, Lori Ginzberg, and Molly Ladd-Taylor, eds. *Root of Bitterness: Documents of the Social History of American Women*. 2d ed. Boston: Northeastern University Press, 1996.

Daly, Maria Lydig. *Diary of a Union Lady, 1861–1865*. Edited by Harold E. Hammond. New York: Funk and Wagnalls, 1962.

Hamilton, Gail [Mary A. Dodge]. "A Few Words in Behalf of the Loyal Women of the United States by One of Themselves." New York: *Loyal Publication Society*, no. 10, 1863.

Henshaw, Sarah Edwards. *Our Branch and Its Tributaries; Being a History of the Work of the Northwestern Sanitary Commission and Its Auxiliaries. . . .* Chicago: Alfred L. Sewell, 1868.

Hoge, Jane C. [Blaikie]. *The Boys in Blue; or Heroes of the 'Rank and File'*. New York: E. B. Treat, 1867.

Livermore, Mary A. *My Story of the War: A Woman's Narrative of Four Years Personal Experience . . . .* Hartford, Conn.: A. D. Worthington, 1889.

Livermore, Mary A. *The Story of My Life*. Hartford, Conn.: A. D. Worthington, 1897.

Martin, Edward Winslow [J. Dabney MacCabe]. *The Secrets of the Great City; A Work Descriptive of the Virtues and the Vices, the Mysteries, Miseries and Crimes of New York City*. Philadelphia: National Publishing, 1868.

Masur, Louis P., ed. *"The Real War Will Never Get in the Books": Selections from Writers during the Civil War*. New York: Oxford University Press, 1993.

Moore, Frank. *Women of the War; Their Heroism and Self-Sacrifice*. Hartford, Conn.: S. S. Scranton, 1866.

Olmsted, Frederick Law. *The Papers of Frederick Law Olmsted*. Edited by Charles E. Beveridge. Baltimore: Johns Hopkins University Press, 1977–90. Vol. 1: *The Formative Years, 1822–1852*. Edited by Charles Capen McLaughlin and Charles E. Beveridge. Vol. 2: *Slavery and the South, 1852–1857*. Edited by Charles Capen McLaughlin,

Charles E. Beveridge, and David Schuyler. Vol. 3: *Creating Central Park, 1857–1861*. Edited by Charles E. Beveridge and David Schuyler. Vol. 4: *Defending the Union: The Civil War and the U.S. Sanitary Commission 1861–1863*. Edited by Jane Turner Censer. Vol. 5: *The California Frontier: 1863–1865*. Edited by Victoria Post Ranney, Gerard J. Rauluk, and Carol F. Hamilton.

Parson, Emily Elizabeth. *Memoirs of Emily Elizabeth Parson, Published for the Benefit of the Cambridge Hospital*. Boston: Little, Brown, 1880.

Peck, Thomas Bellows. *Henry Whitney Bellows: A Biographical Sketch with Portrait*. Keene, N.H.: Sentinel Printing, 188-).

Phelps, Mrs. Lincoln, ed. *Our Country, in Its Relations to the Past, Present, and Future. A National Book, Consisting of Original Articles in Prose and Verse, Contributed by American Writers*. Baltimore: John D. Toy, 1864.

Report of the Superintendent of the New England Soldiers' Relief Association, December 1862. Founded by Sons of New England resident in New York, April 3, 1862. New York: n.p., 1862.

Richards, Caroline Cowles. *Village Life in America, 1852–1872, Including the Period of the American Civil War as Told in the Diary of a School-Girl*. New York: Henry, Holt, 1913.

Sala, George Augustus. *My Diary in America in the Midst of the War*. London: Tinsley Brothers, 1865.

Schuyler, Louisa Lee. *Forty-Three Years Ago: or the Early Days of the State Charities Aid Association, 1872–1915: An Address, February 25, 1915*. New York: United Charities Building, 1915.

Six Hundred Dollars a Year, A Wife's Effort at Low Living, under High Prices. Boston: Ticknor and Fields, 1867.

Stanton, Elizabeth Cady, Susan B. Anthony, and Matilda Joslyn Gage. *History of Woman Suffrage*. Rochester: Susan B. Anthony, Charles Mann, 1881. Vol. 1: *1848–1861*. Vol. 2: *1861–1876*. Vol. 3: *1876–1885*.

Stillé, Charles J. *How a Free People Conduct a Long War*, Loyal Publication Society no. 13. New York: Anson D. F. Randolf, 1863.

Stillwell, Leander. *The Story by a Common Soldier of Army Life in the Civil War, 1861–1865*. Erie(?), Kan.: Franklin Hudson Publishing, 1920.

Strong, George Templeton. *The Diary of George Templeton Strong*. Edited by Allan Nevins and Milton Halsey Thomas. 4 vols. New York: Macmillan Company, 1952. Vol. 1: *Young Man in New York, 1835–1849*. Vol. 2: *The Turbulent Fifties, 1850–1859*. Vol. 3: *The Civil War*. Vol. 4: *Post-War Years, 1865–1875*.

Wormeley, Katherine Prescott. *The Cruel Side of War: Letters from the Headquarters of the United States Sanitary Commission during the Peninsular Campaign in Virginia in 1862*. Boston: Roberts Brothers, 1898.

INDEX

Abandoned wives, 6n. 8
Abbey, Hannah, 260
Abell, Mrs. Ira, 93
abolitionism: H. W. Bellows on, 67–69; black suffrage and, 268; Blackwell family and, 39; R. Cormany and, 24; expectations of, 50; female participation in, 15n. 28, 94n. 17; F. L. Olmsted and, 62n. 22; societies for, 199
Adams (N.Y.), 93, 223
Advisory Committee of the Boards of Physicians and Surgeons of the Hospitals of New York, 78
African Americans. 22n. 5, 45, 93–94, 182, 268. *See also* freedpeople; Slavery
Agnew, Cornelius R.: Bellevue nursing school and, 271n. 8; on employees, 180; sister-in-law of, 203, 204n. 22; soldiers' home proposal and, 246; G. T. Strong and, 244; USSC posts of, 80–81
agrarian women. *See* rural women
Alabama (N.Y.), 142
Albany (N.Y.), 157
Albany County (N.Y.), 184
Albany Sanitary Fair (1864), 217, 218, 260
Alcott, Louisa May, 25
Aldrich, Jeanie, 111
"Alert Clubs," 110

Alexandria (Va.), 143
Alfred Centre (N.Y.), 145
Allen, Delilah, 102–3, 139, 143
All Soul's Church (N.Y.C.), 40, 57, 58; abolitionism and, 67–69; Schuyler family and, 42; USSC identified with, 163; war explained to, 73
Altoona (Pa.), 100, 259
Altoona Society, 98, 100
Ambulance Corps, 175
Amenia Aid Society, 94–95, 257
American Bible Society, 157, 158
American Revolution: Confederate nationalists and, 75n. 54; evocation of, 20; female contributions to, 6, 45; republican motherhood and, 7; standing armies and, 32
American Temperance Union, 157
American Tract Society, 157, 161–62n. 43
American Unitarian Association, 58n. 14
Anderson, Benedict, 4n. 6
Annapolis (Md.), 239
Anthony, Susan B., 268, 272
Antietam, Battle of (1862), 111, 118
antislavery movement. *See* abolitionism
Antwerp (N.Y.), 93, 95, 144, 259
Arcadia (N.Y.), 259
Argyle (N.Y.), 143

Dickinson Centre (N.Y.), 99, 258
disabled veterans, 194, 234–38; H. W.
  Bellows on, 245; in Hartford, 256; Knapp
  on, 243–44; in New York City, 246
divine right of kings, 67n. 30
Dix, Dorothea, 43–44, 78, 107n. 50, 195,
  198–99n. 1
domesticity. *See* household labor, women's
  unpaid
domesticity, ideology of, 11–13; Civil War
  and, 45–46, 252, 273–74; female
  patriotism and, 31, 211; women's
  prerogatives under, 55, 88–89, 253;
  weakening of, 126. *See also* gender
  compromise
Dorcas Societies, 34; in Cornwall, N.Y., 44;
  in Lodi, N.Y., 101
d'Oremieulx, Mrs. T., *152*, 271
Douglas, Ann, 55n. 11
Douglas, Camp, 198n. 1
Douglas, John Hancock, 119
draft (conscription), 32, 110, 145, 148
Dunstan, Caroline, 26
Dutchess County, 217

East Hadden (Conn.), 136–37
East Hampton (N.Y.), 135n. 25, 137
Easton (N.Y.), 142–43
Eddy Aid Society, 99, 257
elite: charges against, 136, 144; Confederate
  women, 34n. 36; disabled soldiers and,
  235; men and women, 150, 183, 271;
  postwar careers of, women, 270; soldiers'
  aid societies and, 34, 159. *See also* New
  York City elite
Elizabeth (steam-barge), 119
Ellsworth (N.Y.), 98, 101, 104
Elmira (N.Y.), 240
Emancipation Proclamation, 13, 201n. 13,
  206
Emerson, Ralph Waldo, 58, 60, 71, 72
Enlightenment philosophers, 7n. 11
Episcopalians, 270
Europe: fair committees in, 203;
  Metropolitan Fair and, 213n. 46;
  nationalism in, 67, 74; travel in, 250, 266;
  veteran institutions in, 237
European liberal philosophy, 7
European women, 9
evangelicals: conflict with, 58n.15, 58–59n.
  16; female benevolence and, 160;
  perceived excesses of, 60; in Rochester,
  94n. 17; urban elite men and, 54; CC and,
  164n. 49
Evans, D. W., 227
Evans, Mrs. H., 222
Evans Centre (N.Y.), 261

Evening Express (N.Y.C.), 207
Evening Post (N.Y.C.), 27n. 21, 210
Exeter (N.Y.), 226

fairs, 95, 198–219, 222, 225, 271
Faneuil Hall (Boston), 24
Fayetteville (N.Y.), 90, 224
female patriotism, 4, 5, 51, 126, *127;*
  during American revolution, 7n. 10;
  Civil War concept of, 30–31; Civil War
  impact on, 274–75; flag production and,
  26–27; Livermore on, 22; loss of loved
  ones and, 29, 261; the press and, 37, 47;
  USSC and, 57, 123, 124, 139–40, 171,
  262–263
feminism: C. Beecher on, 11; Civil War
  and, 45–46, 47, 269–70; coverture and,
  15–16; cultural myths and, 9; in France,
  13n. 23; homefront women and, 260;
  261–62; material, 269–70; postwar, 270,
  272, 274, 275; postwar attack on, 273;
  reform activists and, 126; Vaughan on,
  14–15
field hospitals. *See* military hospitals
Field Notes, 47, 48
Field Relief Corps, 175–76
Fifteenth Amendment, 269, 273, 274, 275
Finley, Clement, 116
First Unitarian Church. *See* All Soul's
  Church (N.Y.C.)
First Vermont Heavy Artillery, 243
Fish, Carl Russell, 32n. 32
Fish, Mrs. Hamilton, 203, 204
Fisk, Mrs. M., 106
flags, 26–27, 37, 97
Flanders, Mrs. C. B. W., 47
Floral Temple (Metropolitan Fair), 210–11,
  212
Follett, Mrs. E. A., 136
Fort Monroe, 261
Fort Sumter: H. W. Bellows and, 68;
  Brooklyn women and, 34–35; M. Daly
  on, 20; New York women and, 38; USSC
  founders and, 78; war fervor and, 19
Fostin, A. F., 260
Fourteenth Amendment, 269, 275
France, 54, 60
France, Mrs. M. H., 99, 257
Frank Leslie's Illustrated Newspaper, 41
fraud allegations. *See* corruption allegations
Fredericksburg, Battle of (1862), 118, 119,
  131
Fredrickson, George, 60–61n. 19,
  122–23n. 1
freedpeople, 3, 94n. 17, 270n. 5
French Revolution, 13n. 23
Fuller, Mrs. David, 261

fund raising, 33, 110, 117, 118–20. *See also* fairs

Furness, Horace Howard, 155–56, 159

Gage, Frances Dana, 47–48
Gage, Matilda Joslyn, 268, 272
Galena (Ill.), 20
Gallatin, Mrs. Albert, 210
Gay, Elizabeth Neall, 23
gender compromise: C. Beecher on, 11; domestic ideology and, 12–13; female reformers and, 14, 46; material feminists on, 269; warwork and, 16–18, 126–27, 247, 274–75
gender relations: citizenship and, 7; Civil War and, 51; class and, 55–57; in early republic, 6–7, 45; economic value and, 16–17; feminist critique of antebellum, 126; nationalism and, 30–31; Republican ideology and, 16–17; romantic, 28–29; USSC leaders and, 81
Geneva (N.Y.), 103
German immigrants, 245
German Ladies Aid Society of Buffalo, 95
Germany, 74
Gettysburg Address, 201n. 13
Gibbs, Oliver Wolcott, 65n. 28, 81, 181, 182, 246
Ginzberg, Lori, 8n. 14, 46, 94n. 17, 126n. 8, 274n. 13
Godey's Lady's Book and Magazine, 13, 30
Godkin, Edwin L., 177n. 17
Gordon, Julia, 135, 138
Goshen (N.Y.), 155
gossip, 141, 183, 204
government hospitals. *See* military hospitals
Grand Anti-Slavery Festival (1851), 199
Grand Hall of the Fair Building (Metropolitan Fair), *209*
Grant, Julia, 36
Grant, Ulysses S., 20, 36, 198–99n. 1, 221, 269–70n. 4
Graves, Mrs. William W., 136n. 29
Great Britain. *See* Britain
Great Central Fair (Philadelphia, 1864), 214–15
Greeley, Horace, 154n. 12
Green, Mrs., 145
Griffin, Mrs. William Preston, 271
Griffith, Martha, 258
Griffith, Mrs., *152*
Grinnell, Helen, 23
Grinnell, Moses H., 57n. 13
Grove, Captain, 105

Hadley, William Hobart, 102, 118, 130, 156
Hale, Edward, 154n. 12

Hales Eddy (N.Y.), 222
Hamilton (N.Y.), 226
Hamilton, Alexander, 42
Hamilton, Mrs. Alexander, 203
Hamilton, Mary, 150, 151, 153, 154–55
Hamlin, Hannibal, 40
Hammond, William A., 116, 158, 187
Hardin County (Iowa), 100
Hardy, Jane, 135, 224
Harmony (N.Y.), 142
Harper's Weekly, 118, *127, 209, 212*
Harris, Elisha, 54, 80
Harsen, Jacob, 54
Hart, Helen, 29
Hartford (Conn.), 150, 151, 155, 255
Harvard College, 58
Harvard Divinity School, 57
Harvard Unitarianism, 58–59n. 16
havelocks, 35–36, 97
Hawley, Mary, 29
Hawthorne, Nathaniel, 186n. 43
Hayden, Dolores, 269
health. *See* medical problems
Hebrew Women's Aid Society of Philadelphia, 93
Henshaw, Sarah, 31, 35–36
Herald (N.Y.C.), 205n. 25, 214
Hester, S. H., 222n. 7
Hicks, Mrs. W. Scott, 260–61
Hills Grove (N.Y.), 103
Hoadley, David, 129
Hoag, Julia, 261
Hoboken (N.J.), 105, 222
Hobsbawm, Eric, 74
Hoge, Jane C. [Blaikie], 198, 199–200, 201, 269–70n. 4
Holmes, Oliver W., 186n. 43
Home for Disabled Soldiers (N.Y.C.), 246
Home for Soldiers' Wives and Mothers (D.C.), 239
Home for the Friendless (Chicago), 198n. 1
Home for the Friendless (N.Y.C.), 210
Home Missionary Society, 161n. 43
Homer, Winslow, 97
Homestead Act (1862), 48
hospitals: Dix and, 43; fairs and, 216; forwarding donations to, 92; in New York City, 54, 78, 271; for veterans, 235. *See also* military hospitals
Hôtel des Invalides (Paris), 237
household labor, women's unpaid: accusations concerning, 147; assumptions about, 100; C. Beecher on, 9–11; economic valuation of, 8, 16–17, 126n. 8, 258–60; material feminism on, 269; nationalist purposes and, 3–6; political significance of, 37, 49; sentimentalization

of, 2–3, 12–13, 89, 97, 103n. 40, 210–11, 275; USSC objectives and, 57, 87, 247; USSC valuation of, 216; wartime visibility of, 45, 51, 103–4, 126, 168, 263, 272; WCRA and, 52, 183. *See also* domesticity, ideology of; warwork
Hovey, William, 232, 233n. 39
Howe, Julia Ward, 107n. 50
Howe, Samuel Gridley, 107
Howell, Rebecca, 105
Howland, Eliza Woolsey, 96, 107–8
Hudson (N.Y.), 157
Hudson River region, 157
Hughes, Caroline, 224
Hunt, Kate, 214
Hunting, S. S., 224n. 14
Huntington, Cornelia, 135n. 25
Hurlbert, William Henry, 119
Hurn, Ethel Alice, 20n. 2

ideology of gender spheres. *See* domesticity, ideology of
Illinois, 199n. 1
immigrants, 245, 246
income tax. *See* taxation
Indian costume, 217
Indian Department (Metropolitan Fair), 208–10
Indian wars, 79, 208–10. *See also* Seminole War (1835–42)
industrial capitalism. *See* capitalism
inflation, 137–38, 222–23, 245n. 68
institutional care. *See* hospitals; sanitaria proposal; soldiers' homes
insurance companies, 81–82, 117
Irish immigrants, 245, 246
Italy, 74
Ithaca (N.Y.), 135, 224

Jackson, Mary, 27
Jacksonian era, 11, 12, 60, 144
Jenkins, John Foster, 80, 180; Blatchford and, 256; Bloor and, 232; dissatisfaction of, 233; on fairs, 215, 225; G. T. Strong and, 244
Jewish women, 93
John, Hannah, 258
joint property claim, 15–16, 269
Judd, Harriet Steward, 23

Kelley, Mary, 211n. 43
Kerlin, I. N., 105–6
Ketchum, Morris, 129
Ketchum, Mrs. Morris, 203
King, Thomas Starr, 117, 233
Kingsley, J. C., 223–24
Kirkland, Mrs., 186n. 43

Knapp, Frederick Newman, 180; Bloor and, 165, 230–31, 232; Cooper Union address of, 228; Home for Disabled Soldiers and, 246n. 72; Hunting and, 224n. 14; Jenkins and, 233; F. L. Olmsted and, 249–50; questionnaire of, 245; responsibilities of, 80; L. Schuyler and, 192–93, 195; veteran issue and, 238–39, 241–44
Knickerbocker Kitchen (Metropolitan Fair), 208

Ladies' Committee (Metropolitan Fair), 203, 204–5, 207, 213
Lancaster (N.Y.), 260
Lancey, S. Herbert, 156–57, 159–60
Landes, Joan B., 13n. 23
Lane, Mrs. David, 271n. 8
Leach, William, 274n. 14
Legal Tender Act (1862), 137
Leiber, Mrs. Francis, 203
lemon incident (1863), 177
Leslie's Illustrated Newspaper, 41
Leslie's Monthly, 36
Lewis, Charlotte, 100, 259
Liberal Christian, 58n. 14
life insurance companies, 81–82, 117
Lily, 14
Lincoln, Abraham: Antwerp women and, 93, 95; Brockett on, 2n. 2; M. Daly on, 145–46; Hadley on, 156; manuscripts of, 201n. 13; military supplies, funding for, 32–33; troop calls of, 19, 24, 110; USSC and, 79, 81, 91; war powers of, 148
Lincoln, Mary Todd, 145–46
Lincoln Home (N.Y.C.), 246
lint-making, 35, 99
Lippincott, Mrs. Augustus, 103
Lisle Centre (N.Y.), 261
Livermore, J. E., 261
Livermore, Mary: on female loyalty, 22; feminism and, 269; on middle-class women, 25; Northwestern Sanitary Fair and, 198, 199–200, 201; postwar activism of, 270; on suffering of women, 29; on U.S. flag, 26, 27; on war fervor, 19–20, 24; on waste, 38
local aid societies. *See* soldiers' aid societies
localism: H. W. Bellows on, 67, 245; CC and, 161; Civil War and, 75; concessions to, 184; fairs and, 198–202; federal principle and, 171; F. L. Olmsted on, 109; political, 147–48, 148n. 1; replacement of, 74–75; "rural" mentalities and, 71–72; Stillé on, 172; G. T. Strong on, 65; Union League Club and, 181
Lodi (N.Y.), 101
Logan, John A., 29

Logan, Mary, 29
London *Daily Telegraph*, 105
Long Island, 216, 217
Longfellow, Henry W., 154n. 12, 186n. 43
Louisville (Ky.), 239n. 52
Low, A. A., 216–17
Lowell Institute, 59
Loyal Publication Society, 4n. 7, 182, 251
Lyndon (N.Y.), 135n. 25

Manifest Destiny, 75n. 54
Mariposa Company, 176, 178, 249
market economy. *See* capitalism
married women, 6n. 8, 126. *See also*
   coverture
married women's property acts, 15–16, 46,
   269
Marsh, Mary, 23, 34–35
Mason, Mrs. S. C., 226
Massachusetts: aid societies in, 186; asylums
   in, 107n. 50; economic hardship in, 223;
   questionnaire responses from, 152;
   WCRA work in, 17, 91n. 9. *See also* New-
   England Women's Auxiliary Association
material feminism, 269–70, 273
Mather, Mrs. Henry, 184
Maxwell, William Quentin, 122n. 1
May, Abby, 196, 233, 274n. 14
Mayflower, The, 24, 47, 48, 49
McClellan, George Brinton, 208
McClellan, Mrs. George Brinton, 208
McFadden, Mrs. S. L., 135
McPherson, James Birdseye. 221
Meade, George Gordon, 221
Mecklenburg (N.Y.), 143
Medical Bureau. *See* United States Medical
   Bureau
medical personnel. *See* nurses; physicians
medical problems: *Bulletin* on military, 187;
   and death rates of soldiers, 110; of
   discharged soldiers, 243, 261; F. L.
   Olmsted on military, 114–15; of recruits,
   40, 79, 81–82, 114; of L. Schuyler, 266; of
   women, 10–11, 103–4. *See also* disabled
   veterans; sanitarianism
Memphis (Tenn.), 239n. 52
Metropolitan Fair (1864), 202–15, 216, 219,
   228, 271n. 8
Mexican War, 32
Michigan 27th Volunteers, 224n. 14
Midwest, 35, 131
military draft, 32, 110, 145, 148
military hospitals: S. Bucklin in, 31; *Bulletin*
   reports from, 186, 187; canvasser reports
   on, 155; distribution channels to, 261;
   Field Relief Corps and, 175–76;
   homefront women in, 2, 105, 106;

household manufacture for, 3;
   management of, 53; in Mississippi Valley,
   132; nurses for, 39, 44, 78; paid agents in,
   162; in Philadelphia, 34; rumored
   corruption in, 142–43; supply needs of,
   52, 95–96, 107–8, 118–19; testimonials
   from, 130–31; WCRA and, 193; in West,
   199n. 1; visitation in, 151, 229–30
military physicians: *Bulletin* and, 189; Field
   Relief Corps and, 175; ignorance of,
   115–16; rumored corruption of, 130, 142,
   153; supply distribution and, 119
military recruitment, 32, 114
military uniforms, 25, 33, 35, 36, 38
Ming, Harriet, 139
ministers, 158, 161n. 43, 162, 176
Minturn, Robert, 129
missionary societies, 161n. 43
Mississippi, 15n. 29
Mississippi Valley, 132
Missouri, 199n. 1, 234n. 42
Monroe, Fort, 261
Moore, Frank, 1–2, 246n. 71, 272
Moore, Mrs., 222n. 7
moral suasion, 13, 14, 46
Mott, Valentine, 42
mustered-out soldiers. *See* veterans

Nantucket (Mass.), 223, 259
narratives, Civil War, 1–4, 18, 23n. 6
Nash, Cavendish, 203, 204n. 22
Nashville (Tenn.), 239n. 52
Nast, Thomas, 21, 127
National Academy of Sciences, 80
National Invalid Corps of the Sanitary
   Commission (proposed), 236
nationalism, 147; H. W. Bellows on, 57,
   197; citizenship and, 69; in the
   Confederacy, 4n. 7, 75n. 54;
   cosmopolitan rationalists and, 71–76;
   difference from European, 67; northern,
   4; F. L. Olmsted on, 69–70; G. T. Strong
   on, 70; unpaid household labor and, 45;
   USSC as vehicle for, 183, 190, 220, 235.
   See also female patriotism
Nevins, Allan, 122n. 1
Newark (N.J.), 139
Newberry, John Strong, 131, 166, 177, 180
Newburgh (N.Y.), 224
New England, 57n. 13; Bloor tour of, 230;
   competition in, 164n. 49; corruption
   rumors in, 174; nationalism of, 72; origins
   of elite New Yorkers from, 71; secession
   crisis and, 69; superiority of, 62
New England Rooms (N.Y.C.), 240
New England Soldiers' Relief Association,
   240n. 54

New-England Women's Auxiliary Association, 83n. 70, 153, 164n. 49, 196n. 66, 233, 274n. 14

New Jersey, 6n. 8, 17, 91n. 9, 152, 186

New Orleans, 4n. 7, 239n. 52

New York Association for Improving the Condition of the Poor, 43n. 55

New York Board of Charities, 270n. 5

New York City: archives in, 251n. 10; bonnets sold in, 27n. 21; bourgeois houses in, 8–9n. 16; CC headquarters in, 158; economic growth of, 58, 168–69n. 62; fair in, 202–15, 216, 219, 228, 271n. 8; hospitals in, 39, 54 , 78, 271; institutional housing in, 246; lemons in, 177; medical establishment of, 84; nationalism in, 70; philanthropy in, 42–43, 101, 266, 270–71; proposed convention in, 79; reformers in, 39, 63; regimental march in, 20, 21; riots in, 59, 61, 182, 205–6, 243; Union meeting in, 26; USSC work in, 81, 233; veterans in, 192n. 55, 240, 245. See also Central Park (N.Y.C.)

New York City elite: Central Park and, 63; Civil War and, 67–69, 76; class relations and, 63, 65, 205; Metropolitan Fair and, 206, 207, 210, 213; as nationalist leaders, 71–73, 74; USSC and, 54, 57, 60, 61, 84, 168, 169, 172; women: concerns about female benevolence, 38–39; —, havelock making by, 35–36; —, Metropolitan Fair and, 203, 204–5, 207 210, 213; —, militarism of, 24; —, "visiting" in public hospitals by, 270–71; —, WCRA and, 40, 42, 44, 83, 84, 154

New York City Metropolitan Police, 177

New York City WCRA office. See Cooper Union WCRA office

New York Daily News, 211

New York Evening Express, 207

New York Evening Post, 27n. 21, 210

New York Herald, 205n. 25, 214

New-York Historical Society, 2n. 1

New York Infirmary for Women and Children, 39, 40, 85

New York Juvenile Asylum, 43n. 55

New York Medical Association, 78

New York National Freedmen's Relief Association, 270n. 5

New York Seventh Regiment, 20, 21, 36

New York Sixtieth Regiment, 111

New York Soldiers' Relief Association, 240

New York State: aid societies in, 90, 93–95, 98–99, 104–7, 186; "Alert Clubs" in, 110; anti-slavery festival in, 199; appropriations by, 108, 240; Bloor tours of, 164, 230; Bush tour of, 226; canvass work in, 157; CC inroads in, 223; charitable institutions in, 270, 271; economic hardship in, 101; D. W. Evans tour of, 227; fairs in, 217; fraud rumors in, 142; Hadley tour of, 156; monetary estimates from, 259–60; personal sacrifice in, 261; questionnaire responses from, 135–36, 152; USSC identification with, 241–42; warfront news in, 111; WCRA work in, 17, 91n. 9

New York State Charities Aid Association, 271

New York State Inebriate Asylum, 245n. 68

New York State Lunatic Asylum, 210

New York Times, 33, 130, 207, 243

New York Tribune, 40, 206, 207, 210–11

New York Union League Club, 181–82, 203, 248

New York Unitarian Association, 58n. 14

New York World, 208, 213

Nichols (N.Y.), 135

Nightingale, Florence, 60, 79n. 62, 187

North Billerica (Mass.), 100–101, 223

North Pitcher (N.Y.), 136

Northwest, 31

Northwestern Sanitary Commission, 83n. 70, 198, 199

Northwestern Sanitary Fair, 199–201, 202, 207

Norton, Charles Eliot, 69n. 39

Norwalk (Ohio), 110n. 59

nurses: Dix and, 43, 44, 79; housing for, 239; recruitment of, 53, 78; rumored corruption of, 142, 153; training of, 39, 40, 84

Oberlin College, 24

O'Daniels, Mrs. A. M., 135n. 25

Olmsted, Frederick Law, 57, 61–63; Agnew and, 180; antebellum reform and, 54; army investigation by, 114–15; Blatchford and, 164–65; Brink and, 131; on Civil War, 172n. 2; club proposal and, 181, 182; Connecticut resistance and, 150, 151; credibility issue and, 129–30; cross-class vision of, 205; disillusionment of, 127, 166; dissatisfaction of, 234; exhaustion of, 249–50; Field Relief Corps and, 175; Furness and, 156; homefront observations by, 76; individualism decried to, 171–72; on larger purposes, 123; "Loyal Women of America," 91–92, 93, 110; on masculine discipline, 55; on Medical Bureau, 116–17; on "natural aristocracy," 72; on new mentality, 119; on patriotism, 69–70; portrait of, 64; post

railroads, 200
Randall, Mrs. Henry, 105, 167
Reconstruction, 268
recruitment, 33, 114
Reed, Clara, 257
reform movements: elite men and, 54; fairs and, 198; women and, 13–15, 46, 94n. 17, 126. *See also* abolitionism; civil service reform
Reilley (pickpocket), 211n. 43
religious revivals, 158, 164
religious tracts, 158, 159, 161
Republican Party: CC and, 161; Civil War and, 50; gender/property assumptions of, 16–17; Metropolitan Fair and, 210; New York laborers and, 206; nominal support of, 118; opposition to, 222; responsibility of, 103; USSC and, 82, 139, 153, 169, 181
Revolutionary War. *See* American Revolution
Rhode Island, 91n. 9, 186
Rice, Mrs. William B., *152*
rights. *See* woman's rights
Richards, Caroline Cowles, 26–27
Richmond (Va.), 4n. 7
Ripley, Sarah Alden, 23
Roberts, Helen, 259
Rochelle (Ill.), 257
Rochester (N.Y.), 94n. 17
Rockdale (Pa.), 34
Rodgers, Daniel T., 67n. 30
Rogers, Eliza, 223
Roman Catholic women, 93
romantic relationships, 28–29
Rome (Italy), 214
Roosevelt, Theodore, 246n. 71
Rose, Anne C., 23n. 6
Rosenzweig, Roy, 61n. 20, 63n. 25
Rouse, Mrs. B., 131–32
Rousseau, Jean-Jacques, 7n. 12
Ruggles, Samuel, 129
rural children, 199n. 4
"rural" mentalities, 72
rural women: *Bulletin* and, 188; emulation by, 44; generosity of, 101–2; local benevolence and, 104; modesty of, 257–58; quilting bees of, 34
Ryan, Mary P., 104

St. Louis, 93–94, 201, 234n. 42
St. Luke's Hospital (N.Y.C.), 270
Sala, George Augustus, 105–6
salaries, 162–63, 180, 237
San Francisco, 249
sanitaria proposal, 242, 244
sanitarianism, 60, 77

Sanitary Commission. *See* United States Sanitary Commission
sanitary fairs, 95, 198–219, 222, 225, 270
Saratoga (N.Y.), 37
Satterlee, R. C., 53
Saunders, Mrs., 224
Schenectady (N.Y.), 155, 218n. 59
Schermerhorn, Mrs., 214
Schofield, John McAllister, 221
Scholl, Mary, 94
Schultz, Jane Ellen, 25n. 12, 272
Schurz, Mrs. Carl, 210
Schuyler, Eliza L., 58n. 14; H. W. Bellows and, 70–71; Elizabeth Blackwell and, 40; correspondence of, 113; elite women and, 102; F. L. Olmsted and, 93; WCRA executive committee and, 42
Schuyler, George Lee, 42, 58n. 14, 70
Schuyler, Louisa Lee, 42–43; on "Alert Clubs," 110; associate managers and, 153–55; on battles, 220–21; Elizabeth Blackwell and, 40; Bloor tour and, 230; Boston branch and, 196; branch rift and, 190–91; *Bulletin* and, 184–89; canvassers and, 155, 156, 157, 159; on CC, 165; closing work of, 264–66; in Connecticut, 150–51; on corruption charges, 130, 167, 173n. 5; on fairs, 217, 218; final offensive of, 226–29; on government responsibility, 107; Mrs. Green and, 145; institutional inspections by, 270–71; last letters and, 255–56; leadership by, 182–84; lint rumor and, 174n. 7; mentioned, 58n. 14; on F. L. Olmsted resignation, 179; organizational history and, 250–51, 266; Parrish and, 253; Pennsylvania colleague and, 160; personal contacts of, with homefront women, 113; portrait of, *185*; postwar plans of, 266, 270, 271; provincial loyalties and, 109–10; questionnaire of, 132–146, 149, 151–53, 172, 188; Mrs. Randall and, 105; remonstrances by, 194; reorganization plan of, 192–93, 198, 225, 240; on self sacrifice, 101–2; Stillé and, 163; O. Wait and, 142; on WCRA appeals, 44; Mrs. Wheeler and, 104; Woman's Council and, 195, 197
Schuyler, Philip, 42
Scott, James C., 123n. 2, 141
Second Connecticut Regiment, 26
Sedgwick, Henry D., 57n. 13
Seminole War (1835–42), 32
Sennell (N.Y.), 107
Seventh New York Regiment, 20, 21, 36
Seward, William Henry, 90
"sexual contract," 7n. 11. *See also* gender compromise

veterans, 194, 244–47; alcoholism among, 245n. 68, fear of, 242; Knapp and, 241, 242, 244; labor competition and, 245n. 68, local aid societies and, 239–41, 252, 255. *See also* disabled veterans

Vicksburg (Miss.), 117–18, 177

Virginia, 270n. 5

Vorhis, Mrs. C. L., 138

Vosburgh, Jennie, 139, 143

wages, 161, 162–63, 180, 237

Wait, Ophelia, 139, 142

Wall Street (N.Y.C.), 178

Walpole (N.H.), 57n. 13

Ward, Lydia R., 93

war profiteering, 144, 168, 174

warwork, 16, 17, 37, 148–49, 225; assessments of, 261, 263; burdens of, 99–100, 125, constraints on, 102–3; defined, 5; gender compromise and, 247–48; legacy of, 271, 272–74; F. L. Olmsted on, 109; political awareness and, 126; the press and, 44; suspension of, 111–112, 156; USSC and, 53, 179, 192, 196, 254, 255; at war's end, 256, 258; WCRA and, 44, 52, 83–84, 110, 184

Washington (D.C.): Connecticut agent in, 150; contraband slaves in, 22n. 5; corruption in, 142; inspection tour of, 54, 78–79; institutional housing in, 239; lobbying in, 182; nurse organization in, 43; personal distribution in, 261; troops for, 19; USSC work in, 80, 178, 233, 238, 243, 249–50; wagons leaving, *231;* WCRA work in, 83, 92n. 13, 133; Woman's Council in, 194–97

Waters, Mrs. C., 99, 260

Watertown (N.Y.), 37, 106, 218

Watson, Sarah, 23

Watts, Alice, 38

West Point (N.Y.), 80

Western Sanitary Commission, 177, 234

Wheeler, Mrs., 104–5

Wheeling (Va.), 92n. 13

Whigs, 71; H. W. Bellows and, 57, 60, 253; Democratic Party and, 72n. 45; war expectations of, 50

White, Leonard D., 32n. 33

White Sulphur Springs (W. Va.), 111

widows, 6n. 8, 237, 261

Williams, B. B., 135

Willink (N.Y.), 99, 111

Wisconsin, 20n. 2, 27

Wolcott (N.Y.), 260

Woman's Central Relief Association, 17–18; appropriations of, by USSC, 79; associate

managers, 153–55; —, admonitions from, 184; —, Bloor and, 130–31, 233; —, *Bulletin* and, 188, 189n. 51; —, convention of, 228–29; —, correspondence with, 255–56, 264; —, councils of, 197; —, final correspondence with, 265; —, hiring of, 195; —, proposal for postwar role of, 253; —, successes of, 196–97; —, supervision by, 194; H. W. Bellows and, 42, 52–54, 84, 89, 192, 264; Bloor and, 83, 164, 230; Brooklyn fair and, 216–17; *Bulletin* and, 186, 188; canvassing campaign of, 226–27; CC and, 165; cloth distribution by, 110; complaints to, 142; on contributions, 194; Cooper Union office (*see* Cooper Union WCRA office); correspondence with, 101, 100–6, 112–13, 255–56; demise of, 263–66; early work of, 43–45, 89; fairs and, 216–19; former workers of, 271; founding of, 40, *41,* 42; as intermediary, 126; introspection in, 225; "Loyal Women" and, 91n. 9; male canvassers and, 155–57, 252–53; Metropolitan Fair and, 202–3, 228; *New York Times* complaint and, 130; F. L. Olmsted and, 80n. 64; peace and, 254; peak affiliation with, 111; questionnaires, 132–46, 149; —, of associate managers, 188–89; —, disorganization revealed by, 222; —, negative results of, 172; —, positive interpretations of, 151–52; —, on rumors, 141; questions to, 138; reorganization of, 192–93, 198, 240; special status of, 190–91; takeover of, 83–86, 268; Vernon correspondent and, 99–100; veterans and, 236, 240; Washington inspection team and, 78

Woman's Council (1864), 193–97, 229

Woman's Journal, 270n. 4

woman's rights: Bloor on, 262; Brockett on, 273; raised expectations for, 45–49; Vaughan and, 2, 14–15. *See also* citizenship; citizenship, female; feminism; suffrage

Wood, Robert Crooke, 78

Woolsey, Abby Howland, 96, 107–8, 271

Woolsey, Harriet R., 214

Woolsey, Jane Stuart, 20, 24, 27, 29, 35

Woolsey, Sarah Chauncy, 26

World (N.Y.C.), 208, 213

Young Men's Christian Association, 157, 158